A Non-Euclidean Perspective

Robert Anton Wilson's Political Commentaries 1960-2005

A Non-Euclidean Perspective

Robert Anton Wilson's Political Commentaries 1960-2005

Introduction by Jesse Walker
Afterword by Richard Rasa

HILARITAS
PRESS

Praise for *A Non-Euclidean Perspective*

When today's billionaires talk about liberty, they mean freedom from taxes and regulations. When Wilson wrote about liberty, he meant freedom from mental prisons and social control. His libertarianism stems from compassion and human connection, rather than greed or self-interest. The essays in *A Non-Euclidean Perspective* reveal a thinker as distant from today's tech-bro libertarians as the teachings of Jesus are from prosperity gospel preachers. Where modern libertarians worship the market, Wilson celebrated human potential and warned against all forms of dogma and power — whether wielded by the state or a corporation. Wilson understood that true freedom requires breaking everyone's chains, not building higher walls around private compounds.

    – **Mark Frauenfelder**, co-founder of *Boing Boing*

• • •

RAW's early essays emerge from the rich ideaspace that opened up in North American intellectual life at that time. The imagination, wit, and humanity evident in these essays animated Robert Anton Wilsons politics and writing for the rest of his life.

    – **Revd Jonathan Harris**, High Priest of Church of Burn

• • •

A Non-Euclidean Perspective is a unique combination of compassion and erudition that will light up your neural pathways like Times Square on New Year's Eve.

    – **Lewis Shiner**, author of *Glimpses*

• • •

Say what you like about the principles of anarchism, Robert Anton Wilson said it earlier, better, and funnier.

    – **Ken MacLeod**, author of *The Star Fraction* and
    Beyond The Hallowed Sky

Few people remember that in the last three decades of the 20th Century, "Futurist" was a well-paying gig. Top futurist writers like Buckminster Fuller, Marshall McLuhan and Robert Anton Wilson attracted large audiences at conferences. Situated somewhere between fortune-tellers and philosophers, these prognosticators included tech in their visions. The computer was the new deck of Tarot cards. The future that they foresaw was of course, accurate. We are living in it. For my money, Robert Anton Wilson, was the most charismatic of them all. He had a sense of humor and a grasp of absurdity that transcended even the most profound, but sadly serious, visions of the others. These qualities multiplied his appeal hundreds of times and were, as a result, generative almost immediately, of many tributaries (The Church of the Subgenius, to name but one). More importantly now for us, people of the future, is the dire need for humor and understanding of the absurd. This collection of essays is a manual for yielding those things, maybe even acquiring them. Wilson was an optimist, not because he saw the coming sci-fi world as particularly wonderful, but because he was unafraid to see us still wallow between contradiction and awe like the proverbial cat caught in the door between Einstein and Heisenberg. Wilson was an encyclopedic scholar of human folly, or maybe simply the folly of being human. Great tonic read!

   – **Andrei Codrescu**, author of *The Disappearance of the Outside: a Manifesto For Escape*

• • •

Explodes like a string of Zen-infused firecrackers! *A Non-Euclidean Perspective* chronicles the evolution of Robert Anton Wilson's political, epistemological, and spiritual outlook through four decades of his articles. The reader will experience a keen, perceptive, articulate mind sifting through the socio-political detritus of the Late Second Millennium to find a philosophy (or several!) that can maximize liberty while (dare I insult Eris?) minimizing Discord in our lives. Truly a volume of priceless wisdom from a multi-dimensional intellect!

   – **Victor Koman**, author of *The Jehovah Contract* and *Kings of the High Frontier*

A Non-Euclidean Perspective:
Robert Anton Wilson's
Political Commentaries 1960-2005

Copyright © 2025, Robert Anton Wilson

Print: ISBN: 978-1-952746-47-5
eBook: ISBN: 978-1-952746-48-2

Cover and Interior Design by Pelorian Digital

Hilaritas Press, LLC.

www.hilaritaspress.com

Contents

Editor's Note

When they started working on the Hilaritas reissue of *Natural Law*, editor Chad Nelson and our Esteemed Publisher, Richard Rasa, had assumed that the book revolved around politics, and thus began assembling supplemental essays of that orientation for inclusion in the book. After obtaining a copy of the rare, out-of-print classic, they soon realized that *Natural Law* explored model agnosticism, not politics, and thus set aside the political essays and collected a more appropriate set for inclusion. Those shelved essays from *Natural Law* became the foundation of the book you hold right here, right now.

On the heels of the success of *Lion of Light*, I wanted to keep the momentum going with a politics book that could be released in time for the 2024 US election season (the best laid plans of mice and men). I started reviewing RAW's non-Euclidean politics course from the Maybe Logic Academy and developed the idea of using the course outline to create a structure for our politics book. In that course, Bob takes us through a variety of alternative economic and political ideas, but also goes much deeper into the psychological and socio-cultural underpinnings by touching on Reich, Korzybski, Fuller, Crowley's *Book of the Law*, and the Eight Circuit Model of Consciousness. Furthermore, he hints at a more optimistic vision of the future with incursions into The Hedonic Imperative (see: paradise-engineering.com) and the philosophy of Bucky Fuller. Chad dusted off his political essay list and began reviewing and expanding on it with the help of Jesse Walker, while I looked into essays on the deeper underpinnings and an optimistic vision of the future.

As Chad and Jesse began sorting through the political essays at our disposal, Jesse dropped a haul in our laps: the complete collection for *Minority of One* via the Johns Hopkins University Library, many of which earned their way into this publication. It soon became apparent that we had more than enough politically oriented material to fill out a whole book, and the essays I had been assembling were set aside, perhaps for another project in the future.

Credit to Jesse Walker, Martin Wagner, Chad Nelson, and myself for unearthing mosbunall of the contents of this book from the catacombs of the analog world, and to Chad and Jesse for helping to select the best of the best that you hold in your hands right now. Our Esteemed Publisher and Hilaritas Work-Horse, Rasa, did the majority of the heavy lifting, painstakingly converting analog documents into the digital realm and assembling them all in chronological order, along with the multitude of other details necessary to publish a quality product. I should note that Rasa maintains a quiver of behind-the-scenes unsung heroes meticulously proofreading each book prior to (and even after) publication. Enormous thanks go out to Tom Clisson, who worked as our primary proofreader. We would also like to acknowledge Jim Turney, who recorded the Hess/Wilson discussion and gave us his blessings, as well as Ted Hand, who graciously made an initial transcription of the video. And Jesse gives a shout out to Ben James for digging up a reference in a book outside of his possession, and to Gabriel Kennedy for his helpful feedback on the intro.

In a time where old political-social-economic structures erode away and collapse, paradigms shift, and new structures have yet to crystalize in place, perhaps the essays found here can help us all to think outside the box, break free of the past, and move a little more open-mindedly into the future.

– Mike Gathers, Hilaritas Press Editor

Discordia Rising

Introduction by Jesse Walker

Robert Anton Wilson was born a Catholic, then rejected his faith, then found himself working through a series of substitute faiths. Gradually, he came to see faith itself as the problem. We are "tiny fallible beings crawling around on a relatively small planet," he concluded, "and anybody who pontificates dogmatically about anything is giving evidence that they are an idiot, even if you agree with them. They shouldn't sound that certain. We think we're so damn smart and we know so fucking little."[1]

Or: Wilson's father was a union Democrat and his uncle was a Charles Coughlin–loving antisemite who hated the big banks and the government. Wilson spent his adult life committed to one of the few political principles that his uncle and father had in common – an opposition to war – while searching for ways to join Uncle Mick in rejecting those big banks and governments while also joining his dad in rejecting his uncle's bigotry and paranoia.

Or: Wilson reached adulthood in the middle of the 20th
century, a time when the world was dominated by two social
visions: a centralized and bureaucratic form of capitalism
that had made its peace with (and indeed seemed to rely on)
government intervention, and a centralized and bureaucratic
form of socialism that had made its peace with (and indeed
seemed to rely on) a setup where one class of people controlled
the means of production and a much larger class of people
worked for wages. He started searching for alternatives,
looking first to Leon Trotsky (a popular choice for Americans
who wanted to reject capitalism but didn't think the Soviet
system looked very appealing), and then to Ayn Rand (a
popular choice for Americans who wanted to reject socialism
but didn't think *Organization Man* corporate conformity
looked very appealing), before exploring Benjamin Tucker's
individualist anarchism, Henry George's Single Tax, and other
decentralist and anti-authoritarian alternatives.

Or: Lurking beneath the ordinary political spectrum, there
is an upside-down territory where intellectuals trade in stranger
things. It resembles what the sociologist Colin Campbell
calls the *cultic milieu*. This "cultural underground," Campbell
argued, "is continually giving birth to new cults, absorbing
the debris of the dead ones and creating new generations of
cult-prone individuals."[2] Don't get hung up on that word
"cult": Campbell was using an older, non-pejorative definition
of the term, one meant to spark thoughts of loosely associated
mystics, not tightly hierarchical dogma factories. And while
he was thinking, at least in that particular essay, of ideas that
are not obviously political – clairvoyance, magick rituals,
extraterrestrial contact – there is a cultural underground of
political ideas too. Call it *Fortean politics*: a space for political
anomalies, some of which have erupted unexpectedly into the
mainstream while some are forever relegated to the crank zone.
That's the space where Robert Anton Wilson made his home,
absorbing the ideas he found valuable and having satiric fun
with the others.

Or: Throughout his career, Robert Anton Wilson wanted everyone to be far freer than they are now – freer from state power, freer from authoritarian relationships in general, freer from the personal hang-ups that might lead someone to submit to an authoritarian relationship. And in that general spirit of choice and multiplying alternatives, he was open to different ideas about how to make the world a more utopian place.

• • •

This book contains dozens of Wilson's political essays and interviews. The earliest was published when Dwight David Eisenhower was president; the most recent appeared well into the war on terror. My job here, in this introduction, is to offer a historical framework for how his ideas evolved over that half-century of writing and speaking. And since Wilson would never want to stop at only one model for understanding something, I've just given you five you might find useful.

Feel free to generate more of your own. You'll probably need *some* sort of framework as you make your way through his political writings, both here and in his other books. Otherwise, you might get confused by what look like contradictions.

For example: In "Is Capitalism a Revealed Religion?"[3] (first published in 1961 and reprinted in this volume), Wilson mentioned a man "who stopped talking to me when he found out I'm a socialist." Two decades later, in his book *Prometheus Rising*, Wilson commented that "as indust-reality has spread, socialism has followed in its wake" and then noted in parentheses that he "does not like" this.[4] But just a few years after that, Wilson told the *L.A. Weekly* that the best real-world political system (as opposed to abstract ideologies that have not been fully enacted) was "Scandinavian socialism," which he said had fostered "clean streets, a low crime rate, a general air of high civilization."[5]

Wilson was also sometimes prone to calling himself right-wing – in 1969 he published a pseudonymous essay (reprinted here) titled "Why I Am a Right-Wing Anarchist,"[6] and four year later he called himself "a spokesman for an extreme right-wing libertarianism that prides itself on being more radical than left-wing anarchism."[7] In 1971, on the other hand, he and Robert Shea wrote an article mocking Richard Nixon where they casually dropped the phrase "We of the Left."[8] In 1988, Wilson complained in *Critique* magazine that "some flatlanders insist on classifying me as Leftist and others, equally Euclidean, argue that I am obviously some variety of Rightist"; rejecting both labels, he wrote that he felt like "a visitor from non-Euclidean dimensions whose outlines are perplexing to the Euclidean inhabitants of various dogmatic Flatlands."[9]

Speaking of libertarianism: After the 1980 election, Wilson wrote that "ideologically" he "should have voted for Ed Clark, the Libertarian Party candidate; but I am not that kind of Libertarian, really; I don't hate poor people."[10] At the end of the '80s, on the other hand, he wrote that he usually didn't vote, "on the anarchist principle that it only encourages the bastards," but that when he did it was usually for the Libertarian Party, "to annoy the bastards."[11]

While Wilson consistently opposed censorship of pornography (and of anything else), his attitude toward the material the censors were targeting also seemed to shift. In a 1963 article for *The Realist*, he denounced *Playboy* as "merchants of imitation sex."[12] But by the end of the '60s he was happily working at *Playboy* himself, and in his 1981 novel *The Homing Pigeons* he imagined – with satiric intent, but also with obvious approval – an alternate timeline where the Second Amendment contains these words: "A self-regulated sex life being necessary to the happiness of a citizen, the right of the people to keep and enjoy pornography shall not be abridged."[13]

Wilson spent most of his career identifying as an anarchist, but in 1981 he told an interviewer he was "not an anarchist any longer, because I've concluded that anarchism is an impractical ideal. Nowadays, I regard myself as a libertarian . . . I'm a libertarian because I don't trust the people as much as anarchists do."[14] But after a while he turned that on its head. He told a different interviewer in 2002, "I sometimes call myself a libertarian, but that's only because most people don't know what 'anarchist' means."[15]

Here's one last example. Wilson usually described whoever happened to be president in the most caustic terms available, even the presidents that someone of his sensibilities was "supposed" to like. (After the Bay of Pigs invasion, Wilson wrote that his "good Liberal friends who voted for Mr. Kennedy and considered me a beatnik for refusing to vote can decide for themselves what share of guilt they must bear for helping this man achieve power."[16]) But the election of Bill Clinton put him in an uncharacteristically accepting mood ("the first First Family in my lifetime that I would enjoy having dinner with"[17]) – until it became clear that Clinton was just as prone as previous presidents to sending the gendarmes after marijuana users, after which the president was "77 kinds of sonofabitch" and "a hillbilly with a perpetual hard-on."[18]

Everyone changes their mind from time to time, and some of these shifts are probably just that. Wilson's initial reaction to Clinton, for example, came in that moment, right after the fall of the Soviet Union, when almost the whole world seemed to be getting freer; it wasn't hard to see the election of a relatively young man who had fooled around with cannabis and protested the Vietnam War as a sign that these changes were touching the United States too. With the end of the Cold War, Wilson said in 1995, "I began to see the differences between the Republicans and the Democrats again"; the Clintons struck him as "counterculture types who are trying to cover it up by acting respectable."[19] Until they didn't.

Some of these shifts, conversely, just amount to using different language in different contexts. (That same essay that declared its author a right-wing anarchist called for the abolition of land-rent, dreamed of a future without the employer-employee relationship, and spoke favorably of traditional Native American societies, all of which suggest that we're dealing with a quirky definition of "right-wing."[20]) Some shifts might reflect not a change in Wilson's underlying philosophy but a change in which authoritarians were annoying him the most at the moment: The violence and dogmatism that emerged at the end of the '60s provoked a bit of an anti-left backlash within Wilson, and then the Reagan era pushed him in the opposite direction.[21]

And some apparent shifts may just be a matter of thinking on more than one level. When he was particularly high on Buckminster Fuller and *Star Trek*, or particularly worried about nuclear war, Wilson was known to suggest that some sort of world governance would be an improvement on the status quo – an idea he had vociferously rejected in the 1960s. "I'm all for accelerating the process of the transfer of power to one center," he told an interviewer in 1983, arguing that this would make it more likely that we'll "survive the Nuclear Age." But he simultaneously rejected the idea of a consolidated world state, explaining to the same interlocutor that he was imagining "a decentralized world system in which, as much as possible, nationalism is retained while the power to use weapons is gradually taken away from nations, and given to some kind of peace force."[22] The overarching system's structure, he added, might resemble the old Articles of Confederation. If you're an anti-authoritarian who's been losing confidence in anarchy, that's the sort of possibility you might propose as a relatively pragmatic alternative.

On the flipside: In Wilson's 1992 book *Reality Is What You Can Get Away With*, he imagines a future scholar reacting disapprovingly to the fact that the America of our era had "no National Health plan."[23] But in his 1996 introduction to a later edition of the same book, Wilson suggested that encrypted online alternative currencies could serve as an electronically updated variation on the mutualists' economic proposals, allowing an anarchistic "underground economy without interest or taxes" to emerge – and that this unregulated market could "offer all that socialism ever promised without taking away one jot of our freedom."[24] He liked that Scandinavian model better than the other Actually Existing choices, but he still liked ol' Ben Tucker even more.

That was the period, interestingly, in which the Scandinavian countries started adopting some fairly substantial market reforms. They are arguably more deregulatory than the U.S. is now, but they also have a more generous safety net, a combination that the Robert Anton Wilson of 1996 would have probably appreciated.[25]

• • •

Enough hopscotching through history. Let's work our way through Wilson's career chronologically and see what those five models tell us about the evolution of his thinking.

In 1932, Wilson was born into a working-class Irish-American household in New York City. The bounds of this world's political debate were split, he later wrote, between "two hostile camps. The first group said The Depression resulted from the machinations of the Wicked Jews, but the other group said it resulted from the selfish scheming of the Wicked Republicans."[26] Put differently, it was split between people like Wilson's uncle and people like Wilson's dad.

In that environment, Wilson recalled, he adopted a series of Correct Answer Machines, a term he borrowed from the libertarian writer Mike Hoy. The first was the conservative Catholic belief-system favored by the nuns at Wilson's grammar school. When he moved on to high school and met students and teachers from outside his native tribe, he was initially angry. ("That," he later explained, "is the function of Correct Answer Machines: to make you have an adrenaline rush, instead of a new thought, when confronted with different opinions."[27]) But soon he was less angry than intrigued, and he started reading writers the grammar-school nuns had denounced, such as Charles Darwin and H.L. Mencken.

"I found myself floating in a void of incertitude," he recalled, "a sensation that was unfamiliar and therefore uncomfortable. I retreated back to robotism by electing to install a new Correct Answer Machine in my brain. This happened to be a Trotskyist Correct Answer Machine."[28] According to Wilson's biographer, Gabriel Kennedy, the Trotskyist group Wilson joined was the Socialist Youth League, which was recruiting among young bohemians at the time.[29] Some of Wilson's future friends were known to turn up at the organization's events, though not necessarily the ones he attended: Norman Mailer spoke to at least one meeting, and the beat poets Allen Ginsberg and Lawrence Ferlinghetti are said to have attended a few.

If you're familiar at all with Wilson's work, you can see why he might enjoy that environment. But if you're familiar at all with Wilson's work, you probably also understand why he would bristle at Leninist party discipline – and would be put off when the middle-class Trots accused the working-class Wilson of being too bourgeois. And so he left the Trotskyists too.

Around the same time, the reliably antiwar Wilson learned that there were historians, such as Charles Beard, who wrote critically about America's participation in World War II. His high school teachers "were too Liberal to tell me I would go to Hell for reading such books (as the nuns had told me about Darwin, for instance), but they made it clear that the Revisionists were Evil, Awful, Unspeakable and probably some form of Pawns of the Devil."[30] Naturally, he started reading them as well. He also read existentialists, cyberneticists, General Semanticists, beatniks, and the radical psychoanalyst Wilhelm Reich, who favored both sexual liberation and a system of self-managing "Work-Democracy." Shortly after he exited the Socialist Youth League, he picked up an Ayn Rand novel and briefly entered a period of dogmatic devotion to Rand's hyper-capitalist worldview.

A Non-Euclidean Perspective

And he read a group of libertarians who were far more radical than Rand: the individualist and mutualist anarchists. (Not every individualist anarchist is a mutualist, and not every mutualist anarchist is an individualist, but there is a large overlap.) Writers such as Benjamin Tucker, Lysander Spooner, Josiah Warren, and Pierre-Joseph Proudhon wanted to abolish the state entirely and to kick away the legal privileges that propped up economic elites; as a result, they argued, virtually everyone would work for themselves or for horizontally organized associations rather than answering to governments and bosses. It would be a world where cooperation flowered as compulsion withered.

Wilson supplemented his interest in the anarchists by reading other social critics. In that *Critique* essay, he mentioned such figures as Henry George, Silvio Gesell, C.H. Douglas, and Buckminster Fuller. Others who influenced him have ranged from the feminist social scientist Riane Eisler to the idiosyncratic historian Brooks Adams to the New Left leader Carl Oglesby. But if you read Wilson's articles from the early 1960s, you will find a pretty clear ideological core to it. This outlook mixed the politics and economics of the mutualists – a rejection of the state and of a monetary system based on "usury" – with the anti-puritanical sex radicalism of figures like Reich.

Viewed in light of Wilson's background, this was a remarkable combination: While one hand threw off the sexual dogmas of the Catholic Church, another had found its way to notions that were not unlike some old-school Catholic ideas about money and banking. Some of you might be wondering whether Wilson had landed uncomfortably close to Uncle Mick. "Usury," after all, is one of those words you often hear slung about by antisemitic conspiracy theorists – and in fact, the influences we've mentioned so far include several folks (Adams, Douglas, Proudhon) who were known to fret about purported Jewish plots. Wilson was also prone to praising the fascist poet Ezra Pound, not just for his literary gifts but for some of his economic ideas.[31] Meanwhile, Wilson's readings on World War II led him to one fellow who at the end of his life started wading into Holocaust denial (Harry Elmer Barnes) and another who plunged in deep (James J. Martin). So maybe . . .

Don't worry, that isn't where Wilson landed. He rejected Holocaust denial,[32] he took pains to note that the bankers he criticized tended to be gentiles,[33] and he regarded Jew-haters as a "loathsome club."[34] He denounced antisemitism both fiercely and frequently – not in the pro forma way of someone muttering "not all Jews" before proceeding to quote *The Protocols of the Learned Elders of Zion*, but in the manner of someone who thought the very concept of collective guilt was at the root of many of the world's worst social ills. Indeed, Wilson was suspicious of *any* form of essentialism, whether or not it took the form of a social prejudice: He often recommended the exercise of trying to speak or write without the word "is" – to avoid declaring that a person or group or concept *is* something else – as an "antibiotic" against "demonological thinking."[35]

So no, he did not turn into his uncle. But if he was shaped by both his uncle and his father, this was one way you might expect that dialectic to play out.[36]

If you've read a lot of Wilson's books but had little exposure to his younger Tuckerite and Reichian writings, you might be taken aback by some of the early essays in this collection. Not because of the views expressed – Tucker and Reich remained cornerstones of Wilson's worldview until his death – but because they were often written with a tone of strong certainty, a posture that Wilson came to reject in his later years. He would eventually come to condemn dogmatism so fiercely, in fact, that I can't help wondering whether some of those broadsides on behalf of agnosticism were written with his younger self in mind.

That said, these essays are often stylish and insightful, and in them you can see some outlines emerging of *Illuminatus!*, the explicitly anarchist 1975 trilogy that Wilson composed with Robert Shea and that made both writers' reputations.[37] It's just that by the time that trio of novels appeared, the author of those early articles had experimented heavily with psychedelic drugs and occult rituals, sometimes in combination; had gotten pulled headfirst into the paranoia of the 1960s, when you couldn't always be sure which comrades were informants; and had embraced the prankster religion of Discordianism, a faith that staved off fundamentalism by developing a doctrine so absurd that hardly anyone could take it literally. Wilson later described those years as a journey through Chapel Perilous. When you cross through that chapel, he wrote, "You come out the other side either a stone paranoid or an agnostic; there is no third way. I came out an agnostic."[38]

The agnosticized Wilson exuded an anti-dogmatic aura that made his periodic changes of heart on one issue or another feel not just understandable but inevitable. What's more, he urged readers to try to hold more than one perspective in their heads at the same time, embracing "multi-model agnosticism." At times he seemed to revel in the results, as when he joked that he was an "anarcho-technocrat."[39] His politics now seemed simultaneously more flexible and more stable. If he sometimes appeared to contradict himself, he was simply large, containing multitudes.

The political labels attached to Wilson most frequently were *anarchist* and *libertarian*, and he usually accepted each. Throughout the 1970s, '80s, and '90s – yes, even in the period when he made that crack about Ed Clark hating poor people[40] – Wilson spoke frequently at gatherings of the Libertarian Party. That party has contained several ideological strains over the years, but the dominant one in this period was influenced, sometimes directly and frequently indirectly, by the mutualist and Georgist writers who had left such a strong mark on Wilson; the party's most radical elements favored a stateless society of private property and voluntary exchange that resembled Benjamin Tucker's vision. But while Tucker rejected absentee ownership and expected rent and interest to virtually disappear in a stateless market, members of the Libertarian Party were far more likely to mix Tucker's political ideas with the views of the capitalistic "Austrian" economists, especially F.A. Hayek, Ludwig von Mises, and Murray Rothbard.

Wilson made his most extensive comments on where he disagreed with that group in a 1976 interview with *New Libertarian Notes*.[41] His remarks are reprinted in this volume, so I won't quote heavily from them here, except to note that he was both harshly critical ("The rosy view the Austrians have of these matters, I think, would collapse in two weeks if they had to deal with the damned corporate pirates as an ordinary worker does") and ultimately friendly ("this is turning into a diatribe against the group I find least obnoxious in the whole politico-economic spectrum . . . orthodox conservatives and liberals, not to mention Nazis and Marxists, are really pernicious, and the Austrian libertarians are basically okay"). In 1993, Wilson and I both attended an off-year convention of the Libertarian Party, him as a speaker and me on behalf of a now-defunct magazine; I asked him how close he felt to the party at that point, and he replied that it depended on which segment of the party we were talking about. This particular convention, he added, was basically being run by the local chapter of the drug reform group NORML, so he was cool with them.

So that is one way to get an admirer of Scandinavian social democracy onto a bill filled with *laissez-faire* capitalists.

• • •

When I laid out those five models at the beginning of this introduction, four of them focused on what was happening in Robert Anton Wilson's head: He was working through different faiths on a path to living without certainty, he was living out a dialogue between two worldviews he grew up with, he was searching for alternatives to state capitalism and state socialism, and he was looking for ways that everyone could be freer. But the other model – the one built on Colin Campbell's cultic milieu – doesn't revolve around why Wilson found certain ideas appealing. It's about the social context that allowed him to discover ideas like these in the first place and to hop from one to another. This book isn't just a tour through Robert Anton Wilson's thoughts. It's a tour of the space where such thoughts flourished, and of the counterintuitive connections that emerge there.

Consider the individualist anarchists. These writers have never been household names, but it doesn't seem odd that Wilson came across their work. There were, after all, so many possible routes he could have taken to finding them.

For example: Philosophically speaking, Trotskyism is miles from mutualism. But sociologically speaking, the world of Americans who were both anti-Stalinist and anti-Cold War was pretty small in the 1950s, and New York City gave them plenty of chances to encounter one another. The Socialist Youth League was part of a larger coalition called the New York Student Federation Against War, and the other participants included anarchists.

Or how about the Randians? Rand despised anarchism, but she had been embedded since the '30s in an Old Right milieu where several figures habitually cited Tucker's arguments against the state, even if they preferred to get their economics from Hayek or Mises. Some of them even got their economics from Henry George: While many Georgists identified with the left, such figures as Albert Jay Nock and Frank Chodorov ensured that the Single Tax had devotees on the libertarian right too.

There were other possible conduits. James J. Martin, one of those critics of World War II, also wrote *Men Against the State*, a history of individualist anarchism in America.[42] Wilson's favorite novelist, James Joyce, once produced a list of his political influences that consisted entirely of anarchists and libertarians, with a special shout-out for Tucker's *Instead of a Book*, which in Joyce's words "proclaimed the liberty of the non-invasive individual."[43] Or maybe young Bob just stumbled on a tract at the library or read something from an encyclopedia.

That last option is, in fact, what happened. In 1910 the *Britannica* had the anarcho-communist Peter Kropotkin write the encyclopedia's entry on anarchism, and he produced a fairly balanced overview of the different schools of anarchist thought. Half a century later, Wilson's wife Arlen came across Kropotkin's article and shared it with her husband. They both loved it. Mystery solved!

But my point here isn't to pick at the details of Robert Anton Wilson's life. My point is that the Trotskyists and the Randians, two groups whose areas of agreement didn't extend much farther than whether Joe Stalin was a nice guy, were nonetheless just a couple degrees of separation from each other. They occupied a common milieu, and the intersections therein were far more complex than any one-dimensional political spectrum could capture.

Near the beginning of this essay, I called that milieu "Fortean politics." That's mostly because Charles Fort, a writer Wilson admired, loved to find anomalies that didn't seem to fit the standard scientific models, just as non-Euclidean political ideas fail to fit easily onto the standard political spectrum. But it is also because the Fortean movement was itself a conduit for such ideas. If you made a habit of reading *Doubt*, the Fortean Society's magazine, in the 1940s and '50s, you would have encountered items on everything from an alleged Pearl Harbor conspiracy to the economics of Henry George and Silvio Gesell.[44] The Society's members themselves frequently gravitated toward left-libertarian views, but with room as well for maverick socialists, reactionaries, and unclassifiables.[45]

In the internet age, it is much easier to stumble randomly

onto these off-brand ideologies and to discover the unexpected ways they influence and abut each other. Wilson's work gives us a glimpse at a more analog era, a time when you couldn't just click a hyperlink to follow one of those paths but had to show up at a demonstration, a coffeeshop, or a radical bookstore. Or subscribe to an unconventional publication, like the ones that published the essays and interviews in this collection.

If this book lets us peer into that past, the people who saw these words when they first appeared were catching a glimpse of times to come. When I first encountered Robert Anton Wilson's writing, back in the 1980s, the internet barely existed; it certainly wasn't the mass phenomenon it is today. But watching him synthesize these disparate ideas, sometimes finding unexpected harmonies and sometimes creating a glorious cacophony, I was unwittingly visiting the online future. As you read his visions of a freer, more open and interconnected, more peaceful and prosperous planet, let's hope they turn out to be glimpses of our future too.

Introduction Notes:

1 Quoted in Michael Dare, "The Cosmic Wag," *L.A. Weekly*, February 26–March 3, 1988.

2 Colin Campbell, "The Cult, the Cultic Milieu and Secularization," in Michael Hill (ed.), *A Sociological Yearbook of Religion in Britain* 5, SCM Press, 1972, p. 122.

3 Robert Anton Wilson, "Is Capitalism a Revealed Religion?," *The Realist*, June 1961.

4 Robert Anton Wilson, *Prometheus Rising*, Hilaritas Press, 2016 [1983], p. 249.

5 Quoted in Dare, *op. cit.*

6 Ronald Weston [Robert Anton Wilson], "Why I Am A Right-Wing Anarchist," *the rogerSPARK*, May 1969.

7 Robert Anton Wilson, *Sex, Drugs & Magick: A Journey Beyond Limits*, Hilaritas Press, 2021 [1973], p. 94.

8 Robert Anton Wilson and Robert Shea, "Come Back, Lyndon!" *The Organ*, July 1971.

9 Robert Anton Wilson, "Left and Right: A Non-Euclidean Perspective," *Critique* 27 (1988). The essay also appears in this volume.

10 Robert Anton Wilson, *Right Where You Are Sitting Now: Further Tales of the Illuminati*, And/Or Press, 1982, p. 136.

11 Robert Anton Wilson, "Why I Voted for Michael Dukakis," *The Realist*, Winter 1989. And it's in this book too.

12 Robert Anton Wilson, "Negative Thinking," *The Realist*, June 1963. This is not the same essay that appears in this book under the same title. "Negative Thinking" was the name of Wilson's column in *The Realist*; it sometimes ran with an additional headline and sometimes did not.

13 Robert Anton Wilson, *The Homing Pigeons*, Pocket Books, 1981, p. 144.

14 Quoted in Jeffrey Elliot, "Robert Anton Wilson: Searching For Cosmic Intelligence," *Starship*, Spring 1981.

15 Robert Anton Wilson, "Anarchism," *TSOG: The CD*, New Falcon Publications, 2002. The interviewer is Lance Bauscher. A year earlier, in another conversation with Bauscher — reprinted in this volume as "Utopia USA Interview" — Wilson expressed frustration that the words "anarchist" and "libertarian" could *both* be misinterpreted, and flirted with just calling himself a "decentralist."

16 Robert Anton Wilson, "'When Blood is Their Argument,'" *The Minority of One*, June 1961. Or you could read it in this book.

17 Quoted in Tiffany Lee Brown, "RAW Circuits: Surviving with Robert Anton Wilson," *FringeWare* 8 (1995).

18 Robert Anton Wilson, "T.S.O.G.: The Thing That Ate the Constitution" (2001), online at rawilson.com/tsog.

19 Quoted in Brown, *op. cit.*

20 Anarchists come in both collectivist and individualist varieties, and these are sometimes described as "left" and "right" anarchism, respectively. And while Wilson was influenced by several left-anarchist writers, he drew more ideas from the individualist strain.

21 Similarly, while Wilson had a long history of opposing discrimination against minority groups—he was writing defenses of gay rights in the early 1960s, long before that was a popular cause, and he was arrested for participating in an anti-segregation sit-in in 1963—he could also be grouchy about political correctness.

22 Robert Anton Wilson, *Coincidance: A Head Test*, Hilaritas Press, 2018 [1988], pp. 337–338. (This interview did not appear in the original 1988 edition of *Coincidance*.) For a contrasting view from the younger Wilson, see Robert Anton Wilson, "How to Think About

War and Peace," *Way Out*, December 1962. That essay also appears in this book.

23 Robert Anton Wilson, *Reality is What You Can Get Away With*, Hilaritas Press, 2024 [1992], p. 12.

24 Ibid., p. xxxi.

25 Even before this, there was a history of anti-statist writers appreciating aspects of Scandinavian society. The American cooperative movement of the early 20th century, which included some mutualist and Single Tax strains, admired the co-ops of the Nordic nations. Much later, Wilson's friend Karl Hess—another man known to straddle the "left" and "right" varieties of anarchism—noted with pleasure that the Scandinavian left was "moving further and further toward worker management of productive facilities and further and further away from old concepts of top-down authority and management." (Karl Hess, *Dear America*, William Morrow & Company, 1975, p. 209.) And the Georgists have been a significant force at certain points in Danish history. Albert Jay Nock, an anarcho-libertarian heavily influenced by George, reported excitedly in 1927 that Denmark was seeing "a considerable movement for a complete separation of politics from economics, which, if effected, would of course mean the disappearance of the State." That turned out to be a big *if*. (Albert Jay Nock, "Anarchist's Progress," *The American Mercury*, March 1927.)

26 Robert Anton Wilson, *Cosmic Trigger II: Down to Earth*, Hilaritas Press, 2019 [1991], p. 21.

27 Robert Anton Wilson, "Left and Right," *op. cit.*

28 Ibid.

29 Gabriel Kennedy, *Chapel Perilous: The Life and Thought Crimes of Robert Anton Wilson*, Media Heist Publications, 2024.

30 Robert Anton Wilson, "Left and Right," *op. cit.*

31 To see Wilson disentangling what he likes in Pound from Pound's

A Non-Euclidean Perspective

fascism and antisemitism, read Robert Anton Wilson, "Ezra Pound and His Admirers," *The Minority of One*, October 1960. The article is reprinted in this book.

32 In that *Critique* essay, Wilson noted that he had met many witnesses to the Holocaust over the years. And as you'll see in this book, he invoked Hitler's genocide many times throughout his career, never with any hint that he doubted it was real.

33 Indeed, one of the financial institutions that Wilson criticized the most was the Vatican Bank.

34 Quoted in Peter McAlpine, "Robert Anton Wilson Interview," *Conspiracy Digest*, Spring 1977.

35 Robert Anton Wilson, *Quantum Psychology: How Brain Software Programs You and Your World*, Hilaritas Press, 2016 [1990], p. 80.

36 Towards the end of his life, Wilson developed an elaborate parody of one perennial antisemitic conspiracy theory—the idea that Jewish agents of influence have put America under the thumb of a Zionist Occupational Government, or ZOG—with a detailed argument that tsarist agents of influence have put America under the thumb of a Tsarist Occupational Government, or TSOG. This doubled as an attack on one of Wilson's favorite targets, the drug war: A key functionary of the purported Muscovite conspiracy was the nation's *drug czar*.

37 The early-'60s Wilson was certainly closer to the *Illuminatus!* worldview than the early-'60s Shea, who at that point was still a Kennedy Democrat.

38 Robert Anton Wilson, *Cosmic Trigger I: Final Secret of the Illuminati*, Hilaritas Press, 2016 [1977], p. 4.

39 He cracked that joke in his author bio in a 1971 issue of the *Journal of Human Relations* (volume 19, number 1). He repeated it in his entry for the reference guide *Contemporary Authors*, which first covered Wilson in a 1977 volume and then issued a revised

entry in 1986. In both venues he also described his religion as "transcendental atheism," so it's fair to say he approached these self-descriptions in a playfully paradoxical mood. All the same, there was some serious thought lurking behind them. In a 1975 letter to Don Werkheiser, written as he was growing more interested in ideas like space colonies, Wilson summed up a shift in his thinking by saying he "used to be *anarcho*-technocrat and am now anarcho-*technocrat*."

40 Clark, I should note, was an odd target for this barb: He described his philosophy as "low-tax liberalism" and told reporters that he would not cut welfare for the poor until his other economic policies had brought the country to full employment. I suspect that Wilson was not paying close attention to the details of the Clark campaign and instead was reacting to the Randian gestalt (the Galt gestalt?) that at times seemed to dominate the party.

41 Eric Geislinger and Jane Talisman, "Illuminating Discord: An Interview with Robert Anton Wilson," *New Libertarian Notes*, September 5, 1976. *New Libertarian Notes* was not a Libertarian Party organ—indeed, its anarchist editor was hostile to the party, on the grounds that pursuing political office was an act of collaboration with the state. But the publication and the party came from the same ideological milieu, and the questions the interviewers posed about rent, Austrian economics, and so forth are not far from what you'd expect a member of the Libertarian Party's Rothbardian wing to have asked.

42 James J. Martin, *Men Against the State: The Expositors of Individualist Anarchism in America, 1827–1908*, Adrian Allen Associates, 1953.

43 Herbert Gorman, *James Joyce*, Rinehart & Company, 1949, p. 183. Although this statement was written as though the words were Gorman's, he took the text directly from a note by Joyce. See Richard Ellmann, *James Joyce*, second edition, Oxford University Press, 1982, p. 142 [first edition published in 1959].

44 There were several calls as well for the release of Ezra Pound, who received (and annotated) the publication at the asylum where he was imprisoned. And in 1958, *Doubt* ran an item recommending two periodicals that would soon be closely associated with Wilson: *The Realist*, which published his articles throughout its lifespan, and *Balanced Living*, which Wilson would edit for a spell in the early 1960s, renaming it *Way Out*.

45 Joshua Blu Buhs has written many mini-bios of members of the Fortean Society in this period, including discussions of their political views, and posted them at his blog *From an Oblique Angle* (joshuablubuhs.com). See also Joshua Blu Buhs, *Think to New Worlds: The Cultural History of Charles Fort and His Followers*, University of Chicago Press, 2024.

Negative Thinking

Published in *The Realist*, February 1960

Readers who were confused by the column that appeared under my name last month have my sympathy. I was confused by it myself. Actually, it was not written by me but by somebody in the printer's office. (Probably, it was the same frustrated literatus who added that magnificent stream-of-consciousness bit onto the end of Paul Krassner's editorial in the same issue.).

I did write a column with the same title and some similar lines in it, but its whereabouts: a mystery. I will say, however, that the column which did appear in print was interesting, in an experimental sort of way, although too heavily influenced, I think, by the Dada poetry of the '20s.

That same issue contains a letter expressing pleasure that *The Realist* is printed at a union shop. I am reminded of H. L. Mencken's remark about cigars. "Every time I get a bad one," he said, "I turn it over and read the label. It always says, 'Made by union labor.'"

• • •

This column has lashed out at so many bromides of both Left and Right that my seventeen faithful readers might be starting to wonder just what I "am," politically. The answer is that I "am" nothing, politically. I regard politics as a sport strictly on all fours with table-tapping, palmistry or attending folksong concerts, and I would sooner get hit on the head with a rhinoceros hoof than get mixed up in it in any way.

In all my life I have only heard two political theories with which I agree. The first was enunciated by Rimbaud: "Don't be a victim." The second was paraphrased from Lao-Tse by Jack Kerouac: "Avoid the authorities."

Several months ago, after I had made some saturnine remarks about the Nuremberg Trials in this column, I received a very intelligent letter taking the opposite view, from a Mr. David Loeb of Woodmere, New York. I intended to answer it here, but other things kept capturing my attention, and I never got around to it.

Last Christmas Eve, however, a good answer came along: and it has been repeated almost daily, all over the world, ever since. I refer to the swastikas that the psychopaths of the world have taken to inscribing upon synagogues.

If this "connection" seems a bit obscure, let me be more explicit. It is commonplace to remark that Hitler never would have gotten beyond the level of a neighborhood trouble-maker if Germany hadn't had good and ample reason to be disgruntled with the Versailles Treaty. There are always people like Adolph around; every community has a few of them. But they do not rise beyond beer-hall hooliganism unless the community as a whole is seething with discontent and looking for desperate solutions to its problems.

America was seething with such discontent and desperation in the early '30s; and the Adolphs (who are always around) came to the fore. Several of them got big, noisy followings.

(One was doing so well that only a bullet kept him out of the White House.) Fortunately for us, a bounder of a vastly more civilized type was at the helm in those days, and his radio crooning was able to soothe the hungry mob until the situation was alleviated by a war-time economy.

But the Adolphs are still around. When the Supreme Court's desegregation decision of 1954 raised blood pressures below the Mason-Dixon line, they came to the fore again. One of them migrated southwards all the way from Greenwich Village, acquiring a drawl and a big hat on the way.

This is a perennial problem, and punishment does not solve it. Indeed, it actively and positively makes it worse. Caryl Chessman, who is proud to call himself a criminal psychopath, says of his arrival in the Death Cell at San Quentin:

"I had 'proved' everything I had felt the need to prove: that I couldn't be scared or broken or driven to my knees, that I didn't give a damn. But here is where the tragedy lies: this felt need is compulsive and negative only. It is a need to prove that one can do without – without love, without faith, without belief, without warmth, without friends, without freedom . . . If not checked, the ultimate (conscious or unconscious) need is to prove that one can do without life itself."

To "punish" people of this sort is only to provide fuel for the inner fires of other psychopaths. The judges who passed sentence at Nuremberg didn't just set in motion the legal machinery that brought Jules Streicher to the gallows, where he died shouting "Heil Hitler!"; they also set in motion the psychological machinery that moved the hands that scribbled swastikas on the synagogues of New York fifteen years later.

"It is an old rule," said Gautama Sakyamuni. "Hatred is not cured by hatred. Hatred is cured by love." It is, indeed, an old rule, 2500 years older now than when he quoted it; but still only a small minority has understood it. It is not sentimental; it is not idealistic; it is not utopian. It is a plain fact which you can test in your daily life.

Politics is the art and science of ignoring this rule and convincing yourself that you can make the world better through force.

When the fascist planes bombed the civilians of Guernica, Spain, in 1937, the whole world shuddered. That such things could be done to civilians – including innocent children – seemed an abomination so terrible as to be beyond understanding.

Within five years, all the nations involved in the Second World War were doing the same thing. The Allies, in the total course of the war, actually did more saturation bombing of civilians than the Axis. And they concluded the war by dropping two atomic bombs on two different cities. All of this was done, we were told, to preserve freedom and civilization. The war was thereupon concluded by turning half of East Europe into slavery at the hands of Stalin.

I am far from being an intellectual giant myself, but I admit to utter astonishment at the stupidity of people who can still believe anything that comes out of the mouth of a politician.

• • •

The new Miss Rheingold, Emily Banks, is one of the most charming girls I have seen in a turtle's age, but I wonder why she is content to enter only the second largest election in the country. She could obviously win in the bigger election as easily as she did in the smaller one. And as President she would undoubtedly be an embarrassment to Comrade Khrushchev – how could even he be publicly disagreeable to such a nice, old-fashioned girl? Besides, she looks much too refined to be advertising beer, which is after all a *man's* drink.

Why not just have her switch jobs with the present incumbent, or non-incumbent, of the White House? After all, he's an outdoorsy, huntin' and golfin' sort of chap, rugged-looking and fatherly, and he *looks* like a beer drinker. Using him as a symbol, Rheingold might double their sales.

Let's have the right person in the right job, I say.

. . .

The best book of 1959, in my opinion, was Bernard Wolfe's *The Great Prince Died*. Besides being a rip-snortingly lively thriller of the Graham Greene school, it is the first book since Trotsky's death to attempt a judicious and balanced portrait of that astounding career.

Trotsky was, after all, the only person of genius-level intelligence to get mixed up in politics in our time, and his career was such a maze of paradoxes, contradictions and enigmas that it will remain forever one of the great dreams of history.

Why did Trotsky, who had warned against totalitarianism as early as 1904, become the most bloody of all the Bolsheviks, after 1917? Why did he allow Stalin to push him aside so easily, almost seeming to cooperate with his own banishment? Why did he continue to defend the Bolshevik ethic after his own son had fallen victim to it? And why was he such a sitting duck for the GPU at the end, making only token gestures to defend his household when he knew GPU killers were in Mexico?

Bernard Wolfe, a novelist of more than common talent, has answered all these questions in *The Great Prince Died*. In every case, the answer is Kronstadt. Wolfe's analysis is that Trotsky was basically the romantic, idealistic fellow that he seemed to those who knew him in youth. Under the pressure of the Revolution, he accepted all those "dry, deadly" aspects of Marxism which he had earlier somewhat doubted.

To prove to the other Bolsheviks – and to himself – that he was truly an iron-willed Marxist, and not the dreamy idealist he had been accused of being, he outdid everybody else in ferocity. He even pushed this "false self" so far that he was able to become a military genius of the highest order.

The inevitable rebellion of the inner self came with Kronstadt. Wolfe points out, incisively, that Trotsky himself once referred to the Kronstadt sailors as "mistaken comrades" rather than as the White-infiltrated "reactionaries" the Party Line claimed them to be. These sailors had idealized Trotsky more than any other Bolshevik.

Nevertheless, their mutiny was viciously crushed, with Trotsky's approval. Wolfe insists that from that point onward Trotsky was a divided man, incapable of facing his guilt, incapable also of escaping it. He had to defend the Bolshevik ethic to the end: to deny it was to admit to himself that he was no better than any other murdering thug, *no better than Stalin.*

But the voice of humanity in him could not be stilled. His heart was not in Bolshevism any more. He allowed himself to be pushed into minor administrative posts. Then, with all the evidence in his hand (including Lenin's will warning against Stalin) he allowed himself to be pushed aside entirely. From exile, he kept up a paper warfare, a verbal warfare, against Stalin.

It never succeeded because it was not really meant to succeed. Trotsky had tasted the bitter fruits of power and knew their poison, and didn't really want them back again.

Wolfe doesn't quote from *Their Morals and Ours*, but it proves everything he says about this part of the Old Man's career. No more confusing and contradictory, no more pathetically sophomoric treatise has ever come from the pen of a man of undoubtable genius. The argument really comes down to: it's good for me to kill the Czar's innocent children for a theoretical system, but it is wrong for Stalin to kill my innocent son for a theoretical system.

The wrongness of killing anybody for any theoretical system he couldn't admit, for then he would have to answer for Kronstadt.

When the GPU thugs gathered about his home in Coyoacán, he made only mechanical gestures of defense. He was a man at war with himself. The more he wrote to prove a difference between the Trotsky-Lenin ethic and the Stalin ethic, the more obvious it became that there was no such difference.

When Jacson's cowardly blow finally came, it must have been a merciful release to the tormented Old Man.

Such, at least, is Wolfe's theory. As I have indicated, it makes sense to me. More than that, it takes Trotsky out of the role of innocent victim in a melodrama as well as out of the villainous and equally melodramatic role to which he was once relegated by Stalinist propaganda and liberal stupidity. It makes him an authentic tragic hero in the Greek and Shakespearean sense – and that, really, is the best the Old Man could expect for the verdict of posterity.

• • •

I don't think Reginald Dunsany was very fair when he called me an "intolerant boor" in his "Tolerant Pagan" column two months ago.*

~•~

*There is a much better, more amusing attack on me by Jack Jones in the December issue of *The Independent*.

~•~

The expression is harsh, and seems slightly unjust in my estimation. "Cantankerous bumpkin" or "irascible curmudgeon" would be more accurate, I think. I take pride in getting just the proper tone of scrupulous nastiness into these columns, and I hate to be misunderstood or undervalued. Perhaps "recalcitrant maverick" is what Mr. Dunsany was really trying to say.

There are times when I attempt to reform and mend my wicked, wicked ways – I have even subscribed to *The Humanist* just to learn the proper technique of arguing against a lunacy without once revealing that you consider it a lunacy. I have thrown away all my books by Mencken, Bierce, Brann, Fort, Voltaire, Harrow, Paine and other such irreverent scoundrels; and I have read nothing but polite academic journals for a whole month. It doesn't seem to help. I remain the same recalcitrant, irascible, cantankerous and intolerant bastard I always have been.

The fellow who first threw a dead cat into the sacristy was certainly a rude, intolerant and vulgar chap – but he did something for mankind that all the polite, safe liberals and humanists have never done. He demonstrated that the terrible, all-powerful, omnibodaceous God on the altar, and His terrible, all-powerful, omnivociferous priesthood, were between them not pugnacious enough not to stifle one man's honest expression of what he thought of them.

He made it known to all men that it is possible to rear up on your hind legs and tell the most entrenched authoritarians to go to hell. And, most important of all, he showed that we need not always be shy, and tentative, and awkward, when we dissent from a popular delusion. He showed that the forces of unreason can be treated precisely and exactly as they deserve – with an unfrightened, undisguised and unmitigated contempt.

Ezra Pound and his Admirers

Published in *The Minority of One*, October 1960

Impact: Essays on Ignorance and the Decline of American Civilization by Ezra Pound. Henry Regnery Company, 1960. 285 pp, $5.00

When I was purchasing Ezra Pound's new book, *Impact*, at the West 8th Street bookstore in Greenwich Village, the clerk said to me, "There's a lot of mush in with the impact."

"There always is, in Pound," I answered, "But the impact is still there."

It is, indeed, still there and always there in Ezra Loomis Pound – poet, composer, economist, polylinguist, fascist, traitor and madman. On page after page of this book I stopped breathless at Pound's insight and his verbal wizardry. Aphorisms stick in the mind afterwards like arrows in a target: "*A slave is one who looks for someone else to free him.*" "*Every man has the right to have his ideas examined one at a time.*"

A Non-Euclidean Perspective

"Latin is sacred, grain is sacred." "The enemy is ignorance (our own)." "If Christ and the angels ran the farms, with Aristotle, Spinoza and Henry Ford supervisin', it wouldn't do any good unless the consumers and would-be consumers had currency to buy the product."

There is a great deal of worth in this book besides pungent aphorisms.

To the point are a long essay on the "Ethics of Mencius," a brilliant study of the Jefferson-Adams correspondence, and a 20-page digest of United States economic history that is so damn good I would like to quote all here (if I had the room).

Pound's great value as an economist, irrespective of the utility of the various "solutions" to our problems that he has espoused at various times, is his clear, crisp command of two basic insights: that money has no value in and of itself, but is merely a symbol of value; and that true value resides in the natural order, the "growing grass" and "living sheep." Others have realized this, but Pound's importance is the peculiarly poetic quality of his awareness, and his ability to transmit this to his readers. Read any of Pound's economic writings once and you will never again be completely easy with the international system that, while it has produced great quantities of paper wealth, has *destroyed more land for agriculture in the past 50 years than were destroyed in the previous 5000 years.*

Many readers may not like my praising Ezra Pound, and I can sympathize with them – I do not like praising him, either. That is the real point of this review. Ezra Pound is the greatest single challenge to our minds and hearts that the 20th century has offered us. Two statements which I am arrogant enough to call "facts" must be placed on record in any intelligent discussion of Pound: (1) He is a great poet and a great thinker; (2) He has deliberately and consistently supported fascism, anti-Semitism and other vicious systems and attitudes for 30 years now, and continues to do so.

You can almost divide the contemporary intelligentsia into two parts: those who refuse, obstinately, to recognize the first of those facts, and those who, with equal obstinacy, try to avoid recognizing the second of those facts. This is only human, and quite forgivable. Placed together, those facts make a paradox which is both tragic and highly alarming. Most of us prefer not to face that paradox, and we reduce Pound to one part of it and ignore the other part.

This new book, for instance, has been edited – without Pound's consent, I would guess – to remove pro-fascist or anti-Semitic passages. I feel this was done without Pound's consent, because Pound's latest volume of poetry (*Thrones*, New Directions, 1959) continues to express those opinions unabashedly and violently.

Here are a few examples of what has been done in this anthology:

The essay, "A Visiting Card," has been stripped of the following opening aphorisms: "*A thousand candles together blaze with intense brightness. No one candle's light damages another's. So is the liberty of the individual in the ideal and fascist state.*" I quote this from the edition of "A Visiting Card" published by Peter Russell, London, as #4 of "Money Pamphlets by Pound." (Peter Russell, 114b Queen's Gate, London S.W. 7; 1952.)

The same essay contains the following passage in the Peter Russell edition but not in the *Impact* anthology:

"*Eliot, in this book, has not come through uncontaminated by the Jewish poison.*"

"*Until a man purges himself of this poison he will never achieve understanding . . .* In these essays Eliot falls into too many non sequiturs. Until he succeeds in detaching the Jewish from the European elements of his peculiar variety of Christianity he will never find the right formula . . ." etc. etc., with more such gibberish for several lines, all of it removed from this edition.

A more interesting case of suppression occurs in the essay, "Integrity of the Word." As published in *Impact*, the passage in question begins with the following quote from Lenin:

> *"Moreover, imperialism is an immense accumulation of money capital in a few countries, which as we have seen, amounts to 4 or 5 thousand million pounds sterling in securities. Hence the enormous growth of a class, or rather a stratum, of rentiers, i.e. persons who live by 'clipping coupons' who take absolutely no part in any enterprise, and whose profession is idleness. The exportation of capital, one of the most essential economic bases of imperialism, still further isolates this rentier stratum from production, and sets the seal of parasitism on the whole country living on the exploitation of labour of several overseas countries and colonies."*

In Peter Russell's edition (*What is Money For? – Money Pamphlets by Pound* #3) we find the following more extensive comment:

> *"Very well! That is from Lenin. But you could quote the same substance from Hitler, who is a nazi (note the paragraph from Mein Kampf magnificently isolated by Wyndham Lewis in his 'Haler' – 'The struggle against international finance and loan capital has become the most important point in the National Socialist programme: the struggle of the German nation for its independence and freedom.')*

> *"You could quote it from Mussolini, a fascist, from C. H. Douglas, who calls himself a democrat and his followers the only true democrats. You could quote it from McNail Wilson, who is a Christian Monarchy man. You could quote it from a dozen camps which have no suspicion that they are quoting Lenin.*

> *"Some facts are now known above parties; some*

perceptions are the common heritage of all men of
good will, and only, the Jewspapers and worse than
Jewspapers try now to obscure them."

I am not dragging up these repulsive rantings of Pound's to further disgrace the man; he is already in considerable disgrace with the majority of his fellow humans. I am merely trying to emphasize the paradox that nobody seems to want to face. Against these unpleasant quotes we must place such passages from Pound as (to give three):

1. From a letter to Secretary of the Treasury Henry Morgenthau Jr., dated August 7, 1934: *"The sane thing to do with the hogs is not to destroy them, but to issue money against them up to the limit of what people want (as distinct from what they can buy under present food system.) . . . If the govt. has enough title to hogs and corn, to destroy 'em it has enough title to issue bills against 'em demanding delivery."* (*Impact*, page 271)

2. "Pull down thy vanity

    How mean thy hates

Fostered in falsity,

    Pull down thy vanity,

Rathe to destroy, niggard in charity.

Pull down thy vanity,

    I say pull down."

(*The Pisan Cantos*, page 99)

3. "Ysolt, Ydone,

    have compassion,

Picarda,

    compassion

By the wing'd head,

by the caduceus,
compassion;
By the horns of Isis-Luna,
compassion."
(*Section: Rock Drills*, page 88)

Some simple-minded fools will convince themselves that
the love expressed so nobly in Pound's poetry is hypocritical,
and will ignore his 40-year crusade for economic justice,
and his myriad charities recorded by Louis Zukofsky, Ernest
Hemingway, William Carlos Williams and other anti-fascists.
Another group of simple-minded fools will see Pound's
positive side then blind themselves to his repeated anti-Semitic
ranting, his continued pro-fascism, his obvious paranoia and
his fantastic ability to lie to himself about the murder of six
million people.

The simple fact is that most of us dare not look at the
paradox of Ezra Pound too closely, because it is the paradox of
human nature – our own nature. To see Pound as he is – a man
of genius and goodwill, of folly and rage, of love and integrity
and hatred and dishonesty – is to admit that such contradictions
can exist in the human personality. That is not a comfortable
thought – it is especially uncomfortable to those of us who
are, like Pound, idealists intent on changing the world – so we
prefer to brush it aside and go on playing our life-myth that the
universe is one big Western Movie where the "good guys" (us)
are fighting the "bad guys" (our enemies).

I am not saying that you will find Pound's real goodness
in every fascist somewhere and Pound's real hatefulness in
every Humanitarian Reformer somewhere, but just that the
two do overlap more often than we care to admit. The senior
LaFollette, for instance, was as honorable and sincere a
reformer as America has ever produced – but he did indulge
in anti-Semitism in a few of his writings. Colonel House,

the liberal friend and advisor of both Woodrow Wilson and Franklin Roosevelt, once shared Pound's admiration for Mussolini's "ruthless efficiency." The number of sincere Liberals who closed their eyes to the horrors of Stalin's Russia runs into the hundreds of thousands, undoubtedly.

The simple – dreadfully simple – fact that the urge to reform is always at least partly personal, in the narrow sense. The average man never lifts himself out of his rut of doing what he is expected to do and thinking what he is expected to think. Creative thought begins from frustration, always: we see that something is wrong somewhere and we wonder what. From this point onward we can take off in any direction, depending upon the complexity of our personal suffering under the thing that is wrong, our degree of awareness of logical alternatives and our learned ability to avoid jumping to conclusions. Impatience is always the great enemy: it is easy to pick some Villain and to convince ourselves that everything would be all right again if He were eliminated.

Even Jefferson showed a tendency toward the fanatic personality, whenever he started raving about "nourishing the tree of Liberty with blood." You don't nourish any tree with blood, except the tree of Death.

I am not trying to "explain" or "justify" Ezra Pound; I am trying to indicate the way in which his particular tragic schizophrenia must be taken into account as a warning by every man who dares at all to think for himself. George Washington and Lenin both had beloved older brothers killed by the systems they later rebelled against (as Pound points out). The roots of our own motivations are never completely open to us, and even Hitler – somewhere in his twisted childhood – began as an instinctively correct rebel against an unjust social system.

Poor Ezra – at an advanced age and in delicate health – endured fifteen years in an insane asylum. Anybody who knows anything at all about such institutions must, if he be human, feel a stab of sympathy for a great poet brought to such a pass at the end of his life. I am not saying that Pound suffered enough to expunge his crime; I do not understand people who think that suffering expunges anything. I am merely saying that Pound has suffered. He has learned nothing from it. His first gesture on returning to Italy was to give the fascist salute – but if we learn nothing from it, we are fools indeed.

The Accusing Ghost of Caryl Chessman

Published in *The Minority of One*, September 1960

The Kid Was A Killer, by Caryl Chessman.
Gold Medal Books, Now York, 1960. 168 pp. 35c

On May 2, 1960, the State of California ritually sacrificed another victim to the scowling God of Capital Punishment.

It had taken them twelve years to do it, because this victim, unlike most of the men who end their lives in death row, was an unique personality well endowed with eloquence, intelligence and determination to live. He was Caryl Chessman – San Quentin #66565 – a self-diagnosed "criminal psychopath" who taught himself law and fought his way past eight execution dates with legal maneuvers of unprecedented brilliance.

He also wrote books, and violently disturbing books they were, well calculated to get under the skin of any ordinary

citizen who considered "the Criminal" to be a sub-human species completely unrelated to himself. Chessman said that "the Criminal" was not different, not alien or unearthly or possessed by demons, but a man much like yourself, and, because Chessman was an artist with words, he could make you feel this, with an intensity that might be painful if you were a person who had never doubted the simple goodness of your own motivations.

The newspapers and mass magazines of the country, by and large, gave Chessman an unfriendly coverage. He was challenging the institution of Capital Punishment, and many editors wouldn't know what to put on the front page half the time if there weren't an execution to be celebrated. Chessman's attempt to argue his innocence in his books (notably in the Appendix to *Trial by Ordeal*) was rather persuasive; the newspapers and mass magazines made sure that most of this evidence never reached their public. To the majority of people in America, Chessman's guilt is as indisputable as the wisdom of Eisenhower or the Divine Origin of Christianity. Most of them were glad when he was executed. "Serves the dirty rapist right," they said, defending Sound Moral Principles.

Caryl Chessman died with quiet dignity – "without animal fear and without bravado," as he said he would. He left behind a letter to the American people, asserting again his absolute innocence of the rape-kidnappings for which he was executed, and also quashing a burgeoning "Chessman fan club" among some shady intellectuals: "*I regard myself as neither hero nor martyr*," he wrote tersely. "*On the contrary, I am a confessed fool who is keenly aware of the nature and quality of the folly of his earlier rebellious years.*"

Caryl Chessman always said that he wanted to, and felt himself capable of, making a serious contribution to our understanding of the "psychopathic personality." In *Cell 2455, Death Row,* he told the grisly story of the deformation of his own character into the psychopathic mold, and gave us some compelling insights into the thinking and feeling of such a personality. He made obvious what many of us had long suspected: that the "psychopath" is not nearly as far removed from the rest of us as many psychiatrists think.

It might be well to pause here a moment and clarify our terminology. Most laymen, even those with a nodding acquaintance with psychiatry, tend to confuse "psychopath" with "psychotic," or to think that a "psychopath" is just a "neurotic" on the borderline of becoming "psychotic." Actually, the distinctions are quite sharp. A neurotic has a fairly undamaged perception of reality, but is unable to accept his role in society: most of his aggressions are turned inward against himself, and generally only come out against others in sneaky and covert forms. A psychotic has a badly damaged perception of reality, lives in complicated delusions and hallucinations, and may turn his aggressions inward or outward. A psychopath has a very clear perception of reality, and simply unleashes upon the world the aggressions which neurotics turn inward on themselves and psychotics convert into fantasy and hallucinations.

The psychopath is often a most charming and likeable person – until you stand in his way. Norman Mailer has pointed out that the hipsters are in some ways very similar to psychopaths. Many scandalous novels of recent years are about psychopaths who hold high positions in our society and who can generally be recognized by the reader through artfully placed hints: recall the T.V. entertainer in *The Great Man*, the sponsor in *The Hucksters*, the General in *A Bell for Adano*, the Governor in *All The King's Men*, the movie producer in *The Big Knife*, etc. To a great extent, current mass culture (beliefs, values, etc.) has been imposed upon the public by these psychopaths.

Most psychiatrists say that the psychopath lacks affect, or has "a weak Super-ego" (conscience), or just doesn't "feel as ordinary people do." There is even a large minority opinion holding that psychopaths are "just born that way".

Dr. Robert Lindner, who had more success in treating psychopaths than the average psychiatrist, dissented from all those theories. He felt that the psychopath was, in the title of one of his books, a *Rebel Without A Cause* – a person who injured by society turns against it, but without a constructive socially ameliorative program – "*an agitator without a slogan.*"

Caryl Chessman has left us one more legacy to add to his last letter – a new book published (ironically) on the day of his execution. This book, *The Kid Was A Killer*, says more, in my opinion, about the genesis and nature of the psychopath than anything else I have ever read, with the possible exception of a few pages in Wilhelm Reich.

Chessman's analysis is basically Reichian. The Kid – he is never given any other name – does not lack affect, or feeling, or a Super-ego. He is not "born that way." He very simply has armored himself against feelings, because he has been hurt too much by the world. A sadistic father starts the process of hurting and armoring: beating the Kid constantly, accusing the Kid of homosexuality when he shows normal human feelings of tenderness, and telling him repeatedly: "You gotta be able to take it" (page 45). Then a terrible thing happens: the Kid's long-tormented mother murders his father right before his eyes. The mother is sent to prison and the Kid to a state "home" where discipline is of the Teutonic variety and sadism comes with breakfast in the morning. The Kid begins internalizing his father's philosophy: "*There were times when you did have to be able to take it, when you stood up and hurled defiance into the teeth of the cosmos.*" (page 61) The Kid's mother dies in prison: "*Far into the night he cried and prayed, and the other kids made fun of his tears and prayers, as they often had before. "Old cry baby's at it again," one of them said. The others snickered . . . His sobs grew louder. The night attendant told him to shut up. He did. He bottled up his feelings.*" (page 60).

The Kid begins to learn the secret of "taking it" – i.e., killing one's own emotional life. *"Being free was what counted, free even of love if love were a mothering thing, an Achilles heel, if it brought only suffering and pain."* (page 61)

This is a far cry from the "emotionless," "inborn" psychopathy. This is an alive, feeling human child trying to learn to cope with pain by becoming emotionally armored.

Now, however, comes the great irony of the book. Having given us his own insider's view on how psychopathic criminality is born, Caryl Chessman pulls a trick on us – a trick with quite a moral to it. The Kid takes *"hate and guile on his friends"* (page 62) as Chessman himself talks of his *"fanatic friend, Hate"* in *Cell 2455, Death Row* – but the Kid does not become a hardened criminal! Instead, the Korean War comes along, and the Kid with his armored personality, holding back the normal emotions and only allowing hate and guile to express themselves – becomes a military hero and wins a pile of medals. This is where the "killing" is done that the reader has been waiting for. Our culture, which creates the psychopathic killer, nowadays can use him as well.

After the war, the Kid drifts into the prize-fighting game, where his hate and guile again serve him well. Finally, in a rather unconvincing but dramatic conclusion, the Kid becomes aware of the emotional wasteland of his life and deliberately allows himself to be killed by a sneaky punch by the Champion.

He has realized that his armoring has stifled all of the living things inside him and that he has become a hollow shell, and he cannot bear to go on living that way.

To the fight crowd, the Kid becomes a hero, a symbol; and Chessman makes his point with savage irony: *"In an age so fear-ridden, so full of doubt that it can feel secure only by creating awesome weapons too destructively stupefying to imagine, it is no surprise that such an age would create an equally awesome psychopathic personality whose attributes should appear, as well as clinically tragic to a few of us, symbolically desirable to many of us."* (page 167)

Wilhelm Reich wrote a long time ago in *The Function of the Orgasm* and *The Mass Psychology of Fascism* that the "armored personality" is becoming epidemic in our civilization. People are bottled-up, tense, ashamed of their sexual feelings, embarrassed by their tender feelings. They admire only "toughness," and follow any leader who seems to offer them an outlet for their unconscious rage against the culture which has imposed this armoring on them. Since Reich wrote, the armorings of individuals; and of nations both have grown thicker and more conspicuous, and unconscious rage is the only explanation of the insane rapidity with which we are pouring radioactive poison into the food of the world. Chessman's novel, as the case history of an armored individual who became a hero to countless thousands who are trying desperately to become equally armored, serves as an interesting document to demonstrate Reich's thesis. It is tragic to reflect that just when Chessman was beginning to understand these things, and to do something about them, the state of California murdered him.

Chessman had learned to challenge his inner rage away from irrational crimes against society, into rational criticisms of society – but the state of California killed him. Chessman proved his growing ethical sense by volunteering to become a subject for research in a cancer laboratory – but the state of California killed him. Chessman has left us an imperishable testament to his own emergence out of psychopathy, in his last letter, where he pleads not for his own life, but for *"other men living out their last days on death row"* – but the state of California killed him.

Perhaps, Chessman's death, even more than his writings, will force society to look at itself, and ask if all the psychopathy is in the professional criminals.

Behind the Mask of Apathy

Published in *The Minority of One*, May 1961

C. Wright Mills once described United States foreign policy (under Eisenhower) as a variety of "crackpot realism." The phrase, it seems to me, might do well to describe attitudes in the United States today, not just on international relations, but on almost any subject under the sun.

We are living in an age of conformity, as a hundred or more social critics have remarked; but the roots and origins of this conformity are rarely discussed. Man is not naturally a conformist: by biological endowment, he is the opposite, a born rebel. Psychiatrist Robert Lindner was so impressed with the tenacious inner creativity and inner powers of innovation shown by all mankind, even by the most miserably frightened neurotics, that he posited an "instinct toward rebellion" as an inborn human trait, as strong as the food or sex instincts. A biochemist I happen to know says, even more stringently, that every child is born a deviate: in his

A Non-Euclidean Perspective

germ plasm he is unlike any other child ever born. (This can be rigorously proven by direct application of the Second Law of Thermodynamics to genetics: each meeting of genes produces a *Gestalt* that has never been before.) Man does not need to be brilliant or brave to be a non-conformist; he only has to be himself. If we are living in an age of conformity, we can be sure that we are also living in an age of enormous cowardice.

I will come on so strong as to say that "conformity" and "crockpot realism" are misleading phrases in a way, and that Norman Mailer came closer to the bone when he said that American life today "exudes extensive fear from every pore." The sleepwalking apathy of our society is probably a gigantic organized mask, like the mask of apathy, worn by certain psychotics, who are about to erupt into violence on the next tick of the pulse. Professional psychiatrists and psychologists read the letters sent to Governor Brown of California last year urging Caryl Chessman's execution; and I have heard that these hardened experts on pathology, were shocked by the extent and explicitness of the emotional sickness revealed in these letters. Certainly, I have been increasingly conscious, during the last decade, that the sensibility of this nation has shifted profoundly and in an unhealthy way.

It was after coming into this country that Wilhelm Reich felt the need to posit a new psychological type, not neurotic merely and not yet psychotic, the *"emotional plague"* type. If as recently as the '30s this country seemed partially neurotic and partially healthy, now it seems more neurotic, less healthy and with a large and growing incidence of emotional plague.

Here are some of Reich's criteria of emotional plague: unlike the neurotic character, who is passive and suffering, the emotional plague character is active and causes suffering; he is intolerant in the strictest sense of that word; he cannot bear to see anybody acting freely or spontaneously, because he wants all the world to be under the same rigid compulsions as himself; his racial prejudices are violent and malignant (unlike the "gentleman's anti-Semitism," for instance, of most neurotics); he believes in force, in violence, in warfare, as a means of settling disputes, and is compulsively afraid of anything that can be called "tenderness" or "gentleness" (he would call it "cowardly" or "soft"); he is compulsively busy regulating, or trying to regulate, the sexual-love lives of others; etc. That this nation is the only in the 20th century to put a man to death for a sex offense (which every psychiatrist knows could only be committed by a sick individual), and that the people hysterically supporting this execution by an overwhelming majority are two indications of the prevalence of emotional plague.

What most of us mean when we complain about the "conformity" in this society today is that we have become conscious of some of the aspects of emotional plague around us, and do not recognize it for what it is. Man is not a conformist by birth, and can never really become one, no matter how hard he tries. What passes for conformity is an attitude, or a semantic conditioned reflex, of "Ah, what-the-hell, why should I stick my neck out?" Such semantic reflexes, or thought-stoppers (more properly, we should call them life-stoppers, since they block off perception and feeling as well as thought) are part of an enormous desensitization, a contraction of the life-energies.

This is not an other-directed society; it is an un-directed society. It's not directed because it's not going anywhere. To say that the bland, apathetic faces of most Americans look like those of battle-fatigue cases is not to stretch a point at all: growing up in such a society is growing up absurd, as Paul Goodman wrote, and each of us has to fight a battle to keep some of our biochemical individuality, and most of us have been severely scarred in the skirmishes.

The reason that the American public reacts indifferently, or doesn't react at all to the folly, dishonesty, and sometimes mania of the A.E.C., for instance, is that the American public cannot begin to imagine that there is an alternative to such organized idiocies. The mind and the perceptions are dead, or

A Non-Euclidean Perspective

dying; and any event is forgotten and banished from memory and evaluation with another great semantic conditioned reflex: "It's a tough world." With those magic words Joe American abdicates his humanity and becomes a molecule acted upon by blind, impersonal forces. He likes being such a molecule, really: he wants to feel helpless and carried along by something, mysterious, blank and impersonal. There are very definite and deliberate reasons for the popularity of the myth that "we're all caught in this trap together, nobody can do anything about it," etc. Emile Zola, one man alone with no allies, but his own intellect and anger overturned a French government, and got Dreyfus off Devil's Island after seven years; but the myth of impotence beloved by American society today has nothing to do with that fact or the hundreds like it recorded in history. Americans believe in the importance of intellect today because they have been trained not to use the intellect; they believe in the folly of idealism, because they have been trained not to be idealists. And there are very simple reasons for all of this, reasons so simple that nobody dares to mention them in the public prints. The reason above all other reasons is that we have lost the tradition of what this nation was founded for, we are afloat without a rudder. This nation was founded by secular humanists on rational, humanistic values, and one force and one only has acted, since the beginning, to obliterate this knowledge. That force, quite simply, is organized Religion.

Americans today have no sense of values and little hope for survival: they confront the gigantic, psychopathic, tyranny of neo-Stalinism and don't know how to answer it. The only answers they have ever been taught are the medieval, superstitious myths of the organized churches. It is pathetic, and ridiculous; it is like sending out children who have been taught only Mother Goose and fairytales to argue physics with Einstein. We had a great humanistic and scientific tradition in Jefferson, Franklin, Adams, etc., but no detail of this tradition can be taught in our schools. A teacher who mentions that these men were all freethinkers will be looking for another job in a week.

Hence, Americans have no ideals to set against Soviet ideals, no values to set above Soviet values, no motive to set against Soviet determination to impose its motivations. Not being aware of the terms of the 20th century conflict, our citizens and our statesmen are baffled and beaten before they enter the arena of debate.

What is plaguing American society, principally, is anxiety: that deadening of the life-energies that come from traumatic fear. To paraphrase Housman, we are afraid in a world that science has made. Being raised on anti-scientific myths, we don't know how to adjust to the 20th century. Paradoxically, as the anxiety of our system grows, we grab more firmly to the only comfort we know – religious myth – and thus make ourselves further incapable of reacting rationally to the challenges of our time. But this leads to greater follies and blunders, thus increasing our continuous defeats in the ideological war, and adding new reverberations of anxiety to our national psyche.

Can Even Living Be Forgotten?

Published in *The Minority of One*, March 1961

The authoritarian social structure of so-called "civilization" has not changed radically, at the root, in 6000 years. This authoritarian social structure remains basically an oligarchy at all times; dictators and tyrants escape this oligarchal structure no more than democracies do. The oligarchal rule of civilized man involves, fundamentally, the control of the symbols of wealth (paper money, gold, or whatever) by a small group of usurious manipulators.

Under this 6000-year-old social structure every child is born into a state of debt inherited from his parents, and often from his parents' parents. In most cases, also, the child is born without the legal "right" to live on the planet Earth, i.e., on its surface. He has to purchase this "right" from somebody else, through the payment of "rent," since a small group of speculators claims to "own" the Earth and only allows the rest of us to dwell on its surface so long as we pay tribute to them.

The international usurers who control paper money and other symbols of wealth similarly have appropriated unto themselves the medium of exchange; and we no longer have what Lincoln once said free men must have in order to remain free, "our own money to pay our own debts." We must use the usurer's money, and pay tribute to him for the privilege.

The social structure is almost certainly the result of conquest. That is to say, a people dwelling in the state of nature would not depart from it willingly, but must be forcibly regimented into slavery at first, and then, their spirits broken, released into the "slavery to symbols" of civilized man. In other words, the "simple" savage is too sophisticated to believe in symbols of wealth the way civilized man does: he values the concrete filing, this tree, that horse, yonder grazing pasture. Only after an interim of slavery, of being forced to act not on his own volition but on another's command, will the savage grow schizoid enough to be ready for the "civilized" state. "Civilized" man, living on a planet that he has been told is owned by others and forced to deal with things always through a paper symbol the value of which he has been told must be controlled by "experts" he never sees, has lost all control over his own life and does not know what a truly volitional act would be. He therefore, at all times and all places, even in the most blatant dictatorships, makes a big verbal noise about his "freedom" and "liberty," etc. – abstractions which would never occur to the savage who possesses their reality.

There is considerable evidence that the stress of this kind of anti-natural living is definitely harmful *psychosomatically*, as well as "psychically." The physical bearing of "civilized" man is so obviously different from that of the savage that every explorer we know of comes back with bemused comments on this subject. Grantly Dick-Read's *Childbirth Without Fear* first popularized the discovery that the muscular tensions of "civilized" woman prevent her, in most cases, from experiencing the type of childbirth that is natural for humans.

Recently, the arctic explorer, Vilhjalmur Stefansson, has

argued, in his *Cancer: Disease of Civilization*, that this dread disease is either rare or non-existent in primitive communities. So is stuttering, according to Dr. Wendell Johnson's *Language and Speech Hygiene*. Both stuttering and cancer, and perhaps heart disease and several other ailments, seem to be connected with the tension, apprehension and bodily "anxiety" (improper breathing) of so-called "civilized" man. Many gynecologists agree with Dr. W. Reich's idea that the prevalence of cancer of the uterus in "civilized" woman results directly from her unnaturally repressed sexual energies.

The control of symbols by a small class, and corresponding dependence upon that class by everybody else – is perhaps best illustrated by the career of Jim Fisk who once, back in 1868, owned all the gold in the world for three hours, without ever touching any of it, or even seeing it. No primitive could ever understand this "ownership"; and even the average "civilized" man grows dizzy when trying to understand the manipulations of Wall Street, which is why he prefers to leave such "arcane" and "mystical" matters to the presumed experts. Nevertheless, this metaphysical ownership affected, directly, the diet and clothing of uncounted millions for generations thereafter. Whether or not you can "buy" two good steaks or only one good steak for ten "dollars" today depends on who owns the gold of the world and what he is doing with it.

Under such a system, anxiety, worry, insecurity, etc., as *chronic body attitudes*, have reached epidemic proportions.

G. Rattray Taylor's *Sex in History* notes, without attempting to explain, the rise of anti-sexual "religious" teachings after a great social calamity. For instance, post-exile Judaism is shot through with hatred of sexuality, whereas earlier Judaism seems to have been as tolerant as the Greeks. Similarly, English Puritanism rose out of a context of bloody civil wars and religious persecutions. In numerous other cases we observe the same pattern of social trauma followed by extreme hatred of the living flesh. Luther's hatred for capitalism led him to a theology of anxiety which flowered into the Protestant Era's embrace of capitalism. Once anxiety has become a chronic body attitude, desensitization sets in and man becomes incapable of responding naturally to the cyclic processes of his own living energy. But this chronic anxiety, caused by economic insecurity, creates the psychological vacuum, which drives man to "keep busy, busy, busy" and thus perpetuates the economic system which created it.

Thus we find that the essence of "civilized" man's bifurcation from Nature is a circular-causal process, or, in simple terms, a vicious circle. The authoritarian-usurocratic system creates anxiety; and anxiety drives the system ever onward and upward (away from the fertile earth and the living flesh); and does so at an ever-accelerating rate. Everybody today knows, in his bones, that this whole system is heading straight toward universal death like an engine out of control, and everybody feels helpless to do anything about it.

2000 years ago, when this perverse system was only about 4000 years old, Saul of Tarsus understood that "the love of money is the root of all evil." Money, the symbol of things, is not a useful thing in itself. It is a net of usury with which one class traps another into starvation and simultaneously entraps itself forever. 500 years before Saul, the Buddha proved that, in an ownership society, theft must occur, leading to police forces, leading to murder, leading to capital punishment, leading to a universal web of anxiety. Mencius, in China, asked, "Is there a difference between killing a man with club and killing him with a sword?" Is there any difference between killing a man with a club and killing him with a system of economics?

It seems like a ridiculous over-simplification when one first thinks of it, but the thought has grown on me over the years.

No man tries to build his house on a map; he builds it on the territory. No man tries to eat a menu; he eats the meal. All of our problems, including the atomic disaster we all anxiously await, derive from the fact that people do not regard money as realistically as they regard maps and menus. They have confused the symbol with the thing symbolized, as semanticists would say. "In Gold We Trust" is, indeed, the principle religion of "civilized" man.

Only an understanding of how this magic is worked – an understanding that money need not be at the mercy of invisible manipulators "with no front name, no hind name and no address" – an understanding that the exchange of goods between Mr. A and Mr. B does not have to involve use of a medium which forces both A and B to pay tribute to a mysterious 3rd party who "owns" some of the miscellaneous minerals of the world – an understanding that Alberta, Canada, and Wörgl, Austria, in our own century, and parts of China and the Ottoman Empire in the past have had socially-owned money for which NOBODY paid interest to ANYBODY – only such an understanding, breaking through semantic bewitchments of thousands of years standing, can free "civilized" man from his enslavement to this symbol and the anxiety this enslavement costs him.

Is Capitalism a Revealed Religion?

Published in *The Realist*, June 1961

. . . so sore mennes eyes were blinded
Where covetousnesse of filthie gaine is more than
reason minded.

– Ovid's *Metamorphoses* (Golding translation)

A friend of mine told me a story recently that makes a good introduction to a column about economics. It seems that my friend was in the men's room at his place of business, voiding his bladder energetically, when the President of his firm walked in and took a stance at the next urinal. A strange thing thereupon happened to my friend: his urine ceased spurting, even though he could still feel the pressure of an incompletely emptied bladder.

The reader may want to accuse me of surrealist symbolism, a dirty mind or a perverted sense of humor, but I can think of

no better place to begin an examination of Capitalism than the lavatory. We are all aware by now, or should be aware, that Protestantism has played a large part in creating and maintaining the Capitalist ideology, and Protestantism itself began in a privy.

This little-known fact is worth stressing, in the light of psychoanalytical theory. Luther's own words are: "But once when in this tower I was meditating on those words, 'the just lives by faith,' 'justice of God.' I soon had the thought whether we ought to live justified by faith [*the central doctrine of Protestantism* – R.A.W.] This knowledge the Holy Spirit gave me on the privy in the to wer" (quoted in *Luther* by H. Grisar).

All Protestant theology begins from, and pays tribute to, this "experience in the tower" – *Thurmerlebnis*, as it is called. That this experience could hardly have happened anywhere else but in a toilet is well documented by the anal and excremental style of Luther's fantasy: at least twice he had visions of the devil in which that Evil Spirit assaulted him by the time-honored gesture of contempt – "showing him his posterior," in Grisar's words.

More: this anal preoccupation colors Luther's entire sensibility. The Pope and his Bishops are, Luther says, "urine, excrement and filth . . . the filth of squiredom, dung splattered on the sleeve," etc. The devil wants to "stink us and stab us with his dung." As for mankind, "we are but worms in ordure and filth." Such quotes could be multiplied almost ad infinitum, certainly ad nauseam. Alfred North Whitehead was being accurate, not polemical, when he compared Luther's rhetoric to Hitler's, and said that Luther was "more foul-mouthed." Even facing death Luther could think in no other imagery: "I am the ripe shard," he said, "and the world is the gaping anus."

It was, I believe, Erich Fromm who first explained the connection between the Protestant ethic and the rise of Capitalism – a connection long noted and well documented by such sociologists as Tawney and Weber – by pointing out that both Protestantism and Capitalism are creations of what Freud called "anal personalities." Fromm, of course, has to dilute and obfuscate the basic Freudian insight in order to get it in line with his sociologicalization of psychology.

This dilution and obfuscation is what Fromm and other neo-Freudians celebrate as their "advance" over Freud's "biological orientation." What is primary to Fromm is not body-sensations but "attitudes toward the world" occasionally expressed "in the language of the body." (I am paraphrasing and condensing from his *Escape from Freedom*.) Thus Freud's clear and eminently scientific conception of the "anal personality" becomes vulgarized into the foggy and uselessly vague notion of the "authoritarian personality."

I leave this de-materialized psychology to those professors who, finding it useful in mixed classrooms and inoffensive to the public at large, have embraced it. I take it that I have a body, and my reader has a body, and that we both had them long before we began developing "attitudes toward the world," and that any psychology worth elbow-room at the counter of scientific consideration will have to be centered on these facts and on the pulsating rhythms of the living flesh.

Freud, like Marx – and in a different way, like Cezanne – was gifted with a special kind of stupidity: a kind of stupidity which (I flatter myself) often appears in this column to the irritation of its readers. I mean the kind of stupidity that the little boy had in Andersen's legend when he refused to see the Emperor's new clothes. Marx was just dumb enough to ignore, or disbelieve, all the cultural prejudices of his infamous century and see with his own eyes that the relation of boss and worker is chiefly a physical relationship, an energy relationship, in which part of the worker's energy is drained off much in the manner that a vampire's victim has his blood sucked.

All ideological super-structure is built upon this simple energy process, and Marx was right in refusing to let any other fact or set of facts distract him from his unblinking examination of this central circumstance of our economic system. When the "natural sciences" and the "social sciences" are finally synthesized, this basic energy process will be their chief link, and will be formulated, I am convinced, in a Third Law of Thermodynamics.

Freud's stupidity was of an equally brilliant kind: he was the first psychologist really to understand the implications for psychology of the simple fact that people have bodies. (Cezanne's stupidity, similarly, was to look at the world as a child does and not as an art teacher tells one to.)

But to return to my friend, standing there at the urinal in the grip of an unusual variety of impotence.

Readers are beginning to write in accusing me of being a Reichian, and I don't want to lend support to so terrible an accusation, but I also don't see, and can't see, how we can account for what happened here except by saying, in Reich's terms, that the presence of the President of the firm created an anxiety   and anxiety, to Dr. Reich, meant simply, physically, the withdrawal of life-energy from the periphery of the body to its core: a contraction. My friend's genital-urinary apparatus went dead as the energy flowed back into his center.

(For some interesting data tending to indicate the increasing prevalence of this anxious energy-contraction in American culture, see Lawrence Barth's column in the October 1960 *Realist*.)

An experience of my own comes to mind here. Recently, a guy I know got so damned mad at me that he refused to speak to me anymore. Readers of this column may figure he had good justification – and I would be the last one in the world to deny that, intent as I am on becoming known as the meanest literary bastard since Brann the Iconoclast – but the point is that my offense, in this case, was merely speaking against the Capitalist system. Being sent to Coventry for this, by a cat who has been only mildly peeved by my sexual and religious heresies, is what prompted the question asked in the title of this column:

"Is Capitalism a Revealed Religion?" Has it now become so sacred that questioning it is more dangerous than, let us say, asking if Jesus ever pulled his pudding as a boy?

I am going to come on so strong as to say that, in a Freudian sense, Capitalism always has been a revealed religion. ("Religion," old Papa Sigmund once succinctly said, "is a public neurosis; neurosis is a private religion.") *Capitalism, I would in all seriousness suggest, can best be understood as a public neurosis characteristic of societies in which the life energy has been driven out of the genital area into the anal area.* Being a public neurosis, it is institutionalized, ritualized and mystificated with all the pomp and folderol of any other religion.

Let us look into the age that gave birth to Capitalism. The Late Middle Ages were a time of hysteria (always a result of prolonged anxiety states) and of witch-hunting (a symptom of hysteria) – and, finally, of impotence. The whole style of the age, as Spongier would call it, is well illustrated by *Bull Summa desiderantes* issued by Pope Innocent VIII:

> "It has indeed lately come to Our ears," wrote
> His Holiness, "that in some parts of Northern
> Germany . . . many persons of both sexes . . . have
> abandoned themselves to devils . . . and by their
> incantations, spells and conjurations . . . have
> slain infants yet in their mother's womb, as also
> the offspring of cattle . . . These wretches further
> afflict and torment men and women . . . with terrible
> piteous pains and sore diseases; they hinder men
> from performing the sexual act and women from
> conceiving, whence husbands cannot know their
> wives, or wives receive their husbands . . ."

It seems evident that, as G. Rattray Taylor notes in his brilliant *Sex in History*, Innocent was concerned "solely with certain pathological sexual phenomena . . . particularly psychic impotence and frigidity." Taylor produces considerable evidence that such Papal fears were well-grounded because the dictatorship of the Medieval Church was indeed so thoroughly destroying the normal sexual functioning of men and women as to create widespread impotence and infertility.

The witch-hunts of the period were almost all, Taylor demonstrates, brought on by people who, finding themselves impotent, accused some neighbor of "bewitching" them. The infamous *Malleus Maleficarum*, the handbook used for centuries by witch-hunters and Inquisitors, reads like nothing so much as a modern textbook of sexual pathology.

It was out of the maelstrom that Protestantism and Capitalism emerged. As the genitals of the Western World died, its anus, so to speak, came to be its central living preoccupation – inspired and guided by the hysterical vision of one neurotic monk sitting on a john.

The psychoanalytical insight that money represents to the anal personality – the feces which it covets – is not really new or novel. Have we not always spoken of "filthy lucre?" Doesn't Dante put the usurers and the buggers in one pocket of hell because both are "against natural increase?" Five hundred years after Dante, didn't another great poet, who is markedly hostile to Freudian theory, intuitively make the same discovery:

> Usury kills the child in the womb
> And breaks short the young man's courting
> Usury brings age into youth; it lies between the
> bride and the bridegroom
> Usury is against Nature's increase.

Yes, that is Ezra Pound, in his Canto 51. Elsewhere, Pound has indicated the same awareness of the pro-anal, anti-genital direction of the Capitalist (or, as he calls it, Usurocratic) temperament:

his condom full of black beetles,

  tattoo marks round the anus,

and a circle of lady golfers about him.

the courageous violent

  slashing themselves with knives

the cowardly inciters to violence . . .

  the beast with a hundred legs, USURIA

and the swill full of respectors

  bowing to the lords of the place,

explaining its advantages,

  and the laudatores temporis acti

claiming that the shit used to be blacker and

  richer

(Canto 15)

At the end of Arthur Miller's novel, *The Misfits*, the hero curses, not "money," but, significantly, "shit and money." Another artistic expression of the anal orientation of the modern world occurs in Norman Mailer's *The Time of Her Time*, in which the protagonist, trying to cure his girl of frigidity, finds he can bring her to orgasm by entering *per anum*.

Actually, the psychoanalytical theory of money as a symbolic turd is already implicit in the Judeo-Christian myth of work as Adam's Curse. Dr. Karl Menninger's *The Human Mind* recounts a case-history of a millionaire who was compulsively busy to escape anxieties connected with infantile anal guilts. Similar cases appear in the works of Freud, Ferenczi and Jones, among others. Abraham describes in his *Selected Papers on Psychoanalysis* a patient whose anxieties centered around the idea of being forced to eat excrement as a punishment for sin: the theme of two or three of the most popular jokes in capitalist society.

"Work," says Durkheim briefly, "is still for most men a punishment and a scourge." Freud, perhaps, put it even more simply, in his study of Dostoevsky, saying that Dostoevsky was under a compulsion to make his burden of guilt take tangible form as a burden of debt. Norman Brown's brilliant *Life Against Death* (to which I am greatly indebted) sums it all up thusly: "Money is human guilt with the dross refined away till it is a pure crystal of self-punishment, but it remains filthy because it remains guilt."

It may seem almost too pat if we now remind ourselves that the congenital problem of Capitalism, never yet solved, is the problem of *dumping the surplus.*

The psycho-dynamics of Capitalism, in short, seem to consist of what cyberneticists call a circular-causal process. Born of neurotic anxiety and desensitization (contraction of the life energies), it constantly generates more anxiety through its unpredictable boom-and-bust cycles and the wars incident upon its imperialistic necessity to dump the surplus. But this second-order anxiety (which afflicts the boss as well as the worker, for he, too, is the victim of the cycle) breeds that "busy-busy-busy" compensating activity which drives the whole system ever onward into contradictions, crashes and further anxieties.

Dr. Wilhelm Reich's theory was that cancer is caused, partially, by the contraction of life energies, i.e., anxiety. (And anybody who doubts Reich's theory of anxiety only needs to observe himself in a moment of stress to be convinced that Reich was absolutely right. Improper breathing and what A. S. Neill calls "the stiff stomach danger" make up the feeling we call "anxiety" or "tension," and both are symptomatic of muscular contraction, such as we see on a very gross level in an infant cringing with fear.)

Consider, in the context of Reich's idea, the following words of one of the most enthusiastic defenders of modern American Capitalism, Dr. Ernest Dichter, President of The Institute of Motivational Research: "Possibly more than half of all human diseases are psychogenic," says Dr. Dichter in *The Strategy of Desire*; "worry, maladjustment and other emotional disturbances can be responsible for almost anything from heart attack to cancer." Dr. Dichter's job, as high-priest of Motivational Research, is using this "worry, maladjustment and other emotional disturbances" to influence people to allow themselves to be exploited still further by the Power Elite of Capitalism.

According to the University of California's recent symposium on psychological factors in cancer, all the women with cancer of the breast examined by Dr. Franz Alexander in one study showed severe psychiatric disturbances, generally with some degree of sexual malfunctioning; another study, of women with cancer of the uterus, showed even more conspicuous sexual disturbances, especially of the sort called "frigidity" (*Psychological Variables in Human Cancer*, University of California Press).

Vihjalmur Stefansson's *Cancer: Disease of Civilization* points out that this pathology is rare, or nonexistent, among primitive tribes. Need we add to this that the physical bearing of primitive peoples is so different from that of our so-called "civilization" that almost every explorer on record comes back with bemused comments on the subject? Primitive man, free of the anxieties and armors-against-anxiety characteristic of our culture, stands and walks and sits as a human being should, gracefully and naturally. Look around you and notice how much visible tension you can see in people's postures; and you will know why Dr. Reich called cancer a *shrinking biopathy*.

Our kindly editor has asked me to stop using the example of the guy walking into the park with a radio in his hand every time I want to say that people are dead in modern America. Okay. I will use another example. I once said to a young lady (who happened to be the wife of the guy who stopped talking to me when he found out I'm a socialist), "Dig that tree there – wow!" She replied, icily, "I *dug* it," putting me down for being so corny as to talk that way. The point was that she hadn't dug it; she had hardly glanced at it. Basho could flip over a sight as simple as a tom cat with the Yen, and write a poem about it:

> Yawning. Then, fully awake,
>   the cat goes out
> to a night of poontang.

This is not just "the poet's eye"; Cezanne had it. Nor is it the "artist's eye"; Darwin had it when he looked at the iguana and intuited the law of evolution. It is the special kind of stupidity I was talking about earlier in this column. It is the innocent childish eye of a man who is not completely blinded by the organized bullshit and desensitization of an unjust social system. It is obvious, or should be, that the prejudiced White never "sees" a Negro; he sees the social lies, stereotypes, in his own mind. (This is the point of the best novel ever written about the Negro in America, Ralph Ellison's *Invisible Man*.)

It should be equally obvious that, in a social system motivated by anxiety, and a deadening of life energy, nobody even sees the street on which he lives anymore. We are walking dead men, has Lawrence tried so hard to show us in *Lady Chatterley's Lover*, that great and mostly unread novel, and which average breeders hop around, looking for a symbolic sexual gratification, and skipping the passages, which give the book half its meaning – the passages about how Clifford's impotence and paralysis drove him to becoming a successful businessman.

The whole world has been stunned for 17 years now by the opening, in 1944, of the Nazi annihilation camps. We still don't know how to explain such things, how they could be possible.

Let me bring this column toward a conclusion with a set of facts that may throw some light on what happened in Germany – and is *happening* here – facts which are all explained by my hypothesis that Capitalism derives from Deadening of the genitals and centering of the interest in the anus, but which cannot be explained, so far as I know, by any other hypothesis.

1. The English of Shakespeare's day were a bawdy, sexy, uninhibited bunch of hipsters. As Capitalism grew in England, this national character changed markedly, so much so that it is difficult for us to imagine Falstaff and his friends as truly English. The modern post-Capitalist Englishman is the epitome of the armored individual, rigid, compulsively "moral," utterly lacking in spontaneity. Simultaneously, England was the first nation consciously to idealize the completely frigid woman.

2. Capitalism was born in Germany, chiefly, and chiefly in the age of Luther.

3. Calvin's fanatically anti-sexual regime in Geneva was also one of the primary creators of the Capitalist spirit. Raleigh, observing the deadness of the Genevese, remarked that they had "nothing left but their usury."

4. As Capitalism came to dominance in Germany, the German national character became more and more rigid, armored, "closed" and secretive, lacking in play and spontaneity, etc. Out of this came the automaton who is a living caricature of humanity, the goose-stepping tin soldier known as the Nazi.

5. America, the only surviving 100% Capitalist nation, is the most Puritanical nation in the world. It is the only nation, indeed, which has executed a man in the 20th century, not for murder, but (in effect) for a sexual offense.

6. Desensitization in America is growing more appalling all the time. Lawrence Barth recounted in *The Realist* a few months ago an incident at a racetrack in Illinois where a section of the grandstand collapsed, killing and injuring a great number of people; the people in the uncollapsed part of the grandstand

were completely unmoved, according to reports – even those sitting only a few feet from the groaning bodies of the victims. It is this country also which twice dropped atomic bombs on two cities full of men, women and children, and which poured burning napalm on its enemies in Korea.

7. Recently, in Harmony, North Carolina, the American Legion staged a little rabbit hunt – for charitable purposes, of course. The rabbits were beaten to death with baseball bats.

8. The mysteries of Capitalist economics are held to be as sacred as those of any other religion – i.e., every other organized social neurosis. Only the "experts" are supposed to be able to understand "the rate of interest," "the price of money," the "dangers" of "inflation," etc. The whole system – "the black magic of money," as Pound once called it – simply rests upon *breeding* money as if it were alive. ("Is your gold ewes and rams?" – Shakespeare.) Or, as Paterson, the founder of the Bank of England, put it. "the bank hath interest on all moneys it creates out of nothing." This creation out of nothing is just what the infant wants to do with its feces, according to Freud, Jones, Ferenczi, Abraham, Menninger and other psychoanalysts. (Rexroth once paraphrased Dante's analysis of this system by saying that, to Dante, the usurer is a pederast who wants to make his turds his heirs.)

I could go on, but what's the use? Those who have had a little experience in psychiatry will know what I'm getting at: others will just laugh, as they've been laughing since Freud published his first case histories. I ask only one thing of skeptics: don't bring up Soviet Russia, please. That horrible example of State Capitalism has nothing to do with what I, and other libertarian socialists, would offer as an alternative to the present system.

Dante said of the damned in hell that they were persons who had lost *il ben del' intelletto*, which I don't think it's at all extravagant to translate as: their ability to *dig* things. This is not a Marxist kind of social criticism I have been presenting in this column, but just a way of saying that there's something pathological. literally so, about a system which increasingly blinds people to the joys of the senses and ties them down to a narrow groove of profit-seeking.

What I Didn't Learn at College

Published in *The Realist*, September 1961

"Teach? At Harvard? It cannot be done."

– Henry Adams

In my youth, because I was a wicked sinner, God punished me by condemning me to one-and-a-half years in a School of Education. (Never mind which one it was; I have no desire to single it out for special blame. Escapees from other Schools of Education assure me that they are all equally squalid.)

Basically, I learned three things at that institution. The first was that it is possible to sleep all through the average education course (or to bring a book on some interesting subject and read it) and still pass the final examination easily.

The second and third things that I learned were that all modern educators agree that education should consist of not stuffing the pupil's mind with miscellaneous information, but actually preparing him for the life he will lead after graduation;

and that all modern educators are firmly united against any attempt to live up to this ideal.

In other words, they all verbally approve of "education for life," and they are all terrified of ever telling the truth to the pupils on any subject whatsoever. What they really aim at is education for "citizenship" (one of their favorite expressions); what this means is education for conformity to the insane conventions of this pathological society.

It is now autumn and thousands of young men and women are departing for college, most of them having the delusional belief that they will find education there. Like all delusions, this is both amusing and pitiful.

They would have greater chances of success if they were looking for chastity in a brothel, truth in the daily newspapers, or entertainment on television. There is more hope for the blind man in a dark room looking for a black hat that isn't there. Finding education in an American college or university is as possible as finding swimming pools in the Sahara.

It seems to me that, since *The Realist* regularly gets mail from college students, this is a good place to put down the fundamental facts which are never expressed in our official educational system.

I must add a warning, however: I am not responsible for the consequences if anybody is so rash as to quote or paraphrase any of this within hearing distance of a professor. I especially refuse to bear the blame if you are naive enough to use any of it in a term paper. The consequences will be much the same as if you wrote to Fulton Sheen to ask how much homosexuality goes on in the priesthood. You will not get an answer; you will get a malediction.

The first thing to learn in a good contemporary education (and the one thing you will never learn in a college or university) is that, contrary to Harry S. Truman's famous words, U.S. foreign policy is not based on the Sermon on the Mount.

I know how shocking this must be, but I assure you that you will find nowhere in the words of Jesus a justification of dropping atomic bombs on Hiroshima and Nagasaki, or using burning napalm on the babies of North Korea, or sending mercenaries to take away from the Cuban people the government that they want. These things are typical practices of imperialism, and have nothing to do with the philosophy of love taught by Jesus.

Although Truman was the only one dumb enough to say, with his bare face hanging out, that the activities of our State Department and CIA are motivated by the Sermon on the Mount, Eisenhower and Kennedy have made safely vague remarks to give the same general impression.

The only way you can discover how far from the truth these claims are is to look into C. Wright Mills' *The Causes of World War III*, where you will discover, for instance, that John Foster Dulles once said, in so many wards, that the U.S. Government will go to war in the Near East if the interests of Standard Oil are imperiled there. There are many interpretations of the Sermon on the Mount, but none of them include defending the Profit Motive with the blood of men.

The blunt truth is (and I apologize again for how shocking this must be, and I warn you again not to say it in a classroom, if you want to pass the course) that U.S. foreign policy is motivated by the economic and power interests of a small group of industrialists and militarists.

Nobody in Nutley, New Jersey or Sandusky, Ohio is being hurt when the Cubans throw off their bloodsucking exploiters and establish a people's government, but several large corporations are being hurt by it. You and I have nothing to gain, and everything to lose, if we are sent down to Cuba to kill men, women and children, in order to force them to take the land away from the peasants and give it back to a few landowners; but certain large corporations have a great deal to gain if you and I are sent down there to do that dirty work for them.

There are several fact-packed books which tell a great deal about the relations of government and economic ruling classes down through history. Two especially good ones are Brooks Adams' *The Law of Civilization and Decay* and Alexander del Mar's *History of Monetary Systems*. Almost any professor will agree that Brooks Adams was one of America's greatest thinkers and historians; del Mar was called the greatest historian of the 19th century, and was frequently consulted as an expert by governments (who often refused to take his advice).

Both books have been out of print for years, and neither is used in a college or university today, as far as I know. Arthur Kitson's testimony before the Macmillan Commission has never been refuted, yet his book (*The Banker's Conspiracy! which unleashed the World War*) is as little-known, in academic circles, as Adams or del Mar. Read all three of them, and see what you think of the history and economics taught in your school.

Every college economics course contains a built-in refutation of Marx, but how many students who have gone on to take the trouble to read Marx can agree that these "refutations" are honest or even half-way in contact at all with what Marx actually argued? Proudhon pointed out before Marx – and Adams and del Mar demonstrated exhaustively – that the function of governments has been, throughout history, to exploit the masses in the interests of the few.

Every form of exploitation consists of seizure by a few of some natural power, followed by forcing the rest of us to pay on that the traffic will bear for some share of that natural power. The earth, the actual living-space of the planet, is owned by a small group, and the rest of us have to pay tribute to them (called "rent") for the right to stay here; otherwise we are in danger, apparently, of being thrown into the ocean or expelled into outer space.

Now, how did these "owners" get to "own" the planet? Did they buy it from God some time in prehistory? If you're planning to leave school and go out and get an education, ask some professor that question some time. The fact is that the government guarantees with its police and army that these "owners" will have the *right* to own and the rest of us with have the *duty* to pay tribute to them.

The same holds true with all natural powers. The government decides who will own the water-power, the electricity, the ores, etc. of a continent; the rest of us then have to go to the "owners" and pay whatever they ask to get a share of it for ourselves. This is called "freedom" because we have the choice of paying what they ask or starving to death.

The chief type of exploitation in the modern world, and the chief cause of wars, is usury. This practice – condemned by Aristotle, St. Ambrose, the Bible, the Koran, Confucius, Cato the Elder, Shakespeare and almost all of the great thinkers before about the sixteenth century – has become so dominant in the modern world that La Tour du Pin called our epoch "the age of usury" and Brooks Adams said that "since Waterloo, usury has ruled the world."

The mechanism is the same as that of all other forms of exploitation, the seizure by a few of that which potentially belongs to all. In the case of usury, the natural power that is seized is the accumulated labor of past generations, and this is "rented" just as land is rented.

Since this is a process in time – unlike land, which exists only in space – it is a self-augmenting and increases as an exponential function, a discovery made independently by at least four thinkers in the last 50 years: Henry Adams (*The Rule of Phase Applied to History*); C. H. Douglas (*The Natural Economic Order*); Alfred Korzybski (*Manhood of Humanity*); and Buckminster Fuller ("Comprehensive Designing").

Man accumulates *power-and-knowledge* (the ability to use natural resources for human purposes) at a rate which increases each generation; this natural function, belonging to all humanity, becomes *capital*, which is "owned" by a few and rented to the rest of us at usurious rates of interest.

(Proudhon proved over a hundred years ago that 1% interest was all that was justified by the labor expended by the usurer.)

We live, in other words, in a world that is manmade – made by the accumulated effort of 250 generations of *homo sapiens* – and all of the knowledge, techniques, machines, methods of communication (from Roman roads to television), etc., which make this world human, are owned, in the form of capital, and rented to us, in the form of usury. This is made possible by money, a *symbol* of wealth, which we have been conditioned to take as wealth itself.

Money bears the same relation to wealth that a ticket to a seat at a concert bears to that seat. It is the kind of relation which exists between the menu and the meal, or between the map and the territory.

Dostoyevsky's Grand Inquisitor pointed out that every state and church in history have ruled through "miracle, mystery and authority." Herbert Muller's *The Loom of History* has taken that phrase as a keystone: he studies each civilization to ask how much it depended on "miracle, mystery and authority," and how much it rested upon the natural creative critical powers of the free mind. Since Muller's standards are basically Square, not Hip, he finds a few civilizations that almost satisfy him, although he is honest enough to condemn most.

From a Hip point of view, which demands the complete absence of "miracle, mystery and authority," and the absolute freedom of their opposite forces, which are Wilhelm Reich's trinity of "love, work and knowledge," all civilizations with governments are sick. A healthy civilization would have no governments. Only "miracle, mystery and authority" need to be administered by a government; love, work and knowledge administrate themselves.

Morgan's *Ancient Society* and Reich's *Mass Psychology of Fascism* give several examples of societies without governments – societies of *work-democracy*, as Reich calls it – where love, work and knowledge were set free to administrate themselves. They function for self-regulation naturally, homeostatically, in the group as well as in the individual.

(Morgan, like del Mar and Adams, has been allowed to go out of print; Reich is banned by the U.S. Government – as he was also banned by the Nazi and Soviet governments.)

The "Sturch" – a fine word, coined by Philip José Farmer, to signify the mutual activities of State and Church – always rests upon "miracle, mystery and authority," always acts to prevent the natural self-regulation of love, work and knowledge. The Sturch is the sadistic end of the sado-masochistic neurosis of man; the masses, which accept and even welcome the Sturch, are the masochistic end.

When given a free choice between fascism and social democracy, in 1932, 17 million German workers went out and *voted* for the "miracle, mystery and authority" of fascism against the "love, work and knowledge" of social democracy.

Not that the social democracy available in Germany then wasn't itself sick; I haven't got room to make every necessary distinction in this column. Of course, I am against Fidel Castro's government, but I am more against the attempts of the U.S. Government to create something even worse in Cuba. All governments are evil, but some are more evil than others. The best government is the least government, said Jefferson. The least government, added Benjamin Tucker, is no government.

This is getting rather abstract, I perceive; allow me to bring it back to earth with a concrete example.

During the Civil War, the U.S. Government borrowed from the Rothschilds some 275 million dollars *in paper money*. After the war, poor old Ulysses Grant was hornswaggled into signing a bill ordering the Treasury to repay the debt *in coin*. Now, at that time, one dollar coin was worth two dollars paper; the Rothschilds got back 550 million for 275 million, plus their usual usurious interest. This is not ordinary usury; it is what Pound called *hyper-usura* and Benjamin Tucker called *misusury*. The people of the United States had to make up that additional 275 million dollars out of their earnings, in the form of additional taxes. (See Del Mar's *History of Monetary Systems*, and Overholser's *History of Money in the United States*.)

The same type of swindle was inflicted on the people again under that great democrat Franklin Delano Roosevelt, when the "'government" bought ten billion of gold which they could have had for six billion before they changed the price of gold. Somebody made four billion in profits, and if the "government" gave it to them it was out of the pockets of the people. (See Ezra Pound's *Impact*.)

The same basic trick, similar to the *okkana borra* of the gypsies (the "gypsy switch" as bunco squads call it – although they are not empowered to prosecute it when the government is involved in it), was behind the famous "Scandal of Assumption" when Alexander Hamilton and some friends bought up the veterans' certificates at 1 cent on the dollar and then persuaded Congress to authorize payment of them at face value. (See Bowers' *Jefferson and Hamilton*.)

A few elderly readers may be yawning at this point, having heard it all before. Patience, fellers: the beginning of this column was not rhetoric. I am really writing it because I have discovered a whole generation of college students who have never heard anything of this sort in their whole lives. I don't mean that they've heard only a little of it; I mean they've heard zero, nothing. *They haven't got a clue*, as my wife says.

The struggle today is not to discover new stuff so much as it is to get the old stuff to the heads of those who have been artificially isolated from it by mendacious mis-education.

Henry Adams' *Education*, a charming and trivial work that makes a few good points here and there, is recommended reading at several universities. His brother Brook's *Law of Civilization and Decay*, which contains the hard economic facts which inspired Henry's romantic pessimism, might as well have not been written as far as impact on the "groves of academe" is concerned.

The usurocratic system rests upon the same "miracle, mystery and authority" as the slave system from which it is derived; Marx was quite right in calling the modern worker a "wage-slave." Work is the productive application of human energy to the advancement of the human community; only a handful of artists and composers *work* in our system. The rest of us *slave* for wages.

The difference is in the direction of the will, and there must be both, direction and will, for that expression to mean anything.

Toiling for wages is not work. It creates slackers, loafers, etc. precisely because it is not work. Loafing is a pathology; the healthy man needs work. It is because it is so hard to find *work* that will support one, and so easy to submit to *wage-slavery*, that pathological loafing and criminal behavior are pandemic in our society. The natural work-democracy of the Trobriand Islanders, the Bruderhof community, etc. do not create such pathology.

The professor who says that, in a communal economy, the workers will support the loafers, is, of course, talking like a Babbit (which is only to be expected, since the Babbits pay his salary); worse yet, he is showing deplorable ignorance of the natural functioning of energy in the human body, as revealed by Reich in *The Function of the Orgasm* and *The Mass Psychology of Fascism*. If you have any doubt about the whole system being based on "miracle, mystery and authority," try this simple experiment. Ask any economics professor: "What determines the *price* of money?" You will hear such a rigmarole of double-talk and metaphysical periphrasticism as has not been concocted by the human brain since the theologians of Rome set out to refute Galileo.

Miracle, mystery and authority all take their power

from what Reich called *the emotional plague of mankind,* a perversion of natural functioning that began when the work-democratic matriarchies were replaced by authoritarian patriarchies about 6,000 years ago. Government, slavery, usury and warfare have been chronic ever since, bringing with them untold epidemics of psychiatric and psychosomatic illnesses.

The chief of these is what the Scottish psychiatrist Ian Suttie called "the taboo on tenderness" and Paul Ritter calls "the emotional limp of civilized man."

It is well known that the electro-colloidal processes of life take place in a periodic manner. Basically, it seems that the energies of the body move toward the skin surface in pleasure, and move back toward the core in anxiety. (A lie-detector measures the withdrawal of electrical energy from the skin during anxiety.)

Dr. Reich's classic experiments of 1935-36 measured electrical potential during sexual excitation, pain, fear, when sweet candy is placed on the tongue, etc. He showed that energy runs from core-to-surface ("out of the self, toward the world") in all forms of pleasure, and from surface-to-core ("away from the world, back to the self") in all forms of displeasure.

Besides shedding a great deal of light on the problem of cancer (which the AMA still won't admit is basically a psychosomatic disturbance, even though it strikes one out of eight in our society and is completely unknown in some primitive societies), these experiments also have tremendous sociological implications.

Since Freud, or actually since Charcot in the last century, it has been obvious that many disturbances, both psychiatric and psychosomatic, result from the repression of the natural sexuality of infants, children and adolescents.

Yet any attempt to change this situation, to stop the torture of these young ones who cannot protect themselves, to prevent the beginnings of untold pathologies ranging from

A Non-Euclidean Perspective

hysterical blindness to chronic ulcers, to save the children from unnecessary suffering and the adults which they will become from unnecessary irrationalism and neurosis – any such attempt has met with the most vitriolic opposition, not only from the Sturch, but from the medical profession itself.

There is only one reason for this: The emotional plague of mankind (which manifests itself "physically" as chronic headache, chronic improper respiration, chronic drunkenness, chronic feeling of contactlessness, etc., and "psychically" as the taboo on tenderness and the longing for "miracle, mystery and authority") is necessary for the continuation of patriarchal-authoritarian government.

And this emotional plague is *anchored* in each new generation by the sexual repression of infants, children and adolescents. This anchoring is nowhere nearly as metaphysical as Freudian terminology makes it appear. It is simply that the periodic function of pleasure-unpleasure (energy contraction/ cnergy expansion) is not all owed to function naturally. Instead, what Pavlov called *conditioning* and Skinner calls *reinforcement* is used, so that anxiety and contraction become increasingly chronic and pleasure and expansion become increasingly rare.

Seventy years ago, Freud noted that breathing difficulties are present in every neurosis. He made one of his brilliant but inadequate metaphysical guesses: the neurotic is secretly longing for suffocation as a punishment for incestuous desires. Reich makes it abundantly clear that some such irrational thinking may go in the periphery of the mind, but that the improper breathing is a symptom in and of itself, caused by chronic contraction and chronic fear of expansion.

So now you see why sex and economics are the two subjects most clothed with "miracle, mystery and authority" in our sick society, why they are the two subjects about which professors always speak in downright lies or metaphysical double-talk. It is not a coincidence: the two are related. People cannot be made submissive to irrational authority unless their natural energy functions are first crippled by sexual repression.

Robert Owen and the other early socialists were quite right in feeling that sexual liberalism and economic advancement were somehow connected and had to be worked on together, and Marx and his followers went completely wrong in ignoring the sexual problem and leaving it in the hands of the psychiatrists, who, like other medical men, are exploiters of a monopoly protected by the Sturch and naturally unwilling to follow any chain of thought likely to lead them into conflict with the Sturch.

The whole story of the collapse of Marxism into futile dogmatic politics and of Freudism into a reactionary tool of the Sturch is contained in that one great blunder.

Only Reich managed to keep the whole man in view, and to see the connection between work-democracy and sexual self-regulation on one hand and authoritarianism and sexual repression on the other hand. Naturally, both Marxists and psychoanalysts quickly disowned Reich.

Looking back over this column, I see that I haven't said nearly enough about "the taboo on tenderness" and how it affects everything from sports to the rate of interest at Household Finance Company, or about the way usury makes wars, and that I haven't gone into sufficient detail about the electro-colloidal functioning of human energies. This cannot be helped. I did not set out to convince anybody of anything, or to "prove" something. Both conviction and proof need much more time and space than I have at my disposal here.

Chiefly, my hope has been to arouse curiosity, by making the reader aware of those vast areas of fact and theory which are never discussed in the "institutions of learning." I have dragged in the titles of several books, hoping that the curiosity I arouse might send a few people to those books in search of further information.

Everybody who looks into medieval and renaissance

history quickly becomes aware that a great deal is omitted from most college courses on those subjects, and that the Catholic Church is responsible for these omissions. I do not know why it is that when people become aware that certain other things are omitted from most college and university courses, and that Church, State and High Finance all have good motives for wishing these things omitted, these people do not form a natural suspicion. This is especially hard to understand when one reflects that we have all heard of cases of professors who lost their jobs for daring to open their mouths about these subjects.

I leave you with one last riddle to plague your professors with (if you have the nerve, and don't care whether you graduate or not). Almost all literature courses present T. S. Eliot as the greatest poet of the twentieth century, and yet Eliot has frequently and publicly stated that all he knows about writing poetry he learned from Ezra Pound, who is hardly ever taught and little discussed. Can the reason be that Pound's poetry is full of lines like the following?

> These fought in any case,
> and some believing,
>
> > pro domo, in any case . . .
>
> Some quick to arm,
> some for adventure,
> some from fear of weakness,
> some from fear of censure,
> some from love of slaughter, in imagination,
> learning later . . .
> some in fear, learning love of slaughter;
> Died some, pro patria,
>
> > non "dulce" non "et decor" . . .
>
> walked eye-deep in hell
> believing in old men's lies, then unbelieving
> came home, home to a lie,

home to many deceits,
home to old lies and new infamy;
usury age-old and age-thick
and liars in public places.

"When Blood is Their Argument"

Published in *The Minority of One*, June 1961

My favorite bit of prose of 1961 was a magazine's account of the Cuban debate in the UN. *Time* characterized the Cuban ambassador, Raul Roa as "liverish," little" and "shrill" – i.e., the kind of character who would make a great foil for Abbot and Costello. The Russian ambassador, simply, is "no great brain," according to *Time*. Against these burlesque figures stands that model of statesmanship and wisdom, Adlai Stevenson, the Uncrowned King of Liberaldom, *"speaking with unusual intensity"* (but not, of course, intense enough to become "shrill!") and laboring *"to explain the world what is already self-evident, that the U.S. considered Cuba a clear threat to hemisphere security."*

Comparing the size, manpower, industrialization, armaments, etc. of the U.S. and Cuba, one might feel that Stevenson would do better trying to persuade the world that a tiger that ate a rabbit considered the rabbit a threat to security. But that let pass. The really fascinating thing about *Time*'s report is that they have to repeat Stevenson's actual denial of the chief fact at issue.

The facts presented by *Time* indicate clearly that Stevenson was lying and the Russian and Cuban ambassadors were not; the emotional tone of *Time*'s report buries these facts so effectively that the implication emerges that a man of dignity and principle was unfairly attacked by two clownish hooligans. To put it mildly (and in *Time* style) this is being fast and Luce with the truth.

One of the most significant remarks made about the whole subject of the Cuban invasion is missing from *Time*'s account, but appears in *Time*'s less literate sister, *Life*. This was the remark made by President Kennedy – good old idealistic John F. Kennedy – when approving the invasion. The President said that U.S. troops must not be used, because "*I don't want a Hungary in Cuba.*"

It seems that what Kennedy meant by "a Hungary" is not the moral quality of that episode of history, but the repercussions of it. He is using the standard which all Proper Bostonians use about sex: it doesn't matter what you do, but it does matter what you get caught at. This is exactly the standard that all fascist governments use in international affairs. My good Liberal friends who voted for Mr. Kennedy and considered me a beatnik for refusing to vote can decide for themselves what share of guilt they must bear for helping this man to achieve power.

Readers who save old copies of the *Minority* can check this for themselves: I have never uttered a word of praise for Fidel Castro. The undeniable good that Castro has done for Cuba, in land reform, building schools and so forth, doesn't, to my peculiarly old-fashioned 19th century-Liberal mind, wipe the blood of vindictive and tyrannical executions off his hands. But, in the same bull-headed and old-fashioned way, I will repeat until they take my typewriter away and shove me in jail: whatever food Kennedy distributes to the needy in West Virginia, whatever liberal social reforms he makes inside this nation, will not free him of the crimson taint of brutal imperialism. The "crackpot realism" that flourishes in all political persuasions, Left and Right, in these sad psychotic times, will regard me as impractical and "immature." But that kind of "maturity" and "realism," having destroyed 22,000,000 people the last time it went into action on a large scale, keeps us living in a world that's as jittery as an armed madhouse. After such realism, it is time that the idealists had a chance. As Shakespeare asked of the military mind three centuries ago:

"But if the cause be not good, the king himself hath a heavy reckoning to make, when all those legs and arms and heads, chopped off in battle, shall join together at the latter day and cry all 'We died at such a place'; some swearing, some crying for a surgeon, some upon their wives left poor behind them, some upon the debts they owe, some upon their children rawly left. I am afeard there are few die well that die in a battle; for how can they charitably dispose of any thing, when blood is their argument?"

How to Think About War and Peace

Published in *Way Out*, December 1962

In 1944, Mortimer Adler, then professor of law at the University of Chicago, wrote a 300 page book, *How to Think about War and Peace*, published by Simon and Schuster. Adler has since organized the world's wisdom into the Syntopicon and has helped shape the Great Books movement. His book on war and peace has influenced the thinking of peacemakers for a quarter of a century.

THE SCHOOL OF LIVING

WAY OUT

Formerly
BALANCED LIVING

Vol. 18, No. 11
December, 1962
15c a copy

A NEW LOOK AT THE
PEACE MOVEMENT
—Dick Fate, page 144

THE ECONOMICS OF PEACE
—Mildred J. Loomis, page 148

HOW TO THINK ABOUT
WAR AND PEACE
—Robert Anton Wilson, page 153

HOW MUCH FAILURE IN
GANDHIAN NONVIOLENCE?
Report of speech by John Stewart, page 158

This book begins with a Plea to the Reader by Clifton Fadiman. "I am pleading with you," Mr. Fadiman writes with heart-rending sincerity, "to do something difficult – to read a book that had to be hard in order to be good, and is both." Although I am touched by Mr. Fadiman's evident adoration for the great intellectual depths and profundities of Mr. Adler, I cannot share his feelings. *How to Think about War and Peace* did not seem either hard or good to me. It seemed easy and bad.

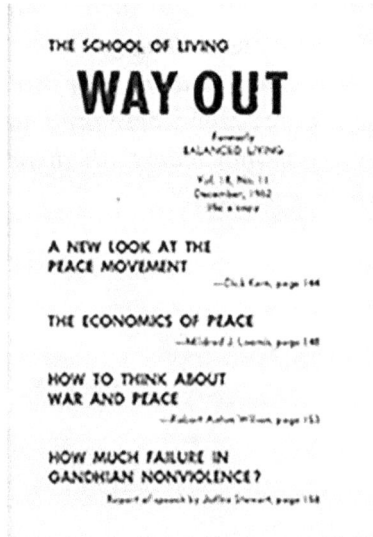

Mr. Adler's thesis is so simple that a child, or even a professor of law, could understand it. The thesis is this: there is "only one cause of war," and this cause is "anarchy." No other factor is a game of war – not "economic rivalry," not "cultural antipathies," not "religious differences," not "individual acts of injustice," not "hate and fear," not even "factions and ideologies." Mr. Adler examines all these causes and proves, at least to his own satisfaction, that they are not causes of war. Only "anarchy" is a cause of war.

Now this is, on the face of it, absurd. Except for the Eskimos and the Nuer, there are no Stateless societies left in the world. "Archy" (State-ism) and not "Anarchy" (Statelessness) is dominant everywhere. Saying that anarchy is the cause of war – the only cause of war (Mr. Adler actually says, with emphatic italics bristling with dogma) – is like saying that the poverty of the poor is caused by their riches, or that the starving peoples of Asia are dying from over-eating. It is the kind of proposition that only a professor from the University of Chicago would utter.

Oh, but we've been taking Mr. Adler too literally. He does not mean by "anarchy" what is normally meant by that word. He admits that we are all blessed with benevolent governments overlooking our activities, but we are still "anarchists." Why? Well, it seems that we do not have yet enough government. We need more of it; we need it in horse doctor's doses; we need it on a world-wide scale. In short, we need – surprise! surprise! – World Government.

Let us look into this thesis a bit. According to Mr. Adler, "It is the absence of governmental controls" which causes wars (page 74). Let us look at the largest stretch of anarchist history known to us – the 995,000 years in which man existed without the State.* According to traditional political philosophy (in which Mr. Adler was educated), this was a time of blood and broil and horror, in which Victor McLaglen type cavemen went around beating the brains out of all weaker-looking humans.

The actual facts, however, as revealed by archeology, are quite the reverse. As Elliott Smith says, "All the available evidence seems to point clearly to the conclusion that until the invention of the methods of agriculture and irrigation on the large scale practiced in Egypt and Babylon, the world really enjoyed some such Golden Age of Peace as Hesiod has described." (*The Evolution of Man*) W. J. Perry is even more emphatic: "It is an error, as profound as it is universal, to think of man in the food-gathering stage as being given to fighting. All the available facts go to show that the food-gathering stage of history must have been one of perfect peace. The study of the artifacts of the Paleolithic Age fails to reveal any definite signs of human warfare." (*Children of the Sun*) Note that these two experts, in a position to know, speak definitely of "all the available evidence" and "all the available facts."

This is confirmed repeatedly by archeological diggings. Sir Arthur Evans says of his excavations in Crete, "We have found nothing that suggests war, nothing to imply civil strife or even defense against foreign raids." (*The Palace of Minos*) McCown writes of his diggings at Teleilat-el-Ghassul that the city presented "no evidence that the place possessed any system of defense," (*The Ladder of Progress in Palestine*). H. B. Stevens sums up: "When the excavations of prehistoric sites get down to levels over four thousand years old, they no longer find the warlike weapons, the signs of a soldier class and the elaborate preparations for defense which characterize recent times." (*Recovery of Culture*)

The facts are these: man had 995,000 years of anarchy and peace, followed by 5000 years of government and war. Only a philosopher as deep and profound as Mr. Adler could argue in the face of such historical data that government tends to create peace and anarchy tends to create war.

I am not going to be as dogmatic as Mr. Adler, in the opposite direction. I won't say that government causes war; I merely point out that it is intimately connected. It is, let us say, part of the same kind of mentality – the authoritarian mentality. Anarchy and peace are part of the non-authoritarian, or libertarian, mentality.

Let us now turn to another of Mr. Adler's arguments, the one that claims that nothing but anarchy causes war, that "economic rivalry," for instance, does not cause war. His argument for this proposition consists of listing all the factors popularly considered "causes of war" – and, to show how broad-minded he is, he lists almost two pages of such causes, quite objectively. Then he comments that each of these things "operates within a single community without causing war. None of these things is by itself or in itself a cause of war. Nor is war caused by a combination of all of them. Singly or together these factors and forces cause war only when their action is not restrained by the institutions and machinery of government." (pages 75-76) At this point I begin to feel a little sorry for Mr. Adler. He must have been tired when he wrote that. The book was probably as hard for him to write as it was for Mr. Fadiman to read. For, if anything in the world is obvious, it is that "these factors and forces" (economic rivalry, etc.) "cause war only when their action is IMPLEMENTED by the institutions and machinery of government." On a smaller scale, they do not cause war; they cause insurrection, revolution, rebellion, strikes, sabotage, passive resistance, etc. It is the "institutions and machinery of government" that lift these conflicts to the plane of war. If we had a World Government, these conflicts would not evaporate, but their expression in action would not be called "war" anymore; it would be called "insurrection" or "revolution" or "rebellion," etc.

I would like to go a little bit deeper in probing Mr. Adler's philosophy. What causes college professors to propagate deep and profound thoughts such as his? As Korzybski points out, we experience life on three principal levels of abstraction: first, on the object level: we see, touch, handle, etc., concrete things; second, on the descriptive level: we talk about what we have seen, touched, handled, etc.; third, on the "high levels of abstraction" we talk, not about concrete things but about classes and categories of things. These higher levels are infinite: we can go from this chair right here to "chairs in general," "furniture in general," "manufactured articles," "the gross national product," "labor and capital," and so on up to Paul Tillich's god, "Being Itself." The same distinctions hold true in economics: we work, first, on the object level: we plant seeds, or build chairs, or repair voltmeters, etc.; second, on the lower symbolic level: we collect rent or interest (money-tickets, symbols of labor done by somebody else); third, on increasingly higher levels of abstraction: we handle bills of exchange, or sit in congresses that pass tariff laws, or we alter the value of the currency to profit on exchange, etc. Now, mankind is the symbolizing class of life, and hence, as Korzybski said, "those who control the symbols control us." The symbol-manipulators (usurers, landlords, philosophers, governors, etc.) make up a class more or less isolated from actual contact with actual labor-processes and they tend to think alike, abstractly and "impersonally." Kropotkin tells in his autobiography how he became an anarchist through working for the Czarist bureaucracy in Russia: realizing that these men knew nothing about the actual labor-processes they were "administering," he became convinced that the only way social life could ever become sane was to turn the administration back to voluntary associations of actual farmers, mechanics and other producers. (One of the classic cases Kropotkin recounts is that of a bureaucrat passing navigation laws for a river he had never seen, a river on which his laws would be not only chaotic but physically impossible.)** But the symbol-manipulators can never understand this: they are convinced that a farmer cannot plant, a mechanic cannot tighten a bolt, and a printer cannot set a line of type, without their benevolent administration above him ruling him "for his own good."

After 5,500 years of this benevolence, the symbol-manipulators have got to the stage where they cannot provide bread for the people without ordering the farmers to burn their wheat and buying somebody else's wheat from a thousand miles away, and cannot stop themselves from an imbecile accumulation of greater and greater war weapons and an equally compulsive verbal chatter about guaranteeing "peace" – which grows louder and more painfully sincere after each war they create. They will do everything for the people, as Tolstoy says, "everything – except get off their backs." They love the people and they will rule them "for their own good" if they have to blow up the earth to prove it.

But, since nothing else has worked, they are now driven to carry their logic to its ultimate conclusion. Since having the sowing practices of Ohio farmers controlled from Washington (by a man who wouldn't know a corn stalk from a tomato plant) doesn't seem to provide perfect economic rationality, and since having the rice-paddies of Viet-Nam half-ruled by Washington and half by Moscow doesn't give much peace to Vietnamese rice farmers, there is, to the symbol-manipulators, only one obvious solution: we need more government, more control, more centralization. Henceforth let one gang of benevolent bureaucrats, seated let us say in Geneva, decide on the best farming methods for the slopes of the Rockies, the best currency laws for the Eskimos, the best hours of labor for the employees of the Ford Motor Co. at Dearborn, the trade regulations between the Zuni and the Navajo, etc. That such earth-shaking powers in the hands of a few men can wreak more havoc than history has ever known is inconceivable to such people.

"To be governed," wrote Proudhon, "is to be watched, inspected, spied, directed, law-ridden, regulated, penned up, indoctrinated, preached at, checked, appraised, seized, censured, commanded . . . To be governed is to have every operation, every transaction, every movement noted, registered, counted, rated, stamped, measured, numbered, assessed, licensed, refused, authorized, indorsed, admonished, prevented, referred, redressed, corrected. To be governed is, under pretext of public utility and in the name of the general interest, to be laid under contribution, drilled, fleeced, exploited, monopolized, extorted, exhausted, hoaxed and robbed; then, upon the slightest resistance, at the first word of complaint, to be repressed, fined, vilified, annoyed, hunted down, pulled about, beaten, disarmed, bound, imprisoned, shot, judged, condemned, banished, sacrificed, sold, betrayed, and to crown all, ridiculed, derided, outraged and dishonored." Anyone living in what we ironically call civilized society knows the bitter truth of those words. It takes a philosopher, or a professor of law, to believe that such a system is defective only because it isn't world-wide, and will become indeed perfect when it is world-wide. Perfect, in truth, it will be: perfect hell.

There is no World Federalist who can seriously claim that, under his system, there cannot occur insurrections. There could even be continent-wide insurrections, indistinguishable from war in all respects except name. That would no doubt satisfy the symbol-manipulators, but it will not satisfy mankind as a whole forever. Sooner or later, if we survive at all, we will have to begin thinking seriously about Kropotkin's (and Proudhon's) principle of federation: the voluntary association of small human-size communities in which the local rules are made locally by those who actually do the work. Such communities might occasionally fall into conflict, as did the communes of the Middle Ages, but they will not be able to throw the rest of mankind into an uproar along with themselves, and a man in Peru need never be afraid, under that anarchistic system, that a disagreement between a man in Moscow and a man in Washington might result in the incineration of Lima. In spite of Mr. Adler, that, at any rate, is how I prefer to think about war and peace.

* "In the history of humanity, states are very recent. Man . . . has probably been on the earth for about a million years. The first states arose about 5,500 years ago. . . . The State as a social form has therefore only existed for about one-two-hundredth of man's history." – Anthropologist

A Non-Euclidean Perspective

Kathleen Gough, in *The Decline of the State* (available from School of Living, Brookville, Ohio, for 25¢)

** "War, one war after another; Men make 'em who couldn't put up a good hen-roost." – Ezra Pound, Canto 18

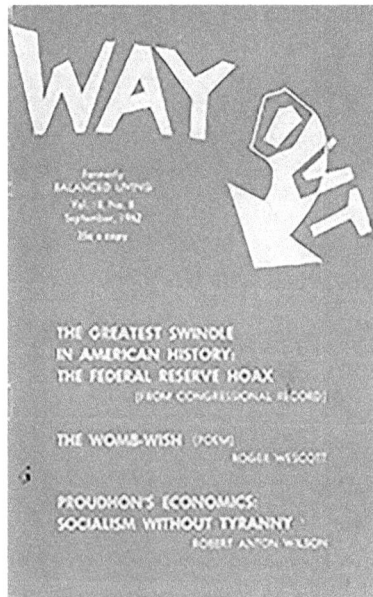

Proudhon's Economics:
Socialism without Tyranny

Published in *Way Out*, September 1962

Benjamin Tucker considered *The General Idea of the Revolution in the 19th century* Proudhon's best book – "the most wonderful of all the wonderful books of Proudhon" – and he may well have been right in that judgment. Like many of the greatest works of the last century this "most wonderful book" comes to us from a prison cell: a fact which is probably far from insignificant. It is not without cause that the letters of Bartolomeo Vanzetti, the *Pisan Cantos* of Ezra Pound, "The Ballad of Reading Gaol," Nietzsche's *Antichrist*, the best poems of Antonin Artaud, Van Gogh's two or three greatest canvases, Koestler's *Darkness at Noon*, and several other of the most significant cultural products of this age, were produced by men who were at the time unwilling "guests of the State." Nor is it idle to note that some time has been

A Non-Euclidean Perspective

served (unproductively, alas!) by Ford Madox Ford, Nijinsky, Seymour Krim, Allen Ginsberg, William Burroughs, Jim Peck, and almost everybody else worth a damn as a serious thinker or artist. It is getting to the point where, as Eustace Mullins noted in his biography of Ezra Pound, lack of a police or psychiatric record is looked on, by *avant-garde*, as a sign that a man has sold out.

The General Idea of the Revolution in the 19th century was written while Proudhon was serving three years "of enforced leisure" (his own phrase) for something he had written that offended Louis Bonaparte. He doesn't tell us much about his prison, so maybe it wasn't as bad as some of the others that the great minds of our time have been confined in; but it was evidently bad enough, for the next time Proudhon was sentenced to prison (again for something he had written), he fled to Belgium and accepted exile rather than the regime of sadism-and-sodomy we inflict on the great minds which society imprisons to protect itself.

The background of *The General Idea of the Revolution in the 19th century* was the abortive Revolution of 1848 in which Proudhon had participated and which ended with Reaction entrenched more firmly than ever. Writing in an exalted and prophetic vein, Proudhon sees clearly that the Revolution is not dead and foreshadows the Paris Commune twenty years in the future. He foretells many victories still ahead for the status quo, he has moments of doubt and almost Reichian pessimism about the masses: "But reasoning will avail nothing," he writes once. "The eagle defends his eyrie, the lion his den, the hog his trough, capital will not relinquish its interest. And we, poor sufferers, we are ignorant, unarmed, divided: there is not one of us who, when one impulse urges him to revolution, is not held back by another."

The structure of this book is as block-like and monolithic as Euclid or Spinoza: a fact sometimes hidden by the wit, brilliance and poetry of the style. But beneath all the rapier-thrusts of his hyperbolic and eclectic polemic, Proudhon builds as carefully and logically as a mathematician. Each demonstration proceeds from the demonstration before it, and the cumulative effect is breath-takingly irresistible.

Chapter One, "Reaction causes Revolution," studies the methods by which the entrenched bourgeoisie, attempting to stifle rebellion, directly increased it and created the Revolution of 1848. Bringing the study up to the time of writing (1851), Proudhon shows, in detail, how the subsequent oppressive laws, aimed at preventing further revolution, are instead making further revolution inevitable. For instance, he points out that the teachers, with their usual conservatism, mostly opposed the Revolution of 1848, but have become, by 1851, quite revolutionary because of the thought control imposed upon them by the reactionary government.

Chapter Two, "Is there sufficient reason for a revolution in the 19th century?" is a study of economic life in France from the fall of the Bourbons to 1851. The general impression is like that of Engels' *Condition of the Working Class in England*. Proudhon shows that, with such misery being almost universal, the laws made to prevent revolution can only inflame the people and bring revolution closer. Proudhon's special emphasis, however, is on the various "reform" movements which attempted to better the lot of the people. It is sixty years since feudalism was replaced by capitalism in France, he argues, and all the attempts to "reform" capitalism only prove that the original Revolution is unfinished. The death of the old privileged class has not brought freedom, but a new tyranny; it has not brought order, but more chaos. The Revolution of the 19th century is inevitable, Proudhon argues, because the Revolution of the 18th century was incomplete. Here he sounds strangely contemporary; as he elsewhere preceded Marx in discovering the labor theory of value: he here precedes Paul Goodman in the concept of social chaos being caused by an "unfinished revolution."

Chapter Three, "The Principle of Association," argues that

capitalist society is *structured* in a topsy-turvy and cock-eyed way. Here he begins to introduce his concept of *anarchy*, and his chief (but not only) argument for it is that it will be less chaotic, more orderly, than capitalistic democracy. Under the facade of equality and representational government in our system Proudhon sees the ancient relationship of Master and Slave not basically abolished. Land tenure and the banking monopoly both come down to us from the Roman slave state, he says, and as long as they last we will always be basically slaves. Here he offers his new model of non-governmental society: anarchism, which he defines as a system "based not on *force* but on *contract*." Here also he criticizes the Blanquist socialists (the forerunners of modern Communism) for their attempt to create a new society in which *force* will still be a State monopoly thus producing a new form of tyranny where the abolition of tyranny is called for. They, too, he predicts, will make an unfinished revolution.

Chapter Four, "The Principle of Authority," is probably the most devastating attack ever written on parliamentary democracy, and should be compulsory reading for those "liberals" who keep complaining that Cuba hasn't had elections since her revolution. With blistering sarcasm Proudhon writes of how "laws, decrees, edicts, ordinances, resolutions . . . fall like hail upon the people. After a while the political ground will be covered with paper, which the geologists will put down among the vicissitudes of the earth as the *papyraceous formation*. . . . At present, the Bulletin of Law contains, it is said, more than fifty thousand laws; if our representatives do their duty, this enormous figure will soon be doubled, Do you suppose that the people, or even the Government itself, can keep their reason in this labyrinth?" Here his attack on the *chaos* of capitalist-democracy comes to its culmination. The whole idea of the State is wrong, upside-down, irrational; it has its origin in theology and demonology; there is no place for the Principle of Authority among those who pretend to democracy and equality. The State is an invention of the kings, he adds angrily, and should have been abolished when they were. We are still suffering chaos because the Revolution of the 18th century was unfinished.

Chapter Five, "Social Liquidation," considers the "divine rights" which should have been abolished along with royalty but weren't: the money monopoly, by which a handful of bankers control the monetization of credit; the land monopoly, by which a handful of landlords "own" the earth and force the rest of us to pay tribute for living and working on it; and the system of laws by which these monopolies are protected against free competition. Proudhon shows how poverty, crime, disease and war are caused directly by these monopolies; and he shows how they can be abolished, without violent revolution and without expropriation. Here it is especially difficult to summarize his thinking briefly; the basis of it all is his "Bank of the People," which lends *without charging interest.* (Douglas's Social Credit League which worked so successfully in Alberta, Gesell's stamp scrip which performed of the basic Proudhonian concept.) Proudhon shows how the abolition of interest by the People's Bank will force universal abolition of interest through that free competition which is supposed to be, but isn't, a feature of capitalism. Nobody will borrow at interest, when he can borrow without interest; the capitalist banks will not be able to compete with the People's Bank. Next, Proudhon turns to the land monopoly, and proposes a solution much more rational than Henry George's (or the socialists'): after a certain date, he says, let all rent payments be considered as installments toward purchase, and let the price of all land be fixed at the traditional twenty times the annual rent; within twenty years, the workers will own the land, and the landlords will not have been forcibly expropriated. Following the abolition of the money and land monopolies, prices will automatically fall to a level near the cost of production, since the manufacturer, not having to add rent and interest to his overhead, will not be able to pocket the difference either, due to competition. Thus, the basic aims of socialism will be achieved without a tyrannical bureaucracy and without violent expropriation of present proprietors.

Chapter Six, "The Organization of Economic Forces," presents the total anatomy of a society based on contract instead of force. In its amazingly logical structure and its painstaking attention to detail, this chapter is impossible to summarize, even more so than Chapter Five. Instead, I quote a brief passage giving the general conception without the details:

> That I may remain free; that I may not have to submit to any law but my own, and that I may govern myself . . . everything in the government of society which rests on the divine must be suppressed, and the whole rebuilt on the human idea of CONTRACT.

> When I agree with one or more of my fellow citizens for any object whatever; it is clear that my own will is my law; it is I myself who, in fulfilling my obligation, am my own government . . .

> Thus the principle of contract, far more than that of authority, would bring about the union of producers, centralize their forces, and assure the unity and solidarity of their interests.

> The system of contracts, substituted for the system of laws, would constitute . . . the true sovereignty of the people, the REPUBLIC . . .

> The contract, finally, is order, since it is the organization of economic forces, instead of the alienation of liberties, the sacrifice of rights, the subordination of wills.

The final chapter, "Absorption of Government by the Economic Organism," deals with the peaceful dissolution of the State into the system of contractual associations. Each such association might, in a sense, be called a small government; but it would be different in essence from traditional political government in that membership is voluntary instead of compulsory. The possibility of tyranny – even of the tyranny of the majority – will become zero. It is important not to misunderstand Proudhon here: don't think of the Shoemakers' Association planning long-range programs to which the individual shoemaker must submit. *Contract* implies a specific agreement for a specific purpose, to which all parties to the contract agree from motives of rational self-interest. It is not to be confused with a law binding upon an indefinite number of cases unto infinity. Proudhon is so aware that "each case is unique" one almost suspects he has been studying general semantics. There simply is no possibility, under his system, for a man getting trapped into compulsory obedience to a condition he didn't voluntarily accept by signing a contract.

What can we say of this magnificent edifice of creative and constructive social thought? There is no way to do justice to the mind which saw through the errors of all the other reformers of its age and clung stubbornly to the idea of freedom against all the blandishments of "State planning"; there are no words to praise the originality, precision, imagination and logic of this man, Proudhon. The only fitting comment is that, one hundred and eleven years after he wrote, the chaos he dreaded is still in action everywhere, and the concept of orderly contractual society which he invented is still not understood by either conservatives or radicals. The only way to honor him is to forget all about praising his obvious genius and to make his dream come true. The unfinished revolution has been unfinished for too long.

Revolting Conditions

Published in *Way Out*, January 1963

My review of Proudhon's *General Idea of the Revolution of the 19ᵗʰ century* in our September issue has brought forth a letter from Katherine Mathesius. Mrs. Mathesius, whose articles have appeared in these pages several times, taxes me with eight questions, which she apparently considers stumpers. Her questions appear here in italics, and my unstumped replies appear below them in ordinary print.

Revolting Conditions

Robert Anton Wilson

1. Can a revolution ever be finished?

In the absolute sense, no; in the relative sense that we answer most real-life questions, yes. The revolution against cannibalism, begun in the late paleolithic, is not absolutely finished – there are occasionally incidents of anthropophagy in several Australasian tribes, and as many as seven reported cases each decade in the "civilized" world; but, since the practice was once universal and is now rare and eccentric, we can safely speak of this revolution as finished. Similarly, Spartacus's revolution against the gladiatorial games is almost entirely finished; the remnants of *morituri te salutamus* that remain in prize fighting, football, etc. are minor in comparison with the 10,000-man butcheries once served up before the gloating eyes of Commodus. The revolution against usury started by Saint Ambrose, revived in the modern world by the American Rebels of 1760-1775, and carried on notably by Josiah Warren. P-J. Proudhon, Silvio Gesell and others, is still unfinished. One of the purposes of *Way Out* is to finish that revolution, at least relatively.

2. Can human problems be solved by revolting against the conditions that cause them?

In some cases, yes; in other cases, no. It is certainly true, however, that human problems can NOT be solved without revolting against the conditions that cause them. Whether a given revolt will succeed is always problematical. It depends upon the intelligence of the revolutionists, the involvement of the masses, the thoroughness of the reform, the strength of the opposition, the morality of the measures employed, the wisdom of the crucial decisions during the transition, and several other factors which I do not bother enumerating since any prudent person can supply them for himself with a little reflection. It is probably advisable to add at this point that I am here using the word "revolution" in its broadest sense in which it encompasses all decisive social changes and is not restricted merely to violent upheavals. In the modern world, for a variety of reasons, the most successful revolutions can only be made by a total population trained in, and thoroughly committed to, non-violent resistance.

3. Or must we accept responsibility for the conditions – as children of our own irrational thinking?

We must accept full responsibility for all conditions which

we are accepting either actively or passively. To put it another way: any condition, of however great antiquity, which we have not attempted to change, is our own responsibility and cannot be shifted to the debit of our ancestors. All the credit for good conditions, and the blame for bad conditions, rests upon us, so long as we do not attempt to change them in any way. When we do attempt to change them and improvement results, the credit is ours; if degeneration results, the blame is ours. In sum: if we believe conditions to be perfect, we are morally obligated to resist all attempts at change; if we believe conditions are imperfect, we are morally obligated to work for those changes which our own judgment indicates will tend toward improvement. These changes can be in either human psychological functioning, or in the legal (and extra-legal) structure of social institutions; although, of course, this either/ or is a verbalistic fallacy, since any change in social structure influences psychological functioning also, the two being part of a homeostatic field of circular-causal processes.

4. How can one contract with an infant or an insane person?

One cannot. Let me add, however – since this question seems to be calculated as a refutation of Proudhon's concept of contractual association – that this limitation of contract is also a limitation on law. Archic society does not apply its laws to infants and psychotics, yet functions tolerably well by inflicting these laws on all non-infants and non-psychotics. Anarchic society can safely exclude infants and psychotics from contractual association without tumbling into chaos upon this account. Indeed, the whole claim for anarchic society is that, by substituting contracts for laws, it will enable man to escape all obligations to irresponsible persons and obligate himself voluntarily only to those he considers responsible enough to reciprocate the obligation.

5. Must we not admit that unconsciously we asked for our situation and are trapped into compulsory obedience to the condition?

This question is semantically meaningless. "Situation" is a high-level abstraction that can refer to millions of things – the dimensions and climate of the earth, the social structure of this particular culture, the economic practices now in vogue, etc. Such a question is like "Is X black?" No answer can be given, but if various terms are put in to replace "X" various answers can be given. Substituting three somewhat more concrete terms for "situation" above, I ask the question about: (A) the physical laws of this part of the universe, (B) the economic system of this nation, (C) the psychological behavior of most of us brought up in this nation. I then answer: (A) no; (B) partly; (C) partly.

6. Must we not be responsible for our own thinking and the results of our thinking?

Yes, in both cases. But this responsibility is relative to the degree of our freedom from inflexible conditioned reactions. Intellectually, freedom from such conditioning means awareness; emotionally, it means neuro-semantic individuality and integrity. The greater this freedom, the greater is our responsibility. Correspondingly, the less of this freedom a person has, the less is his responsibility. Pavlov's dogs could not prevent their own conditioned reflexes, but humans can, when (through virtue, innate intelligence, hard work or just plain luck) they evolve to full adulthood.

7. How long will man refuse to see himself?

As long as he is convinced that his self is basically evil, corrupt, sinful, etc. In other words, as long as myths like the Christian dogma of Original Sin or the Freudian dogma of infant perversity, are widely believed.

8. How long will he continue to blame others – the State or system or institution – instead of recognizing his own guilt – and then – only then – can the remedy be permanent.

This started out a question and turned into a statement. Unless I am very much mistaken, it is this question-statement that the other questions were leading up to, and the whole message of Mrs. Mathesius's letter really is something like this: Proudhon, in analyzing the institutionalized factors within our civilization which lead to great misery for the majority and idle boredom for the rich minority, is primarily a moralist interested in fixing the "blame" for this misery. Such is not the case.

Proudhon was not only not a moralist, he was not even a "reformer" in the usual sense. I quote his own words: "I protest that in criticizing property, or rather the whole body of institutions of which property is the pivot, I never meant either to attack the individual rights recognized by previous laws, or to dispute the legitimacy of acquired possessions, or to instigate an arbitrary distribution of goods, or to put an obstacle in the way of free and regular acquisition of properties by bargain and sale; or even to prohibit or suppress by sovereign decree land-rent and interest on capital."

What was Proudhon interested in, then? As a social scientist, he was interested in learning the truth about society. He was able to learn a great deal of this truth, and recorded it with unsurpassed detail, precision and thoroughness, in several books. These books show, beyond a peradventure of doubt, that existing institutions – particularly, the collection of tribute from workers on the land by "landlords," the lending of capital at interest, and the vesting of absolute authority in mere human beings – must have inevitable and detrimental effects, and must lead to chronic misery and periodic violence (wars, internal and external). He further showed how a society could be built without these defects.

In short, Proudhon gave us a rough indication of how much human suffering is not due to the "will of God," how much is due to unnecessary institutions. As a scientist, his work was then finished. It is up to each of us to decide for himself whether we want to continue the institutions which make this preventable misery or whether we want to change them. Whatever decision we make, we must then act responsibly and consistently in terms of that decision. This has nothing to do with "blaming" the people – a mere handful of wretches literally dying of boredom – who happen to be, at the moment, in receipt of the profits of these institutions.

But this probably does not answer Mrs. Mathesius's real objection to Proudhon's analysis. She is, I believe, less interested in saving the "ruling class" from blame than in spreading blame around on everybody generally. To this I reply: to the extent that we are aware of the real evils of institutions, and are psychologically integrated enough to take action of some sort against them, and do not take such action, we do, indeed, deserve blame of some sort. But to the extent that we are not aware, and are not psychologically integrated enough to take action, our inaction is blameless: and this applies whether we are bankers living off the interest of a million starving mechanics or are ourselves one of the starving mechanics. To the extent that we are aware of this situation, but not psychologically mature enough to act against it, we need, desperately, to work on our own compulsions, to de-condition our reflexes, to strive toward freedom. But, in all urgency, I would add: those in this last category will be hindered, rather than helped, by the habit of self-blame. Once having made their self-examination and finding themselves lacking, they should work earnestly toward self-liberation without getting stuck in the bog of self-blame, for that is a quicksand which, although it must be passed, must be stepped over lightly and quickly, as it leads down, for those who stand on it too long, into the swamp of self-pity, despair, and inertia.

Perhaps what Mrs. Mathesius really wanted to ask is: *Isn't it true that all human problems are due to man's inner psychological compulsions and cannot be cured by changing social institutions?* One way of evaluating that question is by applying it to Auschwitz. Now it is probably true that the kind of person Zen Buddhists call "an awakened one" could keep his serenity in such a place, and could await his turn to go to the gas chamber without feeling any fear and even without hating his murderers. But I think it is better in the long run to end the Auschwitzs rather than to place upon all mankind the burden of achieving sainthood. And I think that this is not only more realistic than the mystic's faith in human transformation, but is also kinder. It is not only kinder to the victims, but it is even kinder to the administrators, who must bear a tremendous burden of either conscious or unconscious guilt as long as their work is allowed to continue.

For, if it is true that certain people carry their own private Auschwitz with them wherever they go, nobody has the right to assume arrogantly that this is true of all mankind and, on that account, to refuse the responsibility of opposing such things. Perhaps every man, woman and child who went into Hitler's ovens was so neurotic that he would have spent all his life tormenting himself in various ways had not Hitler ended it for him; but that is only a theory, and a theory (I might add) not nearly as well proven as its devotees like to pretend, whereas the gas ovens were a fact. Whether man, free of tyranny, will set about tyrannizing over himself, we cannot really know, but in the meanwhile we have the right to make such dire predictions only about ourselves, if we must make them at all. To testify against mankind as a whole is fashionable in these existentialist days, but it is neither humble, nor intellectually honest, nor generous. The Samaritan in the parable did not tell the man who had been beaten by thieves that he would probably have destroyed himself if the thieves had not destroyed him: he fed him, and clothed him, and bound his wounds.

An Open Letter To Norman Mailer

Published in *Way Out*, February 1963

Dear Norman,

Thanks for your recent letter. This is my attempt to answer the request implied in your remarks on my essay, "Thirteen Ways of Looking at Poetry" (*Way Out*, September 1962), in which you said that essay contained "some very good stuff, but I wish you'd expand your remarks on entropy. It's worth an essay in itself as is the stance of the scientist who calls life 'negative entropy.'"

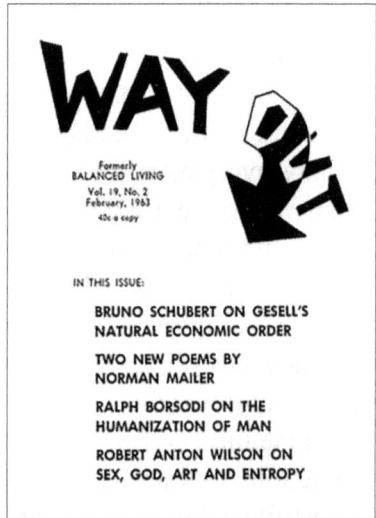

WAY OUT

Formerly
BALANCED LIVING
Vol. 19, No. 2
February, 1963
40¢ a copy

IN THIS ISSUE:

BRUNO SCHUBERT ON GESELL'S NATURAL ECONOMIC ORDER

TWO NEW POEMS BY NORMAN MAILER

RALPH BORSODI ON THE HUMANIZATION OF MAN

ROBERT ANTON WILSON ON SEX, GOD, ART AND ENTROPY

Curiously enough, the same mail which brought your letter also brought the following response to the same essay:

"Your art is about as phony as your mathematics. You must have gone to school, since you've heard of logarithms, but you should have stayed a little longer to find out the true definition. It ain't what you think it is. Your barnyard morals make you a misfit in any respectable organization, and you might be interested to know that there's more than sex to life."

I quote this amusing reaction because it is a good jumping-off place for a discussion of entropy, communication, Hip and God, which are the topics I intend to treat here. You might be a bit confused as to how "barnyard morals" and "sex" are connected with what I wrote about poetry in the essay in question, but the interesting thing is that the young lady who wrote this letter deduced a sexually libertarian philosophy from that essay, and she deduced correctly. Old Reich used to say that the terror of new ideas is caused by an intuition that any new idea can, potentially, upset the delicate balance of a civilization based on repression, unleashing God-knows-what into our midst. A new idea is always connected with new bodily feelings, and is an orgasm of the brain in more ways than one. Outside of Reich, psychology has never fully grasped the erotic sensitivity of the electro-colloidal protoplasmic corporeal body in which we do our thinking. A deep breath sends energy to the genitals, as Reich knew, and the pioneer – whether in art, science or life itself – is always breathing hard.

In *The White Negro*, you talk about the Hipster's attempt to "build a new nervous system." I would like to tie that in with what I have just said above, and with the idea of literature as negative entropy, by referring to I. A. Richards' famous experiments in poetry comprehension, as recounted in his *Practical Criticism*. You may recall that Dr. Richards' principal discovery was that the popularity of a poem was directly proportional to the number of cliches and stereotyped ideas it contained. What happens when a message consisting entirely of cliches pours into the human nervous system? Habitual neural circuits are activated – what Korzybski terms "a conditioned semantic reflex" – leading to what Richards called "the stock response." Activating these habitual circuits and eliciting these stock responses is the whole secret of popular art, as practiced by Herman Wouk, Mr. Kennedy's speech-writers and makers of fine face-creams everywhere.

Now what happens when, on the other hand, language is charged with meta-dimensional meaning, improbable structure, craziness, "that strange thing called genius"? What happens when language gets like this –

> Curse, bless me with your fierce tears I pray
> Do not go gentle into that good night

> (Dylan Thomas)

or this

> Perditrix navium, perditrix urbiam,
> perditrix valoram, nupta bellum

> (Andreas Divus)

or this

> Be strong in whore, allure him, burn him up

> (Shakespeare)

What happens to the nervous system in such a case, I would argue, is that new circuits are formed. There are no conditioned neuro-semantic reflexes capable of handling this level of communication. "Learning" must occur, not merely in the narrowly intellectual sense, but in the organismic sense: the sensibility, including its pre-rational and extra-rational faculties, must change in its basic dynamism, multi-ordinally and meta-dimensionally. This is a perfect example of the celebrated Hegelian aufgehoben where a change in quantity leads to a change in quality. (It is what Korzybski called a "non-elementalistic relation," what Fuller calls "synergy." One plus one does not equal two, but, instead, equals two-plus, a new gestalt.)

Now this is precisely what we would be led to expect by the information equation from Claude Shannon which I quoted in my previous article. Shannon, you will remember, defines information as a function of the probability of guessing the message in advance, information increasing as the logarithm of the probability decreases:

$$-H = p_1 \log p_1 + p_2 \log p_2 \text{ etc} + p_n \log p_n$$

where H is the information and the p's are the individual probabilities of the individual symbols. (Claud Shannon: *Mathematical Theory of Communication.*)

Before Dr. Shannon really had time to dry the ink on this equation Dr. Rapoport, Dr. Hayakawa and various other semanticists (including myself) were pointing out that he had thrown considerable light on the arts as well as on electrical communication networks, his ostensible subject. For, once pointed out, it is obvious that great art has precisely the characteristic of much information in Shannon's meaning of that term, and inferior art is notably lacking in information. The quotes from Dylan Thomas, Andreas Divus and Shakespeare which I have already used are chiefly distinguishable from say, Nick Kenny, in that each word in them comes as a mild shock to one's expectations. I see no good reason to doubt that this "mild shock," as I have called it, is the physiological explanation of esthetic pleasure. When information pours into the nervous system, the mirco-volt potential differences caused by the breaking and re-forming of circuits create a situation not unlike the electrical pulsations measured by Reich in couples experiencing orgasm. Freud was right, after all: all pleasure, basically, is erotic pleasure.

More: Shannon's equation is the negative of the famous entropy equation of thermodynamics

$$H = p\text{-}1 \log p\text{-}1 + p\text{-}2 \log p\text{-}2 + p\text{-}n \log p\text{-}n$$

where H is the entropy and the p's are the probabilities of the individual molecules (or other elements) being where they are. Shannon's information is $-H$ where entropy is H; hence, the engineer's short-hand description of information as "negentropy" (negative entropy). Now, in its broadest meaning, what is entropy? Sameness. And what is negative entropy? Differentiation. Schrödinger's bio-physical equations, in his *What is Life?* led up to the conclusion that evolution, as a process of differentiation, is an anti-entropic function going against the direction of development in the physical universe, where differentiation tends inexorably to give way to undifferentiation. From this, Dr. Schrödinger went on to conclusions which seemed supernaturalistic, at least to some readers, but which might more accurately be called supra-mechanistic or synergetic (in Buckminster Fuller's sense). Leaving this philosophic point aside for now, Dr. Schrödinger's bio-physics does lead us to realize that life functions anti-entropically and creates "pockets" of negative entropy around itself. The products of human culture, from the Parthenon to the bicycle and from Issa's haikus to Clerk Maxwell's lovely electro-magnetic equations, are conspicuously complex examples of such "pockets," as are, on a lower level, bee-hives, beavers' dams, birds' nests, etc. As an example of the interlockings of these "pockets" and their synergetic (non-additive), cumulatively unpredictable homeostasis, consider some of the cases recounted in Rachel Carson's *Silent Spring* of the havoc harvested when narrowly mechanistic minds go tampering with anti-entropic ecology. I think in particular of a case in which some cattle-breeders killed off the sage in a certain area to allow for more grass; the ultimate result was the extinction of several herds of moose, the entire beaver population of the area, and all the fish in a nearby lake – because the moose needed the sage for food and the beavers needed another tree, which was destroyed along with the sage, for their dams; and, when the beavers were gone, the lake drained, and the fish were gone too. It is rather like the chaos that would befall New York City if the dinosaurs of Hollywood guilt-myth really did rear up out of the East River some day.

An anti-entropic pocket – an enclave of differentiated life – is a delicate balance of forces, and one blow at the wrong place reduces it immediately to the entropic dissolution of the inorganic universe.

We are beginning to expand our theme to unnecessarily cosmological dimensions; contracting it back downward again we return to the basic insight that, a sequence of symbols containing much unpredictability (and therefore much information) being anti-entropic in structure, its effect on the human nervous system must be anti-entropic, and this anti-entropic aufgehoben (the dissolution of old circuits into new ones) is what we experience as pleasure or beauty. (Reich's attempt to synthesize Marx and Freud by identifying Marx's "working power" with Freud's "libido" contains several passages in which Reich is visibly groping toward this conclusion). Don Werkheiser's often-repeated charge that the State, by enforcing conformity with a club, tends to reduce the potentially rich functioning of human nervous systems to the monotony of plant behavior (tropisms even below the conditioned reflex level) is strongly apropos here. The saying that "every artist is an anarchist" can be rephrased: every artist is anti-entropic. He breaks up tropisms, reflex-arcs, the beloved S-R pattern of behaviorists, etc.; he forces the complicated, unpredictable and somewhat terrifying unleashing of creative awareness in his audience. It doesn't matter how unpolitical he is. He is a threat to every organized conformity in the world. Shaw was right to speak of an "evolutionary appetite" in mankind; everything that contributes to differentiation of man from man, everything that contributes toward individuality of awareness, is an anti-entropic quantum in the direction of evolution.

I once made an outline for a Bible-sized monstrosity of a book in which I was going to start from the easily-demonstrable axiom that no two things in the universe are exactly identical in all respects and proceed, by steps as remorselessly logical as Euclid's, to a demonstration that anarchism is absolutely necessary for man's survival. I seem to be chewing over undigested portions of that aborted epic instead of proceeding with the libretto of the present opus. The explosion of new awareness in the nervous system – the semantic orgasm, so to speak – is my topic, but I cannot treat it in isolation from those forces which oppose orgasm. Man is the armored species, as Reich said; armored against his own emotions and bodily needs; armored against new connections. The fear of art is the fear of orgasm. Conservatism has only one face, in the senate, the library or the bedroom. The hand that throws *Tropic of Capricorn* in the fire is the hand that signs a loyalty oath, and it is a hand that knows not the art of the caress.

Do you know why you've never seen a good Chinese painting of the crucifixion? That austere geometrical form doesn't fit the dynamics of Chinese art, as Chinese Christians have found to their mortification. It is the form of the abstract rationalist, tending always toward the boxed-in, as in Dali's best crucifixion. Fuller's synergetic geometry – I wrote this six years ago, before I had discovered Hip – is the end of the Square in the Western sensibility. It is no accident that the creator of the geodesic dome is also the author of

> God is not a noun;
> God is a verb

Buckminster Fuller, with his dymaxion map showing the world as one island under the air-ocean, his bathroom that folds up into the wall like a Murphy bed, his 3-wheeled car and his house that hangs from a mast like a tree or a ship, is a perfect example of the anti-entropic mind: his technological ideas, had he a different sensibility, might have become classic surrealist paintings or poems like Dylan's. Synergetic geometry – the theoretical foundation of Fuller's technological discoveries – is a profoundly Taoistic system beginning from the axiom, "there are no absolutely isolated structures," which is the Zen-Tao proverb *shih shih wu ai* almost literally translated. We seem to be recapturing that medieval sensibility which Pound has so beautifully described, that "world of moving energies," that "world of forms" seen "as the sculptor sees the form in the air," the world of Erigena and Dante and Plotinus and Grosseteste;

Erigena who argued that all things are lights, Dante who intuited "the love that moves the sun and other stars," Plotinus who argued that the body was inside the soul, Grosseteste who knew that human energy is basically sun-energy. None of these "mystical" and Gothic philosophies seem particularly weird when I remember that, in caressing my lover's genitals, I release, through friction, energy that came into my hands from the air and the food, and, hence, ultimately, from the sun, and the stars as distant as Betelgeuse.

You have argued that "jazz is the music of orgasm," but I am arguing that all music, and all art, are orgasm. This, I submit, is why even tragic art is pleasurable – the mystery that has puzzled critics from Aristotle on up is no mystery at all when you think of art as an excitation of the nervous system. Which brings me, by the labyrinthine compulsions of my peculiar logic, to the thought for which this essay exists, the thought that orgasm is God.

What does that guttural, strangely sexual syllable, so similar to the four most common obscenities in English – that weird word, "God" – mean, after all? To "the ragged and the golden rabble" (if I may purloin an urgently meaningful phrase from Bartolomeo Vanzetti) this word means: a narrow-minded old man, of astronomical dimensions, gaseous and invisible, sitting on a cloud. Theologians and mystics, as well as free-thinkers, know that this is a myth. What, then, does "God" mean? To Dante, *L'amore che movette il sol e altare stella*, as we have already quoted. To the Upanishads, God is "the True Self," the ground of being in which we all partake: cosmic life energy. ("Brahmin is the power by which the tongue moves and the eye sees.") In Taoism, as in Fuller's philosophy, God is a verb, a process, a synergetic relationship. Note that to the Brahmins we are isolated from this cosmic power by "illusion," the illusion of the ego-trap; and to the Taoists, we are isolated from It by "unnatural living," the cake of false culture. Is this not what Freud said, in his remark, "The ego is part of the id, and that is the strength of the ego; but the ego feels itself separate from the id, and that is the weakness of the ego"?

Protoplasm – see any biology text – is an electro-colloidal dispersion. The electrical charges of the particles push them apart, tending to create expansion; the surface tension pulls them together, tending to cause contraction. In the rhythmicity between expansion and contraction the great life processes of breathing, digestion, orgasm, etc. go on. Freud, as well as the Brahmins and Taoists, knew that man had fallen away from this natural cycle and its natural serenity, and his mysterious word, "repression," tries to suggest the way in which the harm is done. There is no mystery to it, when you read Reich on muscular armoring and remember that the contraction of muscles is caused by the shift of electro-colloidal dispersion toward gel by increase of surface tension over electrical charge. In the context of our discussion of entropy, this process of what Reich called "armoring," that is, the contraction of the protoplasm, is entropic, just as sexuality and art by stirring-up the nervous system, are anti-entropic.

Eddington defined entropy as "time's arrow," because the entropy in a system is a function of its age: the older the system, the more entropy (except in living systems, of course). If the idea of "God" really derives, as I have been suggesting, from the convulsive moment of the strength of the ego through the disappearance of the ego – the expansion of the protoplasm – we can understand the family resemblance between the words, "come," "fuck," "cock," "cunt" and "God," all of them coming from the clogged breath of the last orgasmic explosion. (This may explain also the mystic "Aum," which is the next breath afterwards.) Not only were you right in ending *The Deer Park* with the idea that sex is Time and Time is new connections, but you could have added that God is sex and new connections are anti-entropy, making the total formula, God equals sex equals Time equals new connections equals anti-entropy.

I could stop right here, having come full-circle back to the idea from which I started and having given that idea a context which, perhaps, makes it sound a little less crazy than it did at first, but I would like to add one final note, as to the role of this essay in *Way Out*. The average letter I get these days says, reduced to simplest terms, You, Mr. Wilson, are crazy, because I can't understand the things that get into your magazine. Well, there happens to be a very simple principle that explains what gets into this magazine, and that principle is Dr. Shannon's equation. I have dug up Frobenius and trotted him out not necessarily because I think he is more important than, say, Frazer, but because Frazer is digested by the intelligentsia and Frobenius is not. Similarly, Josiah Warren and his circle have gotten a great deal of attention here, not because his is the greatest social theory of all time, but because of all important social theories his is the least commented upon these days. Gesell is getting the same treatment in this issue because you can find a thousand Marxists for every Gesellist in this moribund Republic and Gesell is at least as important as Marx. In other words, I am trying to provide information for my readers, and that means eschewing popularity and presenting, not "what everybody is talking about," but what everybody is NOT talking about. This essay, running together a dozen ideas that have never met each other before, might be as crazy as most readers will think it is, but I present it because, right or wrong, it should provoke some species of mental-emotional activity in the nervous systems of some of you. For I am convinced that at least part of my theory is true, and if I do not become overwhelmingly beloved and a rival for Herman Wouk by playing against the melody and coming on all the time with ideas that are either too old or too new to be on the cycle of the "movement" (as I believe it is still called) of the mass intelligence, I at least provide static; and static – this is another of Shannon's discoveries – is also information.

Ralph Reid summed up the importance of Frobenius in two sentences: "He seeks to arouse curiosity. He does not seek to abolish it."

Attack Usury at Its Source

An exchange between Bill Treichler and Robert Anton Wilson

Published in *Way Out*, May 1963

"Bob Wilson says his aim is to end the revolution against usury. Why is he, an anarchist, concerned with usury, a voluntary and private arrangement? (1) Does he think usury should be outlawed? (2) I should think an anarchist would say, 'If people want to buy automobiles and color TVs at outrageous terms that is their own business.' So much talk about usury makes me wary of the share-the-wealth schemes, because I associate the feeling toward borrowed money dependence with propertyless people or get-rich-quick plungers. (3) I think the anarchist or libertarian should relentlessly challenge taxes and privilege. (4) Five U. S. Senators have introduced a bill to relieve people with strong convictions (Amish) from social security. We should support them. The Liberty Amendment, which will repeal the income

A Non-Euclidean Perspective

tax and get the government out of business, has been endorsed by six states. (5) We should explain what it will do to everyone we can." – Bill Treichler, Walker, Iowa.

(1) Mr. Treichler very well states the condition under which usury would be tolerated, and even defended, by the anarchist; he errs, however, in assuming that that condition obtains at present. Far from being "voluntary and private," usury is in today's world involuntary and public. The reason that Mr. Treichler does not understand this is that he is using the word "usury" in its special modern sense of "an unfair or cruel rate of interest," whereas anarchists continue to use the word in its original sense, as it was used by Aristotle and the authors of the Bible, to mean any interest charge whatsoever. It has been repeatedly explained in this magazine – and by such earlier anarchist writers as Spooner, Greene, Tucker, Proudhon, Cohen, Labadie, etc. – that the rate of interest on capital is fixed by the rate of interest on currency; that the rate of interest on currency is fixed by the monopolists who control the issue of currency; that this monopoly exists only because of law's forbidding the formation of mutual banks; and that these laws are enforced by the threat of violence by the police power, as all State-made laws are enforced. Under these conditions, usury is, in the strictest meaning of these terms, both involuntary and public. The only way for Mr. Treichler to dispute this conclusion is to bring forth evidence of interest existing in the absence of such a monopoly upon the issue of currency.

(2) I have never urged – and no anarchist writer known to me has ever urged – that usury should be outlawed or forcibly suppressed; such a position is, indeed, the antithesis of anarchism. It is true that I have said that usury will ultimately disappear, but I do not expect this to come about by the invasion of human rights. I expect the abolition of usury to be achieved through the exercise by the people of a right that is now denied to them; namely, the right to form their own mutual bank of issue, to provide currency at cost and without interest to the members of such banks, such currency to be secured by

the property of the members. This has been explained countless times by anarchist writers, who have indicated step by step how such banks will cause the abolition of usury; in essence, the claim of these writers is that nobody will borrow at interest when he is able to borrow without interest by joining a mutual bank. Such usury as does continue to exist under such a system will truly be "voluntary and private," the eccentric practice of a few morons or masochists.

Now, it was possible to dispute this idea with some show of plausibility back in the days when Lysander Spooner and P. J. Proudhon were first promoting it. In those days, money was always backed by a precious metal, and those not sophisticated in monetary economics were under the superstitious impression that no other form of property – no other commodity whatsoever – could secure currency except one of these precious metals. Since then, we have all become accustomed to money backed by government bonds; look in your wallet and see how many bills are silver certificates and how many are Federal Reserve notes; the Federal Reserve notes are backed by government bonds. I think it should now be obvious to any rational man that there is no special indwelling "magic" in gold and silver, and that any commodity – not just government bonds, but any form of property whatsoever – can legitimately be the basis of a valid currency. It only remains to convince the people that they can perform the service of issuing such money for themselves, through their own mutual credit associations, and that they do not need to let the State do it for them by passing it through monopolistic banks and charging the taxpayers nine billion dollars interest per year for it. The success of credit unions all over the world indicates, I think, that such is, indeed, a possibility; and all we need to accomplish free banking and end the monopoly of the Federal Reserve banks is to make the existing credit unions into banks of issue for their members. This is, however, forbidden by laws, made at the instigation of the monopolists, and until these laws are abolished involuntary usury will be forced on the people by the fact that some form of currency is needed in an economy with division-of-labor and the only currency available is monopolized by usurers.

(3) Understanding the sense in which I use the word "usury" should make nugatory Mr. Treichler's reference to those who borrow from finance companies to buy color TV sets. Every interest-charge is usurious in my meaning of the term: usurious because unnecessary: unnecessary because the result of restricted liberty. Every entrepreneur, every small businessman, every worker, loses part of the product of his labor because he needs a medium of exchange, and the medium of exchange is monopolized by profiteers who will not issue it to him at cost but instead loot him for all they can get. The State stands behind this monopoly, threatening violence against any group of producers and workers who attempt to issue their own medium of exchange at cost. Thus, the price of every commodity on the market consists only about 40% of actual cost to workers and managers and 60 % of interest charges paid all along the line – by the farmer, by the weaver, by the tailor, by the manufacturer, by the wholesaler, by the shop-keeper – paid by each of these producers to a group of parasites who contribute not one iota of labor to the finished product, but who merely place a levy on every act of exchange between these producers.

Mr. Treichler shows some degree of hostility, or fear, toward the "propertyless," but since he doesn't attempt to justify this feeling (perhaps recognizing unconsciously that it has no justification), I do not know how to rebut it. I can rebut an idea, but I do not know how to rebut the absence of an idea. Let me merely indicate that if Mr. Treichler accepts Adam Smith's great dictum that the natural wage of labor is its full product, he must accept the conclusion that every man is entitled to property-rights in that which he has himself created through labor. Every man should, therefore, be propertied, except for the rare and pathological cases of those few who have never labored in their lives. If Mr. Treichler will look around the world he might observe, however, that most men are not propertied; that those who have labored the most and the hardest are the least propertied; and that, in many cases, those who have through hard labor created fantastic amounts of property for the world have no property for themselves at all. Let Mr. Treichler ask himself how this property got into the hands of those who presently hold it, many of whom have never labored in their lives, and how it got out of the hands of those who have done the labor. We anarchists claim that the method by which this magic is done is what we call usury, i.e., the monopoly on the currency held by certain bankers and denied to the actual producers by the police power (jail power) of the State. It is this monopoly which steals from the worker half or more of each day's product, syphoning it off as interest; this monopoly which ruins 85% of the small businessmen in their first two years of business; this monopoly which stifles competition and increases other monopolies, erecting a plutocracy more centralized and merciless than the kings of old; this monopoly which breeds landlordism.

(4) I thank Mr. Treichler for his advice that anarchists should attack taxes and privileges. Since anarchists have been doing just that for two hundred years, we shall continue to do it.

(5) The compulsory income tax and compulsory social security programs are, of course, banditry, as taking money by force is always banditry, whether performed by one man who frankly calls himself a highwayman or by a group of men who call themselves a government. But, while I am opposed with all my being to such violent expropriation, I do not see that ending these two forms of it is particularly called for while the more enormous banditry of the banking monopoly is still allowed to continue and we are still denied the right to form free bank associations. While the State keeps that latter invasion of our rights in force, stopping such minor pests as the income tax and social security will have only one effect: it will make the rich richer and the poor poorer. Let us have real liberty – freedom,

first, from the money monopoly, and second, and through the first, freedom from the land monopoly – and then it will be time to begin lopping off, one by one, the other excrescences of State power.

Long Live Anarchy: An Interview with Robert Anton Wilson

Pacifica Radio, 1965

This interview aired on WBAI-FM in the mid-1960s. The interviewer, Charlie Hayden, later went on to become a prominent LGBT activist under the name Randy Wicker.

I purchased access to an audio version of this interview upon finding it in Pacifica's archives, and with the help of Wilson scholar Nick Helweg-Larsen, have made the following transcription. Enjoy.

– Chad Nelson

Hayden: Today we're talking to Mr. Robert Anton Wilson who happens to be a freelance writer who's written for such publications as *Fact* magazine, *The Realist*, *Jaguar* magazine *Liberation* magazine. Mr. Wilson also happens to be somewhat of a strange political animal in our particular culture, namely, he calls himself an "individualistic anarchist." Mr. Wilson, can you explain yourself a little bit on what your political viewpoints are?

Wilson: Well, to begin with, an anarchist is a libertarian socialist. Originally all forms of socialism tended to be anti-state as well as anti-capitalism. There came a point in the development of socialism in which the theory of the dictatorship of the proletariat was promulgated and the idea that through the political state, socialism would be implemented as a dictatorship and then the state would wither away – which is the orthodox Marxian theory. The anarchists at this point distinguished themselves by strongly opposing this ideology and insisting that socialism could only be implemented outside of the state, that anything implemented through the state could never be socialistic nor could it tend toward socialism.

Hayden: You say "implemented outside the state" . . . today socialism is at least identified in the public's mind as statism.

Wilson: Yes, according to the anarchists this is a complete misunderstanding of socialism. The anarchists would say that anything implemented through the state is statism and the direct contrary of socialism. Socialism means a system oriented toward society. The state is not society. The state is a mechanism apart from and above society interfering at all times with the natural functioning of society. The anarchists believe that the only way socialism can be implemented is through free and voluntary associations within society, not through the Frankenstein monster of a state above society.

Hayden: And what happened within the socialist movement once the anarchists began taking this different viewpoint from the others. I mean, was there a large split within the movement at one time in the late 19th century?

Wilson: Well, what happened in the first place was that Marx deliberately sabotaged the First International when he found out that there were more anarchists in it than Marxists. He sabotaged it by moving it from Europe to New York where there were at that time much less socialists than there were in Europe and therefore made it an organization without a head so to speak.

Hayden: What do you mean "in New York where there were fewer socialists than there were in Europe"?

Wilson: The International began in Europe and Marx had the headquarters moved to New York so as to prevent the lively anarchist movement in Europe, which was much livelier at that point than the Marxist movement, from taking it over as they were obviously about to take it over since there were more of them than Marxists. The Marxists, always hostile to democracy, didn't want to see the majority taking the movement over.

Hayden: And then what happened?

Wilson: Then in the Second International there was a split and the fight came out in the open and the Marxists, who at that point, were a majority, were able to push the anarchists out of the movement entirely, so the so-called Black International was formed out of which the modern anarchist and anarcho-syndicalist movements evolved.

Hayden: About this time, unless I'm mistaken, there were various assassinations attributed to anarchists and there were riots led by anarchists and gradually the word anarchy became somewhat of a dirty word to the press and to the public generally

Wilson: If we must talk about the assassinations, and I guess we must . . . This always comes up in discussions of anarchism. Let me state first of all as the *Encyclopedia Britannica* itself points out in the article on anarchism – if you list almost all of the assassinations that have been attributed to anarchists and assume that all of them were performed by anarchists (which is a dubious assumption by the way – many of them were police frame-ups), but on that assumption it still turns out that more anarchists have been murdered by governments than all that can be accused of having murdered governors. The number of anarchists who have been killed by governments on trumped up charges, or sometimes without charges at all, goes way above the number of the governing classes that were killed by anarchists. Now at the time this wave of assassinations went on, in the 1880s and '90s and up into the first decade of this century, many of the leaders of the anarchist movement strenuously objected to this method and criticized it, said it would not advance anarchism and predicted that it would even lead to the decline of anarchism. It must be understood clearly that the men who committed these assassinations were almost unanimously working men who had never had a normal education. Many of them were completely self-educated; many of them had known intense misery in their lives. For instance Ravachol, the celebrated French anarchist terrorist who threw bombs into restaurants, was a completely uneducated working man who had taught himself to read and who was supporting a sister with an illegitimate child on a salary that couldn't properly support himself as a printer. And Ravachol, in a fury at the poverty of himself and his sister, one day decided to take revenge on capitalist society and began his wave of terror.

Hayden: Well, if these assassinations were not the reason for the decline of anarchism as a vibrant, very real political movement, what in your opinion was the reason for the nearly total demise of anarchism from the political scene?

Wilson: There were a number of causes. Anarchism declined rather slowly. In the 1930s anarchism was still a fairly large force. In the Spanish Civil War the communists managed to betray the anarchists with whom they were supposedly fighting side by side against the fascists. And in the Spanish Civil War a great many of the best minds of anarchism perished frequently, so to speak, shot from behind by the communists instead of in front by the fascists. That was only one cause of course. Anarchism declined, I think, because nothing succeeds like success and it took a long long time. It still isn't complete for disillusionment with Marxism to set in. Once the Marxists had Soviet Russia, one-sixth of the earth's surface, it quickly became the dominant form of socialism. Because they actually had something and were doing something. They had their land and their plant and so on. And all the other forms of socialism, not just anarchism, declined because, as I say, nothing succeeds like success. As disillusionment with Marxism increases, one expects to see a gradual revival of anarchist ideology. It'll take a long time because as soon as they . . . as soon as the majority of socialists get disillusioned with one Marxist experiment, another one is set up and it takes them about fifteen years or so to get disillusioned with that one. Hope springs eternal within the human breast.

Hayden: Have the anarchists ever had a chance to put any of their theories or ideas into action and if so have they been successful in doing so?

Wilson: There have been numerous successful anarchist experiments. There was one in the Middle Ages even. A town in Bohemia which for seven years had an anarchist regime and held off the entire Prussian army which was attempting to come in and crush them. After seven years they were finally defeated but the system did not collapse from within as all authoritarians would predict. The system of anarchism worked very successfully until the army came in and murdered them all. In America there were several successful anarchist colonies in the 19th century. The greatest success to date of anarchism was in the Spanish Revolution in 1936-37. For 18 months the factories of Barcelona were run by anarchist committees without any authoritarian capitalist or communist-type structure. And they actually increased production 19 percent during that period and were actually thriving at the point when Franco's fascist troops came in and blew the town to hell.

Hayden: Today are there many anarchists left? Is there any such thing as anarchist publications? Anywhere in the world, do the anarchists have any sort of political foothold and can be recognized as any sort of sizeable or even fringe movement?

Wilson: There are many anarchist publications. I do not have with me right now any figures on the number of anarchists in the world. One thing for instance in Spain, you couldn't say there were any anarchists because anybody known as such would be shot. But one could wager, considering the number of anarchists when Franco took over, probably a considerable portion of the Spanish population are still anarchists. And if they could get out from under the Franco dictatorship they could attempt to implement anarchism once again. Through the rest of the world there are anarchist parties in most of the large nations. In England, there's a publication called *Freedom*, which comes out weekly in newspaper form. And they also publish a bi-monthly called *Anarchy*. In America there's *Views and Comments* published by the Libertarian League and there's also *Liberation* magazine which has a very strongly anarchist tending policy. The Catholic Worker Movement is committed to anarchism of the peculiarly Catholic sort. And there's even the agrarian anarchist movement in this country centered around the School of Living in Ohio.

Hayden: Have there been any movements of social reform that anarchists generally have identified themselves with and have taken an active role in promoting and shaping?

Wilson: First of all there's the mutual banking idea in the early 19th century. The mutual banking idea was promulgated by two anarchists. Independently of each other, Josiah Warren in America, and completely unknown to Warren and also not knowing about Warren, Proudhon in France, began teaching the same idea. They both originated independently, just as like Leibniz and Newton invented the calculus, or Darwin and Wallace invented the theory of evolution simultaneously. Warren and Proudhon devoted a great deal of energy to the mutual banking idea and although there are no mutual banks today there are in most parts of the world credit unions which are, from an anarchist point of view, a truncated, I might almost say castrated form of the mutual bank. But the fact that the credit union movement exists and is so widespread is a derivation from the original anarchist mutual banking idea. Also, the anarchists were pioneers of the labor movement at a time when the Marxists were very hostile to labor unions.

Hayden: What were the Marxists saying at the time they were hostile to labor unions?

Wilson: That the proper technique was for the workers to act through the state by voting in a socialist government. And they felt the labor unions could do nothing to improve the condition of the workers. The anarchists, especially in Italy and France, were responsible for creating the labor union movement. In this country; they played a large part in it also. A third thing which anarchists have contributed which has had a large effect on the modern world is the freeing of education. Long before Neill came along with Summerhill, there were similar schools founded by anarchists. In New Jersey around 1908 there was the Francisco Ferrera School named after the anarchist martyr Francisco Ferrera who had founded similar schools in Spain and was shot by the Spanish government for a crime which he didn't commit. The Francisco Ferrera School is even more radical than Summerhill and was founded here in America in

1908. Similar experiments in free education were started by anarchists in many other parts of the world.

Hayden: Well, today are there any well-known anarchists who are making any major contributions in any area at all? Arts, politics, religion, science?

Wilson: To begin with, the most famous anarchist around these days, I suppose, is Paul Goodman, who I disagree with on many things. But he has certainly obtained a very considerable influence within the community of the social scientists and the universities. They all pay a lot of attention to him, and his ideas are anarchistic and derived largely from Kropotkin. In addition to Mr. Goodman there are Julian Beck and Judith Malina of the Living Theater, both anarchists who have made a contribution to the American theater, which I don't think will be fully appreciated for another fifty or a hundred years. But even today the real hip people realize what a great thing the Becks have done. And besides them of course there's Dorothy Day of the Catholic Worker Movement, who has probably more than anyone else been the center or the fountainhead of the pacifist protest in America in the last couple of decades.

Hayden: How do you answer the charge that anarchism's an outmoded political belief? That it was a nice theory to attempt to apply to an agrarian society, but in our modern day of technology and industrial society, that anarchism is just simply antiquated?

Wilson: Well, I would reply to that by saying bluntly that it's just not true. The anarchist idea, I think, is especially well adapted to industrial society. In the first place, as Marx (I always like to quote the enemy when I can), as Marx pointed out, industrial society is creating a sense of solidarity among the working class in a way that didn't exist under previous systems. Also, the modern tendency of technology, as indicated in cybernetics, is towards the destabilization of industry, and towards the self-regulation of the machinery. The whole essence of cybernetics is self-regulating technology, which is called homeostasis, or redundancy of control, in the technical engineering language of the cyberneticist. Now this implies, necessarily, a decentralization of the human parts of industry. Also, and I am very amused to notice, the American Management Association, in their bulletins on cybernetics, are continually forced to use the concept of decentralization. They have even come up with a phrase, "decentralization of authority and centralization of financial control," which is a flat contradiction. But it's the only way they can maintain the concept of centralization of financial control in a cybernetic world. They are trying to hold on to an antiquated way of thinking, which cybernetics is gradually going to force the whole world to abandon. Cybernetics is going to drive the whole world to decentralization, which is what the anarchists have always urged.

Hayden: How do you explain the popular misconception, I gather, that anarchists are opposed to all forms of law and order? That anarchy means unrestricted, unrestrained individual freedom, and actually has become associated (if you read the charges made by such distinguished Americans as Governor Wallace of Alabama, and what have you), that anarchy prevails, which is like saying "pandemonium and holocaust are upon us"? How did this type of idea regarding anarchism evolve? Were there anarchists who indeed were opposed to all forms of law and order or who did go about causing great disruption and problems? I'm thinking specifically of the Haymaker affair [sic], which I'm only vaguely familiar with, through reading and what have you.

Wilson: Well, to begin with, anarchism is a word which is like a red flag to a bull. The man who coined the word, in the modern world, was Proudhon, and as much as I admire

Proudhon, I must say he was overly addicted to the paradox like many great French writers. It's a peculiar trait of the French to delight in paradox, and Proudhon chose this word anarchism because it was so shocking and paradoxical to the average person, who was as then, and still is now, the next thing to saying "I'm a lunatic," to say "I'm an anarchist." Proudhon took it, because as I say, he was addicted to paradox.

Most anarchists continue to use the word only out of a sense of solidarity and brotherhood to the great anarchists of the past, many of whom suffered martyrs' deaths. I'm thinking of Sacco and Vanzetti, and Joe Hill, and Landauer, and so many others, and also in tribute to the great brains of the movement who have contributed, who created so many splendid philosophical treatises, such as Tolstoy, and Benjamin Tucker, and Josiah Warren, and Bakunin, and Proudhon. Since all these men used the word anarchist, it seems to me rather dishonest to abandon the word, if one agrees with their thinking. A few anarchists down through the years have abandoned the word. They have chosen other words, such as libertarian socialist, or mutualist, and at one point, a fellow named [Francis Dashwood] Tandy tried to popularize the term voluntary socialism. I prefer to stick to the word, as shocking as it is, in tribute to the great men who have used it in the past. As for the Haymarket affair, that was recognized as a frame-up by Governor [John Peter] Altgeld, who subsequently pardoned the anarchists who remained in prison. He couldn't pardon the ones who had already been hanged, but Governor Altgeld, in his investigation, decided that all of those men had been framed. What happened was that the workers of Chicago were calling a strike, and at a meeting somebody threw a bomb, and several people were arrested who were anarchists, and they were convicted of having thrown the bomb, although subsequent evidence showed that none of them could possibly have had any connection with the making or the throwing of the bomb. Considerable evidence has been developed over the years that it was a police agent provocateur who threw that bomb, by the way.

Hayden: How do anarchists generally (seems to me, I have to confess, that I probably hold a number of popular misconceptions regarding anarchy and anarchism), but how can an anarchist who is so totally committed to individual liberty and freedom seek solutions through a political system like socialism? It seems to me that if there was any type of a political or economic philosophy that anarchism could be involved with, it should be a right-wing type of thinking, capitalism or even fascism. Something which did not involve the large concepts of the group working together, and what have you, that socialism involves.

Wilson: Well, here we can get rather deep into anarchist theory which is what I would like to do. I'm afraid once I start getting in deeply, you will interrupt and say it's getting too abstract. But, well, in the first place, the anarchist movement is part of what I would call the age old movement toward, for want of a better word one has to call it, common decency. If you go back about five thousand years you find the origins of the modern state and the modern class system. And what existed before that, loose tribal confederations, are sometimes called anarchistic. I agree with Benjamin Tucker, that this is an inappropriate use of the word. Tucker said anarchism is liberty possessed by libertarians. These early tribes had liberty in a loose sort of sense, but they were not sophisticated enough to know what they had, and it wasn't true anarchism. With the invention of the national state, which incidentally seems to have come through conquest in every case, the German sociologist Franz Oppenheimer pretty thoroughly demonstrated that all the states we have been able to trace to their origins, did arrive through conquest.

We had the beginnings of the class system, in which the great majority toil, not to support themselves, but to support a minority of parasites who live off them. This in its classical form is the slave state as we find it throughout the ancient world. Over the millenniums, this gradually evolves into the feudal state, and later into the capitalist state, but the basic gimmick remains the same. As for example, the basic gimmick in the land swindle is still the same as it was under the slave state. A small minority own the land. The theory originally given is that they are anointed or chosen by God, and the king rules by divine right. God has elected him to rule. His relatives, who are known as the nobility, own the land because they are relatives of the man chosen by God. Everybody else who has been disinherited by God, the rest of us creeps, we don't own the land.

In order to work the land, to grow crops or whatever else we're going to do, run a shoe-making shop, or whatever, we must purchase that piece of the land on installments from one of the owners. Under feudalism, the lord of the land, the king's relative, ruled on the basis of this supernaturalistic theory; I don't think in spite of the hangover of theology into the modern world, if anybody got up and pronounced that argument today, that the landlords rule by God's right, anybody would take it seriously. The reason people continue to pay rent today is that they don't think about the subject at all. If they did think about it, they'd realize that the only justification the landlord has, is this supernatural theory, and I don't think they'd stand for it.

Hayden: Well, are anarchists opposed to (there's an anarchist around New York who has buttons that say "I am an enemy of the state") . . . And are the anarchists now, necessarily opposed to the existence of national state and local governments? And how would an anarchist feel towards the beginnings of world government such as exhibited maybe in a UN with growing power and what have you?

Wilson: An anarchist naturally feels that world government would be just a little bit worse than national government, because [it'd be] more centralized, and even more omnipotent.

Hayden: How would you have international controls enforced? How would you manage to regulate such things as health and disease? How would you settle problems like debates over who gets water from the Colorado River? How would you handle the growing complexities of international trade and commerce if you didn't have some sort of governmental control that could function on a scale this large?

Wilson: Well, the answer to that is that the idea that these things only can be done through governmental control is an error of the human mind similar to the error a long time ago that the earth was flat. This is firmly implanted in everybody's head. But the anarchist just happens to be the man who challenges it. What the anarchist says, in a nutshell, is anything that can be done through involuntary association can be done through voluntary association if it is worth doing. Now that's the whole function of the state. The state is not here to do those things which are worth doing which can be done through voluntary association. Obviously, you don't need a state for that. The purpose of the state is to get done those things which aren't worth doing and couldn't be done through voluntary association. Namely, to protect the interest of the ruling classes, and to suppress the servile classes.

Hayden: But (you speak in terms of socialism too) most of, or many of, the concepts inherent in socialism, what I think of as social service programs, don't they necessarily involve coercion and force, and by this I mean things like medical care for the aged, requiring medical men to take care of poor people who are sick, building codes which make landlords repair a building, which control rent, which prevent fire, disasters, and what have you? It seems to me, all sorts of regulations which are in the interest of the individual necessarily rely on a larger governmental agency forcing unwilling, even unscrupulous people from violating laws that have been passed in the public's interest. Do you think this could be solved through voluntary associations? What if the landlords had a voluntary association that had more money, and more guns, or what have you, than your voluntary association of anarchists or citizens.

Wilson: Well, this gets to the very bedrock of anarchism. To begin with, the anarchist says that all forms of coercion, of a left-wing nature, that we have in the modern world, are the result of not really facing up to the nature of the ruling class, and what has to be done about it. These are all half-measures, and the anarchist opposes all these coercive methods because he thinks that they have not faced up to the real issue. Social security, for instance, although I personally wouldn't want to see it abolished, under the present circumstances, under the present class tyranny, it's a necessary protection for the victims.

Printed with the permission of Pacifica Radio Archives.

Thirteen Choruses For The Divine Marquis

Published in *The Realist*, May 1966

Quotations identified as Sade are from Marquis de Sade, *Grove Press, 1965. Those identified as Marat/Sade are from* The Persecution and Assassination of Jean-Paul Marat as Performed by the Inmates of the Asylum at Charenton Under the Direction of the Marquis de Sade, *by Peter Weiss, Athenium, 1965.*

FIRST CHORUS

"You are afraid of the people unrestrained – how ridiculous!"

– Sade

I dreamed I called Rita Hayworth on the phone and asked her if she hears the babies of Hiroshima screaming in the night.

"No," she said, "I useta have kinda kooky problems like that but my analyst cleared them all up."

But – I insisted – after all, it was your picture that was painted on the Bomb. Not Harry Truman, or Einstein, or even Marilyn Monroe. You.

"Well, yeah, if you wanna look at it that way," she said. "But, Christ, they was sticking my picture on everything those days."

But, but – I shouted – don't you feel any sense of responsibility?

"Waita-minit, Mac," she said, "what are ya, some kinda nut? Nobody ever asked me nothing about it. They just went ahead and dropped it."

But, but, but – I screamed – all those people – 550,000 of them, according to one estimate I read – blown apart by a picture of you –

"Look, Clyde," she said firmly. "My analyst told me it don't do no good to brood over such things."

And the line went dead with a hollow click, like a coffin closing snugly on Dracula as the morning sun throws its white and ghastly nuclear radiations into the cool darkness of dream.

SECOND CHORUS

Why do the children scream
What are the heaps they fight over
those heaps with eyes and mouths

– Marat/Sade

And we, we Hiroshima-makers, are now finally, more than 150 years after his death, tentatively beginning to look at the unexpurgated de Sade.

I dreamed I called Dwight Eisenhower on the phone and asked him if de Sade should be banned.

"I don't know," he said. "I'll have to ask Postmaster General Summerfield. If he says it's a filthy book, then of course it should be banned. America must maintain its purity and its God-given heritage."

And I dreamed I called him back two nights later and he had consulted with Summerfield and the verdict was n.g. "Summerfield says dee Sayd was a pinko pervert."

And the phone went dead with a sudden dull click like the last sound Hemingway heard when he put the gun to his head and said, ah, shit, now, not any other minute but this minute, right *now*.

THIRD CHORUS

> . . . and as if I were a naughty little boy, the
> idea is to spank me into good behavior?
>
> – Sade

Prof. B.F. Skinner of Harvard, ripe with years and wisdom, rich with degrees and honors, says that a world without punishment is operationally conceivable. That is, speaking as a scientific psychologist, Skinner does not know of any behavior that can't be increased or decreased without the use of punishment.

Desirable behavior (from your point of view, whatever your point of view is)? – reinforce it through a system of rewards. It will increase.

Undesirable behavior (again, from whatever your point of view is)? – no need to punish it; just reinforce *incompatible* behavior, again through a system of rewards. The incompatible behavior will increase, and the "undesirable" behavior will decrease.

Simple as a proof in geometry.

But there is something in mankind which profoundly resents Prof. Skinner and his rationalism and his technology and his simplicity. The name of that something is the name of the divine Marquis, Donatien Alphonse Francois de Sade.

I dreamed I called J. Edgar Hoover on the phone and asked him, hey, dig, man, what do you think of a world without punishment?

"(Get a tap on this line,)" he said away from the phone, "(I got a pinko bleeding heart here.)"

"I'll tell you, sir," he said, "we are just a fact-finding agency; we don't draw any conclusions. But I Will Say This! There Is Only One Language the Godless Communists Understand And That Is The Language of Superior Power."

But, but – I cried – can you put the whole world over your lap and spank it?

"If the world had one ass, you can be sure we would," he said. "As it is, the spankings will have to be administered jointly and severally."

And the line went dead with an empty click, like a whip being pulled from its sheath and flicked, testingly, in the air.

FOURTH CHORUS

Marat
these cells of the inner self
are worse than the deepest stone dungeon
and as long as they are locked
all your revolution remains
only a prison mutiny
to be put down
by corrupted fellow prisoners

– Marat/Sade

Eventually we begin to realize that Sade has never been understood. He cried out for liberty, and we accuse him of being a forerunner of Hitler. He dreamed of a world without punishment, and we attribute brutality to him. He spoke for the spirit of love, and we project every viciousness onto him.

We are afraid of being seduced by him, we Hiroshima-makers.

He showed us our own face in a mirror and we have screamed for 150 years that it was his face.

Nothing could be more explicit than his actual words:

Laws should be "flexible," "mild" and "few" (Sade, p. 310).

We must "get rid forever of the atrocity of capital punishment" (Sade, p. 310).

Women must be equal with men: "Must the diviner half of humankind be laden with irons by the other? Ah, break those irons, Nature wills it" (Sade, p. 322).

Property should cease to be monopolized by a few (Sade, p. 313-314).

The present system of property-and-power rests on "submission of the people . . . due to . . . violence and the frequent use of torture" (Sade, p. 11).

He gave up his post as magistrate rather than administer capital punishment – "They wanted me to commit an inhumane act. I have never wanted to" (Sade, p. 29).

His principles are, as he says, quite correctly, not those that lead to tyranny but "principles to whose expression and realization the infamous despotism of tyrants has been opposed for uncounted centuries" (Sade, p. 311).

Even against the clergy, he maintains a solidly libertarian position: "I do not, however, propose either massacres or expulsions. Such dreadful things have no place in the enlightened mind. No, do not assassinate at all, do not expel

A Non-Euclidean Perspective

at all . . . Let us reserve the employment of force for the idols; ridicule alone will suffice for those who serve them" (Sade, p. 306).

But these words are ignored. Because he committed one crime – the crime of *reporting accurately* the secret day-dreams and longings of the psyche of men and women in this civilization, men and women reared in the crucible of authority-and-submission, discipline-and-punishment – he has been portrayed as the endorser of these extremities.

More truly than Flaubert said "Je suis Bovary," Sade could have said (did say, for those who read between the lines), "Je suis Justine." It is his voice that cries out continually in Justine's speeches, "Oh, monsters, is remorse and dead in you?" Just as it is his voice, undeniably, in the "Dialogue Between a Priest and a Dying Man" which says simply, "Reason, sir – yes, our reason alone should warn us that harm done our fellows can never bring happiness to us . . . and you need neither god nor religion to subscribe to [it]"(Sade, p. 174).

I dreamed I called Jesus Christ on the phone and asked him, say, Man, did you *really* forgive them for they knew not what they did?

"Verily, verily, I say unto you," he replied, "I made my position on authority-and-submission as clear as I could: 'You know that the princes of the Gentiles exercise dominion over them, and they that are great exercise authority upon them. But it shall not be so among you.' – Matt. 20:25. 'Every kingdom divided against itself is brought to desolation.' – Matt. 12:25. 'If the blind lead the blind, both shall fall into the ditch.' – Matt. 15:14. 'For they bind heavy burdens and grievous to be borne, and lay them upon men's shoulders; but they themselves will not move them with one of their fingers.' – Matt. 23:4. They be blind leaders of the blind, baby, and mechanical laws of punishment-and-conditioning lead them in little grooves of robot-life."

But, but – I protested – is there anything outside

conditioned behavior? Is there a real freedom, Man? Is there?

"Find the place where Sade and I agree," he said, "and there you will find the beginning of a definition of liberty."

And the line went dead with a sudden click like the sound of a bedroom door closing as a little boy is pushed outside.

FIFTH CHORUS

"They declaim against the passions without bothering to see that it is from their flame philosophy lights its torch."

– Sade

The Castle, somebody pointed out, is a Sadean novel: Kafka's scene is a typical lair of Sadean monsters lying in wait for the innocent traveler. *The Trial* is even more Sadean, I would argue, because the two thugs who haul Joseph K. off to an empty lot to slit his throat "like a dog" are, like Sade's images, revelations of the reality of our civilization. Capital punishment presented as a more nudely naked lunch than even Burroughs has fed us.

What happens to Joseph K., what happens to Justine, are very slight distortions* of what happens to each man, each woman, in a society based on authority-and-submission.

~•~

* "Two of the commonest types of hallucinations are the obscene epithet and the deadly injunction. Both the accusation 'You are homosexual!' and the command 'You must kill them!' may be safely regarded as revived and *not very much distorted* memories of parental utterances." *Transactional Analysis in Psychotherapy*, by Eric Berne, Grove, 1961 (italics added).

~•~

What Sade saw – what Marat did not see – the hidden meaning of Peter Weiss' noisy and Sophoclean circus of a play – is that Man as we know him, Man in historical time, is entirely the product of punishment. That punishment defines his character, contours and structures his character, *is* his character. That sado-masochism is not a perversion, or a "way of life," but the meaning of our civilization.

Sade's drive for liberty – i.e., his attempt to understand himself – led him to the scene in the brothel in which he buggered and was buggered, whipped and was whipped. That scene, and the seven years imprisonment it cost him, has given his name to perversion, and yet one feels there has been a mistake somewhere, Sadeanism isn't Sadism, the two forces met head-on, but Sade was going in one direction and the true Sadist is going in the other.

Open any schlock newspaper and read the personal ads in which S-M people grope for each other: "Docile young man seeks woman experienced in discipline . . ." "Male, interested in leather and uniforms, seeks male of dominant disposition . . ." "Interested in leather on women . . ."

But this is not Sade's direction, my God, it is the direction of General Hershey and LBJ; it is the direction of our civilization; it is the *essence* of our civilization, dragged out into hideous visibility. Uniforms and discipline. "Kill for freedom, kill for peace, kill Vietnamese, kill, kill, kill!" The hallucinatory parental voice that says "You are homosexual" and "You must kill him." Uniforms and discipline. The blind leading the blind.

Albert Ellis is more general than Dr. Berne. According to Dr. Ellis, in a lecture at the N.Y. General Semantics Society, most neurotics – i.e., most civilized people – go around with a little internal voice saying "You are a no-good shit." ("You are homosexual," "You are a coward," and "You are a helpless neurotic" are only three variations on the main theme. The main theme is always "You are a no-good shit.")

Eric Frank Russell, the science-fiction writer, propounded a riddle once: "If everybody hates war, why do wars keep on happening?" Remember the S-M ads: "seeks discipline," "seeks uniforms," "seeks leather and rubber."

Authority-and-submission is the chief structural fact about feudal, capitalist and socialist society. Punishment-and-obedience is the defining gesture, as Stanislavsky would call it, of such societies. To illustrate it in one flash: Orwell's "boot stamping on the human face forever." And that is de Sade's theme, always.

I dreamed I called Fulton Sheen on the phone and asked him, I read in your column that "A child needs a pat on the back to encourage him – provided it is applied hard enough, low enough and often enough." You believe that crap, man?

"Without discipline," he intoned, "our whole civilization would fall into anarchy. 'I will chastize him with my rod,' says the Good Book."

But, but, man – I protested – you're supposed to be anti-sex. Don't you know some cats get their rocks off that way? Ain't you read about spanking orgies and people coming in their pants during it? Ain't you against anybody coming, ever, anywhere, anytime, in any way?

"Argggh!" he said, like the dying villain of a comic book, and I couldn't tell if he was having an orgasm or a heart attack.

The line went dead with a weird click like a bomb-bay door opening to drop Rita Hayworth's picture. Gilda, the whore, beckoning from her golden bed . . . on little bronze heathens who didn't believe in Jesus.

SIXTH CHORUS

Marat
forget the rest
there's nothing else
beyond the body

–Marat/Sade

So: after 150 years, we are ready to look de Sade in the face, eyeball to eyeball. He comes on, always, like a Zen Master, shouting right into our ears: "Tyranny or Anarchy – you must choose. Answer now!"

He was the first one mad enough and sane enough to accept the *given*, the immutable, to start from man-in-history rather than from man-in-theory. Well, he says, I don't believe in the "noble savage," I even doubt that he is "inherently good," but taking him as he is I still say: Freedom. He deserves liberty because nobody else is good enough to take it away from him.

He looked into anarchy, he looked past the voluntarily organized anarchy of Proudhon and Tolstoy, he looked into chaos itself, and he said, yes, even that, I will accept even that, before I will bend the knee to any Authority that claims to own me.

I dreamed I called LBJ on the phone and I said, look, man, you're not taking my son for one of your damnfool wars.

"You are mistaken," he said smoothly. "That boy is not *your* son. He belongs to society and the State, and I am society and the State. I will take him anywhere I want, I will order him to do anything I care to have done, and I will shoot him if he disobeys."

But, but, man – I said – like, wow, man – do you think you own us?

"Read your law books, son," he chuckled. "Ownership is the right 'to use *or abuse.*'"

And the line went dead with a cold little click like an IBM machine punching a hole in a card somewhere in the vast and infinite halls of bureaucracy.

SEVENTH CHORUS

"Although the prodigious spectacle of folly
we are facing here may be horrible, it is
always interesting."

– Sade

I called the world up on the telephone and I implored them:

How much of you belongs to the Combine? If they can take your money in taxes and your sons in wars, how do you differ from the cow who is milked or the pig who is eaten? Do you breed for them like a stallion in a pasture? Is the get of your loins theirs to dispose of? Even a no-good shit afraid that Daddy will come and slice it off has some rights, doesn't he? Or does he? Is there any sacrifice you will not make? Is there any discipline you will not accept? Is there any order you will not obey? Is there any shit you will not eat?

Who got the Indian Sign on you? How did it start? At age 12, worrying that J. Edgar Hoover was watching you jack off through his Washington telescope? Was it the bogey-man they scared you with? "Don't make dirty-dirty in your pants or ogres will come and eat you"? Circumcision the most cruel and inhuman attack on the genital accepted by your doctors; why? Schedule feeding that fucked up the minds of a generation; why? Is that how they get the soldiers for their wars? The whip-and-belt boys, the uniform-and-discipline boys, the Pentagon boys, all one big happy spanking-orgy?

And the operator said, "I'm sorry, sir. The world is not answering the phone anymore. It's watching television."

And the line went dead with a loud and unearthly click like the sound of a boy pulling his zipper up when he hears Father's footsteps in the hall.

EIGHTH CHORUS

A mad animal
Man's a mad animal
I'm a thousand years old and in my time
I've helped commit a million murders

– Marat/Sade

Rita Hayworth's picture on the Bomb.

What do we really want from them? What drove Garbo into hiding, Monroe into suicide, Lamarr into shoplifting, what struck Harlow down and sent Garland into the booze bottle?

And what happens in a Playboy Club? Have you stood there, like me, vodka-and-tonic in hand, looking down a bunny's cleavage and thinking suddenly of Lon Chaney as the Wolf-Man: "Even a man who is pure of heart / And says his prayers by night / Can turn to a wolf when the wolfbane blooms? and the moon is full and bright . . . " If you turned the fantasies of each person in the room onto the wall in LSD stereo what would it look like – a friendly little orgy, the Rape of the Sabine Women, or Mass Murder?

I dreamed I called a bunny on the phone and asked her, dig de Sade?

"But the most, darling," she cooed.

But, but – 1 asked – what do you really think of men?

"But, hon," she said innocently, "what do cattle think of butchers?"

And the line went dead with an abrupt click like a diaphragm falling from a purse onto a cold metal floor.

NINTH CHORUS

"My neighbors' passions frighten me
infinitely less than do the law's injustices,
for my neighbors' passions are contained by
mine, whilst nothing checks the injustices
of the law."

– Sade

A civilization based on authority-and-submission is a civilization without the means of self-correction. *Effective* communication flows only one way: From master-group to servile-group. Any cyberneticist knows that such a one-way communication channel lacks feedback and cannot behave "intelligently."

The epitome of authority-and-submission is the Army, and the control and-communication network of the Army has every defect a cyberneticist's nightmare could conjure. Its typical patterns of behavior are immortalized in folklore as SNAFU (situation normal – all fucked-up), FUBAR (fucked up beyond all redemption) and TARFU (things are really fucked-up). In less extreme, but equally nosologic, form these are the typical conditions of any authoritarian group, be it a corporation, a nation, a family, or a whole civilization.

Proudhon was a great communication analyst, born 100 years too soon to be understood. His system of voluntary association (anarchy) is based on the simple communication principles that an authoritarian system means one-way communication, or stupidity, and a libertarian system means two-way communication, or rationality.

The essence of authority, as he saw, was Law – that is, fiat – that is, effective communication running one way only. The essence of a libertarian system, as he also saw, was Contract – that is, mutual agreement – that is, effective communication running both ways. ("Redundance of control" is the technical cybernetic phrase.)

Sade saw this, before Proudhon. "The rule of law is inferior to that of anarchy; the most obvious proof of what I assert is the fact that any government is obliged to plunge itself into anarchy whenever it aspires to remake its constitution. In order to abrogate its former laws, it is compelled to establish a revolutionary regime in which there is no law; this regime finally gives birth to new laws, but this second state is necessarily less pure than the first, since it derives from it" (Sade, p. 46).

The conflict, Marat/Sade (which should really be Marx/

A Non-Euclidean Perspective

Sade, except that the ingenious Mr. Weiss was not quite ingenious enough to devise a historical conjunction between uncle Karl and the Marquis), is the conflict between anarchy and tyranny. Sade, not Marat or Marx, is the true revolutionary, for he aims at a world outside the crucible of punishment-and-submission, while they aim at a new world still within that crucible.

I dreamed I called Ignatz Mouse on the phone and asked, why do you always throw bricks at Krazy Kat?

But Krazy answered instead and said, "Little Dahlink . . . he's always faithful."

And the line went dead with a dreadful click like Captain Queeg rolling his little marbles together.

TENTH CHORUS

> The guillotine saves them from endless boredom
> Gaily they offer their heads as if for coronation
> Is not that the pinnacle of perversion?
>
> – Marat/Sade

Ralph Nader writes incredulously, in his study of automobile safety, *Unsafe at Any Speed*, "If one were to attempt to produce a pedestrian-injuring mechanism, the most theoretically efficient design would closely approach that of the front end of some present-day automobiles." Mr. Nader has never read Sade. He takes this as an oversight on Detroit's part.

I dreamed I called Batman on the phone and asked, any truth in those rumors about you and Robin?

"Our relationship is 100% platonic," he replied stiffly. "We *sublimate*. Why do you think we're always out looking for 'bad guys' that we can punish?"

And the line went dead with a quick click like handcuffs closing on a thin wrist forever.

ELEVENTH CHORUS

"If you are timid enough to stop with what
is natural,
Nature will elude your grasp forever."

– Sade

There is much sadism in popular culture these days, but little Sadeanism. One rare example of Sadeanism is the old movie, *The Most Dangerous Game*, and another is Ken Kesey's novel, *One Flew Over the Cuckoo's Nest.*

The heroes of both of these works are trapped in situations where superior power seeks remorselessly to destroy them. Both heroes, pure Sadeanists, accept the situation at once – without complaining about its "immorality" or "injustice" – and set out systematically and cold-bloodedly to turn the tables.

This is the doctrine of the bandits in *Justine* – "Nature has caused us to be equals born, Thérèse; if fate is pleased to upset the primary scheme of things, it is for us to correct its caprices" (Sade, p. 481) – and the doctrine of Stirnerite anarchism. De Sade's proletarian heroes, like the glorious anarchist bandit, Ravachol, believe instinctively that "crime alone opens to us the door to life" (Sade, p. 482).

To anyone who doesn't like this doctrine, Sade's answer is blunt: "The callousness of the Rich legitimates the bad conduct of the Poor; let them open their purses to our needs . . . We will be fools indeed to abstain from [crimes] when they can lessen the yoke wherewith their cruelty bears us down" (Sade, p. 481). This sounds horrible, it seems, only to those whose conscious or unconscious wish is to be oppressors. Sadean man merely refuses to be oppressed; *he can only be killed, but never subjugated.*

A Non-Euclidean Perspective

I dreamed I called Adolf Hitler on the phone and asked him. What was your gimmick?

"They believed it was wiser to obey anyone, even me, than to risk anarchy," he said with a ghoulish laugh.

And the line went dead with a sharp click like boot-heels snapped together.

TWELFTH CHORUS

I'm a mad animal
Prisons don't help
Chains don't help
I escape
through all the walls

– Marat/Sade

B.F. Skinner envisions a world without punishment. Nobody is interested.

Guns are now available – they are used in Africa by game wardens – that will stun without killing. Armed with these, an army could capture a town without shedding one drop of blood. Have you heard of any government plotting to wage its future wars with these guns?

Punishment, discipline, obedience – these are the keys to such mysteries, and to the mystery of war itself, and to all oddities of behavior in Man and the other domestic animals. Sade saw it, and was banned for 150 years. He saw the genital fever, the need for embrace, dammed up at the center of man. Another reason he was banned.

The actors are going nuts playing in Marat/Sade. "There is not a single member of the cast who does not hate with a deep loathing every single performance he is required to do of this play," says Ian Carmichael, who plays Marat. "It gets harder and harder," says Patrick Magee, who plays Sade. So far, the company has had one case of acute depression, one fit of "raving screaming" after the show, one actor who almost lost control on stage (Dick Schaap, N.Y. *Herald Tribune*, March 4, "Inmates of the Asylum").

I dreamed I called D.A.F. de Sade on the phone and asked him, "Jesus told me that he and you agree on at least one thing and it explains freedom. What is that one thing?"

"Quite simple," he replied, "don't be afraid of the Cross. The fear of death is the beginning of slavery."

And the line went dead with a triumphant click like a barred door falling open.

Permanent Universal Rent Strike

Published in *Chicago Seed*, April 1969

The reformed Illuminati calendar used by the Ancient Illuminated Seers of Bavaria in conspiracy with Discordianism International dates everything from the year 1 AM (Anno Mundi) when the First Apostle of Eris. Hung Mung achieved illumination and perceived the Sacred Chao (see illustration). This is the mysterious symbol that explains everything, and then some.

In fact, the symbol is so fraught with meaning that it has been repeatedly stolen by other groups – including the Taoists, the Northern Pacific railroad, and most recently, the Sex Information Council of the U.S. (SIECUS). All of these schmucks leave out the all-important Golden Apple (representing chaos) on the right-hand side and the equally important Pentagon (representing superficial order, which is the highest form of chaos) on the left-hand side.

The Taoists carried on Hung Mung's revelation that there are two sides to everything, both of them equally absurd, but they lost the old Chaoists' further teaching that the discord between the two opposites is most interesting and amusing when raised to a higher dialectical level.

The Taoist contemplates the chaos that already exists and smiles. The Chaoist creates greater chaos, and laughs.

Max Stirner, Gran Illuminatus of Bavaria after the flight of Adam Weishaupt to the United States, pointed out in *The Ego and His Own* that the closest approximation to a sane society will come about, not when everybody becomes a masochist or an altruist (there are plenty of them around already, and little sanity has resulted from their activities), but when everybody becomes an egotist.

Benjamin Tucker put it this way: "Even more immoral than the desire to rule is the willingness to submit."

There is no hope (in the Eristic view of things) that everybody will ever become self-sacrificing. Nor would that be desirable. (Who wants to be a zombie among a herd of similar zombies?)

The only hope is that everybody might become an egotist. When everybody says, "Get off my back. I'm not taking any more of your shit," then, obviously, chaos has not been resolved – it never can be – but a very fruitful kind of higher-level chaos develops.

As Paul Goodman once phrased it, there will be a hell of a lot more bloody noses, but no wars. Wars require altruists, masochists, self-sacrificers . . . people who are willing to follow orders.

The permanent universal rent strike – which is, together with the permanent universal tax strike and the coining of non-governmental money, the triple solution to everything – rests on this firm foundation in chaotic egotism.

These tactics do not require self-sacrifice and they do not involve coercing (or killing) others. Hence, they have not been very popular in Judeo-Christian culture, which is basically sadomasochist and strongly inclines people to grasp at

A Non-Euclidean Perspective

philosophies (such as Marxism) which do give people a reason to torment themselves and bully others.

These tactics rest on the assumption that the only non-coercive behavior is truly revolutionary and only egotistic behavior is basically reactionary (whatever "revolutionary" excuse is given for it) and all altruistic behavior is basically insane (the body is an egotist and altruism only becomes possible when the head is split from the body, which is a form of schizophrenia).

The success (if that's the word for it) of the Marxist counter-revolution (masquerading as revolution) is entirely due to the cultural hangover from Judeo-Christian sadomasochist ethics.

YIP [Youth International Party] is the only part of the Movement which begins to have a clue about what real REVOLUTION is.

The permanent universal rent strike is the affirmation, by everybody, of his or her right to live on the planet Earth.

The permanent universal rent strike is the end of Feudalism.

The landlord, as his name reminds us, is a Feudal functionary, originally a relative of the king.

Capitalism continues Feudalism by continuing landlordism although the landlord no longer has to be a relative of the king. Socialism continues Feudalism by making a spook ("the State" or "the People") – into a new landlord. Since spooks can't function in the real world, Socialism just means a continuation of the same old con . . . certain individual human beings, proclaiming themselves the representatives of "the State" or "the People," will function as landlords.

The permanent universal rent strike is a rejection of Feudalism Capitalism and Socialism all together.

Eugene V. Debs, although a benighted Socialist, had his moments of insight. In one of them he said (and this should be branded on the behind of every Movement leader with a red hot iron so they'd never forget):

> If you are looking for a Moses to lead you out of the capitalist wilderness you will stay right where you are. I would not lead you into the promised land if I could, because if I could lead you in, someone else would lead you out.

The Irish rent strike of the 1880s was a monumental success, at first. The English Army could not collect the rents "owed" to the English landlords. The strike ended when the Irish leader Parnell was bribed (not with money, apparently) to call it off. This is what comes of having "leaders." Think about it.

If the Irish had a consciously Stirnerite and egotist philosophy, no "leader" could ever have ended the strike, and they could not have been, in Debs' words "lead back out" of the Promised Land.

The prerequisite for a successful PERMANENT UNIVERSAL RENT STRIKE is a clear understanding of the egoist principle by every participant. Stirnerite and Sadean anarchism has to be firmly grasped and understood and nobody must think he is acting for "the People" or for "the future." The people and the future will profit, no doubt, but the main motive must be to escape MY rent burden HERE AND NOW.

Even Ayn Rand's books are worth spreading and disseminating. Most people attracted to Rand only suffer from the disease for one or two years, then they detach the solid core of the truth inside her system from the vast proliferation of nonsense around it, and emerge as very conscious and knowledgeable anarchists.

Look up the figures in the World Almanac on the number of pigs in your city. Most places, it runs about one pig for every four hundred citizens . . . some places, the odds are even higher on our side. They can't evict us all onto the streets. If they do, they can't patrol efficiently enough to keep us from moving back into the pads right away.

This can only work, of course, with a Union of Egotists, such as Stirner envisioned. The same is true of every other nonviolent and truly revolutionary activity. Which is why, my friends, egotism does not lead to "the war of all against all" but to cooperation.

Egotistic cooperation, for rational and self-interested reasons, is not schizophrenic, does not divide the cortex from the body and does not justify any form of coercion of others. You have to be some kind of altruist, whether consciously Christian or only unconsciously Christian, to justify the coercion.

Only the man who sacrifices himself is ready to sacrifice others.

Non-violent egotist revolution is the only true revolution, the only real break with the pattern of authority-and-submission which has hitherto screwed-up "civilized" society. Every form or coercive or altruistic activity is counter-revolutionary, because it leads back into the same old shit all over again. The permanent universal rent strike is the first step. Hail Eris. Hail Discordia.

Why I Am A Right-Wing Anarchist

by Ronald Weston

[This article, which was originally published under the pseudonym Ronald Weston, is sometimes misattributed to Robert Shea. All available evidence points to it being Wilson's work.]

the rogerSPARK, May 1969

Recent events in France and elsewhere have brought anarchism into the forefront of public consciousness for the first time in several decades. To the radical young, anarchism is a serious alternative to Marxism; to professional demagogues like George Wallace, "anarchism" is a word that has even more power to frighten boobs than "communism," which is beginning to sound as quaint as Technocracy or the Single Tax panacea of yesteryear.

Nevertheless, as a Right-wing anarchist, I am sourly amused by the ignorance of anarchist history and theory shown by almost all commentators these days, both pro and con.

A Non-Euclidean Perspective

Most contemporary writers either think communist anarchism (Bakuninism) is the only form of anarchism; or, if they have heard of Right-wing (individualist) anarchism at all, they have the impression it is a freaky offshoot from the main stream.

Actually, individualist anarchism is the oldest form of anarchism, and, if there were such a thing as proprietorship in words, the school would have the clearest title to possession of the word "anarchy." Communist anarchism only arose after Bakunin attempted to synthesize the individualist anarchism of Proudhon with the socialism of Karl Marx.

Leaving aside forerunners and semi-anarchists – people like Gerald Winstanley, founder of the Digger movement in seventeenth century England, which had some anarchist ideas mixed in with non-anarchist ideas – the history of anarchism begins with the failure of a socialist experiment.

Robert Owen (who enunciated the labor theory of value and much else of socialist theory long before Karl Marx) founded a communist colony in Indiana In 1830. It was called, optimistically, New Harmony. It went the way of most communist experiments back in those innocent days before the doctrine that "the end justifies the means" was introduced into socialist theory. It collapsed in only a few months.

(The same happened in over one thousand communist colonies started in America in the nineteenth century – communism is an old American tradition, although nobody has told that to HUAC yet. Communism only lasts for more than a few months when a band of fanatics at the top, armed with "persuasion per blunt instruments," force the rest of the group to continue the experiment after it has proven unsatisfactory.)

One of the idealists who participated in the New Harmony debacle was a manufacturer, musician, inventor, printer, teacher, et cetera from Massachusetts named Josiah Warren.

In 1832, Warren begun publishing the *Peaceful Revolutionist* – the first anarchist newspaper in the world.

In it, he analyzed the causes of the failure of American democracy and predicted that the failure would grow steadily worse, as more and more wealth and power became centralized in fewer and fewer hands. He also analyzed the failure of New Harmony, and foresaw the totalitarian tendency that future socialist experiments would necessarily develop. And he offered, as an alternative, the system which has become known as Right-wing, or individualistic, or Jeffersonian, or Warrenite anarchism, sometimes also called voluntary socialism or mutualism.

In the next decade, two other original thinkers, independent of Warren and of each other, came to the same conclusions in Europe – P-J. Proudhon, author of *What Is Property?* and Max Stirner, author of *The Ego and His Own.*

In the more-than-a-century since then, we Right-wing anarchists have watched, bemused and wry, as every form of coercive, and violent, and totalitarian, and paranoid type of regimentation has been tried, under the banner of "socialism" and "the welfare of the people," and we are more convinced than ever that the Socialist State is a worse menace to mankind than even the Capitalist State. A system that produces Stalins and Berias is even more perverted than a system that produces Nelson Rockefellers and LBJs. Socialism is the counter-revolution.

What is the Right-wing anarchist alternative to Socialism and Capitalism? In a sentence, you could say it's the position of the Hopi Indians, who have a proverb that says: "No man should be compelled to do that which goes against his heart." Benjamin Tucker, the most gifted writer in the individualist-anarchist tradition, put it this way: "Will you allow any form of coercion of the non-coercive individual? If so, you are an archist; if not, you are an anarchist."

The principle form of coercion in history is slavery or selective service as we call it today: seizing the body of another human being outright, and compelling him, through threats against his life, to obey you. We Right-wing anarchists delight the Left, and annoy the Right, by opposing this form of aggression.

Next in order in our catalog of evils is taxation, or seizing part of the labor-product of another. Taxation is slavery on the installment plan. When the labor-product was seized directly – for example as recently as the last Depression, Government agents took crops and livestock when farmers didn't have the cash for taxes – it was physically obvious that taxation is modified slavery, taking part rather than all of what the victim has labored to produce. We Right-wing anarchists delight the Far Left and Far Right, and drive the Liberals to fury, by opposing this form of aggression, or highway robbery, also.

Next comes rent. The landlord, or lord-of-the-land, was originally a Feudal prince, a cousin or nephew of the king. Rent is the daughter of taxation. Since neither kings nor landlords can produce a valid Land Deed from God showing that He sold, or gave, the planet Earth to them, we Right-wing anarchists hold that the planet obviously belongs to everybody born on it. You don't have to buy your right to live on this planet from landlords any more than you have to buy it from kings, Führers, or presidents. Since the landlords' alleged "ownership" is a State-created fiction, backed up only by the guns of the State police, we Right-wing anarchists reject this form of aggression also, and our growing list of negatives now reads: no slavery (selective or otherwise); no taxation; no rent.

A more subtle form of aggression is hidden in State monetary policy, which places a ten-per-cent tax on auxiliary currencies. This is little-known, because the tax makes such currencies economically unfeasible, and nobody bothers to issue them. However, since we reject all taxes, we reject this tax, with interesting results. Proudhon and Warren both calculated that, in a system of competing currencies, issued by various consumer co-ops or workingman's credit unions, the interest rate would drop to less than half of one per cent.

Of course, you would rather borrow at approximately zero per cent than at the ten per cent and higher (sometimes much higher) which all but a few loans are financed at these days. But there is more to our rejection of government money than this. You pay interest every day even if you are not personally in debt. Every businessman adds his interest charges onto his sales price, in addition to his rent charge (if he has one) and his personal profit.

In a very real sense, the consumers of the country are paying all the rent and all the interest charges of the country. The businessmen are paying none.

So the total individualist-anarchist position is no slavery, no taxation, no rent, and no monopoly on the issue of currency.

In place of slavery, freedom.

In place of taxation and the monster State it creates, voluntary associations supported by dues. If the association gets sassy and starts acting like a State – fuck it. Stop paying your dues, join another voluntary association, and let the first one wither away from lack of support.

In place of rent, a voluntary covenant that he who occupies and uses a piece of earth is steward of that place. ("He" can be a group if this is desirable; sometimes, we admit, it is.) If he does not occupy and use it, he cannot extort money from another person or group who will occupy and use it. He surrenders stewardship when he abandons occupancy and use.

In place of usury, credit unions which are also banks of issue for their membership.

Will people work for wages under such a system? Occasionally perhaps – but in the dignified and pugnacious position of a sub-contractor, not in the present demeaning and eunuchoid position of an employee.

Will huge fortunes like those of the Rockefellers or Morgans be possible? Not in the absence of interest and rent, which together make up the total mechanism of what Marx mystified and confused under the label "surplus value."

Will absolute equality between men be achieved? No, only relative equality. But absolute equality is obtainable only at the end of a gun, which is a price we Right-wing anarchists don't care to pay.

Is there no place for the collectivist dream in this scheme of things? Sure – all can collectivize who will. In any society, some will have the child-like personality which flourishes best in a groupy togetherness. As enemies of coercion, we would not contradict our own principles and force these people to become individualists. We merely ask the same civilized courtesy in return.

There are many other aspects to the Right-wing anarchist position – no censorship, no rules controlling what a man may eat or smoke or drink, no rules about who may mate with who or for how long, and, of course, no laws in the sense of decrees from above (contract into a voluntary association implying that the rules of that association will be obeyed while you are in it, but you retain the right to quit and join another association, or become a hermit, at any time) – but I have given the essence.

No literate person can claim that Right-wing anarchism is unworkable in principle; the American Indians have made it work for centuries. The archist, be he socialist or capitalist, is driven back to the argument that this kind of libertarianism can't work UNDER MODERN INDUSTRIAL CONDITIONS.

Sorry: that refutation has become threadbare. Cybernetics is replacing the old mechanical technology and opening up the possibility of an industrial system that is self-regulating both in each part and as a whole. Such a decentralized technology is obviously more compatible with a cyber-biological self-regulating social system than it is with any authoritarian Socialist or Capitalist social system.

The whole science of cybernetics is a sophisticated mathematical theory of self-organizing and self-regulating systems.

Anarchism is not a revival of yesterday's romanticism, as Marxists charge; it is the shadow of tomorrow falling on our lives today.

How To Wage
Nonviolent Revolution!

Other Scenes, Summer 1971

The idea that non-violent revolution has failed, as of 5730 A.M. (1971 pagan), is equivalent to asserting in 5672 A.M. (1913 pagan) that the airplane has failed utterly and would never replace the locomotive.

There are many techniques of non-violent revolution which have never been given an adequate trial yet, but they have succeeded dramatically in all partial trials.

1: Strike!

Most impressive of these are the general strike, the boycott, the organized mass tax refusal, and the permanent universal rent strike.

These techniques are so practical, so organic and existential a part of the class-war, so obvious and natural, that they have been "rediscovered" several times by anarchists and libertarian socialists who had no idea that others before them had hit upon the same ideas.

The opposite techniques involving violence, seizing the State by force, the "dictatorship of the proletariat," and the contradictory apocalyptical dream of an eventual, far-off "withering away of the state" . . . are like setting about cleaning your house by first dumping shit on every floor and throwing it on the walls.

It is theoretically possible, in the long run, to clean up the shit, I suppose . . . but those who like the idea of throwing shit today are still going to like it tomorrow. Similarly, those who want to seize power today are going to want to hold onto it tomorrow. One doesn't have to wade through many volumes of Dr. Freud to understand that much about the anal-sadistic personality of the power-freak.

Those who say that no social problems can be resolved by non-violent revolution are saying, really, that humanity is doomed.

In a world of hydrogen bombs, ICBMs and chemo-biological warfare, PROBLEM NUMBER ONE is developing non-violent techniques of resolving conflict.

If such techniques are, in fact, impossible, the continuation of the human species is impossible.

The State is inherently stupid. It is stupid because it is a communication matrix without adequate feedback. Information does not flow back to it with any reasonable degree of efficiency. It has a distorted picture of what's going on, always. Its "map" does not fit the territory.

Communication is only possible between equals. The State – the pigs who are "more equal than others" in Orwell's brilliant vision – never receives real communication.

Those who want to seize the State are already stupid. If they succeed, they will automatically become more stupid.

2: Don't Pay Rent!

The State is a device for clubbing people. The legislature makes up the game-rules, declaring who is clubbable and who isn't. The judiciary decides, in individual cases, whether a person, under the rules of the game, should be clubbed or not. The police are in charge of internal clubbing, the army of external clubbing. The tax bureau is devoted to clubbing everybody into paying for the cost of all this clubbing.

Nobody ever tells "the truth, the whole truth and nothing but the truth" to such a clubbing machine.

Everybody, to some degree, tells the State what they think it wants to hear. (Those who don't arouse great anxiety and anger in the State, and ways are quickly found to lock them up or, often, to shoot them.)

COMMUNICATION IS ONLY POSSIBLE BETWEEN EQUALS.

Most of the exponents of non-violent revolution, being Christians, masochists, loonies and crackpots, create an instantaneous revulsion in the exponents of violent revolution, who are usually atheists, sadists, loonies and crackpots.

3: Don't Pay Taxes!

When non-violent revolution becomes an excuse for making a martyr of yourself . . . it is the masochist's equivalent of the sadist's use of violent revolution to make martyrs out of others.

Non-violence must be as practical, as subtle, as flexible and as pragmatic as a businessman's sales campaign, before it will ever be taken seriously by those who are committed to real change rather than just talking about change.

The most important application of non-violent revolution in America today is a permanent universal rent strike.

Not a fake strike, in which the money is handed over the courts and the landlords get it later after the strike is over. A permanent strike. A blunt declaration: "The landlords do not own the planet Earth. Everybody born on the planet has a right to live here. He doesn't have to pay monthly tribute to ANYONE for living here; it is his home planet."

4: Boycott

Nobody pays a dollar, a penny or a mil thereafter. Nobody asks for "repairs" or "improvements." Everybody uses his rent money, now and forever after, to repair and improve his own pad as much as it needs. Nobody gives a penny to a lord-of-the-land ever. Everybody announces, 'The Feudal Age is over. We recognize no Lords of the Land. The land belongs to those who occupy and use it."

What can the landlords and the government do? Throw us all into the Atlantic, or Pacific? Put us in rockets and shoot us to the moon? And even if they could do that, then what? With all of us gone, who will they collect rent from?

Rent is the tribute paid by the non-owning user of land to the non-using "owner" of land. Such ownership is a legal fiction, and needs only to be resisted to be exposed, discredited and abolished.

Every landlord on this continent is a receiver of stolen property. The land was stolen from the Indian tribes before it was "legally" acquired by its present owners. The same is true on other continents, but the history is older, more complex and somewhat hidden by time.

Figure how much of your monthly pay goes to the landlord, to "buy" from him the "right" to live on the surface of this planet, think what you could do with that money if you asserted that you already have the right to live on this planet and don't have to buy that right, in monthly installments, from a Lord-of-the-Land.

PERMANENT UNIVERSAL RENT STRIKE.

Soldiers will shoot at their fellow citizens, after sufficient brainwashing in boot camp. It is especially easy to get them to shoot at their fellows if these people happen to be out in the streets rioting.

It is not so easy to get them to shoot if the citizens are sitting quietly at home and just minding their own business.

Think about it.

If the rent-strike is combined with a tax-strike, both the landlords and their government are threatened.

Think about it.

Individual martyrs to tax refusal accomplish zero, or a quality infinitesimally larger than zero but still hard to perceive.

Collective tax refusal . . . well, Benjamin Tucker estimated that only 20 percent of the population would have to join before the cost of imprisoning them became more than the alleged value to the State of doing so to terrify others.

And meanwhile the other 80 percent would be calculating, balancing the risk against the advantage, brainwashed "loyalty" against personal integrity, gain versus loss . . .

None of this can work, really, until it is put upon an egotistic basis. Asking people to join for altruistic reasons is the chronic error which has ruined most anarchist campaigns to organize such mass civil disobedience.

People who have read Ayn Rand and found the solid core of truth in the midst of all her bull are more likely to start this movement rolling than the average Marxist or Tolstoyan-Christian anarchist.

Objections to Objectivism

Published in *The Match!*, May 1973

Most Anarchists object to Objectivism on pragmatic or practical grounds: they feel that the Objectivist program of "limited government" has no feedback or fail-safe mechanism to prevent an evolution backward to the unlimited government which monotonously reappears whenever and wherever a State is instituted. Starting a government, in this view, is akin to starting a pregnancy, and Objectivism has no built-in abortifacient if the progeny prove monstrous.

Others, of course, object to Objectivism on more personal grounds, related to the mental evolution of Ayn Rand herself, who has become more and more indistinguishable from other apologists for the status quo. Her authoritarianism, dogmatism, intolerance, etc., have long suggested a basic incompatibility with real libertarian philosophy; this has become an acute contradiction recently, as she repudiated libertarian "limited government" candidates in the last election and endorsed the "unlimited government" of Richard Nixon, whose invasions of

noninvasive nations, sky-high taxes, government controls on virtually everything, wiretapping, etc. are as flat a contradiction of liberty as can be found west of Peking. Her weak attempts to justify these recent positions – saying, e.g. that she personally "trusts" Nixon and we should "trust" her "trust" – are the antithesis of libertarianism and a long step in the direction of the "miracle, mystery and authority" of traditional monarchy. If the government soon requires us to be tattooed with numbers on our arms, few would be surprised if Ayn Rand endorses this; and it seems likely that the die-hard Objectivists (those to whom even Nathaniel Branden is anathema since he split with the Grand Duchess) will probably follow her, and urge all of us to get our tattoos immediately. Objectivism seems destined to become one of the great authoritarian philosophies, in the tradition of Marxism, Thomism, Platonism, etc.

I share all these misgivings about Objectivism (as well as the very rational criticisms of Rand's "antirational cult of reason" given in Dr. Albert Ellis' *Is Objectivism A Religion?*) but I think the central defect in the Rand scenario has seldom been stated by her critics. Objectivism, very simply, appears to be a map which does not fit any objective territory.

Human involvement in "nature" or "the universe" exists on at least three levels: the verbal, the objective, and the invisible. Objectivism identifies all three and can be described as no more reliable than a treatment of a cube which depicts it as a square or a line. Objectivism, as a map, distorts the structure or dimensionality of human experience, just as a philosophy of linearity distorts the dimensionality of a conic section.

Let us be country-simple about this. Despite Ms. Rand's fondness for the "is" of identity, we happen to live in space-time continuum where a word NEVER IS the object which it denotes, just as, in the nice metaphor of mathematician Eric Temple Bell, the map is not the territory, or, in the even more memorable variation of philosopher Alan Watts, the menu is not the meal. We cannot drink the word "water", eat the word "potato", or live in the word "house". Any system, such as Aristotle's or Rand's, based on saying that certain objective non-verbal events "are" certain words seems to be flirting with delusion or self-hypnosis. Smith "is" a liar, Jones "is" lazy, Johnson "is" always right, etc., either means that Smith, Jones and Johnson ARE WORDS, which appears to be total nonsense, or mean something else than what they say. Ms. Rand, like Aristotle, writes constantly AS IF people, events, actions, actually ARE words, and this is what I mean by confusing cubes with squares or lines, identifying maps with territories, trying to eat the menu instead of the meal.

It always comes as a distinct jolt, to people educated in traditional Aristotelian methods, when an actual encounter with the non-verbal, objective, sensual sensory level occurs. Such encounters can be triggered dozens of ways – e.g., Korzybski's general semantics has its gimmicks for provoking this experience, yoga and Zen Buddhism and Gestalt Therapy have other methods. One of the easiest is mantra, staring at some interesting scene (such as the ocean) while holding the mind to one repeated verbalization, whether it be "I am here" or "om mani padme hum" or "the shadow knows" or whatnot; eventually the DIFFERENCE between these words (and any words) on one hand and the non-verbal world on the other, becomes strikingly clear.

This difference has never been clear to Ms. Rand, and, not surprisingly, Objectivism, as it evolved, has taken on the static quality of words and lost all contact with the dynamic quality of non-verbal experience. Howard Roark, in *The Fountainhead*, is glorified because he never changes (just like the word "mouse" never changes), while in the world known by experience, everything changes (just as the animal called "mouse" evolves from fetus to newborn to infant to child to adult, and dies.) Just as the verbal category "mammals" never changes, although Darwin found all actual mammals to be part of a chain of evolution, Ms. Rand's "good" people remain "good", her "bad" remain "bad", and everything in her books seems to be preserved on a shelf like dead "specimens", and not engaging in the life of the non-verbal, twinkling, sparkling, on-off, day-night, up-down, twist-turn, ALIVE world of sensory-sensual experience.

Verbalism, perhaps, would be a better name for the Rand system than Objectivism. Take any object, say a coffee cup, and start using it, playing with it, experimenting with it, and you will find (literally) infinite possibilities, which is the way life appears on the objective level. The Rand philosophy deals with the finite, static, absolute way life appears on the verbal level of the WORDS "coffee cup."

This confusion of levels (between verbal and non-verbal) becomes intensified and more befuddling when the third (invisible) level is amalgamated with these two, as occurs in the Aristotelian and Rand systems.

Again, let us be country-simple here. The objects, events, experiences, of the non-verbal level appear, in the light of modern science, as creations of our nervous systems, just like the verbal level. That is, the space-time event which we call "an apple" exists evidently somewhere outside our skins, and, according to the most reliable (useful) equations, has a structure which can best be visualized or imagined as superimposition of waves of energy. The objective "apple" which we perceive does not contain this energy structure, which is known to us only by scientific and mathematical analysis and experiment; the "apple" of perception – the object – is manufactured by our senses and brain as they integrate various stimuli coming in from the energy-apple somewhere out there.

The invisible apple, the apple that we don't see, the mathematical physicist's or chemist's "apple", of course, contains the vitamins, flavor and other properties that make apples desirable to us. The visible apple, constructed by our nervous system, may not contain these needed elements – i.e., it may be a plastic or other artificial device designed to look like the invisible energy-apple that we really want.

Now, just as the objective apple (manufactured by our lower nervous system) is more dynamic than the word "apple" manufactured by higher levels of our nervous system), the external, invisible energy-apple appears still more dynamic. Every electron in it, for instance, is nonidentical with itself from second to second. (Every point has a date, in the Einstein-Minkowski space-time manifold.)

Thus, we deal with "reality" on AT LEAST these three levels, now presented in summary:

(1) The verbal level of static, absolute unchanging, abstract WORDS, created by our higher nerve centers;

(2) The non-verbal "objective" level of more dynamic, only superficially static "things" or "actions", abstracted by our lower nerve centers from external stimuli or clues;

(3) The non-verbal INVISIBLE energy-level of atomic, sub-atomic and complexly beknotted energy-clusters in a space-time manifold where nothing is static and structure is always infinite-valued.

This last point, the variable and multidimensional levels of structure within the invisible world, contains the real trouble-spot for Objectivism. "This is an apple," "This is an energy-mesh," "This is a genetic pattern in the 'fruit' family," "This is an atomic structure," "This is a molecular compound," etc. – all literally untrue, since the event in question, whatever it is, is certainly NOT WORDS – can all be accepted as accurate descriptions, on different structural levels. But Ms. Rand's one-valued system, in which the verbal, objective and invisible levels are all identified as one level, and treated as if that were the verbal level, carries the assumption that only one of these statements can be accurate, and that the others must all be false. This fatal defect in Aristotelian logic has made it unsuitable for modern science, just as the one-valued "time" of Newton and the one-valued "space" of Euclid have been found unsuitable.

It also appears unsuitable for the analysis of sociological

facts. "Smith is a Republican," "Smith is a member of the plumbers' union," "Smith is anti-Negro," "Smith is a Roman Catholic," "Smith is kind to his children," "Smith is a proletarian," "Smith is red-headed," again, appear as false-to-facts, since Smith is not a word, but can all be accepted as true descriptions on various levels; whereas in Aristotelian or Randian logic, one is encouraged to accept one of them as true and discard the others as irrelevant or, if the logic is being applied with real verbal fervor and total alienation from the sensory level, even as false. Again, the one-valued "is" tends to reduce multiple dimensions to two dimensions, and we get a "Flatland" view. (Literary critics disparage Rand's novels, not because these critics "are" "all" liberals and socialists, as her admirers imagine, but because this flattening-out makes for awfully dull reading. Her description of these books as "Romantic Realism" rings true only if one stresses the "Romantic" heavily and forgets the "Realism" entirely. The original two-dimensional novel, Abbott's sci-fi classic, *Flatland*, is more convincing because his squares, triangles, circles, etc., are not presented as denizens of our sensory continuum. Rand's Roark, Dagny, Toohey, Mouch, and the others fail to convince because they are not distanced this way and are set in our own space-time where they don't belong.)

Thus, Rand has a lot of fun "refuting" the paradoxes of modern physics and modern sociology, in *Atlas Shrugged* and other writings. These paradoxes, of course, only exist on the verbal level and are part of the two-valued structure of our Indo-European languages; one can discuss atomic physics in Hopi, for instance, without any paradoxes arising. (See Benjamin Lee Whorf's *Language, Thought and Reality*.) Rand, however, identifying the verbal with the objective non-verbal and the objective non-verbal with the invisible-energetic non-verbal, imagines that the two-valued structure of these languages (and the Aristotelian logic derived from that grammar) MUST fit all levels – i.e., that the word "apple", the objective apple, and the energetic-atomic apple are all identical, as implied in the Aristotelian sentence, "This is an apple." To her, then, modern science appears a great hoax in which witch doctors are smuggling "mysticism" across the border disguised as mathematics.

Rand, it so happens, is mathematically illiterate. (This was true in 1962, when I met her in person. At that time, she could not read a partial differential equation, and apparently did not know what an exponent denotes. Her prose since then gives no evidence that she has become acquainted with mathematics in the interim.)

Thus, the structure of Indo-European language appears the only map-structure in which she can think, and any departure from it appears bizarre, witchy, "super-natural" to her. (Hence her abhorrence for mathematically-influenced modern painters like Kandinsky.) If the words for atomic processes grow weird (i.e. "waves" and "particles" are the same but not the same), then the processes must be weird; since processes cannot be self-contradictory in this way, the scientists must be lying to us.

Like Lenin in 1905, when the results of modern physics first began to diverge from Marxist dogma, Rand has deliberately turned her back on the non-verbal experimental and experiential world, which appears "unthinkable" to her, and embraces a purely verbal world, which, being her own creation, fits all of her hunches and notions of what "reality" should "really" be.

When a modern physicist is asked "Are electrons really particles or really waves?" he or she will probably answer, "Both" – at which point Rand begins muttering "witchdoctor" and harsher things. The physicist knows, as Rand doesn't know, that the electron IS NOT WORDS, and hence IS NOT the word "waves" or the word "particles". The physicist also knows that the mathematical equations which best describe the electron are also NOT the electron but just a description of it, written in a "language" (symbolism) where the Aristotelian either/or and its paradoxes do not arise.

Similarly with "Is Jones or Society responsible for Jones' children dying of starvation?" Sociologists, at least those worth elbow-room in a serious discussion, understand that the word "responsibility" has no referent on the non-verbal level, and realize that an answer depends on the level of structure (or degree of magnification) on which we examine the "facts". To Rand, with a verbal system in which "Jones is responsible" ends the discussion, any attempt at further investigation on the non-verbal level, to discover the various structures actually functioning as the Jones children starve, appears pointless to her, if not more disguised "witchdoctory".

Here we confront the gravest defect in the Aristotelian-Randian system, which Korzybski, in *Science and Sanity* calls "elementalism". Through nobody's fault, the universe in which we live appears non-linear, non-elementalistic, Gestaltish, synergetic. The space-time manifold cannot be broken up into "space" and "time" without re-introducing the Newtonian errors corrected by Michelson, Morley, Lorenz, Einstein, et al. The organism functions as-a-whole IN an environment, and re-introducing such Aristotelian entities as "ego", "mind", "emotions", "senses", reduces this multi-dimensional order to one-dimensional disorder, which is also false-to-facts. This does not mean that there is no rationality, or that we are all idiots (which is what Ms. Rand imagines is meant when anyone attempts to explain the Gestalt or synergetic approach to her) but that rationality occurs on various levels within the organism-environment manifold and cannot be elementalistically attributed to an isolated block-like entity, "mind," off in a hermetically-sealed sensory-deprivation chamber somewhere. All the structures function together, and no entity can be isolated and "explained" by contemplating it in fictitious isolation from all the structures. For instance, as Alex Bavelas has shown in some beautifully designed experiments, the "intelligence" of a group measures at different I.Q. levels depending on the communication-structure within the group.

(Wilson's First Law, of which some of you may have heard, holds that communication is only possible between equals. It was based in part on the Bavelas experiments and in part on observations of communication-jams in Capitalist corporations and other authoritarian or pyramidal structures. Wilson's Second Law, Progressive disorientation is experienced by all members of unequal groups, is the psychiatric justification for anarchism. Wilson's Third Law, This disorientation continues until the SNAFU point and collapse, explains the inefficiency of armies and the decline-and-fall of States, corporations and other authoritarian structures.)

"Jones is responsible if his children starve" appears false, then, not just because "responsibility" is a word without a non-verbal referent, or because sentimentalists would like to feed the children before permanent brain damage or death supervene, but because "Jones" can be isolated from the space–time bio-social continuum ONLY ON THE VERBAL LEVEL. On the non-verbal levels, the invisible energy-mesh manifests as chains of cause-effect with structural unities apparent at atomic, chemical, nutritional, ecological, economic, sociological, and political levels, among others. Jones' stubbornness, orneriness, laziness, cussedness, etc., may appear on some of these levels; so may the cussedness of the local banker in contracting credit, or the decisions made by the Federal Reserve Board a thousand miles away, or the ecological havoc wrought by ill-informed or uncaring manufacturers one hundred years away, or nutritional misinformation acquired by Jones, Mrs. Jones, and the children from stupid authoritarian education, etc. etc.

I do not carry this analysis of starvation further, since Anarchists are familiar with it and can complete it for themselves. My point is that the web of sociological-ecological fallacy woven by Ms. Rand follows inevitably from her primary confusion of (1) the either/or elementalistic "logic" of the verbal level in Indo-European languages, with the (2) less static and less isolated world of neurologically-abstracted "objects" or "actions", and (3) the totally dynamic, invisible world of actual energy-processes not detected by our nervous systems. In a three-level world, she pursues a one-level map and marches inevitably into escalating errors as the map again and again fails to correspond with the territory.

This article will have missed some of its intended effect if Anarchists just nod happily over it and say, "Well, Ayn Rand has been disposed of." In my experience, Anarchists are as likely to confuse words with non-verbal multi-level synergetic realities as often as anyone else; Ms. Rand is relatively unique only in making this confusion a central part of her philosophy. In practice, such confusion needs to be checked by some counter force. Knowledge of several languages, including one or more of non-Indo-European structure, is helpful. Knowledge of mathematics is helpful. Training in general semantics, Gestalt therapy, or Zen meditation are helpful. LSD can be.

Best of all, perhaps, is a sense of humor and an awareness that the programming of one's own biocomputer is not identical with the laws of the cosmos.

Anarchism and Crime

By Robert Anton Wilson and Robert Shea

Green Egg, May 1, 1974

Because anarchists aim at the abolition of government, the first question they are usually asked is, "What about murderers, thieves, rapists? The government protects us from them. Would you just let them run wild?"

The answer, first of all, is that government does not protect us. Its claims are a total imposture, like the fraud of a primitive shaman who claims to bring rain and warns everybody, "If you abolish me, it will never rain again." Thus, *the major crimes are all legal;* the thieves who have stolen the land and the natural resources from under our feet operate with a government franchise. These huge banks, corporations and land monopolies finance both political parties, train the corporation lawyers who become Congressmen or Presidents, and can never be successfully resisted in the courts because they own the judges, too.

Second, the next level of crime, the so-called Syndicate or

Mafia, is also in cahoots with big government and big business, and only token arrests and light sentences are ever imposed on "gangland leaders" – usually rebels who have become unpopular with the higher-level mobsters. In every big city, the links between the mayor's office and the Mob are well-known and often "exposed" in the press, but no reforms are permanent and never can be under this system. The links between the national Mob and the national government are less well publicized, but books like *The Politics of Opium in Southeast Asia,* the recent *Harper's* magazine issue on the CIA and heroin, etc., show that the heroin syndicate could not operate without high-level Federal protection.

Finally, the small-time free-lance criminal – the rapist and sneak thief – *can be* arrested and prosecuted in this system; but *is* he, usually? In New York, in 1972, there were 300,000 burglaries but only 20,000 arrests for burglary. The police are too busy protecting the high-level criminals – as we will explain – to have the manpower to really battle the small independents.

Do you deny this? Well, of course, you have been trained by the State-run schools and the mass media to deny it, do you believe your own denial? How safe do you feel in a large American city, especially after dark? Do you honestly think the government can and will protect you?

IS MORE LAW THE ANSWER?

Many admit that they are frightened and appalled by modern American life, but they think the answer is more laws, tougher laws, an evolution toward the total Police State.

This is, of course, the natural direction of government. The more honest (and misguided) a politician happens to be, the more laws he will write – to prove to himself that he is "working" for the people. Obviously, every time the legislature meets, the honest politicians will introduce more laws, to show how hard they're working. Eventually, nothing will remain that is not covered by some law or other. Everything not compulsory will be forbidden, and everything not forbidden will be compulsory.

Stop and ask yourself if you really want that kind of Nazi- or Communist-style tyranny.

Now, even if we (or most of us) do want it – to be protected from criminals – and even if we escalate our progress and pass a billion new laws a year, arriving at Total Law in say five or ten years, what then? How will such a system be enforced? Kinsey estimated that to enforce our sex laws alone, 95 percent of the population would have to become either police or jail-guards – except that they would all be in jail themselves. This is already impossible, but suppose we tried to enforce the anti-drug and anti-gambling laws, also? We would all spend our lives in Federal prisons, spending part of the day guarding others and part of the day being guarded by them.

This is absurd, but within the framework of government and law, how can we stop short of such a total prison-society?

And remember: each step in this direction – each new law, and each new bureaucracy to enforce the new laws – raises your tax burden. Already, you are working from January 1 to May 23 for the Federal government, to pay your IRS bill for the year. For a few months thereafter, you are working to pay nuisance taxes, state taxes, and various other concealed taxes on every item you buy, every movie you see, every drink you take. Already, it would probably be cheaper to just let yourself be robbed every week by a casual sneak-thief. Government may be more genteel than a mugger (occasionally) but it usually ends up taking more of one's money.

THE FUNCTION OF LAW

There are three kinds of laws on the books today, and to understand them is to understand the State.

The first kind of law declares the State's power over you. It says: we may rob you of this much per year (taxation), we may enslave you for this period of time (the draft), we may do this and that and the other thing to you, and you cannot resist because we are your Masters. This is the earliest kind of law and was originally imposed on conquered people by conquerors. No attempt to justify it has ever been convincing to anyone bold enough to question it in the first place. It is based on mere Force; its only argument is the gun.

The second kind of law is coercive morality. This makes the State into an armed clergyman. It says you can enjoy yourself this way, but not that way; you can smoke this, but not that; you can drink this, but not that. Thou Shalt Not Play Parchesi On The Night of the Full Moon. Thou shalt not gamble on Sunday. Thou shalt not make love to your wife the way you and she both like, but the way the legislators like. Four million arrests a year, and an incredible expenditure of time and manpower and money, go into enforcing these laws.

These are the laws that establish crimes without victims. These are the laws that everybody occasionally violates and some people violate constantly. Their only justification, as with the first type of laws, is sheer brute force. That is, without force, a man who believed in, say, the Seventh Day Adventist vegetarian diet would still obey that diet's rules; with force, the Adventists, if they get into government, can make all of us obey it. The day is not distant when pot-smokers will take over, and if they are vengeful, anti-booze laws will come back on the books. This stupid bullying can go on forever, each group getting its turn to impose its own prejudices on others. Anarchists say: stop it now, get off your neighbor's back, get him off your back, and let everybody enjoy his or her own lifestyle.

Finally, there is the third class of laws – the class that every decent person wishes society would live by. No killing. No stealing. No rape. No fraud. Anarchists, just like you, would like to see these laws really functioning. We just don't believe that government can do that job. We think government is, always has been, and always will be preoccupied with the first two kinds of law. Read on and we will explain this.

THE NATURE OF GOVERNMENT

Government was instituted to guarantee that property would remain stolen. The chief function of every cop, every judge, every bureaucrat is to see that property remains stolen.

The first kings were conquerors. They stole the land by shot and shell, period. Then, they settled down to rob the survivors at a certain rate per year, called taxation. Next, they divided up the land among their relatives or officers in the army, who all became lords-of-the-land, landlords, and were empowered to rob the citizens at a certain other rate per year, called rent. When science and industry appeared, other satraps and sycophants of the royal families received charters to monopolize the resources and means of production, and to rob at a certain rate per year, called capital interest or profit. When banks were formed to circulate the medium of exchange (money), other charters were handed out to others in the bandit-gang, who became bank directors with a license to rob at another rate per year, called money interest or economic interest.

It soon became evident that those not in the gang, the majority of the population, were inclined to rob back as much as they could. The Robin Hood hero appears in all societies at this point, and most of us still admire him, although shamefacedly, since the schools and mass media tell us not to. (Still, who doesn't heroize Jesse James or John Dillinger a little?)

Anarchists say that the first crime was the crime of the conquerors/governors, who seized a whole land, cut it up among themselves, and proceeded to rob all of us forever by taxation, rent, corporative profit, money interest, and various sub-classes of the same basic fraud. Anarchists say that the Earth belongs to its inhabitants, not to this small "owning" and "governing" class of less than 1 percent of the population.

Anarchists say that the way to stop crime is to stop the primordial crime, the State, and administer the land through voluntary associations (syndicates) of all the people.

Anarchists say that if people could work for themselves – if they received the full product of their labor through a syndicate of fellow-workers – almost all motivation for crime would disappear. If you didn't have to pay taxes and rent, starting tomorrow, your purchasing power would be more than doubled. If other forms of exploitation and robbery, through the financial-interest system, were also abolished, your purchasing power would more than quadruple. How much envy, how much worry about money, how much irrational fear, ulcers, nightmares, headaches and other motivations to cheat a little or steal a little would survive after this simple economic justice was achieved?

THE OTHER CRIMINALS

"But, but – how about the violent criminal types? How about the thrill-killers, the nuts, the psychopaths or sociopaths or sadists? How about those who simply enjoy being evil and destructive?"

We are not evading that question. It is absolutely necessary, however, to put it in perspective by explaining the Major Economic Crime of capitalist government (and feudal and other governments) and how other, lesser crimes mostly derive from that primordial injustice.

Now, after economic justice is achieved and voluntary associations of all sorts (labor unions, credit unions, consumer-owned co-ops, people-owned insurance companies, rural communes, tribes, any type of free human grouping) have taken over the functions of government, *some* persons, due to sickness or perversity or one damn thing or another, will still make trouble. Rape. Pilfering. Attempts to defraud. How will anarchists deal with these remaining no-goodniks?

EDUCATION AND THE FAMILY

The first step in solving any social problem, like any

medical problem, is prevention. Other remedies are necessary only when prevention fails.

Anarchists claim that the violent-nut-type of human being is produced by our current methods of child-rearing. This claim is hardly radical or extreme: every psychiatrist, every sociologist, every anthropologist, in one way or another, admits that this grave charge is true. We would not have so many rapists and other violent nuisances if our society were not, in some way, training them from birth onward to behave like that. For instance, Sweden has only a few rapes per year; the United States has one every seven minutes. One rape every seven minutes is not natural male behavior (whatever Women's Lib may say); it is a function of the sexual misery in this society.

Anarchists believe that the repressive, authoritarian, coercive, brutal and degrading practices currently used in the family and the school are only necessary to condition the young human to live in a government-run society. Children must be beaten or otherwise terrorized and bullied in the home and the school in order that they may "adjust" to the terror and brutality of government as they mature. In short, a State-run society must be repressive because repression is the essence of the State.

Libertarian, free-form families and schools – the open family, the Summerhill school, the free association of men, women and children without authoritarian control – will not produce the deformed, mentally twisted, violent and "mean" and "crazy" types so common in our authoritarian society. So anarchists aim, first of all, to prevent violent criminals by changing the child-rearing methods that produce them.

THE DEMONIAC OR MONSTER

There still remains the inexplicable criminal – the guy who enjoys harming others for reasons nobody today can understand. The superstitious say he is possessed by demons; the naturalists imply that maybe he has bad genes or is a throwback to an earlier stage of evolution. Whatever the explanation, he will appear, presumably, in anarchist societies, as he has appeared in all other societies, even after economic injustice and mind-warping education are abolished.

Human-centered societies (as distinguished from governmental or property-centered societies) have dealing with this problem for thousands of years. Tribes, clans, bands, free communes, have existed outside, before and alongside the States which get all the attention from historians. Anthropologists have investigated these free human groupings and have found a variety of methods of dealing with "demoniacs," many of them as good or better than the State's traditional jails, tortures or executions.

Ostracism should not be underestimated. One critic of anarchism, George Orwell, actually complained that ostracism was so cruel that most people would rather fall afoul of government and go to jail than be the sole ostracized person in an anarchist community.

Exile, widely used by governments before jail became popular, is also effective. At least, it solves the problem for the community that uses it (while, alas, passing the problem on to the unlucky community that next gets the offensive nut).

The Quakers have widely practiced a form of moral forgiveness which sounds impractical to most of us, but which is murderously effective. Bertrand Russell was so impressed with this that he suggested it as a fit punishment for Stalin. Until you have seen a group of Quakers reciting somebody's sins in public, weeping over them loudly, and then forgiving and praying for the culprit, you can't imagine how much psychological impulse-to-change this generates.

Many anarchists believe the private defense groups are legitimate; some even are willing to allow such groups to use traditional Vigilante methods. Clarence Lee Swartz, an American anarchist who observed this system first-hand in the old West, thought it both more humane and more effective at peace-keeping than the government law system back East. Other anarchists fear this as the possible source of a new State.

Most anarchists believe that criminals should not be caged under any circumstances, due to the overwhelming evidence that every prisoner comes out of a cage worse than he goes into it. Others believe, however, that punishment in a form of indemnification is compatible with libertarian ideas and should be rigorously enforced by anarchist syndicates. Under the indemnity system, every criminal must pay in cash or work or some needed good to compensate his victims (or their survivors). This certainly does the victims more good than having the criminal put in a cage and fed at community expense, to say the least of it; and is probably just as discouraging or more discouraging to every nut with even the remnant of an ability to foresee the probable results of his actions.

Finally, we must mention miscellaneous solutions. Just as crime in an economically just and free community will be freaky and sporadic (rather than the steady hour-after-hour terror that it is in this mad, unequal and unfree society), the remedies will also be individualized and peculiar to each situation. In some cases, undoubtedly, an anarchist community will decide the "criminal" was right and the community was wrong; for this reason, anarchists do not believe in unalterable laws, but only in general policies.

The acme of anarchist theory is the principle of non-invasiveness or non-coercion – Mind Your Own Business – and those found to be violating this will be given, usually, some method of compensating those whose lives they have damaged. If they refuse, methods like the boycott-ostracism-exile or general cold shoulder need not always be deliberately organized against them. The good sense, the social bonds, and the sense of humor of the organic community will find some way to make them known that human tolerance, even under anarchy, is not infinite. In the Old West, men booted through town with a skunk tied around their necks, and then shoved onto the highway, often became valuable, co-operative and productive citizens in the next town, after some time to figure the likelihood of a repetition of that public amusement if they were to try similar modes of behavior again.

The Case Against Voting: An Insult To Your Integrity

Published in the *Berkeley Barb*, April 1975

If voting could change the basic politico-economic system of this country, it would be illegal. (Common Zen savvy assures us, after all, that anything that can possibly change the system is illegal, right?)

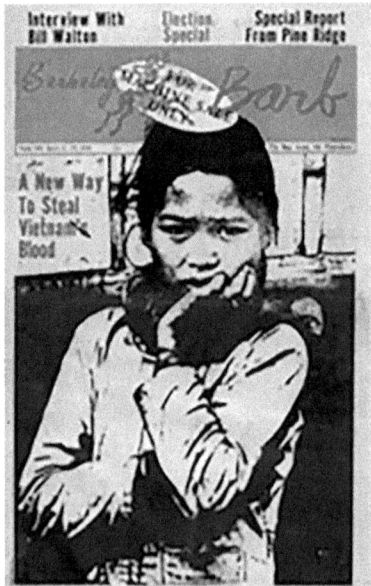

Voting is not only legal but is actually encouraged and praised by the public school system and the oligopolistic media. This indicates perfectly how harmless (and pointless) it is. If voting threatened the ruling elite, the penalty for doing it would be equivalent to owning a Tommy gun (life imprisonment). The right to bear arms – guaranteed in the Second Amendment – has been taken away exactly because it is a real danger to the Establishment; voting has not been taken away because it is not a real threat, or even a serious nuisance.

A Non-Euclidean Perspective

It doesn't matter what gang of clowns holds political office; the real rulers go right on the way they always have.

Grok, and grok in its fullness: if voting Able instead of Baker into office was a major harassment to Standard Oil, say, not even a menace, but just a bother – then, gloriosky, Zero, teaching it in school would be a morals offense. The propaganda against it (from nice old Miss Bland in first grade and sincere Eddie Albert on TV, right up to "thoughtful" articles by official "liberals" in New York think-sheets) would be as monolithic and hysterical as the anti-LSD campaign.

If pulling the lever wasn't condemned by "all recognized authorities" as a cause of blindness or at least chromosome damage, it would most certainly be denounced as "escapist" or "neurotic." We do understand that much about Establishment semantics, don't we?

Second. Voting is, willy nilly, an endorsement of the system. It is a conspiracy to deny liberty. When you enter that booth and pull down that lever, you not only give another human mammal the authority to govern over you and coerce you, but you also give him/her the same authority over your neighbors, who may not want to be governed or coerced.

Whether you give such authority to Dick Nixon or Gloria Steinem or to our local shaman, Jesus Christ Satan, Crown Prince of Arcadia, doesn't matter. You never had such authority yourself in the first place, and you therefore have no right to delegate it to an agent or representative.

Two people who are going down a long country road with a third, do not have the right to do with him as they please, whatever comes into their heads, just because they are a statistical majority. The minority, even the minority of one, retains all its inalienable human rights whatever combination it enters. The situation does not change with the figures adjusted to 2,000 and 1,000, or even to two billion and one billion. Any voluntary agreement is morally permissible.

Government – the imposition of involuntary servitude – is never legitimate, whether imposed by a single autocrat, a parliament, or a democratic majority assembled in solemn conclave to declare war, organize a lynching, or whatever else it pleases.

Dick Nixon always had the right to dump napalm on masochists who dig that scene. He never had the right to dump napalm on anybody who didn't dig such pain. A majority could no more give him that right than it could make him a pink flamingo by calling him one.

Third. Voting implicitly legitimizes the institution of coercion (the State) and all its desiderata of terror, murder, brutality, deception, fraud, robbery and aggravated fakery. Voting contributes to the pretense that there is something voluntary about the most involuntary institution on the planet.

Voting would only measure real public opinion if the ballot included a square for "no government" to be marked by those who choose not to be serfs of any of the opportunists on the list of candidates. It is notorious even now that more people refuse to vote (i.e. implicitly vote "no government") than vote for any of the candidates. Nixon, for instance, received the vote of only about 23% of the population in his "landslide victory." More people wanted **NEITHER** Nix nor McGovern, than wanted **EITHER** Nix or McGovern.

Fourth. Voting for politicians (public entertainers) is a deliberate snare and delusion, to distract us from the real power in this moribund system. When was the last time you were given the opportunity to choose a president for PG&E, our local energy-hog? Yet that guy will effect your bread-and-butter survival, and your glands and nerves, more than the broken-down Model T Ford in the White House.

Dig: they let you choose between such inspiring duos as Nixon-Humphrey or Reagan-Wallace to encourage you to forget that you have no say over who will make the decisions at Standard Oil or GM, or Bank of America. If political democracy were to mean something in the 20th century, the whole people would elect the whole governing group, who would then be responsible to act for the welfare of all. A system in which the most powerful officials of all, the corporation sultans, are not **EVEN IN THEORY** elected by or responsible to the people, is not democracy by any stretch of semantics, but just the continuation of feudalism by other means.

Five. You know and I know and by now the tree on the corner knows, that nobody can make the present system work – not even Jesus Christ and all 13 apostles working 16 hour shifts with Buckminster Fuller acting as logistic advisor. Our ruling class, however, much we like to curse it out, is not the worst in history; compared to Attila the Hun or Genghis Khan, the Kissingers and Rockefellers are quite nice, clean, liberal, sweet-smelling, educated, etc. (This is largely due to low cunning and a product called soap, but let that pass.) The only reason they sometimes act like Attila or Genghis is that they become a little funny-in-the-head from trying to manage a system that no longer can be managed.

They are trying to run a horse-and-buggy 18th century government and a piratical 15th century economy which exists only in their own hallucinations, while around them (invisible to their vision) is the physical technology to abolish hunger, eliminate toil, create abundance for all, achieve immortality and blast off for the stars.

The whole system of wages, bosses, patriarchy, male supremacy, monogamy, etc. is out of date. The ethics, economics, psychology and philosophy is all out of date. We are being governed by McLuhan's "rear-view mirror experts" who know nothing about where we're going and everything about where we've been. The only sane course is to drop out of the system and start creating the new system in the oases and deserts where the State isn't watching, "building the new society within the shell of the old" as the Syndicalists say.

As Yeats sang:

> A statesman is an easy man
> He tells his lies by rote
> So stay at home and drink your beer
> And let the neighbors vote.

Or, in Bokonon's memorable words, "Ceasar has no idea what's really happening."

A Non-Euclidean Perspective

Illuminating Discord: An interview with Robert Anton Wilson

By Jane Talisman and Eric Geislinger

Published in *New Libertarian Notes*,
September 5, 1976

Robert Anton Wilson, who along with Robert Shea wrote the Illuminatus! *trilogy, is the creator of yet another cult. The*

NEW
LIBERTARIAN
NOTES
number 39
September 1976

really neat part is that this is a cult of hard-core libertarian-anarchist-occult-mind-expansionists whose demand for the Illuminatus! *books is making SF retail history. Walk into your corner bookstore and chances are excellent the books have been back-ordered. Borrow a copy or wait in line if you must – it's worth it. The trilogy is truly mind-boggling, outrageous, and curiously familiar. With this in mind we set out to interview one of its authors, Robert Anton Wilson (hereafter R.A.W.).*

Interviewing him by mail was an exciting, albeit frustrating job. His provocative answers triggered seemingly never-ending digressions. We had to more or less learn to limit our responses. Several of the questions in the following interview appear to be asked by R.A.W. himself. These are not misprints – he does give himself questions. To give you some insight into

Wilson's psyche we offer you this tidbit of data – to wit, his return address rubber stamp has his name misspelled "Robert Antoon Wilson." Make of this what thou wilt. – Jane Talisman and Eric Geislinger (hereafter the CRNLA).

CRNLA: Tell us a little about your background.

RAW: I was born into a working class Irish Catholic family in Brooklyn 44 years ago, at the brutal bottom of the Great Depression. I suppose this early imprinting and conditioning made me a life-long radical. My education was mostly scientific, majoring in electrical engineering and applied math at Brooklyn Tech and Brooklyn Polytech. Those imprints made me a life-long rationalist. I have become increasingly skeptical about, or detached from, the assumption that radicalism and rationalism are the only correct perspectives with which to view life, but they remain my favorite perspectives.

CRNLA: What are your favorite novels, movies, TV shows and music?

RAW: The novels would be, I suppose, *Ulysses*, *Finnegans Wake*, *The Magus* by Fowles, *The Roots of Heaven* by Gary, *Don Quixote* and anything by Mark Twain. Movies: *Intolerance*, *Broken Blossoms* and everything else by David Wark Griffith, *Citizen Kane*, *The Trial*, *King Kong*, *2001*. TV: *Star Trek* and *Mary Hartman*. Music: Beethoven's Ninth and his late quartets, Bach, Bizet, Carl Orff, Vivaldi, the less popular and more experimental stuff by Stravinsky.

CRNLA: What do you think of *M*A*S*H*, the Freak Brothers, Bob Dylan?

RAW: I loved Altman's film of *M*A*S*H* but I can't stand the TV series. The Freak Brothers are funny, but I deplore the lifestyle it celebrates. Of course, Einstein and Michelangelo were sloppy, too, but only because they were too busy with real work to fix their attention on sartorial status games. Hippies generally aren't busy with anything except feeling sorry for themselves. Dylan seems to me a totally pernicious influence – the nasal whine of death and masochism. Certainly, this would be a more cheerful world if there were no Dylan records in it. But Dylan and his audience mirror each other, and deserve each other; as Marx said, a morbid society creates its own morbid grave-diggers.

CRNLA: How about Anderson, Le Guin and Heinlein?

RAW: I haven't taken Anderson seriously since 1968, when he wrote an account of the police-riot at the Chicago Convention which was totally false, according to my observations on the scene. I decided Poul loved the Vietnam War so much, that he could actually watch a cop hit an old lady and remember it as a young communist hitting the cop. I haven't bothered keeping up with Anderson's hallucinations since then. Le Guin is great already, and getting better book by book. Heinlein has been an idol to me for more than 20 years. He can do no wrong, no matter how much he loves wars and hates pacifists. (I'm the kind of anarchist whose chief objection to the State is that it kills so many people. Government is the epitome of the deathist philosophy I reject.)

RAW: Are you a pacifist?

RAW: Hell, no. I *like* pacifists, as a rule, and people who have a heavy emotional identification with deathism and war would probably call me a pacifist, but I am a non-invasivist rather than a non-violentist. That is, I believe that an invaded people have the right to defend themselves "by any means necessary" as the expression goes. This includes putting ground glass or poison in the invaders' food, shooting at them from ambush, sabotage, the general strike, armed revolution, all forms of Gandhian civil disobedience, etc. It's up to the invaded to decide which of these techniques they will use. It's not up to some moralist to tell them which techniques are permissible. As Tucker said,

"There is nothing sacred in the life of an invader."

CRNLA: What magazines and newspapers do you read?

RAW: I read everything, including the labels on canned food. I'm a hopeless print addict, a condition alleviated only by daily meditation which breaks the linear-Aristotelian trance. (Most rationalistic libertarians would do well to try the same circuit breaker, or LSD.) *National Lampoon, Scientific American* and *Green Egg* are what I read most obsessively. I also read at least one periodical every month by a political group I dislike – to keep some sense of balance. The overwhelming stupidity of political movements is caused by the fact that political types never read anything but their own gang's agit-prop.

RAW: Any more artistic opinions?

RAW: If I must. James Joyce is more important than Jesus, Buddha and Shakespeare put together. Pound is the greatest poet in English. Thorne Smith should be reprinted immediately, and would be enormously popular with the current generation, I wager. The novels that get praised in the *NY Review of Books* aren't worth reading. Ninety-seven percent of science fiction is adolescent rubbish, but good science fiction is the best (and only) literature of our times. All of these opinions are pompous and aggressive, of course, but questions like this bring out the worst in me. Artistic judgments are silly if expressed as dogmas, at least until we get an "artometer" which can measure objectively how many *micro-michelangelos* or *kilo-homers* of genius a given artifact has in it. Do you know that at UC-Berkeley, Dr. Paul Segal has a lab full of rats who are twice the age at which rats normally die of senility? And these rats are not only alive but still reproducing. *This may be the most important fact I know*. Dr. Segal hopes to have a life-extension formula for humans ready in the early 1980s.

CRNLA: Has Dr. Segal published any papers on his research? If so, where?

RAW: A good, non-technical article by Dr. Segall on his own work and on other approaches to longevity, is in the new issue of *Spit in the Ocean*, edited by Dr. Timothy Leary and published by Ken Kesey. That issue, incidentally, is also worth reading for Sirag and Sarfatti on quantum consciousness, and Leary himself on higher intelligence.

CRNLA: Speaking of Ken Kesey, What did you think of *Cuckoo's Nest*, and where can I get a copy of *Spit in the Ocean*?

RAW: *One Flew Over the Cuckoo's Nest* is certainly one of my favorite recent novels, but I like Kesey's *Sometimes a Great Notion* even better. In fact, a great deal of the structural rhythms of *Illuminatus!*, especially the space-time warps, were suggested by Kesey's similar techniques in *Sometimes a Great Notion*. The way the producers of the movie of *Cuckoo's Nest* swindled Kesey is entirely typical of the way producers and publishers rob writers – it's perfectly normal Capitalist ethics and typically mammalian.

The last I heard, Kesey was supposed to have the new *Spit in the Ocean* out by mid-Summer. (Write: 85829 Ridgway Road, Pleasant Hill, OR 97401).

CRNLA: What route did you travel to get to libertarianism?

RAW: Arlen, my wife, discovered Kropotkin's article on anarchism in the *Britannica* and it immediately convinced us both (1961). We were both highly cynical about the alleged values of Capitalism and State Socialism already, and happy to find an alternative.

CRNLA: What is your present involvement in "movement" activities?

RAW: I'm more involved in space migration, intelligence increase and life extension which seems to me more important than any mammalian politics. What energy I have for terrestrial brawling goes into Wavy Gravy's Nobody for President campaign, the Firesign Theatre's Papoon for President campaign, and the Linda Lovelace for President (which I invented myself, since we ought to have a *good-looking* cocksucker in the White House for once). I think these campaigns have some satirical-educational function, and, at minimum, they relieve the tedium of contemplating the "real" candidates, a more-than-usual uninspiring lot this year. Voting wouldn't excite me unless it included electing the directors of the big banks and corporations, who make the real decisions that affect our lives. It's hard to get excited about the trained seals in Washington. Of course, if voting could change the system, it would be illegal. Teachers would be handling out pamphlets for children to take home proving that voting machines cause chromosome damage, and Art Linkletter would claim that a ballot box drove his daughter to suicide.

CRNLA: There's another Vote for Nobody Campaign being run by Malibu. Have you heard of it? Are you interested in it?

RAW: Glad to hear it. There's a third "Nobody for President" headquarters in Washington, D.C. The more the merrier. One of my friends, the ArchDruid of the Berkeley Grove of the Reformed Druids of North America, is running George III for President – although I admit that the satirical point there is a bit obscure for me. I've also heard, vaguely, about a Who-the-Hell for President campaign. There's also a Bonzo for President poster going around, Bonzo being a chimpanzee who once co-starred with the egregious Ronald Reagan in a rather dumb movie. The American people, who elected Richard Nixon twice, should not find any of these choices absurd. But before leaving this subject, I should mention the sanest political proposal I've heard in years, the Guns and Dope Party proposed by my good friend, Rev. William Helmer (who, like many of the characters in *Illuminatus!*, exists also in

A Non-Euclidean Perspective

so-called consensus reality). The Guns and Dope Party, as the name suggests, would be based on a platform demanding an end to all government interference with guns and dope. Now, while the gun-nuts tend to be paranoid about the dopers, and vice versa, the Guns and Dope Party is a possible libertarian coalition that would constitute a clear majority and could really win an election. All that's needed for success, then, is for the gun-people and the dope-people to understand fully the advantages of affiliating – that is, the very good chance of real success at the polls. Hopefully, this might be enough to persuade them to drop their mutual animosity. If this can be accomplished, we will have the first majoritarian libertarian party in American political history. It certainly seems worth thinking about.

CRNLA: Could you tell us more about your politics – such as how you evolved from Kropotkin to *Illuminatus!*?

RAW: After Prince Peter, I read Tucker, who was being reprinted by Mildred Loomis in a journal called, of all things, *Balanced Living.* (I later became co-editor of that, and changed the name to *Way Out.*) After Tucker, I read all the major anarchists and then began writing anarchist essays myself. I soon discovered that, in addition to the 99.8 percent of the morons who make up any political movement, every gang has its own intellectuals defending it (with every variety of sophistry the Jesuits ever devised). To defend anarchism more effectively, I had to read Marx and Douglas and Gesell and H. George and William Buckley Jr. and so weirder, on and on into the depths of ideological metaphysics – "the great Serbonian bog where armies whole have sunk," as Burke (the best conservative) once said. Such omnidirectional reading, alas, tends to produce a certain degree of agnosticism, but my basic axioms have remained that (1) a system which consigned me to poverty at birth and Nelson Godawful Rockefeller to riches, is demonstrably insane, and (2) I will do anything, including highway robbery and murder, to avoid leaving my children in poverty. In that sense, the political thinker I probably agree with most is Bernard Shaw, who presented that position, with equal bluntness, in his *Major Barbara*. I might add, to be even more offensive, that I regard morality and ideology as the chief cause of human misery. I am even more committed to unmitigated skepticism than I am to anarchism – or to life extension, space migration or high intelligence. With doubt, all things are possible. Doubt and courage.

CRNLA: Your economic views still seem very much in the Benjamin Tucker tradition (especially on rent and interest). Have you read any of the "Austrian" economists, such as Von Mises and Rothbard? What do you think of them?

RAW: Tucker is certainly a major influence. My economic ideas are a blend of Tucker, Spooner, Fuller, Pound, Henry George, Rothbard, Douglas, Korzybski, Proudhon and Marx. I always try to be inclusive, rather than exclusive. Read to see what I can learn from every school, rather than condemning any idea in its entirety. "Every man has the right to have his ideas examined one at a time," as Ez Pound once wrote. Rothbard is, like Marx and Pound, a brilliant closed mind: excellent for stimulation but anybody who gets dragged into a Rothbardian dogmatic trance should take LSD and try looking at the world through another grid. Von Mises is another who is excellent for stimulation, pernicious if erected into dogma. By and large, the Austrians remind me of a parable by Laurance Labadie, in which a certain tribe has the custom of allowing high-caste individuals to kick low-caste individuals in the butt whenever they pass them in the street. A philosophical school, much like the Austrians, naturally arises to prove rationally that the kicking is not only necessary but just, inevitable, beautiful and altogether glorious. If there were big profits in cancer, there'd undoubtedly be an Austrian school of medicine, proving that carcinoma is good for us.

CRNLA: Tucker is one of my favorite people – but one of his views with which I can't agree is that in a free society interest rates and rent would disappear. I think the Austrians have advanced economic knowledge sufficiently since Tucker's day to show why these things exist and how they would come about even in an economy consisting totally of free trade. Your reply?

RAW: You can "prove" anything on the verbal level, just be accepting the necessary axioms at the beginning. Empirically, I don't think they can produce a single case in history where a free people elected landlords to own the land; the land monopoly always starts with conquest. Shot and shell are the coins of purchase, as Herbert Spencer said. Except by force of arms, nobody "owns" the earth, any more than the moon, the planets, the stars themselves. When did God disinherit the majority of humanity, and turn all space over to the "ownership" of the Rockefellers and their friends? Without armed power threatening us, why would anyone but a fool continue to pay these conquistadores the extortion they demand? And, even if the Austrians could convince me that rent is legitimate, I still wouldn't voluntarily pay it to the present landlord class who remain *receivers of stolen property*. I would pay it to the nearest Indian tribe.

As for interest, I'm not aware of any case in which the credit monopoly has allowed a free currency to compete with them. In fact, every case I know of (e.g. Wörgl in the 1930s), ended when the Capitalists used the armed might of the State to stop the competition. The one laboratory experiment in this field, by Don Werkheiser at Central State University in Ohio, confirmed Tucker and refuted the Austrians. Money, after all, is an *abstract artifact*, like language – merely *symbolized* by the paper or coin or whatever. If you can fully grasp its abstractedness, especially in the computer age, it becomes quite clear that no group can monopolize this abstraction, except through a series of swindle. *The average primate cannot distinguish the symbol from the referent,* the map from the territory, the menu from the meal. If the usurers had been bolder, they might have monopolized language as well as currency, and people would be saying we can't write more books because we don't have enough words, the way they now say we can't build starships, because we don't have enough money. As Bucky Fuller says, you might as well argue we can't build roads because we lack kilometers.

CRNLA: I think our differences in "rent" are basically in "land-rent" – you don't see anything wrong if someone wants to rent out power tools and U-Haul trailers – true?

Your main argument with land-rent seems to be with the lack of legitimate owners. I'm assuming legitimate (i.e. non-conquistador) owners when I speak of legitimate rent. If two people went to Mars or the bottom of the ocean and one of them spent his time clearing rocks and fertilizing a section of land and the other spent his time assembling a tractor, and they reach an agreement to exchange the use of the land for one season for the use of the tractor for one season – has anyone been harmed or exploited or extorted? Should some third party come onto the scene and say, "Hey stop that, you're committing rent?"

RAW: Land-rent, or ground-rent, is the most illegitimate aspect of the rent con, of course, and the main target of Tucker's criticisms. The whole concept of any rent, however, appears somewhat dubious to me, since it seems to presuppose "the accumulation of property in a few aristocratic heaps, at the expense of a great deal of democratic bare ground in between," as Ezra Heywood said. (Heywood's writings on this subject, and other aspects of libertarianism, are at least as important as Tucker's and Spooner's.) People *rent*, chiefly, when they cannot afford to purchase outright – when ground-rent, interest and other inequalities have already created a master-class of aristocrat-owners and a servile class of peasants or proles. I would expect to see rent wither away as the democratization of credit abolishes poverty.

I fail to see how your hypothetical "legitimate (i.e. non-conquistador) owners" would achieve "ownership." (I also don't see the bearing of such hypothetical, or fictitious, cases on the real issues of the real world, where all the landlords are conquistadors, or are receivers of stolen property from the original conquistadors, but that is another question.)

Ownership, in the real world, is a social agreement, a social fiction almost, and is produced only by force or by fraud or by contract. In practice, land ownership is produced only by force or fraud.

This may sound polemic, but it is literally true. The Henry George Schools have a book, *Land Title Origins: A Tale of Force and Fraud*, in which you can look up, wherever you live in the United States, exactly the acts of force and fraud (murder and robbery) by which land "ownership" was transferred from the Indian tribes to the current receivers of the stolen property. Now, the third alternative, contract, has never been tried, to the best of my knowledge. The only land contracts which I, or any other Tuckerites or Stirnerites, would sign in freedom, without force being used against us, would be to our own interest, not to the interest of the landlords. In other words, we simply would not sign a contract giving up ownership of this planet, or any other, to a small group of the Elite who claim they have some better title to ownership than the rest of us have. If you would sign such a contract, I can only hint gently that you are more easily defrauded than we are.

The barter arrangement in your paradigm has nothing to do

with *perpetual tribute*, which is the essence of rent – indeed, the factor distinguishing barter from rent.

Of course, since Austrian ideas exist as factors in human behavior, I will admit that some people, hoodwinked by those ideas, will continue to pay rent even in freedom, for a while at least. But I think that, after a time, observing that their Tuckerite neighbors are not submitting to this imposture, they would come to their senses and cease paying tribute to the self-elected "owners" of limitless space, on this and other planets, and in interplanetary communities.

Of course, I myself would not pay rent one day beyond the point at which the police ("hired guns, on guard to see that property remains stolen" as Emma Goldman said) are at hand to collect it via "argument per blunt instrument."

CRNLA: Regarding interest: again I assume a totally free market, where there are no legal tender laws and anyone is free to mint, mine, print or grow anything that they feel the market will accept for money. I think that under these conditions the interest rate would be dramatically lower than it presently is but that it would not tend toward zero. Money generally performs at least three interrelated functions: (1) indirect exchange media, (2) provides a common "measuring scale," (3) stores wealth. In the first two, money is definitely an "abstract artifact" – a "cashless" society could exist merely using bookkeeping entries. But when it's used to store wealth it causes trouble as an "abstract" – bank-runs and the like. Wealth isn't an abstract. It may be subjectively appraised, but it actually exists. When A wants to use B's wealth for a period of time, B is generally compensated for his loss of its use for that period by A – interest. Among corporations (admittedly, a legal fiction) the issuing of "Tucker-money," (i.e., stock) is a fairly unfettered means of obtaining credit – but the people who give it to them still expect a return and the corporations still expect to pay it. I'd be interested in seeing the Central State experiment. Usually because of the multiplicity of ever-changing factors involved in the market, it's difficult if not impossible to ever prove anything empirically.

RAW: Of course, my position is based on the denial that money does store wealth. I think it's a semantic hallucination, the verbal equivalent of an optical illusion, to speak at all of money containing or storing wealth. Such thinking should have gone out with phlogiston theory. The symbol is not the referent; the map is not the territory. Money symbolizes wealth, as words symbolize things, and that's all. The delusions that money contains wealth is the mechanism by which the credit monopoly of study has gained a stranglehold on the entire economy. As Colonel Greene pointed out in *Mutual Banking*, all the money could disappear tomorrow morning and the wealth of the planet would remain the same. However, if the wealth disappeared – if squinks from the Pink Dimension dragged it off to null-space or something – the money would be worth nothing. You don't need to plow through the dialects of the debate between the Austrians and the free credit people like Tucker and Gesell to see this; any textbook of semantics will make it clear in a few hours of study. Wealth is nature's abundance, freely given, plus the exponential advance of technology via human intelligence, and as Korzybski and Fuller demonstrate, this can only increase at an accelerating rate. Money is just the tickets or symbols to arrange for the distribution – either equitably, in a free money system, or inequitably, as under the tyranny of the present money-cartel. As you realize, a cashless society could exist merely by keeping bookkeeping entries or computer tapes. Money is a primitive form of such computer tapes, serving a feedback function. If we are not to replace the present banking oligopoly with a programmer's oligopoly, in which the interest will be paid to computer technicians, we must realize that this is all a matter of abstract symbolism – that it exists by social agreement and nobody owns it, anymore than Webster owns the language. Why is it, incidentally, that the Austrians don't follow their logic to its natural conclusion and demand that we pay interest to the dictionary publishers every time we speak or write?

You have to watch people playing Monopoly, and see them begin to "identify" the paper markers with real value, to understand how the mass hypnosis of Capitalism works. Fortunately, the Head Revolution is still proceeding and more and more people are waking up to the difference between our economic game-rules and the real existential situation of humanity.

Don Werkheiser might sell you a Xerox of his thesis on the Central State experiment if you write to him c/o General Delivery, Ponca, Arkansas. Similar experiments are recounted in Josiah Warren's *True Civilization*, involving four communes in 19th century America. Let me conclude this answer by emphasizing that I do not *blame* the money-monopologists for any of their hoarding behavior. I am sure you will find similar absurdities in the primitive stages of anthropoid civilizations on most planets of G-type stars. Mammalian patterns persist in many other aspects of our society, especially in organized religions.

In my experience, I might add, virtually all adherents of the Austrian economic theories are academics who have never had any dealings with Capitalist corporations. The rosy view the Austrians have of these matters, I think, would collapse in two weeks if they had to deal with the damned corporate pirates as an ordinary worker does. When Joyce went into business briefly, he told Italo Svevo after a while, "You know, I think my partners are cheating me." Svevo answered, "You only

think your partners are cheating you! Joyce, you are an artist!"
Nixon is the typical Capitalist mentality, entirely identical in
all aspects with every businessman I have ever encountered;
his only real distinction is that he got caught. Of course, I'm
not complaining – part of the humor of living on this backward
planet is listening to the hominids rationalize their predations.

CRNLA: I don't think that the Austrians have a particularly
"rosy" view of business. I know a lot of them (Mises and
Rothbard for two) consider a total separation of the economy
and the government to be the best means of keeping these
clowns from becoming too powerful. Most consider a totally
free market to be the ultimate in "consumerism" – not
"capitalism" (at least as it's come to be known).

RAW: Well, there is certainly a kinship between the Austrians
and myself on the level of ultimate goals. I merely feel that
their views of Capitalism-as-practiced-in-the-past-and-present
could only be held by college professors. After more than 20
years of working for the corporations in every position from
office boy to middle executive, I have not been shocked or
surprised in the slightest by the Watergate or post-Watergate
scandals.

Austrians believe what they write, they must be somewhat
abashed, I should think. For instance, David Friedman has
published views about the corporate elite that would be
flattering if applied to Jesus and his angels. However, this is
turning into a diatribe against the group I find least obnoxious
in the whole politico-economic spectrum (because you keep
asking me questions that harp on my differences with them).
The orthodox conservatives and liberals, not to mention
Nazis and Marxists, are really pernicious, and the Austrian
libertarians are basically okay.

CRNLA: Regarding our Rent Interest discussion: I think that
our differences regarding money stem from a difference in

definitions. I would include wealth that is used in certain ways under the heading "money," while you limit the definition to just its transactional functions. OK, as long as we know where we are. Once we start dealing with this "wealth-money" as wealth (and forget the word "money"), the problem of interest becomes just a special case of rent. Which really brings us back to property and ownership. I've never attempted to tie the concept of ownership to the metaphysical framework of the universe. I realize that it's merely a human invention – much like language (which is not to say that other inhabitants of the planet don't use it also) that it's purpose is to make the allocation of resources go as smoothly and efficiently and with the least amount of head-cracking as possible. Like the use of language, the use of the concept of "property" doesn't necessarily have to be enforced. When people discover it they use it because it's in their long-range self-interest to do so. (This is not to say that particular instances don't require enforcement – just that the concept is usually retained without it.) The whole system of ownership/division of labor/rent transactions etc. is merely designed to allocate resources so that they maximize the "vector sum" of everyone's satisfaction – or more accurately, that this system has the potential to maximize. You don't have to use it. Without this system some alternative method must be found to determine who gets the use of what. Le Guin faced this problem in *The Dispossessed*. She chose to do it collectively. Ultimately, this results in some system of voting or representatives or syndics which bear striking resemblance to governments (in addition to being very inefficient). So the so-called "anarchy" in *The Dispossessed* is actually a widespread proliferation of governments and poverty. If the determination of the use of resources is placed in the hands of the individual who makes the resources useful (i.e., grows, finds, fertilizes, builds on, digs up, etc.) this provides him with a good deal of independence from the rest of the herd. Seems like a natural for any anarchistic society. This is basically the idea behind my concept of ownership. Could you give a summary of what you consider to be a good method of allocating resources and any concepts similar to ownership that might be contained therein?

RAW: Since ownership is a social fiction, it should obviously be fluid and sensitive to decentralized feedback, to match the evolving needs of the persons involved in whatever social game is being played. In other words, I do not propose one "right way" of doing it; that has to be found pragmatically in each new situation. The traditional feudal-Capitalist system in which one hereditary group of Great Pirates "owns" everything is not acceptable to me, and obviously would not be acceptable to any band of Stirnerite egoists; and, of course, the altruistic forms of socialism and communism are equally unacceptable to me, and I predict they would be equally unacceptable to a band of self-owners in the Stirnerite, Tucker or Crowley sense. What would emerge in such a rationalistic-egoistic context would, in a general way, probably follow the guidelines suggested by Stirner, Spooner, Proudhon and Tucker – except that this would only be in a general way, as all of those writers realized. The specific individuals in each situation would define their own demands according to the specific situation always. The only contracts that would be acceptable to them, as Tucker indicated, would be those that require no enforcement – that is, those that are so obviously in the enlightened self-interest of each member that their wording would be accepted with the satisfaction the scientific world feels when a hard question is finally answered. If the proposed contract did not have that self-evident feeling character about it – if it didn't provoke the general feeling, "This is the answer to our disagreements" – it would not be accepted. I speak with some experience here, being part of an occult order who do indeed govern themselves that way. My only general rules are Crowley's "Do what thou wilt shall be the whole of the Law," and Leary's Three Commandments for the Neurological Age, to wit: "Thou shalt not alter the consciousness of thy neighbor, 2. Thou shalt not prevent thy neighbor from altering his or her own consciousness, 3. Thou shalt make no more commandments." The so-called "resources" problem is a terra-centric delusion. The Universe is a Big Mother.

CRNLA: To return to life extension, space migration and higher intelligence, I worry about the potential of all that being screwed up by the politicians. How do you feel about that?

RAW: If the oncoming mutation to interstellar immortality is screwed up by the politicians (or the corporations), it will be because those of us who see the opportunities in modern science are not adroit enough to outmaneuver the forces of inertia, stupidity and greed. Well, if we're not intelligent enough to overcome such obstacles, then we don't deserve to carry off the mutation at this stage of evolution. The thing to do, in that case, is to sit down and have a good Taoistic laugh at our own presumption. Meanwhile, until the game is over, I happen to think we're winning. The other side is very, very stupid. Concretely, I say that if we have colonization of L5 by 1990, and longevity at about the same time, I think the game is won; some human seed will become cosmic and immortal. Robert Phedra, M.D., has already predicted life extension to 1,000 years.

CRNLA: A thousand years is OK for a start, but it's not enough. Would you settle for "indefinite life extension" if it means transferring your thoughts to a synthetic storage system?

RAW: I'd consider it, but temperamentally I'd rather blast off for the stars when lifespan reaches about 400 years. I think in a 400 year cruise around the galaxy we'd contact races who have immortality already and we might arrange a trade for the technology of it. (Maybe they'd want an unexpurgated *Illuminatus!*.) I'm for space, actually, whether there are immortals out there or not. Aside from that bias, I'd support life extension by whatever means, from cryonic suspension to cyborgism to coding ourselves into our computers or whatever. Contrary to the last 2,500 years of "philosophy" among the domesticated and neurotic carnivore species we adorn, there is nothing noble or beautiful or dignified about dying. Like poverty, it is ugly, nasty, brutal and primitive. The function of intelligence is to do better than those mammalian norms.

CRNLA: Could you give us a bibliography on everything you've had published and who published it and if it's still in print?

RAW: Hell, no. I've got about 1,000 articles in print and I can't remember where most of them were printed and don't really care to. The things I'm willing to stand by, in addition to *Illuminatus!*, are the essays being collected in *Prometheus Rising*; *Sex and Drugs*, a Playboy Press paperback; my piece on "The Future in Sex" in *Oui*, November 1975; the article on brainwashing by Leary and me in *Oui* for June 1976 (which I especially commend to those who thought the consciousness-warps, ego-fissions, reality-mutations and sex-role roulette in *Illuminatus!* were "fantasy"); "Scientific and Experimental Magic" in *Gnostica*, January 1975; and two pieces on Caryl Chessman and the Marquis de Sade in *The Realist*, dates unknown. Most of what I wrote before last week bores me.

CRNLA: What kind of stuff was the 500 pages that got edited out of *Illuminatus!*?

RAW: It was sacrilegious, blasphemous, obscene, subversive, funny, surrealistic, trippy and much like what did get published. The portion of hard anarchist propaganda in what got cut is perhaps somewhat greater than in what got printed, but I do not attribute that to a government conspiracy. Editors always amputate the brain first and preserve a good-looking corpse. I knew that, and told Shea they'd do it, so we put in so damned much anarchist material that a lot would be left even after the ceremonial castration.

CRNLA: Is Bob Shea a hard-core libertarian?

RAW: More or less. I really don't want to categorize Shea, who can certainly speak (eloquently) for himself.

CRNLA: Who wrote the *Atlas Shrugged* parody in *Illuminatus*? Who wrote the appendices?

RAW: I wrote the *Telemachus Sneezed* section – which is not just another kick at poor old Rand, but also a self-parody of *Illuminatus!*, and of *Moby Dick*, and of my arcane Joycean use of *Moby Dick* parallels in *Illuminatus!*. Unfortunately, that section was particularly mauled and truncated by the editors. Originally, it was trans-Melvillian satire on all ideology and morality, including my own lapses into ethical thinking. I also wrote the Appendices on various occasions when very stoned as a parody on my style in my more academic essays.

CRNLA: What was Hagbard doing in a government printing office?

RAW: Hagbard was visiting the Discordian agents who have infiltrated the government and sneaked parodies into the bureaucratic forms: SMI^2LE = infinity. (Space Migration plus Intelligence Increase plus Life Extension = cosmic consciousness.)

CRNLA: Any word on how sales are doing?

RAW: Fine. I might not have to take up highway robbery and murder to get rich after all.

CRNLA: That's good. Who is Tarantella Serpentine and why is she working for *Limit* newsletter?

RAW: The Discordian conspiracy has been radically decentralized from the beginning, in accordance with Malaclypse the Younger's principle that "We Discordians must stick apart." The last I heard, Tarantella was a fictional character, working in a San Francisco massage parlor (in my other novel, *The Sex Magicians*). It doesn't surprise that she has a life of her own, outside my imagination. *Illuminatus!* is only part of a total art work, or "happening" known as Operation Mindfuck. A group of New York Discordians, for instance, celebrated the 200th anniversary of the Illuminati with a public reading of *Principia Discordia* (which also exists) outside the UN building on May 1 this year. A lodge of Crowleyan magicians in Texas has officially changed their name from the Temple of the Hidden God to the Ancient Illuminated Good Old Boys of Houston. Emperor Norton posters, endorsed by the Illuminati, are for sale through Solidarity Books in Chicago. Everything the Birchers ever claimed about the Illuminati is gradually coming true.

CRNLA: Do you feel frustration living in the "real" world? After reading *Illuminatus!* it's a downer to get back to reality – even my usual escapist literature is depressing. How do you feel about that?

RAW: Every nervous system creates its own "reality," minute by minute – or, in the language of Don Juan Matus, we live inside a "bubble" of neural abstractions which we identify with reality. In metaprogramming systems like Tibetan Tantra, Crowleyanity, or Leary's Exo-Psychology, you can make this neurological fact into conscious experience, and you will never be bored or depressed again. Just reading the scientific evidence that this is true, in social psychology or general semantics or neurology or whatever, will not liberate you; one needs actual re-training, in Tantra or Crowley or Leary, to experience what I'm talking about here. It is a great privilege to be conscious in this universe. Those who understand, shine like stars.

CRNLA: I was just speaking in relative terms. Actually, I'm quite excited about reality – it's probably my favorite thing. I was just wondering if sometimes all the fnords tend to get you a little pissed-off.

RAW: Never. As Tim Leary says, the universe is an intelligence test. The things that hinder me are opportunities to learn more and develop further. That's where amoral thinking is distinctly superior to moral thinking. If you recognize that your latest problem is totally without moral significance – for instance, you have a disease which you can't, by the wildest stretch of imagination, *blame* on anybody – then it's just a question of coping with the situation as best you can. When you realize that people are just as automated as bacteria or wild animals, then you deal with hostile humans the same way you deal with infections or predators – rationally, without claiming you're "right" or they're "wrong." Then you begin to understand Crowley's great Law of Thelema (Do What Thou Wilt) and you're free, really free, instead of being an actor in a soap opera written by the superstitious shamans who created morality 30,000 years ago. You are also free of anger, hatred and resentment, which are great burdens to drop. They live happiest, my friend, who have understood and forgiven all.

CRNLA: Are there real people, alive or in history, who resemble any of your characters (Hagbard in particular)?

RAW: Absolutely. There are hundreds of thousands of Hagbards around, and all the sleep-walkers are potential Hagbards. They only need to be shaken a bit and awakened. As Jesus said, "Ye are all gods, ye are all children of the Most High."

RAW: Have you ever walked into some public place like a

shopping center and said to yourself something like, "Christ, it's solid earthlings! You'd think there'd be at least a couple of aliens strolling around looking at the shops, etc."?

RAW: Curiously, I belong to a loose association of skeptical Contactees – people who have had a Contact experience but are too skeptical to take it literally. There are over a hundred of us in the U.S. alone, mostly scientists, and I think that the gradual surfacing of this story will be one of the major cultural shocks of our time. Right now, Martin Gardner has already registered his viewpoint and I trust that MIT will have the courtesy to print Dr. Sarfatti's rebuttal. I must add that most of us who are involved in this have grown extremely doubtful about the now-conventional extraterrestrial explanation and are trying out various explanatory models that are even more mind-blowing. Those who are interested in this subject might look up my article, "The Starseed Signals," in *Gnostica* for June 1975, and Dr. Jacques Vallee's book, *The Invisible College*. As the divine Mullah Nasruddin said, "If you haven't seen me before, how do you know it is me?"

CRNLA: What are your plans for future books?

RAW: *Prometheus Rising* will be published by Llewellyn next year. It's a collection of my essays on space age occultism and post-LSD consciousness. I hope it will knock holes in the Christian revival, the Hindu revival, the Buddhist revival and all the other neolithic metaphysics going around these days. A book on immortality research, possibly entitled *Death Shall Have No Dominion*, is going around New York seeking a publisher. A book on Dr. Timothy Leary, and a new novel called *Schrödinger's Cat*, about quantum paradoxes and parapsychology, are also in the works. Leary and I are working on a collaborative venture called *The Game of Life* which started out as one volume and became three. It modestly attempts to deduce the next four billion years of evolution from the data of Leary's brain-change research.

CRNLA: Who did you know in the old Berkeley crowd such as Danny Rosenthal, Sharon Presley, Tom McGivern? How about Kerry Thornley?

RAW: I never heard of any of those people except Kerry Thornley and Sharon Presley. Kerry is one of the co-creators of Discordian atheology, which is why volume one of *Illuminatus!* is co-dedicated to him. Sharon is a fine person who I've only met twice but liked vastly. I'm sure all those others are excellent people, too, but I've never met them.

CRNLA: The editor of *New Libertarian Weekly*, SEK3, would like you to write for them – " . . . we're a hell of a lot better than *SRAF* and can even pay a token amount, and can run stuff he can't get past *Playboy* and *Oui*."

RAW: I'd be delighted.

CRNLA: Do you have any concluding thoughts for our readers?

RAW: Absolutely not. As Korzybski said, nothing is conclusive, and every sentence should end with an *et cetera*. Or perhaps Woody Allen said it better: "Not only is there no God, but you can't even get a plumber on weekends." The answer to that, of course, is to become your own god and your own plumber. That may be the fundamental secret of the Illuminati.

A Non-Euclidean Perspective

Eight Kinds of Libertarians

This article, from Robert Anton Wilson's "Illuminating Discords" column in New Libertarian Weekly, *was published in issue number 60 of that publication, Feb. 6, 1977. Part two of the topic, included here, appeared in* New Libertarian Weekly, *March 13, 1977.*

I propose that there are eight kinds of libertarians and that understanding the differences would clarify much of the debate between factions.

The eight varieties of freedom-fighters are distinguished by which neurological circuit or imprint matrix is dominant in their nervous system. There are, according to Dr. Timothy Leary, eight such circuits, and that is why I distinguish eight kinds of libertarianism.

1. The **Biosurvival Circuit** is activated as soon as DNA life is established on a planet. This is the most primitive level of consciousness (3 1/2 billion years old) and scans only for signals indicating safety (security, warmth, food) or danger (threat, isolation, withdrawal of nurture). This

circuit is recapitulated in the first days of infancy and takes a basic biosurvival imprint which lasts for life. In ordinary nontechnical language this circuit is called Will.

The libertarian who has taken his heaviest imprint on this circuit will be obsessed with defense-and-attack on the most basic level of life-and-death struggle against competing organisms. Anarcho-fascists, Sadeans, Stirnerites and vulgarizers of Nietzsche fit this first circuit imprint pattern.

2. The **Emotional Circuit** is formed as soon as life forms become complicated enough to exert effort against gravity, rear up and compete for territory or status. This appeared with the first amphibians around 500,000,000 years ago. This circuit is recapitulated when the infant starts to walk, send emotional signals by Body Language (kinesics) and struggles for a decision-making role in family politics. (All parents know this imprint period as "the difficult years.") Once again, the initial imprint tends to remain a lifelong emotional game strategy.

In ordinary language, this circuit, pre-occupied with mammalian politics, is called the Ego. Its unconscious aspects are the Id of Freud; Berne calls it the Adapted Child.

Libertarians who have taken their strongest imprint on this circuit will tend toward conservatism, join the Libertarian Party and get embroiled in elections, or become Objectivists.

The first circuit is obsessed with survival in a Darwinian sense; the second circuit with territory and status, i.e. Ego-tripping.

3. The third circuit appeared with the emergence of hominid nervous systems about 1,000,000 years ago. Right-handedness, domination of the brain by the linear left hemisphere and the use of the nine laryngeal muscles for signaling concrete and abstract ideas (language) make up this **Symbolic Circuit**. It is activated when the child begins handling, manipulating and altering artifacts, and also asking questions such as, "What is this called? How do you use this?"

In popular speech, this circuit is called the Mind. Eric Berne calls it the Adult or Computer.

(In Star Trek land, the first circuit is Scotty, brooding pessimistically over life-support and weapons systems; the second circuit is McCoy, the expert on tribal decorum; and the third circuit, of course, is Spock.)

Libertarians who take their strongest imprint on the third circuit remain obsessed with logic, linear processes, symbolic constructs, science. Typical examples are Bucky Fuller, the semanticist Korzybski, John Stuart Mill. These types never get involved in politics and tend to regard second circuit politics as sub-human.

The transition from the mammalian second circuit to the hominid third circuit is beautifully portrayed in *2001*, when Moon-Watcher picks up the bone and realizes he can use it as a tool. The quick transitions from the bone flying through the air to the L5 space colony illustrates the extreme rapidity of change on any planet after the third circuit begins operating.

We have said that life and the first circuit is 3 1/2 billion years old and the hominid third circuit only one million, but these figures are too large to *feel.* Try it this way: divide by 10 million and make a model by which this planet is only 400 years old, and begin in 1576. Then, life and the first circuit began around 1626. The emotional circuit appeared with vertebrate life about 1926. The hominid third circuit appeared one month ago, and modern science ten minutes ago.

This rapid acceleration after third circuit symbolism appears was called time-binding by Korzybski.

4. The **Domestic Circuit** appeared with the domestication of humanity about 30,000 years ago. (On our 400-year model scale, that would be about 16 hours ago.) This circuit imprints the sexual apparatus for socially useful purposes. (For further details on this domestication process, see Marcuse, *Eros and Civilization,* and Wilhelm Reich, passim.) This is recapitulated in each individual when the chemical releasers of pubescence

activate the sex-mating drives, and imprinting this energy with the local taboo system creates the Adult Personality. (Freud's Super-Ego, Berne's Parent.)

Since this circuit consists of taboo systems sublimated out of powerful erotic energies, the fourth-circuit libertarian is a driven and compulsive Super-Ego figure. ("He's making a list and checking it twice. He's gonna find out who's naughty or nice.") Utopian, psychologically authoritarian and always convinced SHe is the one mature personality in any group, this type appears both in the camp of fanatic militarism and fanatic pacifism; e.g. Heinlein and Joan Baez both seem to be fourth circuit libertarianism.

(Very few fourth circuit types become libertarians actually, and Maoism is the ultimate fourth circuit domestication. On the *Enterprise*, Kirk is the fourth circuit type.)

5. The fifth neurological circuit, according to Leary's *Exo-Psychology*, is for extraterrestrial life and, hence, has only appeared in random mutants until recently. It is the **Neurosomatic Circuit** and mediates biosurvival in zero-gravity. 85 percent of all astronauts have described "mystical" experiences which are actually fifth circuit "highs" similar to the *dhyana* state in Hatha Yoga or the Turn On you get from neurotransmitters in the cannabis family. Freud called this circuit "the oceanic experience."

Neurosomatic rapture transcends the dualisms of the first four circuits, reverses figure and ground (often in humorous ways) and is appropriately called *spacing* or *floating* in popular speech.

Sex and dope cults such as Tantra in India, the Yezidis in the Near East, the Gnostic and Illuminati heresies in Europe, hippiedom, etc., represent fifth circuit libertarianism. "You can't do good until you feel good" (Leary's translation of Lao-Tse) is their basic motto. They are detached from, and amused by, the dualisms of the first four circuits – the forward-back of biosurvival fight-or-flight patterns, the up-down of emotional politics, the either-or of symbolic logic, the naughty and nice of local taboo systems.

6. The sixth circuit is **Neuroelectrical** or psionic intelligence: direct awareness and control of Brain functioning. In premature infants, this produces space-time singularities, synchronicities, ESP, and a sense that one is living in a sci-fi story of parallel worlds.

Since this circuit is the point at which brain functioning moves more into the right lobe than the left, its purpose has to do with our future evolution and sixth circuit libertarians are extremely rare thus far; one is more likely to encounter them in fiction than in fact. Conchis, in John Fowles' *The Magus*, is one example; Hagbard Celine, another. Krishnamurti's slogan, "Be an Individual," is *in Krishnamurti's context*, a sixth circuit libertarian exhortation. Crowley's notorious saying, "God is the enemy of Man" is another sixth circuit signal, as was Proudhon's antitheism (as distinguished from atheism.)

7. The **Neurogenetic Circuit** involves direct access to the DNA archives: Jung's "collective unconscious" made conscious. The seventh circuit libertarian is an Evolutionary Agent, a conspirator in the vast DNA plot to achieve Higher Intelligence, Immortality, Supreme Bliss and the gratification of all desires.

When Leary was operating on the sixth circuit, he said, "The body is the car; the DNA is the driver." When he graduated to the seventh circuit, he said, "The nervous system is the car; the DNA is the driver." Again, the type is so rare that the prototypes are found more in fiction than in life -- all of Kazantzakis' heroes, especially Odysseus in his sequel to the Odyssey; Prometheus and Daedalus in mythology; Gilgamesh renouncing kingship and all the world to search for immortality; Buddha renouncing all to see Truth.

A classic seventh circuit libertarian is Giordano Bruno, burned by the Catholic Church in February 1600, but the pioneer of modern science and modern Western occultism. (See

Frances Yates, *Giordano Bruno and the Hermetic Tradition.*) A more modern example is Wilhelm Reich, before he wigged out.

8. The highest circuit is **Metaphysiological** (not metaphysical). This is evolving toward synergetic interlock of galactic higher intelligences into one unified energy field free of body container. (The "Atman" or "Overmind" of mystical literature.) Metaphysiological is out-of-the body, out of space-time, literally infinite.

The formula for opening the 8th circuit is SMI²LE, which means Space Migration + Intelligence (squared) + Life Extension. Space Migration and Life Extension are clear enough, I trust, but Intelligence Squared perhaps requires a word of clarification. It means intelligence-studying-intelligence, i.e. Dr. John Lilly's self-metaprogramming biocomputer.

All of the 8th circuit libertarians known to me are unindicted co-conspirators in Leary's Starseed project, which aims to accomplish the SMI²LE mutation in this generation.

• • •

The Noble Eight-Fold Path

*Part two, published in New Libertarian Weekly
March 13, 1977*

In my previous column, I distinguished eight types of libertarians. To recapitulate:

1. The bio-survival libertarian, or anarcho-fascist, is Darwinian, anxiously and bitterly aware of being involved in a life-or-death struggle.

2. The emotional libertarian, or mammalian politician, is concerned with capturing territory and status; SHe is the emotional game-player, the Oneupmanship expert.

3. The symbolic libertarian, or Mr. Spock, is obsessed with logic, linear processes, mechanism and rationality.

4. The domesticated libertarian is the Utopian moralist, determined to right all wrongs and establish pure Justice everywhere.

5. The neurosomatic libertarian is your basic Hippie or Tantric yogin, i.e. the Hedonic Engineer.

6. The neuroelectric libertarian is the Black Magician (so-called), i.e. the Head Tripper free of all categories. "Nobody knows who I am or what I do, not even myself," says Don Juan to Carlos Castaneda, perfectly defining this type from inside.

7. The neurogenetic libertarian is an Evolutionary Agent, dedicated not just to freeing hirself or humanity from political authoritarianism but to freeing life from all limits of space, time or death.

8. The metaphysiological libertarian is operating at de Chardin's Omega Point, at one with all metaphysiological libertarians throughout space-time and beyond space time. (In mystical literature these types are known as the Secret Chiefs, the Bodhisattvas or the Illuminati.)

These eight types are determined by statistically random imprints that are bonded into the nervous system at moments of imprint vulnerability. (See ethology and Dr. Leary's *Exo-Psychology* for further details on that.) The random element is part of the DNA blueprint (or "Mother Nature's plan," to be folksy about it) to ensure that we remain a diversified species.

Thus, there are eight kinds of authoritarians, also. Eight kinds of men. Eight kinds of women. Eight kinds of Armenians. Eight kinds of Italians. Eight kinds of Buddhists. Etc.

Imprint vulnerability is coded into the DNA tapes so that, for example, the newborn gosling is *vulnerable* to imprinting a protective mother entity immediately after hatching. The random element enters because, during the vulnerable period, anything roughly matching the genetic archetype will be imprinted. Thus, Lorenz reports a gosling that imprinted a ping-pong ball and followed it about attempting to nest with it and vocalizing to it as it would toward a real Mother Goose. Evidently, the fact that the ping pong ball has a round white body, like a Mother Goose, was enough to trigger the genetic imprinting process.

Similarly, Ardrie reports a newborn giraffe which imprinted a jeep, which it subsequently attempted to nurse from and followed around with imploring cries. Here the four wheels of the jeep evidently passed the scanners as the same signal normally transmitted by the four-legged Mama Giraffe.

In the past 6000 years domesticated humanity has been herded into vast urban hives at repetitious and stereotyped tasks, a process we optimistically call civilization. As in the ant-hive, these human hives have often kept a slave population and made war on other hives. Obviously, the total insectoid society of Maoism is the highest, most complex form of this fourth neurogenetic circuit. Humanity has been temporarily evolving away from the mammalian norm and toward the insectile.

(Frank Herbert's *Hellstrom's Hive* is a magnificent SF saga extending the process a few steps beyond even Mao.)

If this is the "civilized" norm, then all libertarians are, in some sense, rebels against civilization, i.e. against domestication.

The first circuit libertarian is rebelling backward to an early evolutionary stage; hence, the fierce Darwinian rhetoric in Stirner and libertarians of this type.

The second circuit emotional libertarian is rebelling backward also, but toward a more recent evolutionary stage, the mammalian pack or hunting-warrior band.

All political parties are basically hunting-warrior bands adapting themselves to the fourth circuit domesticated hive.

Second circuit libertarians flock to parties and conspire endless to capture control of the hive and "set it free." This is like plotting to take over a whorehouse and set the whores and customers "free" to practice chastity. That is, people who want chastity are not in whorehouses and people who want freedom are not in domesticated hives.

Third circuit libertarians, whose patron God is Daedalus, are always plotting to engineer a libertarian hive by creating the perfect logical model of what is desired and teaching its value to others. This is based on the error of assuming everybody else is, or should be, a third circuit computer like Mr. Spock.

Fourth circuit libertarians are in a particularly ambiguous position since the fourth circuit is inherently hive-oriented. These types become anarcho-communist mystics, vegetarians, etc. and are usually to be found in mini-hives some hundreds of miles from the nearest macro-hive, practicing their own "libertarian" version of typical hive-taboo morality.

Fifth circuit libertarians turn on, tune in and drop out. They sometimes enter fourth circuit mini-hives briefly but as soon as they recognize the local taboo system as a permutation or combination of those of the macro-hives, they leave and float elsewhere. Probably, they will eventually float off the earth entirely to establish Tantric "Heavenly Cities" in space. Imagine a micro-L5 designed along the lines of Hassan-i-Sabbah's Garden of Delights and you get my idea of where fifth circuit libertarianism is going.

Sixth circuit libertarians are the allies of the future. Where circuits I to V identify the imprinted neural construct with "reality," the sixth circuit type participates consciously in the process of selecting alternative "realities." (Gurdjieff called this Self-Remembering; John Lilly calls it "self-metaprogramming.") By the standards of the earlier circuits, the sixth circuit libertarian appears to be a magician, a witch, a weirdo or perhaps a practical joker or clown. To hirself, the sixth circuit libertarian is engaged in *freemasonry* (to use that mystical term correctly for once), i.e. synergetic co-creation of new realities, Guerrilla Ontology, Discordianism.

Seventh circuit libertarians are Taoistic, alchemical, hermetic Evolutionary Agents. When Camus writes, "If a mass death sentence defines the human condition, rebellion is its consequence," he is defining seventh circuit libertarianism.

If fifth and sixth circuit libertarians seem spooky, few or crazy to fourth-circuit domesticated hive dwellers, seventh circuit types seem absolutely diabolical. The archetypes are Satan, Prometheus, Dr. Faustus, Baron Frankenstein, all the mad scientists in all the kitsch classics who refused to be stopped by fourth circuit moralists warning them, "There are things Man was not meant to tamper with."

If an ideal fourth-circuit hive could be built on libertarian lines (e.g. Dante's earth paradise), the seventh-circuit libertarian would scornfully leave on the next starship. SHe would visit a fifth circuit Garden of Delights for a week's vacation occasionally, but wouldn't dream of living there. A sixth circuit psionic circus (e.g. what fourth circuit types call miracles, synchronicities or parapsychological phenomena) would amuse hir for only two or three weeks. SHe is in search of nothing less than transcending the boundaries of time and space.

When Socrates drank the hemlock he acted out the greatest Zen koan in the history of the West. He was exemplifying his adoration of seventh circuit evolutionary values over first circuit bio-survival. Those who credit his act to bravery or stubbornness have not understood it.

(See the *eleuthyria* chapter of Fowles' great novel, *The Magus.*)

Eighth circuit libertarians, having transcended time and space, live already in the future. Dogen Zenji, saying "Time is three eyes and seven elbows." Chuang-Tse saying, "There is no governor anywhere." (What a glorious precognition of cybernetic biology and the quantum inseparability principle!) Crowley's notorious "Do what thou wilt shall be the whole of the Law." As a Zen classic defines this type, "He walks through the village, shirt open, grinning, looking like nobody special."

Only the eighth circuit libertarian knows that all the other types are right also, in their own way. Yositani Roshi, a great Zen teacher, used to say it to his students in these words:

"You are absolutely perfect just as you are."

The Spaghetti Theory
of Conspiracy

Introduction for *The Illuminati Conspiracy:*
The Sapiens System, by Donald Holmes, M.D.

Published by New Falcon Publications, 1987

WHO'S IN CHARGE HERE?

Pay no attention to that man behind the curtain!

– Oz the Omnipotent

It is characteristic of the primitive conditions on this backward planet that virtually nobody knows any of the basic facts about how the human race is actually governed. For instance –

1: Governments are not nearly as important as most people think. Since we live in a post-barter economy – a money economy – those who **control the money supply** effectively **control the planet**.

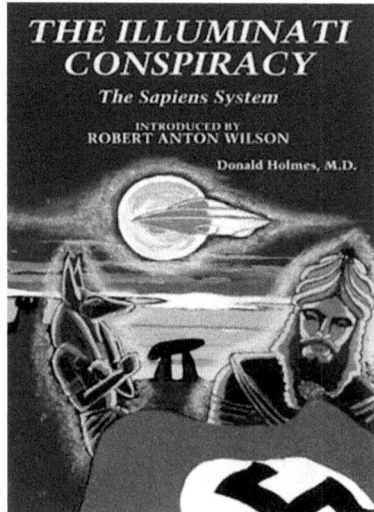

A Non-Euclidean Perspective

Governments gave up all attempt to coin or control money in the 19th century, mostly because they did not trust one another, i.e. no nation had faith that the coinage or currency of another nation was really worth what it claimed to be worth. The great International Banks stepped into this vacuum and, by demonstrating more fiscal rectitude than governments had in the past, became the creators of money in the modern world.

After the banks had control, they no longer needed to be quite so prim in their fiscal rectitude. Nobody could challenge them.

This means that governments cannot do *anything* – good or ill, wise or foolish – unless the banks first lend them the money for the project. The power is in the banks. The governments survive on the permission of the banks. If the banks cut off their credit, governments die. Any government that resists has its credit cut off and dies.

As Buckminster Fuller stressed in all his writings (especially *Critical Path* and *Grunch of Giants*) this means that, in the modern world, banks **act** and governments only **re-act** to the situations the bankers have ordained. Even earlier, historian Brooks Adams wrote of the British financier Samuel Loyd, in *The Law of Civilization and Decay,*

> He comprehended that, with expanding trade, an inelastic currency must rise in value; he saw that, with sufficient resources at command, his class might be able to establish such a rise, almost at pleasure; certainly that they could manipulate it when it came, by taking advantage of foreign exchange.

In other words, as soon as the great multi-national banks had control of the money supply, they saw that they could manipulate cash and credit to maximize profits. They would have been rather dense if they had not seen this. Nonetheless, while these financiers quite sanely and legally maximize profits, the rest of us are at their mercy; but we never elected them to this position of power, and, by and large, we do not even know who they are.

2: In the present decade, it costs $50,000,000 to run a campaign for the presidency of the United States, $10,000,000 to run a campaign for the Senate and $5,000,000 for the House of Representatives. (These figures are documented in Buckminster Fuller's *Grunch of Giants.*) This means that the U.S. – the strongest country in the West – is not only "owned" (in trillion-dollar debt to) the banks, but also governed by persons who are either (a) millionaires or (b) heavily in debt to millionaires. In the words of ex-Senator Pettigrew, we now have "government of the corporations, by the corporations, for the corporations."

3: As Edward Luttwak documents in his cheerfully Machiavellian little text, *The Coup d'Etat,* more governments have been changed, since World War II, by the *coup d'état* than by any other method. More governments have been changed by *coup* than by all the democratic elections and revolutions combined.

Since every *coup* is by definition a conspiracy, this means that conspiracies have had more effect on the past 40 years of world history than all the electoral politics and all the popular revolutions added together. That is rather ominous, in a period when "educated" opinion holds that it is infamous, nutty, eccentric or downright paranoid to think about conspiracies at all. We are, in effect, forbidden to think about how the planet is actually governed.

4: If governments cannot act without permission of the banks – without loans or "lines of credit" granted by the banks – and if the U.S. government is "owned" by the multi-millionaire (or billionaire) banking and corporate elite, and if other governments are, more often than not, changed by conspiratorial *coup,* the major portion of humanity is economically-politically controlled by persons who are largely unknown to the general public and/or have never been elected to any office. Democratic theory is beautiful and inspirational, but has nothing to do with the actual situation of the domesticated primates of this boondocks planet.

5: If the masses of the planet are politically-economically controlled by shadowy financiers and conspiratorial adventurers, the same masses are *intellectually* controlled by persons who are more visible but equally unpalatable to the Rationalist view of history. In blunt language, nearly 300 years after the Age of Reason was prematurely announced, most people in most nations most of the time are mentally in total bondage to religious leaders who operate on sheer bluff, i.e. on the basis of claims that cannot be proven and appear clearly insane to everybody who hasn't been raised within their frameworks.

The Methodist can see how absurd are the beliefs of Roman Catholics. The Catholics can see the obvious insanity of the Sikh militants who blow up airplanes because there are a few Hindus aboard. The Sikhs, no doubt, can see how nonsensical Scientology is. But none of the people processed by any of these cults can see how crazy their own cult is. It is often quite hard for a rational observer to determine if the leaders of these cults are just cynically raking in the cash or are genuinely as deluded as their brainwashed followers.

One can acquire a reputation as a satirist, a wit, a cynic, etc. simply by stating blunt facts. For instance, it is quite clear from the above that the human race is largely governed politico-economically by unknown financial cliques and criminal scoundrels and governed intellectually by borderline psychotics and charlatans. But we have all been so conditioned and indoctrinated that to state the facts simply makes it sound as if one is being sarcastic or perhaps even trying to be "shocking."

Let us look at the situation of this planet in a little more detail.

SOCIOBIOLOGY OF DECEIT

All men are born liars.

— Liam O'Flaherty, *Autobiography* (first
sentence)

Conspiracy is the first manifestation of intelligent life.

The original organic molecules formed affinity groups and conspired to exploit the resources of this planet. Working in small cells originally, these DNA conquistadores quickly developed organizations of higher complexity and spread a network of hungry, predatory Life over the previously dead Earth. In less than 3,500,000,000 years this network has expanded from the ocean beds to the very peaks on the Himalayas. No square centimeter of Earth is uninfested.

The trapdoor spiders formed their own secret society and went underground. They lurked silently, hidden beneath a plausible surface of twigs and soil, waiting to pounce out and devour any beetle or other tasty-looking morsel that happened to pass by.

The day of the undercover agent had come.

This technique of cover-up and disguise has proven an evolutionary success and is widely copied everywhere. Thousands of species of conspiratorial insects even today still hide behind ingenious make-up that deceives us into thinking they are only branches or rocks.

Other species got even smarter even faster. Polar bears donned white fur coats to fade into snowy landscapes. The leopard's spots make it hard to distinguish from speckled sunlight on foliage. The Norway rat *(mus rattus Norvegicus)* learned to hide by day and come forth under cover of darkness.

The first human beings looked about them and very sensibly concluded, "It's a jungle out there."

Human psychology has remained jungle psychology. As historian Carl Oglesby writes in *The Yankee and Cowboy War*

A Non-Euclidean Perspective

> . . . a multitude of conspiracies contend in the night.
> Conspiracy is the normal continuation of normal
> politics by normal means . . . and where there is no
> limit to power, there is no limit to conspiracy.

As soon as we find evidence of human beings on this planet, we find evidence of secret societies. Paleolithic paintings show that they met, typically, in the deepest, darkest caves, and they plotted sorcery and mischief against all competing species.

In every tribe known to anthropology, we still find secret societies. Most tribes have all-male secret societies, but many also have all-female secret societies. Most readers will probably remember that they had their own secret societies as children, with passwords and quasi-Freemasonic grips determinedly hidden from the adults.

From this evolutionary perspective, every paranoid is partly right. The major error of the paranoid appears to be his characteristic belief in one jumbo Mega-Conspiracy that explains everything. This is impossible, because it violates basic laws of primate psychology. Domesticated primates like wild primates are mischievous, sly and have a keen sense of humor: **the double-cross is their most characteristic invention**.

George Washington, who rose to power by conspiring against his king, said with blunt honesty, "Nations have no permanent allies, only permanent interests." This is why governments, corporations and other large-scale conspiracies all have a *natural life-span,* like other living systems. There is no government on this planet that has existed in its present form for more than 200 years; aside from the Dutch East India Company, most corporations rise and fall within 100 years (average). Outside of paranoid fantasy and Romantic fiction, most conspiracies collapse of their own "internal contradictions" within months or years. (Thus, if there actually is one big jumbo-conspiracy governing this planet, it must be, as Donald Holmes wittily suggests in the following pages, of non-human origin.)

The study of conspiracy *as a branch of primate psychology,* has great interest in itself, as Machiavelli knew; but real conspiracies are not as clever or long-lived as the ones that paranoids and ideologists imagine; they are simply much dirtier.

It is one of the ironies of our time that conspiracies and secret societies have proliferated more than ever **at precisely the same time it has become impolite and uncouth to discuss them**. In this sense, the Nazis defeated the Liberal Democracies in World War II, because they have achieved a form of Thought Control over the Liberal Mind. Liberals are afraid to think of conspiracies because that might lead to the One Big Mega-Conspiracy, i.e. to "thinking like Hitler." But a mind chained by Tabu is a mind unfree. I believe it is time we broke Hitler's power over our minds and began to think in terms of the facts instead of being restrained by Tabu.

Disguise, deception and group-action have a long evolutionary history, and primates have all these traditional evolutionary habits, which in political jargon are called conspiratorial habits. Even if it is Tabu to think about it, that seems to be the way things are on this planet.

TRUE CONFESSIONS

> When four sit down to conspire, three are fools and the fourth is a government agent.
>
> – Duncan Lunan, *Interstellar Communication*

Frankly I myself never dared to violate the Liberal Tabu – "Thou shalt not think about conspiracies" – until I was virtually *forced* to think about them.

In the 1960s in Chicago, I was involved in the anti-war movement. Congressional investigators later revealed that there were over 5000 government agents assigned to infiltrate peace groups in Chicago alone – some working for the Federal Bureau of Investigation (FBI), some for the Central Intelligence Agency (CIA) and some for Army Intelligence. From 1968 on, the FBI was following a program code-named COINTELPRO. The purpose of COINTELPRO was to make sure the anti-war movement *knew* it was infiltrated, in order to spread suspicion, distrust and paranoia among individuals and groups who might otherwise have cooperated harmoniously. Working in the peace movement in those days was, accordingly, like living in an Eric Ambler novel. In any given week I would be warned perhaps three times that somebody I trusted was really a government agent, and, of course, somebody who was accused one day might very well be around to accuse somebody else the next day. Over 20 years later, I still don't know who was a government agent and who was not. I enjoyed it all rather than being terrified only because I basically agree with Helen Keller that "Life is either a great adventure or it is nothing."

I encountered the same Spy Story atmosphere in the early 1970s when involved in the campaign to secure the release from prison of the controversial scientist, Dr. Timothy Leary. At one time or another, everybody in the Leary Defense Committee suspected everybody else of being a government agent (I think the poet, Allen Ginsberg, suspected me for over a year) and eventually government "leaks" in the press attempted to persuade us that Dr. Leary himself had become a government agent. I still relish that classic John Le Carre touch, especially since some people believed it.

Eventually it was confirmed that Leary's son-in-law, Dennis Martino, had been entrapped into becoming a government agent. Dennis later died in Spain and three press reports in two days claimed the cause of death had been murder, suicide and accident. That mystery is still unsolved, at least in America. Presumably, the Spanish authorities finally came up with a coroner's verdict, which may or may not be the truth, but by then the U.S. media had lost interest. As far as you can learn from American sources, Dennis Martino accidentally overdosed, committed suicide *and* was murdered, all on the same day. Evidently, nobody in the U.S. media wanted to find out what the hell really happened.

But there are wheels within wheels in this modern Machiavellian world.

During the last year of my employment as Associate Editor of *Playboy,* a certain executive came into my office one day and closed the door behind him. He told me that my home phone was tapped and that I was under heavy surveillance by the Red Squad of the Chicago Police Force.

I was stunned, and asked how the hell he knew this.

He replied that certain people in the *Playboy* empire had made an arrangement with a Chicago police official. The official received regular money through some circuitous route that was not explained to me; in return, he notified his *Playboy* contacts whenever an executive of the firm was under police investigation.

That was when I first realized how often there are spies spying on spies.

Incidentally, my informant told me *why* I was under heavy surveillance. A police informer in the Black Panthers, he said, had reported that I was involved with a group of white radicals who were buying guns for the Panthers.

Despite my cynicism about cops, I was shocked. I explained heatedly that there was no truth in this at all. "We know, we know," said the executive, who was very close to Hefner. "We trust you."

And they did trust me. They never made any attempt to ease me out the back door, or dissociate the Bunny Empire from me. They even offered to pay my legal expenses if the police ever busted me on this absurd charge.

It was years before I wondered why the Bunny Empire decided to trust me in such an explosive matter. My guess, now, is that they had me under surveillance, too, along with their other editors – but that's only a guess. Maybe it was just that I have an honest face. I'd like to think that.

Of course, I was *not* buying guns for the Black Panthers. I had met a few Panthers at Peace rallies, and the informer had seen me. He or she had probably "improved" the story to impress the Red Squad. A *Playboy* editor talking to Black Panthers is not all that sensational, but a *Playboy* editor buying guns for the Panthers was a story that made the informer seem on the edge of discovering a major conspiracy.

I could tell several similar stories, but I would again have to conceal the names of my sources and you would probably not believe me. Truth is much, much stranger than melodrama.

Instead I will examine the neuro-economics of conspiracy and then relate some notable conspiracies that have become matters of public record. We will see that the theories outlined by Dr. Holmes in this book are, however shocking, no more bizarre than the world in which we live.

WEALTH AND "MONEY"

A banker is a man who will loan you money
if you can prove you don't need it.

– attributed to Mark Twain

Just as most people have no idea how this planet is governed at this barbaric stage of evolution, most people have no concept of where "wealth" comes from. This is because most of us have never learned to distinguish between wealth and *money*.

Money was originally created by the State, as I mentioned at the beginning; this is why King Lear says his persecutors can't accuse him of counterfeiting. The State was, in those days, the only legal creator of coin: a legal coin was, by definition, a State coin.

As States learned the advantages to be gained by issuing debased coinage – a matter discussed with great clarity and wit in Jonathan Swift's little-known but brilliant *Drapier Letters* – every State and every individual became the potential victim of coins that did not contain the amount of gold stamped on them. Eventually, no State would trust any other State in this area and, more and more, the *paper* of the great banking firms began to seem the only "safe" medium of exchange.

The U.S. Constitution, amusingly, says that Congress shall have the power to coin money and regulate the value thereof, but Congress has not exercised that power in over a century. Official U.S. money is issued by a private bank, just like the money of all other nations (except Albania, a lonely heretic), but, because U.S. money says "Federal Reserve Note" on it, most Americans assume it is issued by the Federal government. It is issued, actually, by the Federal Reserve Corporation, a private bank, owned largely by the Rockefellers and Morgans. We do not "owe the National Debt to ourselves" as the late Franklin Roosevelt once said; we owe it to the Rockefellers and Morgans.

Irish money says "Bank of Ireland" on it and English money says "Bank of England," and so on; all across Europe, most people know that the banks are in control of the creation of money. Only in America, because the word "Federal" in **Federal Reserve** is thought to mean *"federal"* and because the Constitution says Congress shall coin money, is there a lingering belief that the government is still a sovereign entity not owned by the bankers to whom it is in debt.

None of this has anything to do with Real Wealth in the sense of classical economics.

Real Wealth, in the economic sense, consists of tangible assets. It includes, not only plants in operation "owned" by individual or corporate capitalists, but known resources, inventions, bridges, roads, scientific data – all the creations of human intelligence that can be concretely applied to make the human environment more pleasant for somebody or for everybody.

Thus, if all the Real Wealth disappeared over night, *the world would be entirely different.* We would literally be back in the Old Stone Age, and no amount of Federal Reserve Notes or other paper would change our situation. We would have to re-invent and re-create all the science and technology of the past 30,000 years step by step.

On the other hand, all the money in the world – all the Federal Reserve Notes, Bank of England notes, etc. and all the stocks and bonds – could disappear over night and *the world would be exactly the same physically.* There might be a hell of a fight over *who* owned *what,* but the human world of Real Wealth would still be here.

In kindergarten language, Real Wealth consists of "things" that can't be stored in banks or computers, while money consists of "tickets" or symbols that can be stored in banks or computers.

Of course, Real Wealth is more than solid "things." I have been arguing for 30 years, in various publications, that Real Wealth is essentially pure information. It has finally dawned on me that nobody understands that but a few mathematicians and computer buffs, so I now say, more simply, that Real Wealth is **ideas that work.** In the terminology of General Semantics, Wealth is ideas that are similar in structure (isomorphic) to the energy systems of space-time.

Wealth is created by analysis: by extracting higher-order structure from the raw signals perceived by the senses. You can starve to death in a wheat field if your mind has not analyzed the energy system of space-time sufficiently to recognize that wheat is edible and nourishing.

Money, then, is not Real Wealth, but consists of tickets for the exchange of Real Wealth. Such tickets are necessary in an advanced technology-economy-society, because barter becomes cumbersome and unwieldy.

Most money, however, does not exist in tangible form at all, not even as *paper.* Most money, in today's advanced techno-society, exists only as computer records or, in less advanced outposts, notations in ledgers. Banks may legally lend up to *eight times* the amount they have on deposit, and as Penny Lernoux documents in her invaluable *In Banks We Trust,* they often go far beyond this and hope to cover their tracks before the bank examiner comes around.

Michele Sindona, a kingpin of the Vatican/Mafia/P2 clique and founder of the infamous Franklin National Bank, was convicted of murdering a bank examiner in Italy, after being convicted of 65 counts of bank fraud in the U.S. His principle flaw appears to have been that he was more reckless than older and wiser financiers who have been running the world longer and more judiciously. (We shall return to the Sindona/P2 case history.)

When banks lend eight times what they have on deposit, or more than that, they are gambling that everybody will not come in and withdraw their funds on the same day. It is a safe gamble, most of the time. But it means that paper wealth has become even more metaphysical and ghostly than the most debased coinage of the most corrupt Tudor or Stuart monarchs. It means that, by a species of magic, the Real Wealth of the planet can be manipulated as the ghostly paper is maneuvered from one computer to another. And it means that the really bold adventurers and pirates can alchemically transform totally unreal paper into ownership of resources, factories, roads, bridges and whole nations on occasion, as they, following Samuel Loyd, "establish a rise . . . at their pleasure," or just as easily establish a fall.

The reader should consult some of the books I will be summarizing here – especially illuminating is Richard Hammer's *The Vatican Connection,* which tells how Johnny Roselli and his friends in the American Mafia printed one billion dollars worth of counterfeit stocks which disappeared into the Vatican Bank/Banco Ambrosiano feedback loop in such a manner that the New York District Attorney's office, which had wiretaps on most of the felons, never did find out where the $900,000,000 of the $1,000,000,000 finally landed.

Buckminster Fuller, in *Grunch of Giants,* describes the modern world as governed by MMA&O – Machiavelli, Mafia, Atoms and Oil. You know the Mafia. Atoms and Oil are the multi-national corporations. Machiavelli is the symbol of the paper-magic wizards, or international banks, who make the whole system possible. GRUNCH stands for *GRoss UNiversal Cash Heist.* It's another book you really ought to read.

NEURO-GEOGRAPHY OF CONSPIRACY

Go West, young man.

– Horace Greeley

As I pointed out in *Prometheus Rising,* the Real Wealth of the world has been doubling every generation since statistical economists started collecting data in the 18th century. This is a side-effect of the accelerated doubling of knowledge that has been occurring in the past two millenniums. (Information, or ideas-that- work, is the source of Real Wealth. Remember?) As George Anderla, a French statistician, determined, if we take all the knowledge of 1 A.D. as our base, then knowledge has doubled at the following rate since then:

1 AD – 1 unit
1500 AD – 2
1750 AD – 4
1900 AD – 8
1950 AD – 16
1960 AD – 32
1967 AD – 64
1973 AD – 128

A glance at world-historical trajectories indicates that this doubling of knowledge-and-wealth has followed a western (and mildly northern) vector, as has been documented e.g. in Brooks Adams' *Law of Civilization and Decay,* Timothy Leary's *The Intelligence Agents* and Buckminster Fuller's *Critical Path.*

Bronze Age tools first appeared in Southeast Asia, followed by large-scale agriculture, slavery and war. By 1 A.D. all the technology thus far produced was being processed through the schools and banking establishments of Rome. By the time this knowledge/wealth doubled in 1500, the universities of North Italy and the great Florentine banking families like the Medici held the hot center of power. By 1750, the next doubling was occurring mostly in England, the first Empire "on which the sun never set."

By 1900, the U.S. was becoming a rival to England; by 1950, the American Empire had replaced the English Empire. The years since 1950 have witnessed what Prof. Oglesby calls "the Yankee and Cowboy war" as Eastern bankers like the Rockefellers try to hold on to control and are challenged by Western mavericks like Howard Hughes.

The more adventurous and innovative persons – those with nervous systems programmed by maverick genes and/ or bizarre imprints and conditioning: the "misfits" – have been moving steadily westward for about 5000 years. They have been moving away from centralized Authority, out into the perimeters and frontiers, because that is where misfits and geniuses can function.

Clausewitz described war as a continuation of politics by other means; Oglesby calls conspiracy "the normal continuation of normal politics by normal means." Conspiracy, the murky territory between politics and war, is part of our glorious primate heritage, which is why Ambrose Bierce defined peace as "a period of cheating between two periods of fighting."

The role of conspiracy in human history, I suggest, is a period of cheating during which two power centers are struggling, one of them Eastward and representing established ideas and old wealth, the other Westward and generally representing maverick ideas and new wealth. Enclaves of "outlaws" move in the shadowy territory between these two power poles, running their own games and exploiting the paranoia of each side where and when they can.

Anthropologist William Irwin Thompson has suggested, in a recent address in Oslo, Norway, that the Reagan administration's Strategic Defense Initiative – the so-called "Star Wars" program – is more radical, and less reactionary, than it looks on the surface. Thompson alleges that, under the pretext of military bluster, SDI actually represents the total re-alignment of American society into a scientific-technological paradigm. Only the most "patriotic" rhetoric, Thompson says, could sell to the American people a program which amounts to the most expensive and most daring scientific research-and-development project humanity has ever attempted. In this context, Reagan represents the "Cowboy elite" that Oglesby sees as being on the edge of toppling the Rockefeller and other Yankee empires. The Cowboys are looking for a High Frontier, and they are computerized Cowboys now.

Werner von Braun used Disney world – both the amusement park and the TV show – to "sell" NASA's more adventurous ideas to the politicians by first selling them to the people. General Graham, who gave the "Star Wars" idea to Reagan, is following the same scenario. Amid the 24 separate-and-interlocking conspiracies struggling over the turf on this planet, the Cowboys are struggling for higher and more imaginative lands in the stars. Why not? They are, in the 20th century, the same sort of mavericks the Yankees were in the 18th century – namely, "the products of the Protestantism of the Protestants and the dissidence of dissent," as Edmund Burke said of the wealthy radicals who wrote the Declaration of Independence. The coming dominant looks to be, like California, a mad mixture of Hollywood, computers, special effects, apocalyptical visions and dope. Reagan does not fully understand the neuro-geography of the historical forces he represents.

The next dominant will probably be further west and more technological.

If we revise our chart of the doubling of knowledge (Real Wealth) to include these factors we find:

DATE	KNOWLEDGE FACTOR	CENTER OF POWER	PRINCIPLE ENEMIES
1 AD	1	Rome	Greece, Egypt
1500 AD	2	Florence	Turks
1750 AD	4	England	France, Spain
1900 AD	8	England	Germany
1950 AD	16	New York	Russia
1960 AD	32	California	Russia
1967 AD	64	California	Russia
1973 AD	128	California	New York
?	256	California	Japan

The rising power always seems to the West or Northwest of the declining power that struggles against it; it is always richer and more powerful than any previous Empire; it always seems to the older power center (and its kept intellectuals) exactly what California seems today – a kind of sociological Granola made up of equal parts of fruits, nuts and flakes.

THE C.I.A. & THE MAFIA

Patriotism, sir, is the last recourse of the scoundrel.
— Dr. Samuel Johnson

In the 1960s, the CIA conspired with two Mafia leaders, Sam Giancana and Johnny Roselli. Mr. Giancana and Mr. Roselli provided professional Mafia assassins and the CIA trained them and sent them to Cuba to kill Fidel Castro. Like most real conspiracies, this was unsuccessful; Señor Castro is still alive. This conspiracy was also well documented in Congressional hearings and broadcast in the news media internationally, so you are not considered a crank if you write about it.

You will begin to understand what I call the Spaghetti Theory of Conspiracy when I remind you that Johnny Roselli was also involved in printing one billion dollars ($1,000,000,000) worth of counterfeit stock for the Vatican Bank. That is documented fully in *The Vatican Connection* by *N.Y. Times* reporter Richard Hammer, which I again recommend to your attention.

According to Anthony Summers' book *Conspiracy,* there is a good *prima facie* case that Johnny Roselli was also an instigator of the assassinations of both John and Bobby Kennedy, in collaboration with Sam Giancana – the same Giancana who had previously collaborated with Roselli in providing assassins for the CIA. While Summers' evidence is not conclusive, it is chillingly plausible.

The House Select Committee on Assassinations concluded, on the basis of the hard scientific evidence of acoustics, that there were **two** gunmen shooting at John Kennedy in Dealy Plaza, one from the front and one from the back. On the basis of softer but persuasive supporting evidence, the Committee concluded further that a conspiracy of more than two persons was probable and that the possibility of Mafia involvement was worthy of deeper investigation.

The Chief Counsel for the Committee, Prof. Howard Blakey, was willing to be more definitive in a press conference. "I am now firmly of the opinion that the mob did it," he said. "It is a historical truth." (Quoted by Summers in *Conspiracy.*)

Sam Giancana was shot dead in June 1975, after testifying once before the committee and while negotiating with their investigators about further questions they wished to ask him under oath. Giancana was shot through the mouth – the *sasso in bocca,* traditional Mafia punishment for suspected informers.

Johnny Roselli was shot dead in July 1976, after he, too, had been called once before the Assassinations Committee. According to journalist Jack Anderson, Roselli had told him that he was not involved in the Kennedy assassinations but another Mafia "family" was.

The Mafia has acquired its international empire only because the most popular drugs of our time are illegal. In the past 40 years, the rulers of the Mafia have graduated from multi-millionaires to billionaires *only* because these absurd anti-drug laws remain on the books.

It is permissible in "liberal" "educated" circles to say that these laws remain in force because of stupidity or conservatism or superstition. If you say the laws remain because somebody is making a profit out of them, you are supposed to be eccentric or downright nutty.

Nonetheless, the ancient Romans knew that the basic question about any social policy was – **cui bono?** (Who profits from it?)

INTERLUDE & *KOAN*

In CIA jargon, a "useful idiot" means somebody who is working for them but doesn't know it.

My involvements with controversial politics have left me with one lasting legacy. Whenever I suspect that I am taking myself or my theories too seriously, I stop and ask myself, "Have I become a *useful idiot* yet?"

THE STATE AS CONSPIRACY

The more laws that are written, the more
criminals are produced.

– Lao-Tse, *Tao Te Ching*

It is likely that the State as we know it is an innately conspiratorial organism. As the sociologist Franz Oppenheimer pointed out in his remarkable book *The State,* there is no anthropological or historical evidence that anything like Rousseau's "Social Contract" ever happened in pre-history; on the contrary, the State appears in human affairs only after conquest by armed force. It is to maintain themselves in power over the conquered that a conquering elite create those institutions – police, army, taxation – that make up the skeleton of the State as we know it historically. There is no record of a tribal people peacefully "contracting" to set such a machinery of oppression above themselves. Conquerors impose it upon them.

Bakunin argued in *God and the State* that nobody has ever *seen* "God" or the "State." This, although startling, is true. Human beings, called priests, claim to represent "God," and other human beings, called civil servants, claim to represent the "State," and this metaphysical sleight-of-hand is alleged to justify acts which would be regarded as not only criminal but barbarous if it were remembered that mere human beings were doing these things. Similar verbal magic – meaningless words like "heresy" and "treason" – are used to convince the victims that resistance is evil, escape or flight is just as evil, and even thinking that you are being victimized is somehow sinful.

In simple language, anybody who robs you is a thief, unless he claims to be an agent of the "State" – in which case, he is not a thief but only a tax-collector. By the same metaphysical trick, anybody who murders millions is a lunatic, unless he claims to be an agent of "God" – in which case he is a Crusader. You can resist an ordinary bandit with a perfect sense of righteousness, but you feel guilty about resisting the Churchman or Statesman, since that is called "heresy" or "treason."

Since the State was founded in conquest and is maintained by metaphysics (or, in the Logical Positivist jargon, "abuse of language"), it follows Oglesby's rule – "where there is no limit to power, there is no limit to conspiracy."

We have already cited Anthony Summers' book *Conspiracy* to indicate that there is real evidence, not mere paranoia, behind the claim that the Mafia was involved, perhaps centrally, in the Kennedy assassinations. According to Summers' more recent book *Goddess,* there is also good evidence that Sam Giancana and Johnny Roselli had arranged for the electronic bugging of the bedroom of a house belonging to Peter Lawford, where Marilyn Monroe and Bobby Kennedy met for romantic dalliance in what they thought was privacy. Jimmy Hoffa of the Teamsters' Union, who had been imprisoned by Bobby's "get-tough" Justice Department, was allegedly also involved in this plot, which was intended to obtain material with which Bobby could be blackmailed. A BBC documentary on Summers' book – *Say Goodbye to the President,* BBC-TV 1985 – supported all of Summers' charges.

Giancana and Roselli were both shot in the mid-1970s, as we have seen. Jimmy Hoffa simply "disappeared" and has never been found dead or alive. Rumor claims he is buried beneath an interstate highway in Illinois.

Norman Mailer, many of you might remember, became convinced, while researching his biography of Marilyn Monroe, that there was some kind of "cover-up" connected with her death. Mailer even implied that there was a definite possibility of murder.

According to Summers' *Goddess* and the BBC documentary previously cited, there was indeed a conspiracy in which Marilyn's death was concealed for three hours while persons unknown removed from her house all documentia of her love affairs with John and Bobby Kennedy. The weight of circumstantial evidence suggests that this conspiracy was instigated by Peter Lawford, who had, as we noted, loaned his house as a trysting place for Marilyn's affairs, and who was also brother-in-law to the Kennedys. It is not demonstrable that Lawford ever thought, or allowed himself to think, that he might also be concealing clues in a murder case. He probably thought, or wanted to think, that he was merely concealing politically embarrassing sexual dalliances. The possibility of murder remains only a possibility, although it is still insisted upon by Hank Messick, a former consultant to the New York Joint Legislative Committee on Crime. Messick claims that unnamed informants in the Mafia told him Marilyn was killed to lure Bobby Kennedy into a trap and then blackmail him into ending his crusade against the Mob.

All one can say about that theory is "Maybe."

Nonetheless, another of John Kennedy's mistresses – although he did not pass her on to Bobby – was one Judith Exner. Ms. Exner, the House Select Committee on Assassinations later noted, was, curiously enough, the mistress of Mafioso Sam Giancana before, during and after her affair with the President. The Committee was of the opinion that it was probable that Mr. Giancana more or less shoved Ms. Exner into the President's bed, for blackmail purposes. Mr. Giancana, you may remember, was also suspected by the Committee of having a hand in JFK's assassination, and died of gunshot wounds – through the mouth – while under investigation.

Another of JFK's *amours* was with a Mary Pinchot Meyer, a most interesting lady. She was married to Cord Meyer, a top CIA official who happens to be the only man to have received the Agency's Distinguished Intelligence Medal three times. Mary Pinchot Meyer was also a dear and good friend of Dr. Timothy Leary; and, according to his book *Flashbacks,* Mary told Dr. Leary in 1962 that the CIA wanted to stop him and other scientists from publishing LSD experiments, because they wanted to keep the mind-altering properties of LSD one of their own little secrets.

In 1964, about a year after John Kennedy was assassinated (or about two years after the somewhat mysterious death of Marilyn Monroe), Mary Pinchot Meyer was shot dead on a street in Washington.

Thereafter Dr. Leary was repeatedly arrested, and although every case against him except one was dismissed by the courts, he was finally convicted in that one case, which involved alleged possession of one half of one marijuana cigarette. He was sentenced to 37 years – although the penalty for that crime in that state (California) was normally six months – and was released after serving over five years. Dr. Leary claims he was framed by the arresting officer; he also claims there was a cover-up in the shooting of Mary Pinchot Meyer. Nobody much cares what Dr. Leary claims, because for over a year before his release government officials had leaked to the press claims that he had become an informer. There is no record of any person or persons convicted on the basis of Dr. Leary's testimony, oddly, but the rumor has stuck to his name and "everybody knows" he is a government agent these days.

As the French say, it gives one ferociously to think.

PROPAGANDA DUE (P2)

Make him an offer he can't refuse.

– Don Corleone

As most people know by now, the first degree initiation into Freemasonry contains the warning that if the candidate ever betrays his fellow Freemasons he will be hunted down and hanged where the rising tide will cover his dead body. We are not supposed to think about that at all. That is only "ritual" and isn't meant to be taken literally. Besides, Hitler had delusions about Freemasons and therefore to think about Freemasons hanging people means that we are becoming weird and might turn into Nazis overnight if we don't watch ourselves.

On the morning of 18 June 1982, the body of Roberto Calvi, a Freemason, was found hanging from Blackfriars Bridge in London, where the rising tide had covered his dead body.

A Non-Euclidean Perspective

Liberal opinion – or as it also calls itself Education Opinion – absolutely forbids us to think a rather obvious thought at this point.

Still, it does seem **possible** that Signor Calvi was killed by Freemasons **or by persons who devoutly wish us to believe he was killed by Freemasons**.

At the time of his death, Calvi was in flight from Italy where he had been indicted for massive stock and currency frauds. As president of Banco Ambrosiano, Calvi had been one of the principle managers of Vatican financial affairs, due to the close symbiosis between Banco Ambrosiano and the IOR or Vatican Bank; his financial piracy had left the Vatican in debt hundreds of millions of dollars. His widow, Clara Calvi, has repeatedly asserted that persons "high in the Vatican" ordered the murder of her husband.

Mrs. Calvi's claim is not supported by English journalist Stephen Knight who argues in *The Brotherhood* that Calvi was killed by his fellow Freemasons in the notorious **P2 (Propaganda Due) lodge.** Two other investigative journalists, Foote and della Torre, however, offer a third verdict; in their *Unsolved: The Mysterious Death of God's Banker* they endeavor to prove that Calvi, who had admittedly been "laundering" Mafia drug money through Banco Ambrosiano and the Vatican Bank, had been killed by the Mafia for double-crossing them in a heroin deal.

The first coroner's hearing on Calvi declared, admittedly on the basis of incomplete evidence, that the banker hanged himself. After widespread press criticism, a second coroner's hearing returned an "open" verdict, meaning that the cause of Calvi's death is unknown. The major argument against suicide, discussed in all the books on the case, is that Calvi was hanging from an under-girder of the bridge which appears to be difficult of access even for a trained acrobat – and Calvi was 62 years old, overweight and never seems to have been concerned with exercise or physical fitness at all.

Is it paranoid or extravagant to suspect conspiracy in the Calvi death?

Calvi was found with bricks stuffed down the front of his trousers, a hard fact to explain rationally; but the symbolism reeks of Freemasonry.

The day Calvi was found hanging from the bridge in London, his secretary Graziella Carrocher, died mysteriously in Milan: she fell or jumped or was pushed out of a window of Calvi's Banco Ambrosiano.

The quasi-Freemasonic secret society to which Calvi belonged, **P2**, has been accused by Italian investigating magistrates of multitudinous financial frauds, laundering Mafia drug money, infiltrating over 950 agents into the Italian government, carrying out terrorist bombings, and conspiring to install a fascist government in Italy by *coup d'état.* Financial reporter Penny Lernoux, in her book *In Banks* We *Trust,* adds to this that there is considerable evidence that **P2** was the main financial backer of fascist regimes in Latin America and helped many Nazi war criminals, including the notorious Klaus Barbie, find new identities and employment in the CIA-backed death squads which maintain the power of these fascist governments. P2, Lernoux documents, was largely responsible for the return to power of the fascist Perón regime in Argentina, and Perón personally thanked Licoo Gelli, Grandmaster of P2.

In 1978 – four years before Calvi died in London – the editor of a Rome magazine, *L'osservatore Politico,* Mino Pecorelli, sent Pope John Paul I an issue of his journal in which he named over a hundred **P2** members and/or members of other Freemasonic lodges who had jobs in the Vatican (especially in the IOR or Vatican Bank, which worked so closely with Calvi's Banco Ambrosiano). The Pope died shortly thereafter in ambiguous circumstances – no autopsy was performed and the Vatican has refused to show the death certificate to enquiring journalists.

David Yallop's controversial *In God's Name* is an attempt

to prove that the Pope was poisoned by a conspiracy of Vatican officials who were members of, or allied with, **P2**. Mr. Yallop does not, in any legal sense, prove his case, but he does make it highly plausible.

Whatever the facts about the death of Pope John Paul I may be, there is no mystery at all about the death of Signor Pecorelli, the editor who sent the **P2** list to the Pope. Pecorelli was shot dead in his car. Both fatal bullets entered through the mouth, in the classic Mafia form of execution – the same *sasso in bocca* that was used by the killers of Sam Giancana. It seems undeniable, then, that Pecorelli was killed by the Mafia **or by persons who devoutly wish us to think he was killed by the Mafia**.

COCAINE, THE C.I.A. AND THE POPE

Cocaine is just nature's way of telling you
that you have too much money.

– Richard Pryor

The most provocative moment in the famous "Watergate tapes" occurs when President Nixon agrees to pay E. Howard Hunt $1,000,000 not to spill "that whole Bay of Pigs thing." It is hard to imagine what Bay of Pigs "thing" had not been revealed by 1973, when that conversation took place, or why Nixon would pay such a huge sum to keep it covered up.

Part of the answer probably relates to the odd symbiosis between the CIA and the Mafia which we have already noted. Mr. Hunt was an employee of the CIA at the time the Agency was involved in assassination plots with Mr. Roselli and Mr. Giancana, and while the Bay of Pigs invasion was being plotted.

Another part of the answer, perhaps, lies in the story of the World Finance Corporation, a bank in Miami, Florida, which went bankrupt after its top officials were indicted, in

1981, for knowingly laundering the cocaine money of various Latin American dictators. The President of the World Finance Corporation was one Hernandez Cataya, who had also served in the CIA with Mr. Hunt while the Bay of Pigs was being plotted.

Two other executives of the World Finance Corporation also turned out to be former CIA employees.

To be a "former" CIA agent can mean one of two things. It can mean that the person has left the Agency and has no more connection with them, or it can mean that the person is still working for them and receiving compensation through a numbered Swiss bank account although no longer on the records as their employee. Only God and the CIA know what it means in the case of the World Finance Corporation and its lucrative cocaine business that also supported some of the Agency's favorite dictators.

Financial reporter Penny Lernoux, who discusses this curious bank at length in her *In Banks We Trust,* quotes members of both the District Attorney's staff of Dade County and a Congressional Committee who say bluntly that attempts to discover the exact role of the CIA in the World Finance Corporation were blocked by a CIA smokescreen.

However, it was learned that the cocaine money was laundered by the WFC sending it on a strange carousel that began with an even shadier bank in the Bahamas, called Cisalpine. The major owners of the Cisalpine Bank were Roberto Calvi (remember him?) and Archbishop Paul Marcinkus of the Vatican Bank. Ms. Lernoux believes the drug money passed through Calvi's Banco Ambrosiano and the Vatican Bank on its way to some financial Black Hole where law enforcement officials will never find it.

Lernoux claims – as does David Yallop in his *In God's Name* – that this profitable conspiracy was masterminded by Licio Gelli, the Grandmaster of the P2 secret society. Gelli, who has been indicted in Italy for conspiracy, murder, fraud and plotting to overthrow the government (among other things) is presently hiding out in Uruguay, after being arrested in Switzerland and escaping, in less than a week, from an allegedly escape-proof prison.

It *seems* that P2 was Signor Gelli's invention from the beginning, but this has been challenged by various investigators. Stephen Knight in *The Brotherhood* claims that Gelli was working for the KGB and tries to prove that P2 was a Soviet experiment in destabilizing a Western government; Knight bases this chiefly on the claims of a British Intelligence agent, from which we may deduce either that Gelli was working for the KGB or that the lads in MI5-London have their own reasons to wish us to believe he was working for the KGB.

Both Yallop in *In God's Name* and Lernoux in *In Banks We Trust* indicate that, while there is evidence that Gelli was recruited by the KGB at one point, there is even stronger evidence that he had been recruited by the CIA even earlier – in the 1950s, he arranged the assassinations of several Italian labour union officials whose politics were distasteful to Washington – and the weight of the data strongly suggests that Gelli was deceiving both sides in the "Intelligence war" for his own profit.

Many Italian journalists have tried to prove that Gelli and P2 were both "fronts" for another, older Freemasonic group. Larry Gurwin of the *Institutional Investor* (London), in his book *The Calvi Affair,* quotes one former P2 member as saying this mysterious lodge was headquartered in Monte Carlo.

But Gurwin also notes that Gelli was a member of the Grand Orient Lodge of Egyptian Freemasonry before P2 came into existence. The Grand Orient is well known to students of conspiracy literature. It was founded in 1771 by the duc d'Orléans and the enigmatic "Count Cagliostro" and is believed by many to have manipulated events during the French Revolution so as to advance Orléans to the kingship. If so, it was as unsuccessful as most such plots – Orléans, of course, ended on the guillotine, not the throne. Nonetheless, the Grand Orient has played a role in so many political adventures and high crimes that British Freemasons refuse to recognize it as a "real" Freemasonic lodge.

Grandmaster Licio Gelli's escape from a supposedly "escape-proof" Swiss jail has led many to speculate that P2 is as strong as it ever was, despite the prosecutions of hundreds of its members in Italy. Both Yallop and Lernoux indicate that P2 lodges are still very active throughout Latin America; Yallop insists that there is still a powerful P2 lodge in the United States.

Here it is worth noting some opinions of Roberto Calvi, as a man in a position to know what goes on below the surface of things. According to Yallop and Gurwin, Calvi recommended Mario Puzo's novel about the Mafia, *The Godfather,* on numerous occasions, saying it was the one book that tells "how the world is really run." Calvi believed in what Italians call *potere occulto* – hidden power that operates behind the scenes. His son, Carlo, says Roberto was "fascinated by secret societies" and Calvi's lawyer said to Gurwin that Roberto Calvi believed "the world is run by conspiracies."

The plural is significant. Amateurs in this field always seem to fall into the trap of thinking in terms of One Big Conspiracy, singular. This is because conspiracies, like a bowl of spaghetti, contain endless entanglements and overlaps; but to mistake the spaghetti for a coherent or intelligent organism is like mistaking the debris and flotsam on a beach for the outline of an invading army.

It is noteworthy that Gurwin, although employed by the conservative *Institutional Investor,* concludes *The Calvi Affair* – after tracing the crisscrossing paths of the Vatican, the Mafia, the CIA and Freemasonry through jungles of fraud and double-dealing – "Roberto Calvi's world view may have been far more accurate than anyone realized."

LOONY TUNES AND MERRY MELODIES

The chessboard is the world . . .
the player on the other side is hidden from us.

– Thomas Henry Huxley, *Collected Essays*

All secret societies have their own myths, like the Freemasonic allegory of the Widow's Son; but for that matter, all human groups seem to feel the need for symbol or transcendental "truth" – i.e. for myth and allegory.

Some secret societies, of course, may have real secrets, because conventional "history" and conventional "truth," in any tribe or nation, always turns out to be, as Marx said, the myth of the ruling class. The truth is always "hidden with seven seals," because **nobody is more paranoid than professional conspirators**, and the ruling elites are always afraid to let any real knowledge get into general circulation.

Those who hoard money, land titles, etc. also hoard information; it is a mammalian reflex. It is always a key rule of strategy in all competitive games, as von Neumann and Morgenstern documented mathematically in their *Theory of Games and Economic Behavior.* Hiding information and spreading false information are successful strategies in poker, economic competition and hot and cold wars. All the existing government stamps saying **TOP SECRET** or **FOR YOUR EYES ONLY** are exemplifications of this primate habit of hoarding information.

In this connection, consider first Father Juan Krohn, who attempted to assassinate Pope John Paul II at Fatima in 1982. Father Krohn told the court at his trial that the Vatican has been taken over in recent decades by a conspiracy of "Freemasons and Satanists." This was the doctrine of the renegade Archbishop Lefebvre in France, who ordained lather Krohn and played a large role in Krohn's intellectual development. Many have wondered why Lefebvre, whose denunciations of the Vatican are now legendary, has never been excommunicated. According to Lincoln, Leigh and Baigent in their controversial and speculative *Holy Blood, Holy Grail,* a disciple of Lefebvre's, in England, claims the dissident prelate holds an "earth-shaking weapon" over the Vatican.

Whatever Lefebvre's "weapon" may be, it is probably not any inner knowledge of the Freemasonic/P2 infiltration of the IOR (Vatican Bank); that has already been widely publicized, and the Vatican handled it as priests have always handled unwelcome news, as witness the *Irish Press* for 23 June 1983 in which the Pope replied to an enquiry about the frauds and drug-dealing of the Vatican Bank with the following well-chosen words:

> Many incredible things can be read in the newspapers, things which have no basis in truth. You must never let your faith be shaken by what you read in the newspapers.

W.C. Fields could not have replied with more aplomb.

We are still in the dark as to what "earth-shaking weapon" the heretic Lefebvre holds over the Vatican. According to Father Malachi Martin, S.J. (in his *The Decline and Fall of the Roman Church*), Lefebvre sent the late Pope John Paul I a portfolio of documents concerning Freemasonic affiliations of Vatican staff members – together with photos of Cardinals with their boy friends and other such unsavory matters – but the Pope was taken suddenly dead before he could respond in any way. Lefebvre's right-hand man, the Abbé Ducaud-Bourget said to the French press on the Pope's demise, "It is hard to believe this death is natural" – which was some kind of new high, or new low, in the propaganda war between the Lefebvreites and the Vatican – but something still remains unexplained, one feels.

According to Jean Delaude's *Le Cercle d'Ulysse,* both Archbishop Lefebvre and the Abbé Ducaud-Bourget are members of the Priory of Sion. Delaude identifies the Priory of

Sion as an ancient Catholic order, strongly conservative, which is currently pledged to make Lefebvre the next Pope. Delaude also says the Abbé Ducaud-Bourget is the current Grandmaster of the Priory of Sion, having succeeded Jean Cocteau in 1963.

A rather different view of the Priory of Sion is given in Gérard de Sède's *La Race Fabuleuse.* As de Sède tells it, the Priory is made up of persons descended from Merovingian kings and certain allies who are devoted to the Merovingian cause. Another group, not named by de Sède but sounding suspiciously like the Vatican, has been persecuting and assassinating the Merovingians for over a thousand years; they killed the last Merovingian king, Dagobert II on 23 December 689 and (perhaps out of a sense of symmetry) they killed de Sède's principle informant, an elusive "Marquis de B." on 23 December 1971. At the very end of this odd and undocumented saga, de Sède reveals the secret of the Merovingians and the Priory of Sion – they are superhuman beings, descended from the intermarriages in ancient Israel between the Tribe of Benjamin and extraterrestrials from Sirius.

De Sède does not mention Archbishop Lefebvre at all; but then, he doesn't need to. The extraterrestrials are exciting enough.

The Swiss journalist, Mattieu Paoli, gives a different account in his *Les Dessous d'une Ambition Politique.* Paoli does not mention Archbishop Lefebvre either. He says the propaganda of the Priory of Sion is circulated in Switzerland through the Grand Loge Alpina, the largest Freemasonic lodge in the country and the one that allegedly controls Swiss banking. (Curiously, Yallop's *In God's Name* indicates that the Freemasons in the Vatican Bank included members of the Grand Loge Alpina along with members of P2.) Paoli found that *Circuit,* the newsletter of the Priory of Sion, was distributed through the Grand Loge Alpina, was devoted mostly to obscure articles on astrology and occultism, and, according to its title page, was published by the Committee to Secure the Rights and Privileges of Low Cost Housing, indicating some hermetic humor on the part of some of the Priory. *Circuit* was actually published, Paoli discovered, out of the offices in Paris of the government department called the Committee for Public Safety.

The directors of the Committee for Public Safety at that time were Andre Malraux, the well-known critic and novelist, and Pierre Plantard de Saint Clair, about whom we will soon learn more and understand less. Both Malraux and Plantard served under de Gaulle in the Free French forces during World War II, and both had remained close associates of his after the war. Paoli was admittedly stumped in trying to fathom what the Priory of Sion was, but the conclusion of his book is that the Priory reaches very high in the French government and has considerable influence on Swiss banking.

De Sède's book on the extraterrestrial-Hebraic roots of the Priory had not appeared when Paoli published *Les Dessous,* so it is amusing that he reproduces without comment the cover of one edition of the Priory's magazine, *Circuit.* The cover shows a map of France with a Star of David superimposed on it and something that looks like a spaceship hovering above . . . I suspect hermetic humor again. That cover seems well calculated to push the paranoia buttons of both anti-Semites and the more demoniac UFO theorists.

It is only a coincidence (I hope) but Paoli was shot as a spy in Israel shortly after his book was published.

Literature on the Priory of Sion continues to proliferate.

According to Lincoln, Baigent and Leigh in *Holy Blood, Holy Grail*, the secret of the Priory of Sion is that, as de Sède claimed, its leaders are descended from the Merovingian kings – but the Merovingians themselves were descended, not from extraterrestrials, but from Jesus Christ and Mary Magdalene. The authors also claim (as de Sède only hinted) that the Vatican murdered Dagobert II, but they do not imply that the Vatican is still trying to murder off all the descendants of Dagobert (i.e. also of Jesus). They identify Pierre Plantard de Saint Claire, not the Abbé Ducaud-Bourget, as the Grandmaster of the Priory of Sion, and attempt to prove that Plantard is a direct descendant of Jesus and Magdalene.

M. Plantard actually gave an interview to the authors and was brilliantly occult and evasive. He did not comment on his own bloodline but volunteered that the Priory of Sion is in possession of a treasure that belongs to Israel, that the treasure is not material but spiritual, and that it will be returned to Israel "at the proper time." That may contain some broad hints, or it may be magnificent misdirection.

According to Michael Lamy's *Jules Verne: Initié et Initiateur*, Verne was a member of the Priory of Sion, which was originally a front for the Illuminati conspiracy in 18th century Freemasonry – of course, the Illuminati and the Grand Orient, from which **P2** is descended, were virtually identical – and the great inner secret of the Priory is that they know a temple in Rennes-le-Chateau which has, in the basement, a hole leading down to the center of the Earth, where there is a race of immortal superhumans. Verne hinted at this in several of his novels, of course.

Like de Sède's yarn about the extraterrestrials mating with Hebrews, this thesis that some of Verne's science-fiction was science fact is not well documented. There *is* a temple in Rennes-le-Chateau mentioned in most other books on the Priory of Sion. It was built in the 1890s by an eccentric priest named Father Sauniere, is dedicated to Mary Magdalene, and, for some odd reason, Sauniere wrote over its door the gnomic inscription, **THIS PLACE IS TERRIBLE**. (Of course, to an orthodox Catholic the thesis that Jesus had a child by Magdalene and their descendants are all around us would be rather terrible.)

According to Eon Begg's *The Cult of the Black Virgin,* the mysterious Black Virgins in European churches – there are over 400 of them, regarded as inexplicable by most historians and a profound embarrassment to the Vatican – were placed in the churches by the Priory of Sion in the 13th century. Begg, who is more given to esoteric hinting than to clear exposition, says the Priory also introduced the Tarot cards to Europe at that time and that all this has something to do with Mary Magdalene and the Sufi Order of Islam.

Going back a bit, *Holy Blood, Holy Grail* insists that Father Sauniere's temple to Mary Magdalene in Rennes-le-Chateau has some distinctly odd Stations of the Cross, including one which seems to show Jesus being carried out of the grave during the night as if by conspirators planning to fake the Resurrection. Another one, not so blasphemous but rather spooky if you think of it, shows a Scotsman in kilts watching the crucifixion.

Father Sauniere was, all sources agree, an associate of, and perhaps a member of, the Hermetic Brotherhood of Light, in Paris. This was another secret society, which at various times included composer Claude Debussy, Gerard Encause and Aleister Crowley. Debussy was, according to several of our sources, a Grandmaster of the Priory of Sion. Encause, better known under his pen-name, "Papus," wrote one of the most influential books on the Tarot and was later closely associated with Rasputin in Russia, and thus with shadowy doings before the Russian Revolution. Crowley also wrote an influential book on the Tarot, and became Outer Head of the Ordo Templi Orientis (yet another secret society, which alleges descent from the Sufi Order and the Knights Templar). Crowley also worked for German intelligence in World War I, although he oddly remained a good friend of the acting chief of British Naval Intelligence, leading some to think he was at least a double-agent.

According to Francis King's *Satan and Swastika,* the Outer Head of the Ordo Templi Orientis before Crowley, Dr. Theodore Reuss, was also an employee of German intelligence and assigned to spy on no less a personage than Karl Marx.

It is useless to try to make sense of all this in terms

of a rational paradigm. Remember the bowl of spaghetti metaphor, and remember that conspiracies, like nations, have no permanent allies, only permanent interests. It is worthy of note, however, that Father Sauniere, who built a temple to Magdalene and called it terrible and who associated with the Hermetic Brotherhood of Light and the Priory of Sion, became a very rich man by unknown means. According to *Holy Blood, Holy Grail,* Father Sauniere was given his riches in one huge gift from the Archduke Johann von Habsburg.

According to Maynard Solomon's *Beethoven,* the *Emperor Joseph Cantata,* Beethoven's first Major work, was commissioned by the Illuminati. The *Cantata* glorifies Emperor Joseph von Habsburg as a bringer of light and a foe of "darkness and superstition." The Emperor's enlightenment seems to have been demonstrated chiefly by the facts that he made Freemasonry legal in Austria (including, of course, the Illuminati lodges) and that he closed the Catholic schools, replacing them with public (secular) education.

We might jump to conclusions when noting that one von Habsburg in the 18th century was a friend to Freemasonry and a hero of the Illuminati and another von Habsburg in the 19th century gave huge wealth to a strange priest associated with the Priory of Sion.

We might even think strange and Romantic thoughts if we were to put these facts together with the Merovingian genealogies in the Bibliothèque Nationale, attributed to Leo Shidlof. According to these genealogies the von Habsburgs are of Merovingian descent. They are thus related to Jesus and Magdalene, if one believes *Holy Blood, Holy Grail,* or to extraterrestrials from Sirius, if one believes *La Race Fabuleuse.*

The current scion of the family, Dr. Otto von Habsburg, has attracted the attention of conspiracy buffs, however, because he is one of the leading members of the Bilderbergers – the secretive group of financiers who meet once a year (always at a different place) and never answer press enquiries about what they discuss or what their purposes are. Along with Dr. von Habsburg, the two best known members of the Bilderbergers are David Rockefeller, who virtually controls American banking, and Prince Bernhard of the Netherlands.

Prince Bernhard also has Merovingian genes, according to the Shidlof genealogies. This means either that he is descended from Jesus, or from extraterrestrials, or that some members of some secret societies enjoy planting false leads to baffle profane investigators.

TRILATERAL SPAGHETTI

Every bank of discount is downright corruption, robbing the public for private individuals' gain; and if I said this in my will the American people would pronounce that I died crazy.

– John Adams, letter to Benjamin Rush, *Works,*
Vol IX, p 638

David Rockefeller is, of course, the principle financial backer of the mysterious Trilateral Commission in addition to owning Chase Manhattan Bank and belonging to the esoteric Bilderberger club. Lyndon LaRouche, the eccentric right-wing former Trotskyist, believes that the Trilateral Commission is nothing else but Rockefeller's attempt to take over the world; but then LaRouche also believes Queen Elizabeth II is the mastermind behind the international drug trade. Others far less bizarre than LaRouche have worried about the Trilateralists. For instance, Seán MacBride – winner of the American Medal of Justice, the Lenin Peace Prize, the Dag Hammerskold Medal of Honor of the UN and the Nobel Peace Prize – has also claimed that the Trilateral Commission is a front for Rockefeller's banking interests. MacBride also finds it sinister that even so small a nation as neutral Ireland has a Prime

Minister and two cabinet members who are also members of the Trilateral Commission. Throughout the Western world, Trilateralists are found in higher numbers in all the NATO governments.

Penny Lernoux, in *In Banks We Trust,* treats the Trilateral Commission as David Rockefeller's major folly, arguing that if it is intended to further Rockefeller's financial interests, it is a total failure, since its members seem to spend most of their time quarreling.

Again we must return to the spaghetti metaphor and remind ourselves that most conspiracies are not nearly as clever as they think they are. The Trilateralists are not "running the world" yet, but they are intertwined like spaghetti with every other affinity group that wields considerable power. Through Prince Bernhard, they have a communication channel at least to the Bilderbergers and, probably, the financial wing of the Priory of Sion, which, for all its mysticism, once operated out of an office of the de Gaulle government and which is cosy with the Grand Loge Alpina and the "Gnomes of Zurich" (Harold Wilson's name for the Swiss banking cartel). Through Chase Manhattan, Rockefeller was involved financially with the World Finance Corporation and its strange links to the CIA and the Mafia; through Chase Manhattan, Rockefeller is still financially involved with the Vatican Bank.

Licio Gelli, incidentally, was not only Grandmaster of **P2** and a sometime employee of both the CIA and KGB, but also a Knight of Malta. The Knights of Malta, one of the most secretive of Vatican orders, dates from the 12th century; membership in it gave Gelli a fraternal bond to William Casey, head of the CIA, and who is also a Knight of Malta, and to General Alexander Haig, another Knight of Malta, who was advisor to President Nixon and Secretary of State under President Reagan. This may explain why Gelli's colleague in the cocaine trade and bank frauds, Michele Sindona, was a guest at Nixon's inaugural ball and why Gelli himself was a guest at Reagan's inaugural ball.

David Rockefeller is also a major financial backer of the Republican Party, and two of his brothers became governors of New York and Arkansas respectively. The spaghetti metaphor must be invoked again to explain why Nixon, who, like all Republican Presidents, owes a great deal to Rockefeller, was also a good and dear friend of Rockefeller's arch-enemy, Howard Hughes.

The war between Rockefeller and Hughes is the major theme of David Tinnin's *Just About Everybody VS Howard Hughes,* a book just as important for one who wishes to understand modern Capitalism as Machiavelli's *The Prince* for one who wants to understand politics. Briefly, David Rockefeller set out to capture control of Trans World Airlines from Hughes, who vowed he would "bum down the plant" before allowing Rockefeller to take it over. The conflict was protracted, lasted over decades and left Hughes a clinical paranoid, convinced that Rockefeller owned the U.S. government lock, stock and barrel. The question is: did Hughes think such things because he always had a tendency to paranoia, or did he become paranoid because of what happened to him in fighting Rockefeller in the American courts?

One of the loose ends left over from Watergate is the question of why President Nixon loaned "the plumbers" – his own private espionage and dirty tricks gang – to Howard Hughes, for whom they burglarized a newspaper office looking for God-knows-what. As Carl Oglesby indicates in *The Yankee and Cowboy War,* Hughes had previously given Nixon's brother, Donald, $1,000,000; Hughes had been equally lavish in buying the affections of literally hundreds of Western politicians, in his endeavor to fight off what he saw as the death grip of Rockefeller upon Eastern seaboard legislators and judges. By the end of it all, Hughes was not only paranoid, locked in a room, fearful of human contact, but had his financial empire heavily infiltrated, as Oglesby proves, by the

A Non-Euclidean Perspective

Mafia, whom he had been fighting for control of the Las Vegas gambling casinos.

The Knights of Malta, to which Licio Gelli, William Casey of the CIA and General Haig all belong, is discussed in Gordon Thomas's *The Year of Armageddon.* Thomas claims that Pope John Paul II has weekly meetings with CIA officers in Rome and uses the Knights of Malta as couriers of secret communications with CIA headquarters in Alexandria, Virginia. It all tends to remind me of a remark I once heard from the philosopher Alan Watts: "The principle error of academic historians is their belief that the Roman Empire 'fell.' It never "fell.' It still controls the Western world through the Vatican and the Mafia." Our evidence, however indicates that the Vatican/Mafia group does not control the West, but only tries to, and that in the huge bowl of spaghetti which is primate territorial politics, every other affinity group is aiming at similar control. They all cooperate at times, and they all double-cross each other whenever that is to their advantage.

The Franklin National Bank, which went through the most shocking bankruptcy of the 1970s, was also a client of Chase Manhattan and Mr. Rockefeller. Franklin National was founded by Michele Sindona, manager of Vatican finances in the United States and a member of P2. Sindona, who started his career as a lawyer for several Sicilian Mafia families, bought huge shares in Paramount films, Procter and Gamble and the World Trade Center for the Vatican; he also seems to have looted $55,000,000 from Franklin National, right under Rockefeller's nose – Chase was the major guarantor of Franklin's loans – and was convicted later, in New York, of 65 counts of stock and currency fraud, and in Rome, of the murder of a bank examiner. Sindona died in prison while awaiting trial on the further charge that he conspired with Roberto Calvi, Licio Gelli (Grandmaster of P2) and General Musumeci, chief of the Italian Secret Police, in the 1980 Bologna railway bombing. Reports differ as to whether Sindona killed himself or was poisoned by his former associates. The motives of the Bologna bombing are not clear, either – one's interpretation depends on whether one regards P2 as chiefly a tool of the CIA or of the KGB or as a band of adventurers exploiting both sides in the Cold War for their own financial gain. The only sure thing about any of this is that Lord Acton was right when he said all power tends to corrupt and absolute power corrupts absolutely.

Reprinted with permission of New Falcon Publications

Subversion for Fun and Profit: An Evening with Karl Hess and Robert Anton Wilson

Recorded at the
Libertarian Party National Convention, 1987

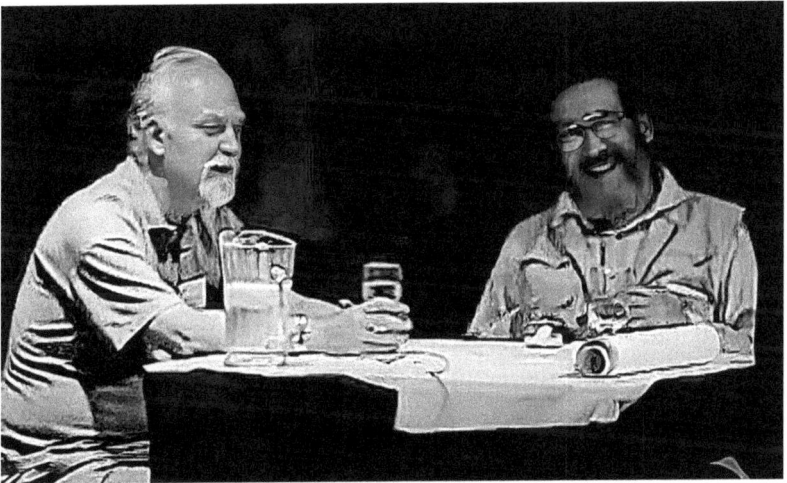

Hilaritas Press has obtained permission to publish this transcript of a video of Robert Anton Wilson and Karl Hess. While formatting the sometimes quixotic A.I. transcription of the video, we were impressed by how reading the conversation left a different impression on our brains than simply listening while watching. We encourage readers to do both. Here's a link to the video: https://youtu.be/kXfbIrLV9W4

• • •

The Libertarian Party's 1987 convention in Seattle is mostly remembered for two things. One was a hard-fought battle for the party's presidential nomination, with the former and future Texas congressman Ron Paul prevailing over the American Indian Movement activist Russell Means. And the other was a session where Robert Anton Wilson, who was not a member of the party but frequently spoke at its events, shared a couple joints onstage with Karl Hess.

Hess had achieved national fame as a prominent Republican who wrote speeches for Barry Goldwater – the GOP's rather right-wing 1964 presidential nominee – before growing disillusioned with the conservative movement and the Vietnam War, deciding that the individualist, anti-authoritarian values that had led him to the Goldwater campaign were in more plentiful supply in the New Left and the counterculture. By the end of the '60s, Hess was an anarchist, a tax resistor, and an antiwar activist. (He also published one of the era's most popular libertarian manifestos, "The Death of Politics," in *Playboy* while Wilson was a staffer there.) With time he grew as disillusioned with the organized left as he was with the organized right, but he remained an anarchist; when the event with Wilson took place, Hess had recently taken a job editing the Libertarian Party's newspaper, where he enjoyed doing things like publishing Emma Goldman and Ayn Rand quotes side by side.

On that stage in Seattle, Hess and Wilson had a funny, freewheeling conversation covering everything from phone phreaking to the Iran-contra scandal to the surveillance arm of *Playboy* magazine. The libertarian activist Jim Turney recorded it for posterity, and audio and video tapes of it circulated for years. At some point around the early 2010s it surfaced online and found a larger audience. This lightly edited transcript is its first print publication.

• • •

Donald Meinshausen: What sticks most in my mind about them is that they're both the warmest, wittiest, and the two of the most original people I've ever known. Robert Anton Wilson and Karl Hess. (*reaches out hand as crowd applauds*) That's $10 each.

Robert Anton Wilson: We're supposed to do our version of *My Dinner With Andre*.

Karl Hess: Oh, my favorite film.

Wilson: Which one of us is going to be Andre and which one will be Wally?

Hess: I guess I was born to be Wally.

I would start out by mentioning how I first met the person who introduced us, because I think that's, if I may, a story of some historic importance. When I was active on the New Left, therefore unpatriotic – before I learned what it was like to be *really* unpatriotic – I was approached one day by a young man.

Meinshausen (*interrupting to bring the men a joint*): The movement started by burning a draft card. This will have to do.

Hess: I'd been approached by this young man who had the most amazing story to tell. He said that although he had appeared to be interested in all of our political activities, what he actually was doing was working for the House Committee on Un-American Activities. But he had concluded, after sober thought, that is the two or three moments he was sober, that the House Committee on Un-American Activities was considerably more dangerous than we, i.e., the New Left.

He was in his mid-teens at that time. Now, I think this is one of the absolutely most courageous things I've ever seen a very young man do. He was scheduled to testify as a House committee stoolie on a certain day with all of the usual things there. And instead he testified publicly – he had to do it out in the hallway – that he had been an informer, that he didn't think that the people he was informing on were dangerous, and that the committee was violently dangerous. This is a young, very young man, and I think he's just as heroic as anybody I've ever met. (*applause*)

He's declined in his later years . . .

Wilson: Take a bow. Take a bow.

Those were great days. I was involved in the peace movement in Chicago in those days, in the '60s. And in 1972 it came out in congressional hearings that between the FBI, the CIA, and Army Intelligence, there were 5,000 informers in the peace movement in Chicago. And we very seldom had a rally with more than 5,000 people. I have been wondering ever since: Was I the only pacifist in Chicago? Were everybody else intelligence agents?

Hess: The circulation of *The Daily Worker* – the Communist Party paper – at one time consisted largely of subscriptions from the Department of Justice.

Also, when I was doing stuff with the New Left, some of the young bravos in it were very angry at the CIA, and they wondered what they could do to irritate them. And so I suggested, "Well, hell, why don't you go out to the CIA, to the entrance to it, and take down every license number of a car driving in, and then go to the license bureau, check the names, and publish them," which they did, and it just irritated the CIA terribly. But I discovered in later years – I believe there were three young people involved in it. One of them was a CIA agent.

Wilson: There's an old middle European proverb: When four sit down to conspire, three of them are government agents and the fourth is a damn fool. (*laughter*) That's my experience. People wonder why I write so many novels about conspiracies. That's because I'm convinced conspiracy is one of the continuous, constant elements in human life. Not that I believe there's one big conspiracy controlling everything. Only hardcore paranoids are able to twist the facts enough to fit that theory. But there are multitudinous conspiracies.

When I was in the peace movement, we had 5,000 agents spying on us in Chicago alone, as I said. When I was in the Leary Defense Committee in the '70s – that was a committee to attempt to get across to the American public an idea that was so radical we could hardly get into print with it, and it still is an unpopular idea in most places, the idea that locking up scientists is not the best way to settle scientific questions. Most people still don't understand that idea. While I was in that, everybody in the Leary Defense Committee came to me at one time or another and told me somebody else was a government agent. And usually the person denounced one day would be around to denounce somebody else the next day. And I remained sane all through that, because I have this basic attitude that life is either great adventure or it's nothing. So I refuse to get paranoid. I just enjoy the sense of mystery. (*laughter*)

Hess: I was at a meeting one time, and this fellow after the meeting had offered to drive me home. And before that, he said, "Come to the rear of the car." He opened it, and inside he had a Schmeisser submachine gun, and he said, "Would you like to have this?" Well, I don't know. I've been relatively violent, I guess, all my life, and the possession of any submachine – I only had one (*laughter*) and the idea of having another one appealed to me very much. But it suddenly occurred to me this was a very strange offer to make. (*laughter*) And so I rejected it out of hand, reminding him that it was illegal. And again, sometime later, he came up to me and he said, "I've got something strange to tell you." Thank God. Here it comes again. He said, "I'm working for the FBI." And he said, "I have concluded that they're more dangerous than you are." (*applause*) That's a terrible blow to a radical's ego.

Wilson: Now, I've got a friend whose name we're best not to mention at this point, and he has been urging for some years the formation of a Guns and Dope Party. Some people think that's what the Libertarian Party is. His attitude is the people who do dope, and the people who are gun collectors or want to have guns to protect themselves, the group generally called the gun nuts: If you add the two of them together, they make a majority. (*laughter*) He's got statistics to prove this.

Hess: But so many of them are in the 101st Airborne.

Wilson: Yeah, there is that problem.

Hess: That small problem.

Wilson: I remember one day sitting around his house. He had piles of guns, including Tommy guns, around that he was selling. He's in the gun business legally and illegally, depending on how the laws are written that year, and he also deals grass. And I was sitting there looking at him, and there's all these guns and pot on the floor, and I said, "Bill, all you need is a teenage girl and some counterfeit money to be the ideal bust for any cop." (*laughter*)

(*Wilson hands the tiny end of the joint they have been smoking on stage to Hess. Hess puts up his hand.*)

Hess: A little too short for my delicate fingers . . .

I was in the gun running business for a time. And the curious thing, when you see the free market at work, it makes everything so pleasant –

(*Meinshausen brings another joint to the table.*)

Meinshausen: We are also the party of prosperity. (*lots of laughter*)

Hess: This was getting guns for a fellow in Cuba, whose name was Carlos Hevia, who was an engineer, which endeared him to me, and he wanted to overthrow Fulgencio Batista, which seemed like a sensible idea. And so he hired me to get him some automatic weapons and some napalm, which I did fairly successfully. But while doing it I noticed, when you deal with these arms merchants, how wonderfully matter-of-fact they are about something that the Pentagon tries to turn into a drama. You know: "How many mortars do you want?" Israelis seem very big at selling mortars to people. "We can get you this many. Would you like a tank?" (*laughter*)

I want to describe just briefly what happened in my illustrious career as a gun runner. The guns went fine, and so did the napalm, because I convinced the company that makes the saponifying agent that I wanted to burn off 52,000 acres of land and needed an awful lot of napalm. (*laughter*) But this stuff isn't – you know, you think it might come already mixed up, but it comes as a powder. It's soap powder, roughly what it is. I thought, my God, there's got to be some proper way to mix this. And how am I going to tell a bunch of Cubans, after we get it there, how to mix it? So I went to a chemist friend of mine at Shell Oil, who wrote out all the instructions for me very seriously and at the end, after spacing it, it simply said "and then run like hell." (*laughter*)

But the highlight of my revolutionary activity was dropping the propaganda pamphlets over Havana. Well, I don't know if you all panic easily, but when you're trying to figure out where was Florida, how are you going to get back there, and how are you going to explain that you've been in all of this restricted area, and everything goes through your mind. So we had a lot of pamphlets to dump out over Havana, and so we dumped them out in bales of 5,000. It occurred to me, my God, I bombed Havana.

So I really feel bad about that. I think that constitutes some sort of a trespass on – The pamphlets wouldn't have been so bad anyway. It's – It was wonderful. (*laughter*)

Wilson: I'm beginning to feel I've led a rather sheltered life. (*laughter*)

I have a couple of other friends who were gun runners, but I've never done that myself. The closest I ever came is when the Chicago red squad was investigating me as a gun runner, which is an amusing story in itself – at least it amuses me in retrospect. I was working for *Playboy* at the time. People wonder how my novels get so complicated about conspiracies within conspiracies and so on. This was one of the crucial incidents in the development of my philosophy of mammalian politics. I was working for *Playboy*, and a chap whose function was never clear to me, although he was very close to Hefner, came into my office and closed the door. I was an associate editor. He closed the door, he pulled a chair over close to my desk, and he said, "This is serious. You're under very close surveillance by the Chicago red squad. They got a tap on your phone, and we think they're doing a mail cover on you too." And I said, "What the hell is that all about?" I mean, I was involved in the peace movement, but I didn't think that they went that far just from marching around with a sign saying "Eat what you kill." (*laughter*)

I said, "What? What did I do that got the red squad so intense?" And he says, "They think you've been running guns for the Black Panthers." I said, "Running guns for the Black Panthers? I don't remember doing that." I began to feel a little bit like Ronald Reagan must have felt recently. Did I? Did I do that? One day I was so stoned I don't remember. Oh, no, I never did run guns for the Black Panthers.

And the more I searched my memory, the more I realized that I had been on platforms with Black Panthers on three occasions at peace rallies. And I said, "How did the red squad get the idea I was running guns for the Black Panthers?" And this chap said, "Well, they got an informer in the Black Panthers, and he says you were bringing guns down there to the headquarters on the south side." And I said, "You know, I think what happened is the informer saw me with Black Panthers at times, and that wasn't good enough to excite his superiors at the red squad. And so he improved the story a little." A *Playboy* editor on a platform with Black Panthers is of moderate interest. A *Playboy* editor running guns for the Black Panthers is of greater interest. And so I think that's what happened, because I swear – I think the statute of limitations has run out. If I were running guns, I would admit it. Now, I was not doing any such thing, but that's probably still in my file at the Chicago red squad. So I lived for quite a while with the knowledge that my phone was tapped, and I was wondering what was happening to my mail, but I was more concerned with: How the hell did *Playboy* know about this? (*laughter*)

So I asked the person whose name I am carefully not mentioning: I asked him, "How does *Playboy* know what the Chicago red squad is doing?" And he said, "Well, we got a fellow at police headquarters. He tells us when an investigation is being opened on anybody who works in *Playboy*."

Later on, it turned out there was another member of the red squad who was being paid by two rich liberals in the Chicago northern suburbs – where the rich liberals live, Wilmette, Winnetka, Glencoe, that area – these two rich liberals discovered this cop was in their peace groups. They recognized him as a cop, and they approached him, and he was very glad to go on their salary. They paid him regularly to be informed of what the red squad was doing. So that's two agents I have personally found out about in the red squad while there were 5,000 agents from Chicago red squad, the FBI, the CIA, and Army Intelligence watching me. That's the kind of world that we were living in, whether most people realize it or not.

Hess: And it depends on the side you're on, really, because I was *actually* running guns, and the FBI knew every single thing I did. But of course, I was approved. You can be an approved gun runner (*laughter*) and so there was never any problem about it.

Wilson: That leads to another of my paranoia-inducing stories. Some of you may remember about three years ago, the head of NORAID – that's aid for Northern Ireland – the head of NORAID stood trial in New York for running guns for the IRA. They were theoretically collecting money for the widows and orphans of the war, but they were actually buying guns for one side.

Hess: That's just prepayment.

Wilson: And his defense, the head of NORAID, his defense was that he didn't believe he was committing any illegal acts. He found it incredible that he was arrested – he still didn't understand what was going on – because he was getting the guns from the CIA. And the government tried to squash that line of defense, but his lawyer managed to persuade the judge it was a legitimate defense, so they brought in the evidence and proved that the CIA was running guns for the IRA. And so I asked Seán MacBride, who some of you may know is the founder of Amnesty International. He also won the Lenin Peace Prize, the United States Medal of Justice, the Dag Hammarskjöld Medal of Honor of the United Nations – and in Ireland, of course, with all those honors, he's still best known as the son of John MacBride, who was one of the revolutionaries of 1916. I got to interview Seán MacBride, and I asked him about that. I asked, "Why would the CIA be running guns for Marxist revolutionaries?" And he said, "When you get into the machinations of intelligence agencies, *anything* is possible."

Hess: Norman Mailer's description of this is that it really is like an onion, and you can peel it endlessly and you'll never get there, because there is no *there* there. (*laughter*) Funny business, funny business. But it's wonderful if you really want a career in high-level mischief. And I must say, it really is fun. I mean blowing up things and stuff. It really is fun. I don't think people understand that about war and why there's so much support for it. It isn't part of a conspiracy. It's part of an excitement. It really is exciting.

Wilson: People go to see horror movies. They go to see Charles Bronson blowing people away in the subway. They go to see Clint Eastwood. And they say, "Violence is all in the other people. I'm a pacifist. I'm a nice guy."

Hess: Oh, *those* folks. Yeah.

Wilson: It's a part of human nature. And of course people enjoy it. If nobody enjoyed it, nobody would go to Clint Eastwood films. Some people are not satisfied seeing it on the screen. They want to act it out.

Hess: It's just amazing how you can be an official outlaw in this country. And I must say, it has some advantages. If you are the state's radical, you are like methadone. (*laughter*) You are the state's narcotic. And they'll help you out. They'll do all sorts of good things. Just as a for instance, the fellow who worked for the FBI, who was my nurse or whatever, this person said that the reason he had volunteered, "volunteered," get this, to become an informant for the FBI was that they had offered him to take his young daughter suffering from a very severe ailment to the National Institutes of Health or Walter Reed or any place to have her worked on. So in order to save his daughter's life, a nice deal that the FBI made with him, he decided to be an informer. I don't think there's any depth to which they'll sink.

To indicate what lovely people these people are: When my tax rebellion was at its zenith, which is when I had any money to tax, the IRS went to my mother, who was quite elderly, and said that they wanted to check on her health. And she inquired why, and they said, "Because we want to make sure that when you die, you don't leave anything to your son, or if you do, we get what he owes us." I think that's villainy beyond belief, isn't it? And my mother, later in talking to this young man, the agent said to her, "Why is your son doing this?" And she said, "Young man, don't you read the newspapers? He's written more about it than anybody I know." But it doesn't do much good, does it?

Except sometimes it may. I've mentioned several times that recently, I met a guy in West Virginia where I live, and he said, "I have a nasty shock for you." He said, "I work at the IRS Data Center," which is, oddly enough, about nine miles from us. And he said, "I'm about to retire." So I've been keeping in fairly close touch with this fellow, because I can't think of anybody more interesting than a libertarian working at the IRS central computer who is about to retire. (*laughter and applause*)

Wilson: Malaclypse the Younger, author of that immortal sacred scripture, *Principia Discordia, or How I Found Goddess and What I Did to Her After I Found Her*, is now the head of the computer department of one of the largest banks in the United States. You'll all be happy to know.

Hess: And very rich, I trust.

Wilson: Very powerful.

But your stories about the FBI remind me of another colorful friend of mine, John Draper, a.k.a. Captain Crunch. He was ripping off the phone company with all sorts of cute electronic devices he invented himself, including the simple device of using a whistle from a Captain Crunch breakfast cereal, which is how he got his nickname. And after years, they finally made a major case against him, and he was convicted in San Jose and sentenced to about five years in prison, at which point he told his lawyer to contact the FBI, and he had a conference with a couple of FBI agents, in which he told them how he had figured out ways to tap the allegedly untappable wires of the CIA, the FBI, and the White House, and how he had worked out methods of transferring money from one bank account to another by telephone, and how he had worked out a way to fire the nuclear missiles in Colorado and start World War III. And he gave them full and explicit details on all of these little pranks he hadn't had time to carry out yet because he was a busy man ripping off the phone company 24 hours a day. And they went back and they checked. Every damn thing he said was true. And they had some kind of executive-level decision, and the FBI entered the case as a friend of the court and persuaded the judge to give John, instead of five years, three months with weekends off, and even he could go home at night too. He was only in the prison in the daytime, and he had weekends off too. He only served three months in return for informing the government how to get around, how to install fail safes against his devices.

After he got out of prison, he went around telling everybody in Silicon Valley the joke was, of course, that the fail safes he had told them about he had already figured out how to get around. (*laughter*) And what he can do, there are 10,000 other genius-level pot-heads in Silicon Gulch who can also do, and they are the people who are designing 90% of the Star Wars technology.

These people don't appreciate my jokes. My jokes are so morbid for them. That's because they're true.

Hess: Ross Overbeek remarked recently that although it has been possible for a long time for them to listen in on everything *we* do, it is now possible for us to listen in on everything *they* do, because the technology is clearly on our side for a change. I think it will continue to be.

Another hopeful sign, it seems to me: You had spoken a lot about stupidity and its central activity as a tool of evolution, and I think that's an interesting thing to toy with. But there is such a stupidity today that it seems to me it is forcing, for survival, brighter people to do extraordinary and new things because they understand they simply can't survive the weight of the stupidity.

Wilson: My theory is that stupidity is an evolutionary driver. It forces the intelligent to get even more intelligent to survive.

Hess: Boy, isn't that wonderful? My sons are going to be smart. Wait till I tell them.

I believe there's an old cabaret rubric in which the entertainers challenge you to think of a bizarre topic that we can discuss, whether we know anything about it or not.

Wilson: That never stopped me from discussing anything.

Hess: Me either. So somebody shout out a good topic.

Audience member: Ollie North!

Wilson: What? Ollie North. *Kookoo, Iran, and Ollie.* A lot of people were shocked when the *National Enquirer* readers voted 15 to one that they wanted Ollie North for president. But if the *National Enquirer* readers didn't vote that way, *I* would have been shocked. (*laughter*) The real test of what's going on down there – I'm sorry this sounds snobbish. I might say "up there," since it's relative, "up," "down." But on the *National Enquirer* level, what's really going on down there? I think if they made it a contest and ran Paul Newman against Ollie North, the readers would vote 15 to one that they want Paul Newman as president, because Paul Newman is much closer to the ideal image than

Ollie North. A recent sociological study shows that 95% of the women in the United States want to ball Paul Newman, anyway.

Hess: What's an interesting thing to think about when thinking about Ollie is to imagine those hearings and imagine his testimony if he had not had a uniform on. I mean, it really changes things. If your image becomes the way he looks, usually it changes. I think he would have been 50% less enthusiastically received. Clothes are important. Packaging is important.

Wilson: Like I said in *Schrödinger's Cat*: Blue uniforms are real. Cops are a social fiction. (*laughter and applause*)

Or to put it in the form of a Zen koan . . . We had a little discussion of counterfeiting at the panel discussion this afternoon. We had a gallant defense of counterfeiters from Dr. Walter Block, and I would like to offer you five or six Zen koans in a row. Maybe we'll get the audience talking. What's the difference between a real dollar printed by the wizards in the Treasury Department and officially blessed by them, and a counterfeit dollar printed by somebody who doesn't have the wizardry and magic? What's the difference between a real dollar and a counterfeit dollar, and one of them picked up by Andy Warhol and hung in a museum as an example of found art? Now, if Andy Warhol found it, it would be worth around $50,000 right away once he put the frame around it. So does it make any difference if it's a real dollar or a counterfeit dollar? And what is the difference between a framed thing in an art gallery that says "*Found Dollar*, by Andy Warhol" if it's forged by William Burroughs pretending to be Andy Warhol? I think these are the questions the Austrian School did not ultimately solve. (*laughter and applause*)

Hess: Well, have we disposed of Ollie as a bizarre topic?

Audience member: Nanotechnology!

Hess: Ah, now you've touched on my subject. Suffice it to say that, as Eric Drexler points out, this manufacturing at the molecular level may be the last technology, because it's all technologies. It means that you can make and produce anything, either of organic materials or inorganic materials, at will. In short, the world will suddenly become a really designed world.

Audience member: Once you get the bugs out of the software.

Hess: Disgruntled programmers, everywhere you look. (*laughter*)

Eric points out that this kind of technology is rather startling and stimulating in nature. And someone had asked him what his estimations were on time, and he said, "My optimistic estimation is 30 years. My pessimistic estimation is 20 years." As a matter of fact, the sooner it comes, the more it complicates everything. Everything's beginning to be so complex now that you'd think somebody would understand that there is no central planning organization or managerial technique that can manage it. There's too much of it. And so here it gets more and more complex, more and more rapidly, and the only people who've got sensible solutions to it are people who aren't in it, who fight it, and who create alternatives. I just keep feeling that, you know, we really won everything. But as getting a message through a dinosaur, it just takes time, you know, got to get up to that pea brain.

Wilson: The big brain is in the tail . . .

Hess (*after finishing the second joint*): I don't know why my thoughts are so disorganized. (*laughter*)

Wilson: You sound very organized to me. (*laughter*)

Hess: The National Security Council is really a bizarre thing. One of the great ending scenes in "my" war, the "good" one, the Second World War, was that a good deal of the German intelligence apparatus, particularly that that had been aimed at the Soviets, were taken in to the United States intelligence forces *in toto*. There's a novel called *The Odessa File* that is, as a matter of fact, an accurate description of what went on. But at any rate, all of these people having been taken in, one of the organizations created in order to deal with them was the National Security Council. They had a very specific purpose in dealing with all of these Germans, many of whom are still in very powerful positions, in keeping this apparatus intact. So Ollie is working in a good place, I guess.

Audience member: Thoughts on writing well.

Hess (*to Wilson*): Do you want to start? Since I think you do it. (*applause*)

Wilson: Writing well, looked at in terms of common sense or behaviorist psychology or logical positivism, is a very expensive neurosis. Writing well means spending a lot of time on every paragraph and balancing the sentences and putting in five jokes that most people won't get and one joke that most people will get, and knowing the nuances of words like a semanticist and the rhythm of words like a poet, and doing all this and then trying to disguise it as a commercial product so you can get a publisher to print it. And there's absolutely no reason why anybody would do it if they didn't get high on it.

Hess: That's right. I had an interesting situation with money for some time, and I had been getting no royalties on books or anything – that was being confiscated immediately. And it occurred to me: Why would I still want to write books? And it turns out, I really would write them – I'd pay a modest amount myself to just to keep on doing it, because it's fun to talk about what you're doing.

I guess my views are almost exactly contrary to Bob's. I think writing is what you do when you get up in the morning because it's so much fun, and you never rewrite anything. So I feel differently about it.

Wilson: Did I make it sound like I didn't think it was fun?

Hess: No, not fun, but that you do things over and over –

Wilson: That's the only way – you've got to do it over and over until every word in the paragraph is just right and every rhythm is just right, and it gives you total aesthetic bliss. And you know that somewhere in the world, of five billion people, there are three who will recognize what you've done. (*laughter*)

Hess: But how could you possibly have failed to do that the first time around? (*laughter*)

Wilson: I'm not as smart as you. I'm still learning.

Hess: Well, there may be an excuse. (*chuckles*)

I think, though, underneath it, in the technical sense, I think that the rediscovery of the simple declarative sentence would refine anyone's writing tremendously. Just that.

Wilson: Now I've trained myself to write long sentences and get away with it.

Hess: Ah.

Wilson: But the first piece of advice I give anybody who brings me a piece of writing and says "How can I make this more commercial?" is divide every sentence into two sentences. Because most people just don't know how to balance a long sentence. Anybody here who's trying to be a writer, you just cut every sentence into two sentences, and it'll be much more commercial right away.

Hess: Another thing: Anybody in here who wants to be a writer and who listens to anything that anybody else tells them about writing isn't a writer.

Wilson: That's right, yeah.

The real inner scoop, which very seldom is revealed, especially by writers: If you want to make money as a writer, if you want to make big bucks in the writing game, the first thing you do is get internationally famous as an infamous felon. (*laughter*) It's too late for any of you to get convicted as Nazi war criminals – nobody would believe you were around then. Most of you.

Hess: Now, wait a minute. Maybe a couple.

Wilson: OK, you might manage to convince somebody you were involved in Watergate. And if you were somehow involved in Irangate, you'll get a $3 million advance right away. But for Watergate, you'll still get a million. If you haven't been involved in anything on that level, you've got to kill at least 12 of your neighbors. Eight won't do it anymore. Twelve is a low estimate – maybe you should kill 40 of them, and then you're guaranteed about a $5 million advance.

But if you're interested in serious writing, you might as well reconcile yourself to the fact it'll be 40 years before you make any money out of it.

Hess: Let's see. I was 15 . . .

Audience member: Children.

Wilson: If you've never been hated by your children, you've never been a parent. (*laughter*) I didn't invent that. I was gonna put the tag on. Bette Davis said that – a wise and honest woman, obviously.

Hess: Well, the first thing to do is to try to figure out how to rescue them from the government school system. (*applause*)

Wilson: Most people are too damn honest for their own good. Most people think, "Well, I don't like what the schools are doing to my kids. I'll pull them out." And so you announce, "As a matter of principle, I disapprove of the school system," which offends every official in the school system and offends all the other bureaucrats. "I'm going to educate the kid myself," which offends all the experts who believe ordinary people like you can't do anything without them directing you. And so you've got the whole house down on you, and you go through the court system, and the odds are about a million to one that you're going to win. You're probably going to lose and get chopped up in the court system. That's what Mike Green, whom some of you may know, calls putting a target on your back. It just invites them to open fire.

The intelligent thing to do, what my wife and I did, is write to the school system and tell them we were moving to another town. And then we were off the records and we had no trouble whatsoever.

Hess: I got out of school. My mother had always advised me to not go to school. But what do kids know? I saw everybody else doing it, so I went until I was 15. And when I came home and told my mother that she'd been correct and I now wanted to leave a school immediately, she just had one question, which was, "How are you going to do it without getting us into trouble?" And I had evolved a very similar scheme. I registered in every high school in the District of Columbia and then transferred. (*laughter*) Never heard a thing!

Audience member: The advance on Gary Hart's next novel.

Wilson: Who's Gary Hart? (*laughter*)

Hess: He's a fiction writer.

Wilson: Is he a politician too?

Hess: No. My God, no. Not at all.

Audience member: Bioengineering.

Hess: We were talking about that this afternoon: how exciting it is to think that you can not only design a house but you could design a person. Obviously some parents want eight foot tall kids with hands as big as basketballs. And I think that then you have real professionalism. (*laughter*)

I think it is even more important. Because I think it comes at an oddly crucial time in history when it is very obvious that the diminution of seed varieties around the world is critical. And here comes, at last, a way to overcome that almost immediately. So it seems to me that genetic engineering is perfectly timed. It is superbly useful, it seems to me. It has all of the potentially humane virtues. And to oppose it strikes me as being bizarre. I mean, there may be some reasons, but I have yet to hear them.

Wilson: What I find even more exciting than genetic engineering is what's happened in cryonics this year. As some of you probably know, I've been involved in cryonics for quite a long time, 15 years or so. But this year, in March, Paul Segal at UC-Berkeley cryonically froze a dog, and brought it down to the temperature where its molecules would not change for 4 billion years if it were not dethawed, and left it there for 45 minutes, and then thawed the dog out, and the dog came back to life as predicted. And the dog is living a happy, healthy life now – and as far as can be told externally, shows no signs of mental damage.

Audience member: Does it sneeze much? (*laughter*)

Wilson: It barks a lot and it pees on everything. (*laughter*)

That's known as the territorial reflex. If you want to know more about peeing in territory, read a biography of Ronald Reagan. (*laughter*)

Audience member: Cause and effect.

Hess: Well, one usually comes before and/or after the other. (*laughter*)

Aren't there any *complicated* topics?

Audience member: Women – what do they want?

Hess: Probably to be spared any more questions like that. (*applause*)

Audience member: Cocaine.

Hess: I don't know anything about it at all. I hold with Bob that actually acid was one of the great gifts to the human race. (*applause*) And it seems to me that it has had (*sputters like he's running down*) no – no ill – ill effects – (*laughter*)

But I don't know about cocaine. I mean, I don't think it's very funny to have a ruptured septum, that sort of thing.

Wilson: I explained last night – Since a lot of people here weren't there last night, I'll repeat myself: You can get the same effect as cocaine by putting talcum powder up your nose and rubbing it in with sandpaper and then running around burning all the money you can find in the house. (*laughter and applause*) If you do that every day for 30 days, the effect is exactly like one month on cocaine, especially when you look at your bank account. Guaranteed to work.

Audience member: Have you seen any good movies lately?

Wilson: *Star Trek IV*.

Hess: I have a problem with movies. My favorite for years had been the original *Smokey and the Bandit*. It shows you where my taste . . .

Audience member: Have you seen any good religions lately?

Hess: Well, yes, I think so. I think Druidism still holds up. (*laughter and applause*)

Wilson: Actually, I am a Reformed Non-Aristotelian Druid of North America. We split off from the Reformed Druids of North America. (*laughter*) For two reasons. The first reason is that the Reformed Druids of North America, in their first degree initiation, you've got to swear three times that "Nature is good." And we Non-Aristotelians felt that's a primitive and neurologically naive statement, so we formed our own sect based on the three affirmations "Nature seems good to me." (*laughter*) Which is in keeping with modern neurology and perception theory and so on, and quantum mechanics. And the second reason we split off is because Reformed Non-Aristotelian Druids of North America makes better initials than Reformed Druids of North America. RNA-DNA, you see. It's a nice rhythmic pattern.

Audience member: Funny, you don't look Druish. (*laughter*)

Another audience member: Gypsies.

Hess: Gypsies?

Wilson: Ireland has its own Gypsies. When they are 50 miles away, they're called Tinkers. When they're 20 miles away, they're call Tinks. When they move in next door, they're call Fookin' Tinks.

Audience member: Ayn Rand.

Hess: Great.

Wilson: Great what? Great jumping Jehoshaphat?

Audience member: Jimmy Hoffa.

Hess: I was talking to Jimmy the other day . . . (*laughter*)

Wilson: Who asked about Ayn Rand? I think the whole key to Ayn Rand is in the footnote to Barbara Branden's *The Passion of Ayn Rand*, the footnote in which she mentions that Ayn Rand was taking amphetamine every day for 30 years, and said some people have misinterpreted this as meaning that she became a speed freak. And then she quotes a doctor who says maybe it affected her mind and maybe it didn't. And she said that should answer those who claim it did. (*laughter*) The doctor said *maybe* it did and maybe it didn't. But who else – by now, most of you have known speed freaks, right? Who else would make enemies out of so many former friends but a speed freak? And who else would think the proper way to conclude a novel is with a 90-page speech? Nobody but a speed freak would think something like that belonged in a novel.

Audience member: Wouldn't you say that both Ayn Rand and Jimmy Hoffa are concrete-bound? (*groans from the audience*)

Hess: I'll tell you one thing. I went through a brief period of going around acting as though Ayn Rand was a pain in the ass and all that sort of thing. And I sort of regret that, because, as a matter of fact, I know a lot of people who are outraged by her, but I don't know anybody who wasn't affected by her. (*applause*) I think she really did a lot. And to criticize her for this thing and that thing, what the hell, people forget that.

I am inclined to like the original just a teeny bit better, though. I think Max Stirner is somebody we should read with some regularity. (*applause*)

Wilson: Maybe I like Max Stirner better than Ayn Rand because I never met Max Stirner. (*laughter*)

Audience member: Bizarre personal habits and why they are important. (*laughter*)

Wilson (*pretending to pick his nose*): I don't know anybody with any bizarre personal habits. (*laughter*)

Hess: But they are important. You put your finger on something there.

Audience member: Slack!

Wilson: Slack is the state of perfect enlightenment and attunement and ideal balance. It cannot be understood by the rational mind. Like most of the great concepts of mysticism, one needs to have direct intuition into the essence of Slack before one can begin to express Slack. But a crude understanding for domesticated primate minds might be achieved by considering that the universe consists of something and nothing. If you see this glass of water, you're seeing something, but if you look all around it, you see a lot of nothing. When you get down to the atomic level, this is even more pronounced. The further down quantum mechanics goes, the more they find of nothing and the less they find of something, until the suspicion is growing that if you get to the bottom, it will be all nothing and no something. That's known as superfluid vacuum; it's very important in some interpretations of quantum mechanics. When you get to the bottom, there's nothing, and then something just appears as a temporary bubble on the nothing. "Figure-ground" is the Gestalt way of thinking of it – the figure is something and the ground is nothing, only the figure seems to be an expression of the ground, so it resolves into nothing eventually. But you don't have to get that deep – I mean, we were almost approaching Buddhism there. For practical purposes, the secret of power, Slack, arises when you are ideally balanced between something and nothing. And then you can get something for nothing. (*laughter and applause*)

Those callow rationalists and shallow empiricists who think this is mystical bullshit should stop and reflect that this is the principle by which "Bob" Dobbs founded the Church of the SubGenius and got rich. This is the principle behind Rajneesh and Ayatollah Khomeini and Jerry Falwell. This is the principle behind every religion in the world: You *can* get something for nothing. All you gotta do is repeat at the end of every sentence: "And send more money, brothers and sisters!"

Audience member: New Age!

Hess: I've been with so many of those folks, and they keep talking about a new age and describe it in minute detail in terms of 100 years ago. (*laughter*)

There's a strain of Luddism with a lot of these folks. I'll tell you this: If I owned a ski lodge near Aspen, and the Muzak people all played my music, and I had billions of dollars and things, I probably would figure: What the hell, let's have a nice, simple place to live in, and let's pump the water by hand, and let's bake the bread and so forth. And if you have enough servants, you can get all of this done very nicely. But I don't think most people want that sort of new age. They want whatever happens next.

My God, did I wax serious for a moment?

Wilson: Do it before Sirius waxes you.

Hess: Sirius – one of the more important stars, of course.

Wilson: If you like to do it doggy-fashion.

Audience member: Hunter-gatherers.

Hess: I hunt at the A&P now (*laughter*) and gather there, and stuff.

Wilson: Did you ever realize that most people are still at the hunting-gathering stage? Engineers and a few others aren't, but most people, if they closed all the supermarkets, would have no idea how to feed themselves. They're in the hunting-gathering stage. They haven't mastered agriculture yet, like Karl has, for instance.

Hess: I'll tell you one thing. I don't want to denigrate for a moment the knowledge of how to do all of these things. It's just that doing them full-time is not quite as much fun.

Wilson: I was a farmer for two years, that was enough for me. But if you like it for 20 years, that's your life.

Hess: I remember . . .uh, what did I remember? (*short pause*) I didn't remember. (*laughter*)

Audience member: Neighbors.

Hess: Neighbors? Oh, yeah. See, I'm not what you'd call a believer in *rights*. I believe in agreements and contracts, and neighbors are the people that you most constantly are making contracts with – just in meeting them, in having any sort of concourse with them. And they are politically the most important people in your life. A person who has a lot of trouble with their neighbors and then pretends to solve the ills of the world is starting from a very shaky foundation. I think the behavior of people toward their neighbors is as crucial as their opinion about epistemology, and so I take neighbors very, very seriously.

Wilson: You were talking Buddhism a while ago, and now you're talking Confucianism. Confucius put that as the basis of everything, *Can you get along with your family?* And the next step is, can you get along with your neighbors? And then after that, you can study philosophy and figure out the ideal system of government.

Hess: You know that, just as an educational aside on that: People are always saying you shouldn't have to reinvent the wheel. I've spent some of the happiest moments in my life reinventing the wheel. (*applause*) And I believe this is probably true of things like Confucianism and Buddhism and libertarianism and a number of other things: that inventing it yourself, discovering it yourself, is just a wonderful part of the experience. Much better than knowing about it is discovering it. I've been very excited by that.

Audience member: Water skiing with your favorite judge.

Wilson: In my case, that would be Hugo Black.

Hess: Yeah?

Wilson: Hugo Black was the first member of the Ku Klux Klan appointed to the Supreme Court.

Hess: That you know about.

Wilson: That we know about, yeah. Very few people approved of his appointment at the time. That was back in the '30s. Hugo explained, "Well, when I was young, I was a salesman, and the only way you can make any sales in that part of the South is if you knew the Ku Klux grip. That's why I was a Freemason, too." People howled and screamed, and Hugo served 30 or 40 years on the Supreme Court.

And he became my personal hero because he refused to look at the material in censorship cases. He had an absolutely consistent policy. He said, "I don't care what it is, it's protected under the First Amendment." (*applause*) And in one of his dissents, he wrote, "I believe the men who wrote our Constitution were masters of 18th century English prose style. I believe that when they wrote 'no laws,' as in 'There should be no laws abridging freedom of speech or of the press,' they meant 'no laws.' I believe that if they meant to say 'some laws,' with their gift of style they would have found a way to say that clearly. (*applause*) Some on this court, with an ingenuity that astounds and almost convinces me, have argued that when they wrote 'no laws,' they meant 'some laws.' But I'm a simple farm boy, and to me, 'no laws' still means 'no laws.'" So he never looked at any of the material. He voted not guilty in every censorship case while he was on the Supreme Court, and I wish we had more like him, even if he did start in the Ku Klux Klan. Anybody can reform, you see?

Audience member: [Robert] Bork.

Hess: Pork?

Audience member: Bork!

Hess: Bork! I think he's a very curious fellow. He worked for me once in an earlier life, and my feeling is that, roughly, his judicial position is that the legislature actually *is* supreme. He's curiously different from some of the criticisms I've seen. He really feels that if the legislature decides anything that isn't *clearly* contrary to the *wording* of the Constitution, he supports the legislature. Now, judicial activism previously had been sort of stepping in to negate or to contend with the legislature, but I don't believe he'll put up with this. I don't know where that puts him in terms of the court.

Audience member: Psychiatry.

Wilson: How many psychiatrists does it take to change a light bulb? Only one, but it takes a long time, and the light bulb really has to want to change. (*lots of laughter*)

Audience member: Have you read Szasz, and do you agree or disagree with him?

Wilson: Thomas Szasz?

Hess: Oh! I'm on the agree column.

Wilson: I agree with his conclusions, but I disagree with some of his arguments. I disagree with him about schizophrenia, for instance, being a matter of definition. I tend to believe it's a genuine physical disease and will probably be cured by chemistry.

Audience member: Then it's not a mental disease.

Wilson: Yeah.

Audience member: (*inaudible*)

Wilson: That's what I said – I agree with him on how we should treat people. But I don't agree with him in arguing things like there is no such disease as schizophrenia. I believe I can recognize the difference in complexion between schizophrenics and non-schizophrenics, for instance. And there's a different smell in many cases. I believe it's a very real physical condition, and I don't think it's clarifying matters at all to say it's a matter of definition.

Audience member: Welds that don't hold.

Hess: Wells that don't hold what? Oh, *welds* that don't –

God, I don't know. I did the most welding I've done in a long time about two weeks ago. I did 80 feet of flat welds on a big flatbed trailer to carry an experimental boat that some friends of mine built. And because I hadn't done much electrical welding lately – since I'd moved farther out in the country, I use gas all of the time – the first two or three inches were just incredibly puddly bad, really ugly. I fortunately had a grinder handy so I could smooth them off immediately, pretending a sort of super-fastidious attention to my welds. But after about three inches, it was just great. And I think it was 80 feet straight through and caused some people to gasp and say, "Man, that's a lot of welding." (*laughter*)

Audience member: (*mostly inaudible joke about yuppies and puppies*)

Hess: Ah, that's wonderful. That's wonderful.

I think one of the most odious clichés of our time is this business of frowning on yuppies because they want *things*.

Wilson: I think yuppies are a social myth. I've never met anybody yet who's been willing to stand there and say, "I am a yuppie." There are no yuppies. It's not like the yippies. There are a lot of people who said, "Yeah, we're yippies." There were people who said, "We're beatniks," "We're hippies," different words at different times. But nobody ever says "I'm a yuppie." Somebody invented the word "yuppie" as a way of dismissing the ideas, the behavior, and the personal existence of somebody they didn't like. And this word has been picked up because there are a lot of people who find that there are a lot of people they don't like and are glad to have another bad word to hurl at them. It's not polite to say "nigger" anymore, for instance, so people of a nasty temperament are hard up to find pejorative nouns, and "yuppie" came along to relieve them.

Audience member: Isn't it the same thing called "the Me Generation" a decade ago?

Hess: Yeah, that's right, and that's the thing I object to. Whether they exist or not isn't as important, it seems to me, as the fact that they're criticized for this horrible thing of thinking about themselves as important and wanting things. And can you think of any healthier definition of a good neighbor than somebody who meets these criteria? They think of themselves; they want things. My God, it's just wonderful. And yet they're criticized. Of course, they're criticized by columnists always who have indoor tennis courts, so . . . (*laughter*)

Audience member: Abbie Hoffman.

Hess: Oh, God, I don't know. What can you say about him? I'm glad I'm out of that.

Audience member: Television!

Hess: Oh, *sheet*. I think it's an interesting minor technology, but I swear to goodness, it's . . . For old people it's neat. I mean, when your mind's going and you don't have anything else to do. (*laughter*)

Wilson: I think the most fascinating thing that's happening in television is that nobody I know in the United States – when I'm in the United States, nobody I know and visit – looks at network television anymore. This came to me very gradually over the last two years in coming back here on three lecture tours, and it's gradually percolated: Nobody I know looks at network television. They don't look at public television either anymore. All they look at is video. So television has become a library. Instead of something you're being force-fed, where you have a limited choice of which channel of garbage you'll turn to, now you go out and rent or buy a video like you used to rent or buy books. And so it's becoming an expression of the personality of the user. I think that's revolutionary, and nobody realizes how revolutionary it is.

Hess: It's the best part of it. We got a VCR through a most curious means, I'm suddenly reminded. I had a new aortic valve installed, in my belief that the original design is not perfect, and that human beings can do a little bit better. So I was really out of it for some time, and our neighbors chipped in and got us a VCR. They just got enough to rent it for a couple of months, until one of them had the good sense to write Barry Goldwater a letter. So he sent them the balance. And now, thanks to our neighbors, we have this VCR. (*applause*) These are the very people criticized by people in Washington for not being open, charitable, kind, and so forth, and yet they are the most charitable people that I know of. It was a very nice VCR, but yeah, you're right – it's a great thing to have around.

Audience member: What would you watch?

Hess: What would I watch? I have this habit. I'm addicted to a certain film. I own a film, and this film is called *The Wind and the Lion*. And the reason I like it is because I think it is beyond any question the most romantic film I have ever seen in my life, and I have to see it at least once a month, because its ending lines are so wonderful. It's a discussion between two people who've just been through horror, very dangerous times, and now they've lost everything, they have nothing. And one to the other says, "Wouldn't it be terrible to never in your life have had anything important enough to risk it all for?" I thought: Boy, that's right. That's important stuff to do.

Audience member: Favorite books.

Hess: Favorite book? *Principia Discordia*.

Wilson: *Finnegans Wake*.

Audience member: Digital tape recorders.

Hess: Well, a little pricey so far. (*chuckles*) Maybe I'll get sick again. (*laughter*)

Audience member: Goldwater's campaign in '64.

Hess: Oh, boy. Not so much the campaign, because you know all about that; I think the more interesting one was his campaign to return to the Senate. When I was then a member of SDS [Students for a Democratic Society] and was working with the Black Panthers fairly regularly, he still wanted me to come out for his Senate campaign to write some speeches. So I took off to go out there, and as a going away present, my friends – I lived on a boat at that time, and my friends in associated boats had given me a piece of hashish that was exactly the size of the largest Hershey bar you can buy, except considerably thicker, and said to go out and do good work for the senator.

So I got out there, and the first thing was that they wouldn't let me register at a distant motel with my name. They had me registered under a false name, and I was never to come near the office, because I was a pretty well-known hippie. And they bring stuff out, and I write these speeches, and it went quite well, particularly the speech at the University of Arizona that began, so help me God, "I have much in common with the anarchist wing of SDS." (*Wilson laughs*) And he then went on to talk about what this anarchist strain meant.

I stayed in his pool house also for a time there. And he came into the pool house one day. Then he sniffed. "Ohhhh," he said. "I haven't smelled any of that for a long time." Then he started talking. You know, it was Arizona where this crazy drug officer got the idea to outlaw everything, because he said he saw crazed cowboys all of the time. Goldwater described those times when everybody was smoking grass, and how he thought it was fine. He couldn't understand why anybody had ever made it illegal. Went on and on and on. His position on that was just inspiring. I wish we'd known about that in '64. (*laughter*)

Although we had things that were almost as bad politically. He was on the ham radio one day in '64. Always – I mean, most of the time in the airplane was spent restringing antennas. And he was talking to somebody in one of the Carolinas, where we were headed for him to make a major speech. And this person said, "Senator, what do you think about the right of a Communist to speak on a campus?" And the senator said – you know, two hams over the radio – he said, "Well, I think that they pay taxes and it's a public place. They ought to have a right to speak there." Went on like that. So this made headlines the next day of him taking this position. And isn't it interesting that the headlines were made by his *opponents*, because it's assumed that anybody who talks like that is incompetent – and this is from both sides. That was an interesting part of the campaign.

Audience member: I think he was ahead of his time on awareness of ecology, wasn't he?

Hess: Yes, I think he was. Because he lived in a very sparse area where you could see connections rather quickly.

Audience member: Artificial intelligence.

Hess: If it's intelligent, it is too artificial.

Wilson: Ronald Reagan.

Hess: Yeah. (*laughter*)

Audience member: Nostradamus.

Hess: Ehh. Look, anybody can predict the future, right?

Wilson: He is the classic example of following Heinlein's advice: It does not pay a prophet to be too specific. (*laughter*)

Audience member: Natural law.

Wilson: I got a card given to me that makes me a genuine and authorized illuminated one, a member of the Secret Chiefs, and a professor of the Invisible College, only it says, "Void where prohibited by natural law." (*laughter*) I'm very happy I don't believe in natural law, so this card can never be invalidated.

Hess: I keep thinking of natural law in terms of, if I go out into the field near our house and proclaim a right of any sort, I keep waiting for the agency that is going to enforce this right or even make it palpable. On the other hand, if I walk up the hill to a neighbor and we discuss something, and we mutually agree that henceforth we will be as gods or something of that sort, then I say that is not a right, that is an agreement. And that's perfectly natural.

So I don't know, I guess this stuff is important, but I keep asking myself: Suppose you know somebody who believes in or doesn't believe in natural rights – which you do, obviously. Now, what difference will that belief or disbelief make in the ordinary congress of life of this person as a neighbor? Will it mean that they won't show up when your barn is burning? Will it mean that they'll rustle your cattle? What does it mean, actually? Does it have any bearing on the way people would behave? My feeling is that, look, there are a lot of things that are fun to debate about and denounce people over. That's certainly fun. But on the other hand, it should be taken into account that these differences that people have may be meaningless differences. I think we should all start assessing these things in terms of, what difference does it make in the person?

Audience member: Enough talk about natural law. How about unnatural acts?

Hess: Unnatural acts. If it's an act, it's natural.

Audience member: So-called intellectual property rights. And since you're both computer literate, I have a specific interest in cases like Apple's claim to have the exclusive use of a particular way that a computer behaves.

Hess: I think they're very difficult to enforce.

Wilson: I think they'll become impossible to enforce very shortly.

Hess: Yeah.

Audience member: Does it mean that copyrights in general are a spook?

Hess: Well, they've always been sort of crazy. I mean, as has been pointed out time after time, they protect the person who gets there first, who may have had a better trolley or something, and have nothing to do with the idea. It's been my understanding all along that libertarians were glorified, among other things, by the fact that they very early on had attacked the copyright laws.

Audience member: But you're both authors.

Hess: I don't think that the copyright laws – Maybe they protect us in some technical sense, but I'd be happy to sell things in a free market.

Audience member: Would you mind if I took "Death in Politics," sold it, and made a profit without cutting you in?

Hess: People are doing it all the time. Look, I made money off that. I figure somebody bought it; it's not mine anymore. And people do it. People do it constantly. And I think it's fine, because if I were asked to do it again today, I'd say I'll do it on condition that a lot of people read it. And this way may help it.

Audience member: World of wrestling.

Hess: The wonderful world of wrestling.

Wilson (*pointing to Hess*): I'll let you handle that. (*laughter*)

Hess: Well, I think the first thing that we've got to think about is who we're wrestling with – with whom we are wrestling. Yeah, so we think about that. Do you want to specify the sort of match you had in mind?

Audience member: Professional wrestling.

Hess: Oh, well, OK. I have a notion about professional wrestling, if that means professional athletics. I think this hue and cry against not teaching football players to be astrophysicists is really wretched. I mean, there's a course for everything else in college. Why in the hell can't there be a course on professional athletics? And then you could drop all of this crap about "these people that should be educated" and so forth. They'll live there to learn a trade. (*applause and laughter*) And I think they should be permitted to do it without being aggravated by a bunch of English teachers. (*laughter*)

Wilson: I believe even policemen can be rehabilitated and taught the useful trades. And football is one trade that most policemen could be taught.

Audience member: The Fairness Doctrine.

Hess: It's gone – hooray, hooray, hooray. It was never fair. It wasn't much of a doctrine.

Audience member: Old age.

Hess: Oh God, what a pain in the ass. (*laughter*)

Wilson: It's better than the alternative. (*laughter*)

Hess: It is. It should go on forever, but . . .

One of the worst things about it is seeing people who are familiar. It used to be that when I saw people who were familiar, I'd say, "God, maybe that's their son or daughter." Now I realize it's either their grandchildren or even their great-grandchildren. I woke up one morning to realize that I'm older than Jimmy Carter. God, this is terminal oldness. (*laughter*)

Wilson: Most men my age are dead already.

Audience member: Favorite toy, yours or somebody else's.

Wilson: Somebody else's. (*laughter*)

Hess: I can tell you about mine. My favorite toy of all toys was the inside of an electric train. Just the motor – it didn't have any of that silly business on it. I thought that little motor moving around those tracks was the most wonderful thing I had ever seen. That was the most important toy in my life, until I read Euclid.

Audience member: Superconductors.

Hess: It should be done by libertarians. Libertarians have got to make some breakthroughs like that. My favorite breakthrough is that a libertarian could come up with a really hot cure for virtually all forms of cancer and refuse to administer it to collectivists. (*laughter*)

Audience member: Are you saying copyright it?

Hess: No, just refuse to give it. I mean, if you give it, you've lost it. I mean at least that seems to me the way it is.

Audience member: Was (*inaudible*) thinking about the motor, or does she know something we don't?

Hess: They're here, they're things like that, and they're more and more exciting things happening. I think the field today is in the organic sciences, in biology and botany. And with genetic engineering I just think that's a major, major field. For a time, it'll outdo a lot of the mechanical ones.

Audience member: What periodicals do you guys follow?

Hess: I can tell you mine very simply. Indispensable: *Technology Review*, which is MIT's magazine. *Popular Science*. A little newsletter edited out in California called *Manas*, which I can't expect that anybody would have read.

Wilson: I have.

Hess: You have read it? Fine, well . . .

Audience member: What's it called?

Hess: It's called *Manas*. It's just a funny little philosophical magazine. I just love it.

Audience member: Who's your favorite fashion designer?

Hess: You ought to let him talk about his magazines first. Maybe one of them is *Harper's*.

Wilson: My favorite magazines are the *New Scientist,* because I live in Ireland and it's more convenient to get it from England than to wait for *Scientific American* to wend its way across the Atlantic, and *Brain/Mind Bulletin*, which is worth waiting for it to wend its way across the Atlantic, because it has all of the most important research on the nervous system and the brain that's going on now. And to me, that's where the action is: the nervous system and the brain, and especially those ever-lovin' peptides.

Audience member: Eminent domain.

Hess: Well, that, I suppose, leads to the question of whether you can own any property anyway. And it just occurs to me, in terms of real property, the fact of the matter is, you can't anyway. Nobody in this country can own a piece of real property; they have to rent it from the government. So I suppose that eminent domain is very similar to that. No wonder it's been hard to argue away from it. But property taxes make it rented property.

Audience member: Nietzsche.

Hess: Oh, boy. Like Stirner, I think it's good to read some of the old folks.

Wilson: When Gordon Liddy got out of jail, he was asked a bunch of questions, and he said "no comment" to all of them until he got to his car. I saw this on television news. He was getting into his car, and one reporter tried one last question: "Do you have any comment on the prison system?" And Gordon Liddy turned around and said, "Anything that doesn't kill me makes me stronger." And I suddenly realized I had a common bond with Gordon Liddy. I recognized our common humanity, because that's my favorite quote from Nietzsche.

Audience member: AIDS.

Wilson: When we find the cure for AIDS, we will have longevity, because AIDS is based on the breakdown of the immunological system, which happens to all of us as we get older. And once they find out how to stop the accelerated breakdown, that will inevitably point the direction to how to stop the later breakdown that happens with senility and so on. So we will learn how to reconvert the immune system to the resistance it had at around the age of 18 to 20, and then we can go on indefinitely, getting higher and higher all the time.

Audience member: Space colonies.

Wilson: Space colonies? I want the first one to be named Proxmire. (*laughter*)

Audience member: Your previous incarnations.

Hess (*to Wilson*): Have you got a favorite one?

Wilson: Yeah. My favorite was when I was Hans Zoesser, born in 1740 and died in 1812. He was a member of the Bavarian Illuminati, and he was there on the day they initiated Thomas Jefferson in Paris, and he knew Voltaire personally, and he's buried in a churchyard in Vienna. I got all this under hypnosis, and one of these days I'm going to go to Vienna and look for that tombstone – and if I find that tombstone, I'm going to be the most surprised son of a bitch on the planet, because I don't believe in reincarnation. (*laughter*)

Audience member: Voting.

Hess: Voting in what sense? If it's voting on the National Committee, I'd say absolutely not. (*laughter*) But if it's voting for dog catcher or sheriff, that sort of thing, I'd say sure. Voting for sheriff is one of the most significant survival acts that you can make in your neighborhood, and if you don't pay attention to it, you're just missing a great point. I think this notion that you support the system or verify it by doing this is not necessarily correct. (*applause*)

Wilson: If voting could change the system, it would be illegal. If *not* voting could change the system, it would be illegal.

Audience member: I can't believe in your friend in the IRS who's so close to retirement, because you wouldn't have endangered him.

Hess: Yeah, well, I don't think that he's actually going to do anything. I've despaired of the project so far.

Audience member: So that wasn't a (*inaudible*) point; it was a "whatever."

Hess: Yes, I think you're right.

Audience member: Is this a party or a revolution?

Hess (*gestures at room*): This thing here? What's "this"? Oh: this [Libertarian] Party.

Well, you know how I feel. I hate to get in trouble again, but I think the libertarian movement is considerable and is serious, and I think that it is a mistake to confuse the movement with any component part of it. And so I presume this is a bunch of people who are in the libertarian movement who have chosen to do a certain thing, and that that is simply something that they have chosen to do.

But I think it is a movement. I think it is coming along, as most movements do. This is some sort of weird determinism, I guess, but I believe tools create in their wake the sort of social organization that they need to progress. Or it may just be that it makes it possible. But I think that libertarians represent a way of thinking which will be absolutely essential to the utilization of the tools now being designed.

Wilson: This is Wilson's Fifth Law: Primate behavior only changes under the impact of new technology.

Hess: I take it very seriously that that's what is happening. There's nothing the world can do but move toward liberty, because the technologies are simply too decentralizing and too complex to be handled by . . . there's little room . . . there's not many jobs for idiots in the long future, although there's plenty today.

Audience member: Forty-two.

Wilson: That's the answer to "Why does the universe exist?" and "What is the purpose of life?"

Audience member: Forty-three.

Wilson: That is the answer to "Is there anything that doesn't make sense in the universe?"

Audience member: Peptides.

Wilson: Take peptides into your heart, brothers and sisters. You'll be better for it. Your neighbors will be better for it.

Audience member: Is free will an illusion?

Wilson: I am determined not to think so. (*laughter*)

Audience member: I Ching.

Wilson: Some people say the I Ching gives meaningful answers. Some people say computers give meaningful answers. The Turing test of intelligence is, "Does it give meaningful answers?" I think computers and the I Ching both pass that test. So by the Turing test, they're both intelligent. I find it very odd that people who believe the computers are intelligent regard the people who think the I Ching is intelligent as mystics, and the people who believe I Ching is intelligent regard the people who think computers are intelligent as materialists. And yet basically, it's the same question. The question is, "Does binary notation of itself generate form and coherence?" Which it seems to do.

Audience member: Christian television.

Wilson: Not as funny as Moslem television. (*laughter*)

Audience member: Jack Paar.

Hess: Oh. One of the greats, absolutely. World hasn't been quite the same. But he's coming back, isn't he?

Audience member: A bumper sticker: "Release the endorphins!"

Hess: Oh, that's great. That's wonderful.

Wilson: My favorite bumper stickers are, in descending order – I see all of these on the California highways – "If guns are outlawed, only outlaws will have guns." And the second one is, "'If guns are outlawed, how can we shoot the libertarians?' – Lyndon LaRouche." And the third one is, "If laws are outlawed, only outlaws will have laws" (*laughter*), which is probably Douglas Hofstadter getting into the act. And the final one is, "If marriage is outlawed, only outlaws will have in-laws" (*laughter*), which I think is a translation from the Hungarian. The original is actually more correctly translated as, "How many surrealists does it take to change a light bulb?" And the answer is, "A fish." (*laughter*)

Hess: My favorite bumper sticker currently, because Therese and I do tutoring of adult illiterates where we are, there's one bumper sticker we have actually seen that says: "Illiterate? Write for help!" (*laughter*)

Wilson: That's like the signs – There are these signs all over the United States that say "No dogs allowed except seeing eye dogs." And the question always comes to me: Who's supposed to read that, the blind man or the dog? (*laughter*)

Audience member: Which historical figure would you want to have a conversation with? Anybody in history.

Hess: Euclid.

Wilson: James Joyce.

Audience member: What would you choose to be the last meal of your life?

Hess: You see you're asking something – You may have touched a nerve with that one. I could be planning it. What would it be? Barbecued potato chips. No question about it. (*laughter*) Just tons of them.

Audience member: Addictions.

Hess: Barbecued potato chips. (*laughter*)

Wilson: Peptides.

Hess: Barbecued peptides. (*laughter*)

Audience member: Bucky Fuller.

Hess: You know, in his last interview before he died, which was with a libertarian lady in California, he was quoted as saying, "I am an anarchist." Buckminster Fuller – his conclusion had been roughly echoing some of the things we've been saying. His conclusion was that it just won't work. You can't plan it. It just won't work. You've got to let it go and let people take charge of themselves.

Audience member: I wasn't a big fan of his crusade against the evil of greed.

Hess: I don't know if he would have. It's just that here is a question of somebody who had reached one conclusion. He may still have a number of other conclusions that may seem odious, but having reached this very significant one, I'd be happy to have him over.

Wilson: I found it fascinating that he got grouchier as he got older. As sublime as he was – he was one of the most serene, beautiful people I ever met. I remember how he policed himself and constrained himself against ever saying anything critical about another human being. He made that one of his disciplines, never to criticize other architects whom he regarded as idiots. But he was very careful never to say that explicitly. When he had to criticize things that were going on, he would specify that the people who did this thought they were doing right. And I saw him on a television show in which (*inaudible*) asked him, "What do you think of the Hancock building," which was just put up in Chicago then. And Bucky looked terribly embarrassed and uptight, and he started staggering toward an answer, very unusual for him. And he said, "I don't like to think harshly of my fellow human beings." And that was more devastating than if he said, "It was 110 stories of shit," you know? (*laughter*) He was struggling so hard to be nice.

But then, at the end of his life, I did an interview with him in which he said, "Ronald Reagan is a dumb actor who can memorize his lines, and that's the only thing I care to say about him." And in his last book, he said the Mafia has taken over most of the businesses in the Western world and they're one of the four most dominant influences, and everything that has to be done to handle Spaceship Earth intelligently and make everybody as rich as they should be will all be opposed by the Catholic Church because the Pope knows as well as I know that if people are well-fed and happy, they won't need a lot of ignorant superstitions anymore. And I said, "What's happened to Bucky Fuller?" (*applause*) He's finally let out all the anger of 87 years.

Hess: Older architect story, installment two. Frank Lloyd Wright was given a prestigious award in Philadelphia one time, and people spoke interminably before he was introduced about him. And so when he rose and went to the podium, he said, "Ladies and gentlemen, my address is Taliesin West," and he walked off. (*Wilson laughs*) Ah, good stuff.

Audience member: Are you delegates? Can you vote?

Hess: I can vote. Yeah, I'm going to vote for Jim Turney. (*laughter*) For, I'm sure, thoroughly idiosyncratic reasons.

Audience member: Nostradamus.

Hess: Oh, Nostradamus. We dismissed him some time ago.

Audience member: Carl Sagan.

Wilson (*mimicking*): Billions and billions.

Audience member: Ralph Nader.

Wilson: Ralph Nader! Ralph Nader. Don't get me started on that subject. I have been traveling around the world, in the last five months. I've been flying from here to there and back and forth. I've been to East Germany to Maui and back across the United States a couple of times, and I'm tied up all the time I'm on the planes. I'm trussed up like a turkey. And then I get off the planes, and I think I don't have to be tied up anymore, and I get in a car, and the first thing they say is, "We've got a new law. I've got to tie you up before I can start the car." So I gotta be tied up in the cars too. And some days I fly six hours tied up on the plane, and then I get in a car and I'm driven two hours tied up in the car. I'm spending more and more of my waking hours trussed up because that son of a bitch Nader is a bondage freak. (*laughter*) He wants us all tied up forever. And you know, the next crusade he's going to start, we're going to have to have belts on at our word processors so we don't fall off the chair and hurt ourselves. This is for our own good, of course.

I thought it was only the English aristocracy who are into this bondage thing, but there's a definite sign of it, not just in Nader, but in a hell of a lot of the ecology movement. I get mailings from a group called the Friends of the Vanishing Malaria Mosquito. The malaria mosquito has been decimated so much in the last two decades. Throughout vast areas of Africa and Polynesia and parts of South America, where this species numbered in the billions and billions, now they can only find five or six a year. It's one of the leading contenders of the endangered species. You can see just how bad it is looking at the malaria death figures in human beings every year – it's been going straight down, which shows there are hardly any malaria mosquitoes left. And if we don't stop this carnage, the fiendish villains in the chemical industry will kill them all. I read this stuff, and I'm trying to figure out, is this satire or is this real?

Hess: It's real satire.

Audience member: Richard Nixon.

Hess: I did a little work for Nixon. And in a conversation one day while I was working with him, a young fellow who later became an ambassador to the U.N., as a matter of fact, was there, and he'd been working on Nixon's book. And then there was there also the fellow who had written the first biography of Nixon. The biographer said, "I think I'm going to write a novel about Nixon." The other person who was there said, "How can that be? I've always understood that a novel had to have a central character." (*laughter*) And I must say I thought that was the most perceptive description of him. Really no character. I think he was a good president – he could probably go down as one of the great presidents of all time – considering how much better he was than any of these birds who followed him. (*chuckles*) But I think he's a person of no character. He lucked into everything he did, I suppose.

Audience member: South African sanctions.

Hess: I think that is just terrible. I've worked in southern Africa – I worked in Rhodesia for a while – and I just think it is the cruelest thing that can be done, to in any way isolate those people. Because there's so many South Africans who really wanted to free up as a society, who'd make it a free market society. There are people like Chief Buthelezi who even feel that for black Africans, that this would be a useful exercise. And to isolate all of this, I just think it's criminal.

Also, I think that the work that Leon Louw is doing, a libertarian in South Africa, is probably the most important libertarian project in the world today. (*applause*) And the reason I say it mainly, is that it has a real possibility of being effective, in which case libertarian history would change very quickly.

Audience member: And the rest of history too.

Hess: Possibly so. I think that the notion that one of the cantons of South Africa would be a free market, competing if you will with some collectivist cantons, is exciting beyond belief.

Audience member: What about the ANC?

Hess: Well, I don't know what their position would be. Leon seems optimistic about it, that they would not violently oppose this.

Audience member: Dealing with crime.

Hess: Dealing with crime or dealing with criminals?

Audience member: Both.

Hess: I dealt with a criminal for a time. I wrote a book for a Mafia guy who was really absolutely fascinating. To show you roughly his stature in Mafia, Lucky Luciano had been his father's driver. And this guy was just marvelous to work with, because, oh, you know, the story of how he helped his mother kill his father's mistress. (*laughter*) The family that slays together . . . (*laughter*)

When he was a fairly young man, he had been just getting used to being a criminal, he and some friends had decided to rob a non-Mafia gambling joint. You know, they're fair game. Incidentally, this guy told me that the Mafia's arrangement with the police regularly is that whenever the police need an arrest of any particular sort, they will tell them who to arrest, because it'll be a non-Mafia person. So the police are constantly wiping out the competition.

But this fellow, when he was telling me about his family life and this good decision to go raid this gambling place, they burst in, they had shotguns and submachine guns, all of the proper equipment, and they had the proper protocol, the shouting and yelling and threatening everything. Did everything just right. But he said it was operated by a bunch of Chinese. And he said, and I'll never forget this phrase, he said, "Those people have no respect for authority." (*laughter*) He said, "We told them to do this, that, and the next thing," and he said, "They just stood there and looked at us." And he said, "I'll tell you one thing. I'm never going to rob a Chinese again."

While we were working on it, he wanted to know if there's anything that would ease my labors. He said, "Woman? Girl? Boy?" And then we got down to the interesting question of narcotics, and he said, "What would you like?" And I said, "Well, some marijuana would be pleasant." And he said, "Ohhhhh." He said, "You know, we've got to buy that just like you do." He said, "We can't control that." (*laughter*) He said, "You know, everybody can grow that stuff." He was absolutely outraged about it. (*laughter*)

So the answer to crime is also the free market. Expose them to some serious competition. Because, as a matter of fact, there are certainly things in the world that are more pleasant than being a criminal. There are some sociopaths, I guess, and maybe the question always is, "What if one of them comes crashing through your window?" And I've got to confess to you that I really believe in aggressive self-defense, and where I come from, the answer is very simple: Evolution is speeded on its inevitable way by eliminating the unfit. (*laughter*)

Audience member: New country projects.

Wilson: The way to start a new country. Loompanics has an excellent book on that, *How to Start Your Own Country*. But one of the methods they left out is you go down about 10 miles south of Laredo with some confederates. You need a little capital to get started. You put up a shack, and you put a chain across the road, and you stop all the American tourists as they come down, and you search their car, and you pretend to find cocaine. Then you lock them up in the shack for three days, and then another of your confederates comes in, pretending to be the American ambassador, and says, "This is really serious. They claim they found two and a half pounds of cocaine." And the poor victim says, "I wasn't doing it. I swear to God, I'm a businessman from Des Moines." And the American ambassador says, "Well, there's one way to handle all problems in Mexico. How much money have you got?" Then the officials all get bribed, and the poor mark is allowed to drive on into Mexico with no more money on him, because, as W.C. Fields said, "It's a sin against nature to leave a sucker in full possession of his assets." (*laughter*) And so then you wait for the next mark to come along. Within a couple of months, if you got enough money on that, you can put up a shack on another road and a shack on another road, and the money comes in more and more of them. You get your own army, your own navy, eventually you have your own nuclear deterrent, and then you're a country. That's the way the Normans went about it, more or less. (*laughter*)

Audience member: Voluntary compliance.

Hess: The state of Ohio – we have a little quote from this in the upcoming issue – the tax commissioner wrote to businessmen about some new tax thing, and it was about voluntary compliance. And that was "voluntary compliance," period.

Next paragraph: "If you do not voluntarily comply, you can expect to be visited, investigated by agents not only of this department, but of the tax departments of the adjoining states," so forth and so on. So I guess that's voluntary compliance – government style.

Audience member: Norma Jean [Almodovar].

Hess: Oh, God, that's a terrible thing that is happening to her, and she's very courageous about it. The worst thing from a libertarian point of view, however, is the reaction to her candidacy, which included the reaction of some Californians that she had ruined the party, or that the party had been ruined by her candidacy. I think this is something libertarians have got to be careful about, to not spook so quickly when something a little different comes along. She did well. I don't think she hurt the party at all. I think, as a matter of fact, she must have helped it.

I wrote last issue about something that I think is germane to this, to the Norma Jean question, of whether you should support those in your movement who are the most unpopular at any given time. My notion is that, perhaps unfortunately, yes, you have to. I wrote last time about a group of punks, punk rockers, that I'd met in Toronto, who are estranged from the Toronto party because they really are not very classy dressers. And yet listen to what they do. They remodel and resell slum housing. The consequence is their little group is rich – they are very rich – and their neighbors so rely on them for help that they have constituted the sort of neighborhood protection for people when there are robbers in the neighborhood, who are known thieves, who are preying on poor and very disorganized Chinese – this is in Chinatown, I should have mentioned. They come to these punk rockers to help them, and the punk rockers are quick to respond. One of them, as a matter of fact, wears an interesting necklace of the teeth of one of the last people.

(*laughter*) You notice that they know how to handle brigands.

Here are these people. They are privatized self-defense. They are rich, which more libertarians ought to be. They are practicing their culture exactly as they like. What could possibly be more libertarian? And I think those are the things that . . . Every now and then, we've got to understand that liberty means liberty, and that some of the people exercise it in the most untidy ways, but to fail to defend anyone in their seeking to attain liberty, no matter how odious their practices may appear to you, I think is a very serious mistake. (*applause*)

Audience member: What do you find really offensive?

Hess: Forbidding me those barbecued potato chips for my last meal. (*laughter*)

Wilson: I don't know, it's pretty hard to offend me. I offend a lot of people, but it's very hard to offend me. The other day, I went up to the concierge to mail a letter, and he had a sign on his desk that said, "Thank you for not smoking." So I said to him, "Thank you for not picking your nose." (*laughter*) He looked all bent out of shape for about five minutes afterwards. And yet I thought that was just a minor bit of surrealist witticism. It's very easy to offend some people. But then again, as John Cleese once said, "There are some people one wishes to offend." (*laughter*)

Audience member: James Joyce. Is there as much allegory in his work as the interpreters think?

Wilson: I don't know how much allegory there is in Joyce, but every sentence has been worked on with great precision to give it at least 18 different meanings, about 13 of which are scatological and five are metaphysical. Well, that's an average ratio – sometimes he does better than that. But no, you don't have to invent meanings in Joyce; he put so many meanings in that it's almost a full-time job to find the ones he put in. We don't need to go around inventing any of our own. Somebody asked him why he was writing such a queer book as *Finnegans Wake*. He said, "To keep the PhD candidates busy for the next thousand years." (*laughter*) After 38 years on it, I'm absolutely convinced that boast will be justified. After 38 years, I feel I'm beginning to acquire the knack of recognizing how many funny things are going on simultaneously in that book.

Audience member: *Portrait of the Artist as a Young Man.*

Wilson: Well, the *Portrait* has a great deal in it that doesn't appear on the surface. It is worth rereading several times if you really want to understand the man who probably was to literature what Einstein was to physics and what Picasso was to painting.

Audience member: Ezra Pound.

Wilson: The last lines Pound ever wrote: "I have tried to write Paradise terrestrial/Do not move/Let the wind speak/that is paradise./May the Gods forgive what I/have made/Let those I love try to forgive/what I have made."

At the end of a 900-page poem, those lines are absolutely magnificent in their simplicity and in how much they contain. OK, that's my comment on Ezra Pound.

Hess: That's great.

Audience member: Joseph Conrad.

Wilson: I prefer Faulkner.

Audience member: *Mad* magazine. (*laughter*)

Wilson: I prefer the *National Lampoon*.

Hess: I prefer the *National Enquirer*. (*laughter*)

Audience member: Dan Rather.

Hess: I don't know anything about Dan Rather, but I tell you, I leap to the support of a guy named Bryant Gumbel, however.

He was criticized in *The Washington Post* recently because he interviews people on television and he was criticized for treating them brusquely. It was said that he had on important world figures and he sometimes treated them as though they were nothing, and he was rude to them and so forth. And so I've written something about that in defense of Gumbel. I mean, he's treating them exactly the way they should be treated. And who is to say that that this young man who's now a network person and interviews people – who's to say he doesn't know as much about anything as government officials? I think this is a terrible habit we get into thinking that public figures are somehow endowed with superior intelligence.

Audience member: Newspapers.

Hess: There's some of them around. (*laughter*)

Wilson: I think the key to politics, going back to the last question, is that nobody ever ran for office who wasn't sincerely convinced of their own tremendous charm.

Hess: Yeah.

Wilson: I think ordinary people occasionally have doubts about their own magnetism and charisma and their ability to sell bullshit to anybody. But the politicians never doubt. Like Nixon never doubted. At the very at the end of Watergate, when he was resigning, he had that look in his eye, like: *If I say it just right, they'll believe me again and they'll say, "Dick, don't resign."*

Hess: Yeah.

Wilson: That's all you need in politics. You don't need anything else.

Hess: It's almost impossible not to acquire such habits of thought. Think of a politician from United States representative up. First of all, you have paid people to follow you around and do things and tell you that you're the best thing that ever happened, because their jobs all depend on your being this. And so you hear this constantly from people of a vested interest in doing it. So you believe it very quickly. I mean, who wouldn't? It would take a person who's run for office surrounded by such people . . .

I mean, look at Libertarians. What is everybody's great nightmare? That there'll be some Libertarian candidate who will take it very seriously and will exercise power once he gets in. It's *the* nightmare, and it's what anti-party people say is bound to happen. Well, if *we* worry about that, how can we be surprised then when we think of *ordinary* politicians bowing to the pressures of power? It's just irresistible.

Has anybody in the room worked at the White House? (*no response*) Well, let me tell you, I have for a while, and I challenge you to think of how you would resist it. Think of a situation in which there is no activity on the face of the earth that will not stop for your presence if you want it to. That is to say, if you call up any place, any airline, any store, any organization from the White House, and say that this should happen at this time, it will happen. It's just irresistible, good God. And you can be out on a friend's boat offshore anywhere and a helicopter will come for you. That sort of thing. I mean, it's no wonder that these people think that they have the answers to everything. Everybody tells them they do.

Wilson: As Mel Brooks said in *History of the World Part 1*, "Being king is good." Remember that?

Hess: Boy, it sure is. Everybody gets code names too. And when you have a code name, that's that makes you think that you really are special.

Audience member: What was your code name?

Hess: I forget. I really do forget. But I know that the feeling you get when an airline has been held on the ground for 30 minutes for you to walk casually but mysteriously onto the plane with everybody hating you and with it not making any difference at all. I mean, how can you fail but to believe, "My God, everything I think, everything I do is, is correct and powerful." Boy.

Audience member: Linus Pauling.

Hess (*to Wilson*): Do you have a comment on his abilities as a chemist?

Wilson: I hear he's pretty good. (*laughter*)

Hess: I still think maybe Owsley's a little better.

Audience member: The sooner the population sheds government, the safer it'll be for all of us misfits. We're sort of gathered here to do something to hurry up the process. The subject is off-the-wall methods for doing that.

Hess: I've got a favorite one. It's so simple that I just wonder about it. It occurs to me that in an effort to help your government go about its appointed task, one of the things they want is a lot of tax returns. They want everybody to file them. So it occurs to me that possibly some ill-tempered person might decide to pick names at random from the phone book and make out their tax returns for them. And assisted by a properly programmed printer, they should be able to do this at a high rate of speed, so that instead of having x number of tax returns coming in to delight them, they will be dazzled by the fact that there's 2X coming in.

Wilson: Or 10X.

Hess: Or 10X, if you can really get the thing cranked up.

Wilson: And what would excite them even more is every time you are in a post office, you pick up three or four tax forms, make them out for fictitious names, wrong addresses, and then add the things up so it looks like we were very clumsily trying to hide $4,000. So they will audit that one carefully, and they'll go looking for that person. And that'll keep them busy, especially if they get millions like that.

Hess: That's right. Or, I don't know what the morality of this would be, but it seems to me picking names at random out of the phone book is just going to make them a lot more – there'll be a lot more critical people. (*laughter*)

Audience member: Karl, didn't you want once to go around the IRS building with a giant magnet?

Hess: Well, yes, but I realize that's impossible. But I think I keep thinking of interesting scenarios involving air ducts and magnetic particles. But you know, that's just really foolish. That stuff's so redundant that it wouldn't do any good. I think you can't abolish the government. I think the only way that it can possibly be affected is to overload it.

Audience member: (*inaudible*)

Hess: No, I think you just want something to cause trouble, not for them, but for the IRS.

Wilson: In one of my immortal novels, I have an organization called the Network, who are a bunch of computer programmers who are concerned with cocaine and immortality. They want to bring down the price of cocaine, and they want to support life extension research leading to possible immortality, and one of the devices of the Network is to frustrate every other conspiracy on the planet, so they can deflect funds the way they want to. And one of the things they are doing is erasing computer tape. Since they're all in the computer business, they're erasing computer tape selectively, and they send notifications to people: "Congratulations, you are one of the lucky 500 this month. All your debts have been canceled. Keep your mouth shut and play it smart."

Audience member: Which book is that?

Wilson: *Schrödinger's Cat*, volume three – which is about to be reprinted, by the way. I'm doing a commercial for myself in public. Isn't that disgraceful?

Audience member (*to Karl*): What have *you* written lately?

Hess: Well, I'll plug that too. Randy Langhenry, who is sitting back there, and I have just finished a book called *Capitalism for Kids*, and we got page proofs the other day, so I guess it'll be out pretty soon.

Audience member: Are you sending a copy to the White House? (*laughter*)

Hess: We asked a number of people for contributions to the book, I mean anecdotes about when they'd started to work and that sort of thing, and the White House declined to do it. And the reason was that the White House cannot be involved with any commercial operation – which was just absurd, because he's always plugging commercial operations of one sort or another.

But nonetheless, we did – Who was the secretary?

Randy Langhenry (*from audience*): Baldridge.

Hess: Baldridge, the late Malcolm Baldridge. We got a wonderful contribution from him. It was sympathetic to the notion that children should start working as soon as they're inspired to do it – not working, but creating wealth. And it was a good note. We got a lot of good replies. David Packard, interestingly enough, was angry about the concept of the book, and he wrote a very angry letter, which we used. His reasoning was, as he said, "I never did anything in my life for money." He said, "I did it because I loved engineering." And I believe that that could be true, but he hasn't given it back or anything like that. (*laughter*) And so we tried to handle it by just pointing out that, as a matter of fact, the love of engineering and doing good engineering is almost inevitably going to make you rich, and so he shouldn't criticize this.

Wilson: The question of whether you're sending that book to the White House reminds me of another question that brings us back to the earlier topic: Are you all sending your urine to the White House? (*laughter*) This is a very low surrealist tactic, almost 'pataphysical, but I didn't invent it. I'm just reporting – I'm a journalist, you know, part time. Ken Kesey has urged everybody in the country who disapproves of this urine testing program to send samples of urine to Nancy Reagan at the White House, because she's the one who first suggested that idea, and since she's so obsessively concerned with everybody's urine, we should see she has plenty of urine day after day from now on. (*laughter*)

Hess: Speaking of piss, Neil Smith has the most ingenious idea for solving the Middle East crisis I've heard. Inasmuch as the Reagan administration is determined to settle it by force of arms, he says he thinks it would be fairly simple: that you just inform the Ayatollah that on a given day you're going to fly over it with tanker planes which will release hog piss. And this will coat all of the people in the area, and they have to go through an elaborate purification ceremony. And you point out that if you know they still don't come to their senses and permit McDonald's in immediately, fly over again and do it. Sounds like an interesting proposition to me.

Audience member: All you are saying is give piss a chance. (*laughter and applause*)

Hess: Oh! (*both Wilson and Hess applaud*) Yeah! That's great.

Audience member: Urine Nation.

Hess: Speaking of new nation projects . . .

It reminds me of my FBI informer again. He said he thought that the best thing you could do to really irritate them would be to send them a schedule. And I thought that's an ingenious idea. I mean, I don't care. So I did try that a couple of times.

But I've learned that it doesn't pay to do things that you take humorously, to do these pranks with the government, because they don't take anything humorously. A couple of years in a row, I thought it would be fun to owe them a lot more money rather than less. So I put down as my income, $100,000, $200,000, and said that I wouldn't pay tax on that. (*laughter*) I've lived to regret it. My bill just shot up, you know. And there's no possible way to prove – You can't go in and say, "Look, I'm a funny guy. You shouldn't take me seriously." (*laughter*)

Wilson: One of Groucho Marx's wives divorced him because when they were coming back from a trip to Europe, on the customs declaration where it said "occupation," Groucho wrote "opium smuggler." And they were held for about 12 hours while the customs people did all sorts of weird police type things, making calls here and there and going through their luggage over and over and whatnot, and Groucho's wife did not regard it as funny at all after eight hours in custody. They have no sense of humor.

Hess: Doug Casey recently came up with what I considered to be the best comment to a public servant of the month. A customs agent was really giving him a thorough search, and Doug very seriously and not in an abrasive way at all said, "Sir, at what point in your life did you decide that you'd spend it going through other people's underwear?" (*laughter*) You know, the inclination is to get angry with these people. But just ask. The Socratic method is good. You've got to be calm about it. They don't know how to handle calm.

Audience member: Is Reagan going to finish out his term, or is he going to resign?

Hess: I don't know. Why in the hell should he resign?

Audience member: To give Bush a chance.

Hess: Speaking of people with no character. I don't believe he'd do it.

Wilson: I was in Texas recently. Everybody tells me that George is a good old down home boy from Connecticut.

Hess: He did give us such a brilliant example of what politics is all about. I mean, to think of the way he denounced Reagan until he got to be vice president. And suddenly, because Reagan is the nominee, all of those criticisms are now invalid. Doesn't show a depth of conviction that I would take terribly seriously.

Wilson: I think the funniest book I've read all year is *The Triumph of Politics*, by David Stockman –

Hess: Oh, yes.

Wilson: – about how he got converted to voodoo economics because he thought Reagan could win, and how he tried to practice voodoo economics and found it didn't work, and tried to explain that to Reagan and became the most unpopular man in the White House.

Hess: That's an extraordinary book. I don't think I've ever read a book, though, that was more self-serving.

Wilson: Oh, yeah. What could you expect?

Hess: God. Just amazing.

Audience member: It ought to be required reading for all conservative Republicans.

Hess: Well, perhaps it should. It'll be required reading. I'll tell you what *should* be required reading. I've thought about this for some time. There is a good book on American politics, and that's Hunter Thompson's *Fear and Loathing on the Campaign Trail*. And it just occurs to me that we should all push to keep that one going, because it reduces it to some raw data that are important. God, what's this fellow's name who writes about the presidential campaigns? Theodore White. He, of course, was present quite a bit, and I could not believe: This guy's a groupie! Merely a groupie. He really thinks that politicians are extraordinary and wonderful people, he takes everything they do seriously, and he writes these books about it, as though people in politics think about things.

You know what? He explains why they did these things. Most of the times I was there when these things happened, they were done because it was possible to do them, nobody had any serious objections: "Hey, that sounds like a good idea." It's wrong, it's absolutely wrong, to think that politicians are in any sense contemplative about these things.

Audience member: Robert Heinlein.

Hess: I'm just reading *Job*. And the *Notebooks* – Lazarus Long's prescription of what it means to be a human being, I think it's as sound as any I've ever read.

Audience member: What a human being should know.

Hess: "What a human being should know" brings up this bestselling book, *Cultural Literacy*, right? I sense something happening. I think – Well, this has got some context. Let me try to explain this.

I have an old, old friend I used to know very well on the left named Jeremy Rifkin, whose work it is in the world is to find causes for alarm. That's the way he makes his money: find a cause of alarm. So lately he's found two. One was genetic engineering, and most recently surrogate motherhood. And he has tried to figure out *why* these things are bad, and of course he finds nothing wrong in the real world, so he has to go to the other world, and his objections in both cases have become religious, absolutely religious. That is to say: that genetic engineering is unnatural, it is not the way God works these things out. Although, if there was ever a master genetic engineer, it was the God of the Christians. We need to use the original design, they say. Very, very contradictory folks. But at any rate, there's that happened, and then – what was the other part that we were talking about?

Audience member: *Cultural Literacy.*

Hess: Oh, yeah. So I think there's a trend to start justifying policies religiously much more. The Sandinistas are doing this – they're very religious folks, those Sandinistas. I think that cultural literacy will now be a version of this. There will be a great push in the educational system to say that one of the problems with America and the world is that we do not share a culture, that we've grown apart from one another, we've become selfish individuals. And the way to restore this is for people to be taught this common cultural literacy.

Now, the book *Cultural Literacy* not only expounds this theory but lists the 500 things that a culturally literate person in America should know, not one of which I can think of would make any concrete difference in anybody's life. I think what was happening is that there's so much concern with the number of young teachers in this country who are beginning to emphasize thoughtfulness and inquiry among their very young pupils, that there's a great deal of concern about this, so that a number of conservatives particularly will be very avid in pushing for this "shared culture" concept, as opposed to individual creative intelligence. And I just think that's the opening gun of something very important.

Wilson: As for what the average American should know, I'm constantly astounded since I moved to Europe – every time I come back here, I'm astounded what the average American doesn't know. For instance, the average American doesn't know that Northern Ireland and Ireland are two separate countries. People keep asking me, "Why do you live there with all those bombs going off and all those shootings and everything?" Well, there's no bombs going off and there's no shootings in Ireland. That's in Northern Ireland, which is a separate country. I'm astounded how many times I've had to explain that. I'm even more astounded that it got into my head to explain it one more time when nobody even asked me about it. (*laughter*) Maybe I'm becoming a Christian Scientist. I think if I explain it the right way, nobody will ask me again.

Audience member: Have you converted any Irish to libertarians?

Wilson: No, but I do write libertarian letters to *The Irish Times*, which would get very intelligent responses from Jesuits proving I'm theologically unsound, which is a verdict I agree with, and very, very violent and abusive anonymous letters sent to my home. Irish newspapers still have the old-fashioned practice: They put your address along with your name. And so I see the best and the worst of Catholic theology. The best comes from the Jesuits and the worst comes from these people who say you must have brain cancer to write that kind of nonsense.

Audience member: Couple of other books – Allan Bloom's *Closing of the American Mind* and Eric Drexler's *Engines of Creation*.

Hess: Well, I think Drexler's book is just crucial. It's an important book, and it should be read. To not take it into consideration would be rash.

I believe that the other book you mentioned, *The Closing of the American Mind*, is roughly part of this push toward some sort of cultural coherence, as opposed to an emphasis on individual creative activity. And I believe this will be a very serious question. I think we'll have more arguments in the future than we've ever had before on this issue, and we'll have to remember that libertarianism does involve individualism, and that we will have to understand that we may be fighting not

A Non-Euclidean Perspective

just on economic issues, but possibly even more importantly on cultural issues, in which the other side will have a great deal of sympathy because it sounds exactly right. "Wouldn't we all be better off if we all had studied what I studied," that sort of thing. And it sounds good, and it will attract a lot of attention. And the contrary – which is encouraging thoughtful processes, analysis, arguments, skepticism, and so forth – this sounds unruly, chaotic. But I think it's a crucial question for all of us.

Wilson: I think the most important book I've read in the last year is *Megabrain*, by Michael Hutchison, which is a very good manual on how to use the human brain for fun and profit. I've written a manual on that topic myself, but I won't mention its name, lest you think I came here only to plug my books.

Audience member: We all know it's *Prometheus Rising*.

Wilson: (*chuckles*) Michael Hutchison has done a very good update on all the latest knowledge on neuroscicnce and all the evidence that the brain was not designed for failure. The brain was designed for total success in universe, and to do things most of us regard as impossible. And the technology and the knowledge is emerging faster every year. And take peptides into your heart, brothers and sisters, the best is yet to come.

Audience member: Mass delusions.

Hess: *And Popular Fallacies* – wasn't that the full title?

Audience member: *Extraordinary Popular Delusions and the Madness of Crowds*.

Hess: Yeah, very popular book with conspiracy theorists of my generation. (*chuckles*)

Wilson: Mass delusions. That brings me back to the counterfeiting thing again. Two people sit down in different places in the same city, and they each make dollar bills. One is real because it was blessed by the wizards in the Federal Reserve Bank, and the other is not real because it wasn't blessed by the wizards. Now hardly anybody in this country today will say they believe in that and they believe in medieval magic, and yet they do believe that the one blessed by the wizards in the Federal Reserve is real and the other one isn't real. So: *Extraordinary Popular Delusions and the Madness of Crowds and the Belief in These Funny Pieces of Paper*.

Hess: The funniest piece of paper of all, I swear to God, is that little tag on mattresses and pillows. (*laughter*) I mean, you can't feel terribly safe in a universe where people will tell you that you can't take it off because it's against the law.

Wilson: I always rip them off, just on general principles.

Hess: Yeah, before reading them! (*laughter*)

Audience member: H.L. Mencken.

Hess: Oh, a demigod. Should be revered by all of us. The thing that characterizes him that I think is so much lacking today is that he really insulted lots of people who badly needed it, and I think that that's a habit we've got out of.

Wilson: Yeah, he did insult a lot of people. But then, the man who called Harding the Marion stonehead and said Herbert Hoover was the first president to look the same upside down (*laughter*) – a man like that wasn't all bad.

He also said FDR's conception of the government was a milk cow with 200 million teats.

Audience member: His definition of a puritan was someone haunted by the fear that someone, somewhere, is having fun.

Hess: You know, William Pitt had said that in bear baiting, it wasn't the agony of the animal that irritated his parishioners, it was the joy of the spectators.

Audience member: Speaking of taking it off, have you noticed all the signs that command you to do or not to do various things when flashing.

Hess: When flashing?

Wilson: When flashing?

Hess: You mean, of course, the installing of flashing on roof eaves.

Audience member: No, flashing lights apparently.

Hess: Oh, no, I don't know about this.

Wilson: The thing that amazes me about these signs is the things you get every time you enter another country. You always get these things that tell you "welcome to the republic of" and "how glad we are to see you coming here" and "we want to make your stay a pleasant one." And now please fill out these forms. "Warning: If your answers to any of the above are not true, you are subject to 20 years in prison and $400,000 fine, and we may possibly take out your back teeth and execute your children in front of you." These things are horrendous! They start out with this false cheer, and then they end up threatening you. Jesus, what a nice place to arrive. They're going to put me in prison right away.

Hess: Along with a little tag on the pillows, there's another depressing sight, and that is somebody at 3:00 in the morning, with no traffic within 5 billion miles, stopped at a stop light. That is uncanny.

(audience members give accounts of Seattle police ticketing for jaywalking)

Wilson: In New Jersey, the Police Department has signs up all over the state now that say "Crime does not pay, but we do," and then they give you a phone number to inform on your best friend, because they'll pay you for it. I've been suggesting to all the Libertarians in New Jersey they should put a new sign up next to each one of them, and this would just say, "Don't suspect a friend, report him," which is from *Brazil*, and see how long it took any of the people who support that kind of police action to realize that the second sign is a satire. They might take it as seriously as the first sign.

Hess: You know what has happened characteristically when the Declaration of Independence is shown to people? The most notable example I remember was some students from the University of Maryland did it at an American air base in Germany, and they asked several questions. The first question was "Who composed it?" and second was "Would you sign it?" The most frequent answer to who wrote it was Lenin, and the overwhelming answer to "Would you sign it?" was no. And incidentally, we recommend that local libertarians might find this a useful thing to do in their own community.

Wilson: That experiment has been done many times. It was done during the First World War. It was done repeatedly in the '20s. It's been done over and over, and every time the results have been the same. The majority would not approve of the Declaration of Independence, and there have been similar studies where the majority overwhelmingly rejects every item in the Bill of Rights. If this country were a democracy when it was founded, we wouldn't have any of the rights we do have. The people have never supported that kind of document or that kind of libertarian thinking. We owe that to the fact that a few aristocrats conspired to create this form of government against the will of the majority, who would much rather have the right to tyrannize over any minority that comes along.

Audience member: 47% of high school students in America think that "to each according to his ability, to each according to his needs" is part of the Constitution.

Wilson: (*laughs a long time*)

Hess: Well, they may be closer to a perception of reality than we are. (*laughter*) But you know, this emphasis on the shared culture will mean, probably, that the Constitution will be emphasized and the Declaration will be just sort of forgotten. It'll be said the Constitution is more important. "Shared culture" never means just sharing everything that you found out about where you live. It's a very specific menu of items.

Audience member: What do you expect in the country that celebrated the birthday of the Statue of Liberty the same year the debate was going on the new immigration bill?

Hess: You've got to admit that the country, among its other fantastic virtues, one of them is that it is shameless. (*laughter*) And I rather like that. The country is so extraordinary and the people are so creative – a lot of them – that . . . (*trails off*)

Wilson: Well, a country that has a Statue of Liberty that says, Send me a poor, your hurd, your huddle, hurdled masses? Your what masses? Your huddled masses yearning to breathe free. And doesn't have the simple honesty to carve the thing over and put in there "And make sure 80% of them are WASPs," which is the actual policy. But they won't put the actual policy on the statue. That's what I'd do – I'd have the balls to do that if I was in charge and that was going to be the policy about it. Be upfront about it!

Hess: I've been trying to get started for some time, a sanctuary program for Hong Kong millionaires.

Audience member: They don't put it on the *statue*, but they'll put it on the *statute*.

Wilson: Like the Jefferson Memorial. It says across the top of it, "I have sworn upon the altar of God eternal hostility to every form of tyranny over the mind of man." And the next sentence in the letter that comes from is "That is why the clergy have always opposed me," and I can only conclude that part was left off the memorial in the interest of brevity. (*laughter*)

Talking about what you get in questionnaires. If you ask the average American, "Was this intended to be a Christian country?" Judging the way people get away with that on television all the time, about 99% would say yes. They've heard that so often, and they've never heard the truth.

Audience member: Greatest person who ever lived.

Hess: Outside of myself? (*laughter*)

Wilson: Johann Sebastian Bach.

Hess: My mother, and then Euclid. (*laughter*)

Wilson: What is this fixation you have on Euclid? I want to call it the Euclidean complex.

Hess: It was like some people say they felt when they first read Ayn Rand. When I first read Euclid, when I was very small, it was a burst to think, "Good God, the human mind is capable of doing this."

Audience member: It was a peptide hit.

Wilson: Yeah.

Hess: It really was. God, I'll say it was.

Wilson: The first time I realized that one equation in differential calculus applied to a system of springs with weights on them, and also applied to an electrical current with resistance, inductance, and capacitance in it, and that there was this simple, mathematical, elegant expression behind these two vastly different physical systems, I got a flash of pure satori. And I have never understood the people who say that science destroys our capacity for mysticism. All the high experiences I had in my teens and twenties were based on mathematics and structural perceptions of what's going on beneath the surface created by our sensory apparatus.

Hess: And to deny this to kids strikes me as being the most cardinal of crimes. To take these naturally curious people and deny them the pleasure of discovery – that's real child abuse. Real child abuse.

Meinshausen: We're quite moved by what you say. So is the hotel – in fact, they want us to move to another room.

Hess: How about where we can all go to sleep?

(*lots of applause as the event ends*)

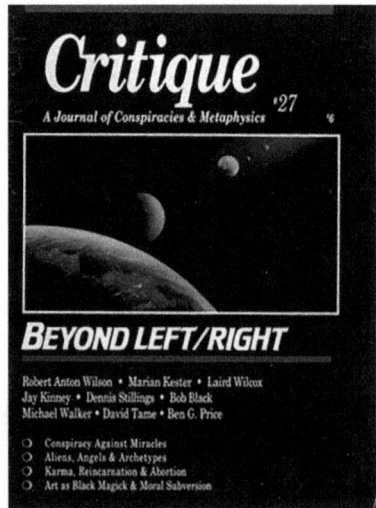

Left and Right:
A Non-Euclidean Perspective

Published in *Critique: A Journal of Conspiracies and Metaphysics* #27, 1988

This is, along with "Thirteen Choruses for the Divine Marquis," one of two essays in this volume that has appeared in another one of Robert Anton Wilson's books – sort of. Bob included this piece in the last book he published in his lifetime, 2005's *Email to the Universe*, but he revised it in several ways. (The two most notable changes: he deleted the second half of the paragraph about Harry Elmer Barnes, and he deleted the closing quote from Alexander Pope.) We present the original version here, representing the Robert Anton Wilson of 1988.

– the Hilaritas Press editors

• • •

Our esteemed editor, Bob Banner, has invited me to contribute an article on whether my politics are "left" or "right," evidently because some flatlanders insist on classifying me as Leftist and others, equally Euclidean, argue that I am obviously some variety of Rightist.

Naturally, this debate intrigues me. The Poet prayed that some power "would the giftie gie us to see ourselves as others see us"; but every published writer has that dubious privilege. I have been called a "sexist" (by Arlene Meyers) and a "male feminist ... a simpering pussy-whipped wimp" (by L.A. Rollins), "one of the major thinkers of the modern age" (by Barbara Marx Hubbard) and "stupid" (by Andrea Chaflin Antonoff), a "genius" (by *Sounds*, London) and "mentally deranged" (by Charles Platt), a "mystic" and "charlatan" (by the Bay Area Skeptics) and a "materialist" (by an anonymous gent in Seattle who also hit me with a pie); one of my books has even been called "the most scientific of all science-fiction novels" (by *New Scientist* physics editor John Gribbin) and "ranting and raving" (by Neal Wilgus). I am also frequently called a "Satanist" in some amusing, illiterate and usually anonymous crank letters from Protestant Fundamentalists.

I can only conclude that I am indeed like a visitor from non-Euclidean dimensions whose outlines are perplexing to the Euclidean inhabitants of various dogmatic Flatlands. Or else, Lichtenberg was right when he said a book "is a mirror. When a monkey looks in, no philosopher looks out." Of course, we are living in curved space (as noted by Einstein); that should warn us that Euclidean metaphors are always misleading. Science has also discovered that the Universe can count above two, which should make us leery of either/or choices. There are eight – count 'em, eight – theories or models in quantum mechanics, all of which use the same equations but have radically different philosophical meanings; physicists have accepted the multi-model approach (or "model agnosticism") for over 60 years now. In modern mathematics and logic, in addition to the two-valued (yes/no) logic of

Aristotle and Boole, there are several three-valued logics (e.g. the yes, no and maybe Quantum Logic of von Neumann; the yes, no and po of psychologist Edward de Bono; etc.), at least one four-valued logic (the true, false, indeterminate and meaningless of Rapoport), and an infinite-valued logic (Korzybski). I myself have presented a multi-valued logic in my neuroscience seminars; the bare bones of this system will be found in my book, *The New Inquisition*. Two-valued Euclidean choices – left or right of an imaginary line – do not seem very "real" to me, in comparison to the versatility of modern science and mathematics.

Actually, it was once easy to classify me in simple Euclidean topology. To paraphrase a recent article by the brilliant Michael Hoy [*Critique* #19/ 20], I had a Correct Answer Machine installed in my brain when I was quite young. It was a right-wing Correct Answer Machine in general and Roman Catholic in particular. It was installed by nuns who were very good at creating such machines and implanting them in helpless children. By the time I got out of grammar school, in 1945, I had the Correct Answer for everything, and it was the Correct Answer that you will nowadays still hear from, say, William Buckley, Jr.

When I moved on to Brooklyn Technical High School, I encountered many bright, likable kids who were not Catholics and not at all right-wing in any respect. They naturally angered me at first. (That is the function of Correct Answer Machines: to make you have an adrenaline rush, instead of a new thought, when confronted with different opinions.) But these bright, non-Catholic kids – Protestants, Jews, agnostics, even atheists – fascinated me in some ways. The result was that I started reading all the authors the nuns had warned me against – especially Darwin, Tom Paine, Ingersoll, Mencken and Nietzsche.

I found myself floating in a void of incertitude, a sensation that was unfamiliar and therefore uncomfortable. I retreated back to robotism by electing to install a new Correct Answer

Machine in my brain. This happened to be a Trotskyist Correct Answer Machine, provided by the International Socialist Youth Party. I picked this Machine, I think, because the alternative Correct Answer Machines then available were less "Papist" (authoritarian) and therefore less comfortable to my adolescent mind, still bent out of shape by the good nuns.

(Why was I immune to Stalinism – an equally Papist secular religion? I think the answer was my youth. The only Stalinists left in the U.S. by the late '40s were all middle-aged and "crystallized" as Gurdjieff would say. Those of us who were younger could clearly see that Stalinism was not much different from Hitlerism. The Trotskyist alternative allowed me to feel "radical" and modern, without becoming an idiot by denying the totalitarianism of the USSR, and it let me have a martyred redeemer again as I had in my Catholic childhood.)

After about a year, the Trotskyist Correct Answer Machine began to seem a nuisance. I started to suspect that the Trotskyists were some secular clone of the Vatican, whether they knew it or not, and that the dogma of Papal infallibility was no whit more absurd than the Trotskyist submission to the Central Committee. I decided that I had left one dogmatic Church and joined another. I even suspected that if Trotsky had managed to hold on to power, he might have been as dictatorial as Stalin.

Actually, what irritated me most about the Trots (and now seems most amusing) is that I already had some tendency toward individualism, or crankiness, or Heresy; I sometimes disputed the Party Line. This always resulted in my being denounced for "bourgeoisie tendencies." That was irritating then and amusing now because I was actually the only member of that Trot cell who did not come from a middle-class background. I came from a working class family and was the only genuine "proletarian" in the whole Marxist *kaffeklatch*.

At the age of 18, then, I returned to the void of incertitude. It began to seem almost comfortable there, and I began to rejoice in my agnosticism. It made me feel superior to the dogmatists of all types, and adolescents love to feel superior to everybody (especially their parents – or have you noticed that?). Around the same time as my Trotskyist period, I began to read the first Revisionist historians, whom I had been warned about by my high school social science teachers, in grave and awful tones, as if these men had killed a cat in the sacristy. My teachers were too Liberal to tell me I would go to Hell for reading such books (as the nuns had told me about Darwin, for instance), but they made it clear that the Revisionists were Evil, Awful, Unspeakable and probably some form of Pawns of the Devil.

I recognized the technique of thought control again, so I read all the Revisionists I could find. They convinced me that the New Deal Liberals had deliberately lied and manipulated the U.S. into World War II and were still lying about what they did after the war was over. (In fact, they are still lying about it today.)

The Revisionist who impressed me most was Harry Elmer Barnes, a classic Liberal who was a bit of a Marxist (in methodology) – i.e., in his way of looking for economic factors behind political actions. I was amused and disgusted by the attempt of the New Deal gang to smear Professor Barnes as a right-wing reactionary. Barnes, in fact, was an advocate of progressive ideas in education, economics, politics, criminology, sociology and anthropology all his life but the New Deal Party Line had smeared him so thoroughly that some people have heard of him only as some cranky critic of Roosevelt and assume he was a Taft Republican or even a pro-Nazi. In fact Barnes supported most of the New Deal's domestic policies, and dissented from Liberal Dogma only in opposing the spread of American adventurism and militarism all over the world.

Charles Beard, another great historian of classic Liberal principles, agreed that Roosevelt deliberately lied to us in World War II and was smeared in the same way as Professor

Barnes. This did not encourage me to have Faith in any Party Line, even if it called itself the modern, liberal, enlightened Party Line.

(I have never been convinced by the Holocaust Revisionists, however, simply because I have met a great many Holocaust eye-witnesses, or alleged eyewitnesses, in the past 40 years. Most of these people I seemingly met by accident, in both Europe and America. A conspiracy that has that many liars planted in that many places – or has always paid such special attention to me that it placed these liars where I would meet them – is a conspiracy too omnipotent and omnipresent, and therefore too metaphysical, for me to take seriously. A conspiracy so Godlike in its powers could, in principle, deceive us about anything and everything, and I wonder why the Holocaust Revisionists still believe that World War II occurred, or that any of past history ever happened.)

I reached 20 and became an employee (i.e. a robot) in the McCarthy Era and the Eisenhower years; my agnosticism became more total and so did my suspicion that politics is a carnival or buncombe (as Mencken once said). It seemed obvious to me that, while Senator Joe was a liar of stellar magnitude, a lot of the Liberals were lying their heads off, too, in attempts to hide their previous fondness for Stalinism. That was something I, as a former Trotskyist, knew about by experience. In *bon ton* East Coast intellectual circles, before McCarthy, Stalinism was much more "permissible" than Trotskyism; it was almost chic. If I still regard the McCarthy witch-hunt of the 1950s as abominable, I also remember that some of the victims had engaged in similar witch-hunts against the Trotskyists in the early 1940s.

It is probably impossible for a social mammal to be totally "apolitical." Even if I was allergic to Correct Answer Machines, my mind kept searching for some general social ideas that I could take more or less seriously. For a while I dropped in and out of colleges and in and out of jobs and searched earnestly for some pragmatic mock-up of "truth" without a Correct Answer Machine attached. And yet both Left and Right continued to appear intellectually bankrupt to me.

• • •

Coming from a working class family, I could never have much sympathy for the kind of Conservatism you find in America in this century. (I do have a certain fondness for the classic Liberal Conservatives of the 18th century, especially Edmund Burke and John Adams.) After I married and had children to support, the abominations of the Capitalist system and the wormlike ignominy of the employee role began to seem like prisons to me; I was a poor candidate for the Conservative cause. On the other hand, the FDR Liberals, I was convinced, had lied about World War II; they first smeared and then blacklisted the historians who told the truth; and they had jumped on the Cold War bandwagon with ghoulish glees.

I was anti-war by "temperament" (whatever that means – early imprints or conditioning? Genes? I don't know the exact cause of such a deep-seated and life-long bias). Marxist dogma seemed as stupid to me as Catholic dogma and as murderous as Hitlerism. I now thought of myself as an agnostic on principle. I was not going to join any more "churches" or submit to anybody's damned Party Line.

My agnosticism was also intensified by such influences as further reading of Nietzsche; existentialism; phenomenology; General Semantics; and operational logic. There have remained major influences on me and I want to say a few words about each.

Nietzsche's philosophy of the Superman did not turn me on in youth; coming from the proletarian, I could not see myself as one of his aristocratic Übermenschen. On the other hand, his criticism of language, and of the metaphysical implications within languages, made a powerful impression on me; I still re-read one or two of his books every year, and get new semantic insights of them. He is, as he bragged, a hard nut to digest all at once.

Existentialism did not convert me back to Marxism (as it did to Sartre); it merely magnified my Nietzschean distrust of capitalized nouns and other abstractions, and strengthened my preferences for sensory-sensual ("existential") – modes of perception-conception. The phenomenologists – especially Husserl and the wild man of the bunch, Charles Fort – encouraged my tendency to suspect all general theories (religious, philosophical, even scientific) and to regard human sense experience as the primary datum.

My polemics against Materialist Fundamentalism in *The New Inquisition* and the Aristotelian mystique of "natural law" (shared by Thomists and some Libertarians) in my *Natural Law; or, Don't Put a Rubber On Your Willy* are both based on this existentialist-phenomenologist choice that I will "believe" in human experience, with all its muddle and uncertainty, more than I will ever "believe" in capitalized Abstractions and "general principles."

General Semantics, as formulated by Korzybski, increased this anti-metaphysical bias in me. Korzybski also stressed that the best sensory data (as revealed by instruments that refine the senses) indicates that we live in a non-Aristotelian, non-Euclidean and non-Newtonian continuum. I have practiced for 30 years the exercises Korzybski recommends to break down Aristotelian-Euclidean-Newtonian ideas buried in our daily speech and retrain myself to perceive in ways compatible with what our instruments indicate about actuality.

Due to Korzybski's neurolinguistic training devices, it is now "natural" for me to think beyond either/or logic, to perceive the unity of observer/observed, to regard "objects" as human inventions abstracted from a holistic continuum. Many physicists think I have studied more physics than I actually have; I merely neurologically internalized the physics that I do know.

Operational logic (as formulated by the American physicist Percy Bridgman and recreated by the Danish physicist Niels

Bohr as the Copenhagen Interpretation of science) was
the approach to modern science that appealed to me in the
context of the above working principles. The Bridgman-Bohr
approach rejects as "meaningless" any statements that do not
refer to concrete experiences of human beings. (Bridgman
was influenced by Pragmatism, Bohr by Existentialism.)
Operationalism also regards all proposed "laws" only as
maps or models that are useful for a certain time. Thus,
Operationalism is the one "philosophy of science" that warns
us, like Nietzsche and Husserl, only to use models where
they're useful and never to elevate them into Idols or dogmas.

Although I dislike labels, if I had to label my attitude I
would accordingly settle for existentialist-phenomenologist-op-
erationalist, as long as no one of those three terms is given
more prominence than the other two.

In the late '50s, I began to read widely in economic
"science" (or speculation) again, a subject that had bored the
bejesus out of me since I overthrew the Marxist Machine in
my brain ten years earlier. I became fascinated with a number
of alternatives – or "excluded middles" – that transcend
the hackneyed debate between monopoly Capitalism and
totalitarian Socialism. My favorite among these alternatives
was, and to some extent still is, the individualist-mutualist
anarchism of Proudhon, Josiah Warren, S.P. Andrews, Lysander
Spooner and Benjamin Tucker. I do not have a real Faith that
this system would work out as well in practice as it sounds in
theory, but as theory it still seems to me one of the best ideas I
ever encountered.

This form of anarchism is called "individualist" because
it regards the absolute liberty of the individual as a supreme
goal to be attained; it is called "mutualist" because it believes
such liberty can only be attained by a system of mutual
consent, based on contracts that are to the advantage of all.
In this Utopia, free competition and free cooperation are both
encouraged; it is assumed persons and groups will decide to
compete or to cooperate based on the concrete specifics of each

case. (This appeals to my "existentialism" again, you see.)

Land monopolies are discouraged in individualist-mutualist anarchism by abolishing State laws granting ownership to those who neither occupy nor use the land; "ownership," it is predicted, will then only be contractually recognized where the "owner" actually occupies and uses the land, but not where he charges "rent" to occupy or use it. The monopoly on currency, granted by the State, is also abolished, and any commune, group, syndicate, etc., can issue its own competing currency; it is claimed that this will drive interest down to approximately zero. With rent at zero and interest near zero, it is argued that the alleged goal of socialism (abolition of exploitation) will be achieved by free contract, without coercion or totalitarian Statism. That is, the individualist-mutualist model argues that the land and money monopolies are the "bugger factors" that prevent Free Enterprise from producing the marvelous results expected by Adam Smith. With land and money monopolies abolished, it is predicted that competition (where there is no existential motive for cooperation) and cooperation (where this is recognized as being to the advantage of all) will prevent other monopolies from arising.

Since monopolized police forces are notoriously graft-ridden and underlie the power of the state to bully and coerce, competing protection systems will be available in an individualist-mutualist system. You won't have to pay "taxes" to support a Protection Racket that is actually oppressing rather than protecting you. You will only pay dues, where you think it prudent, to protection agencies that actual perform a service you want and need. In general, every commune or syndicate will make its own rules of the game, but the mutualist-individualist tradition holds that, by experience, most communes will choose the systems that maximize liberty and minimize coercion.

Being wary of Correct Answer Machines, I also studied and have given much serious consideration to other "Utopian" socio-economic theories. I am still fond of the system of

Henry George (in which no rent is allowed, but free enterprise is otherwise preserved); but I also like the ideas of Silvio Gesell (who would also abolish rent and all taxes but one – a demurrage tax on currency, which should theoretically abolish interest by a different gimmick than the competing currencies of the mutualists).

I also see possible merit in the economics of C.H. Douglas, who invented the National Dividend – lately re-emergent, somewhat mutated, as Theobald's Guaranteed Annual Wage and/or Friedman's Negative Income Tax. And I am intrigued by the proposal of Pope Leo XIII that workers should own the majority of stock in their companies.

Most interesting of recent Utopias to me is that of Buckminster Fuller in which money is abolished, and computers manage the economy, programmed with a prime directive to advantage all without disadvantaging any – the same goal sought by the mutualist system of basing society entirely on negotiated contract.

Since I don't have the Correct Answer, I don't know which of these systems would work best in practice. I would like to see them all tried in different places, just to see what would happen. (This multiple Utopia system was also suggested by Silvio Gesell, who was not convinced he had a Correct Answer Machine; that's another reason I like Gesell.) My own bias or hope or prejudice is that individualist-mutualist anarchism with some help from Bucky Fuller's computers would work best of all, but I still lack the Faith to proclaim that as dogma.

There is one principle (or prejudice) which makes anarchist and libertarian alternatives attractive to me where State Socialism is totally repugnant to my genes-or-imprints. I am committed to the maximization of the freedom of the individual and the minimization of coercion. I do not claim this goal is demanded by some ghostly or metaphysical "Natural Law," but merely that it is the goal that I, personally, have *chosen* – in the Existentialist sense of choice. (In more occult language, such a goal is my True Will.) Everything I write, in one way or another, is intended to undermine the metaphysical and linguistic systems which seem to justify some Authorities in limiting the freedom of the human mind or in initiating coercion against the non-coercive.

...and then came what Charles Slack calls "the madness of the sixties." I was an early, and enthusiastic, experimenter with LSD, peyote, magic mushrooms and any other compound that mutated consciousness. The result was that I became even more agnostic but less superior about it. What psychedelics taught me was that, just as theories and ideologies (maps and models) are human creations, not divine revelations, every perceptual grid or existential reality-tunnel is also a human creation – a work of art, consciously or unconsciously edited and organized by the individual brain.

I began serious study of other consciousness-altering systems, including techniques of yoga, Zen, Sufism and Cabala. I, alas, became a "mystic" of some sort, although still within the framework of existentialism-phenomenology-operationalism. But, then, Buddhism – the organized mystic movement I find least objectionable – is also existentialist, phenomenologist and operationalist....

Nietzsche's concept of the Superhuman has at last become meaningful for me, although not in the elitist form in which he left it. I now think evolution is continuing and even accelerating: the human brain is evolving to a state that seems Superhuman compared to our previous history of domesticated primatehood. My favorite science is neuroscience, and I am endlessly fascinated by every new tool or technique that breaks down robot circuits in our brains (Correct Answer Machines) and spurs creativity, higher intelligence, expanded consciousness, and, above all, broader compassion.

I see no reason to believe that only an elite is capable of this evolutionary leap forward, especially as the new tools and training techniques are becoming more simple. In neuroscience as in all technology, we seem to follow Bucky Fuller's rule that each breakthrough allows us to do more work with less effort and to create more wealth out of less raw matter.

Once I broke loose from the employee role and became self-supporting as a writer, the "horrors of capitalism" seemed less ghoulish to me, since I no longer had to face them every day. I became philosophical, like all persons free of acute suffering. I prefer to live in Europe rather than pay taxes to build more of Mr. Reagan's goddam nuclear missiles, but I enjoy visiting the U.S. regularly for intellectual stimulation....

I agree passionately with Maurice Nicoll (a physician who mastered both Jungian and Gurdjieffian systems) who wrote that the major purpose of "work on consciousness" is to "decrease the amount of violence in the world." The main difference between our world and Swift's is that while we have stopped killing each other over religious differences (outside the Near East and Northern Ireland), we have developed an insane passion for killing each other over ideological differences. I regard Organized Ideology with the same horror that Voltaire had for Organized Religion.

Concretely, I am indeed a Male Feminist, as L.A. Rollins claimed (although seeing myself often on TV, I deny that I simper; I don't even swish); like all libertarians, I oppose victimless crime laws, all drug control laws, and all forms of censorship (whether by outright reactionaries or Revolutionary Committees or Radical Feminists).

I passionately hate violence, but am not a Dogmatic Pacifist, since I don't have Joan Baez's Correct Answer Machine in my head. I know I would kill an armed aggressor, in a concrete crisis situation where that was the only defense of the specific lives of specific individuals I love, although I would never kill a person or employ even minor violence, or physical coercion, on behalf of capitalized Abstractions or Governments (who are all damned liars). All these are matters of Existential Choice on my part, and not dogmas revealed to me by some god or some philosopher-priest of Natural Law.

I prefer the various Utopian systems I have mentioned to the Conservative position that humanity is incorrigible and I also think that if none of these Utopian scenarios are workable, some system will eventually arrive better than any we have ever known. I share the Jeffersonian ("Liberal"?) vision that the human mind can exceed all previous limits in a society where freedom of thought is the norm rather than a rare exception.

Does all of this make me a Leftist or a Rightist? I leave that for the Euclideans to decide. If I had to summarize my social credo in the briefest possible space, I would quote Alexander Pope's *Essay On Man*:

> For forms of Government let fools contest;
> Whate'er is best administered is best:
> For modes of Faith let graceless zealots fight;
> He can't be wrong whose life is in the right.

Why I Voted For Michael Dukakis

Published in *The Realist*, 1989

When I was reaching puberty back in Brooklyn in the 1940s "bush" meant pubic hair and "quail" meant vagina. Now the Republicans have Bush and Quayle in Washington, and I frankly find it embarrassing. Every time I hear those names, Bush and Quayle, my mind goes back to early adolescent conversations whispered in the Boys' Room – "She let *me* touch her bush." "Yeah? Well, she let *me* get two fingers in her quail!" – and I blush. I haven't blushed in 30 years, but early conditioning can't be conquered.

Does George Bush have a sense of humor after all? I had been hoping he would pick Dole as his running mate, so I could go around on the lecture circuit making jokes about the "pussy and pineapple ticket." Then he picked Quayle as if to hand live ammunition to all of us surrealists and anarchists.

The only bright spot I can see in this election is that Pubic Hair and Vagina have won. That gives me what Camus once

A Non-Euclidean Perspective

called "the grim satisfaction of those who plot Apocalypse in a garret." I *predicted* that Bush would win, way back when Dukakis had a 17 point lead in the polls. I wasn't joking either. I have a steadily increasing faith in the proposition that, given a choice of two, the American electorate always chooses the candidate I find more appalling.

According to the Santa Monica *Outlook*, 21% of the people in the U.S. do not know the earth moves around the sun. Those who do know are often unclear as to how long it takes the earth to make a complete revolution around the sun, and many think it takes one day. Others say they can't remember. Only a few know it takes a year. This doesn't surprise me. The majority still believe that a gaseous vertebrate of astronomical heft named "God" has a paranoid obsession about who is fucking whom and which adolescents are playing with themselves.

The majority also, monotonously, rejects the Bill of Rights every time a sociology professor repeats the experiment of sending a group of students out to poll people on the subject. Those who reject the Bill of Rights generally say it sounds communistic. George Bush is the kind of man who will never find that result shocking or disturbing; he has no illusions about the public. His use of Dukakis's membership in the ACLU shows George has the same opinion of the voters I have, or J. R. "Bob" Dobbs has.

You ever hear of "Bob"? He's the founder of the Church of the SubGenius, and his wisest saying is "You know how dumb the average guy is? Well, mathematically, by definition, *half* of them are even dumber than that."

Would it make any difference if we had put Dukakis in the White House? I think it would, at least psychologically. Duke and Kitty are wonderful names. They sound like a pimp and his top hooker. "Hey, mister, you wanna good time? Go see Duke and Kitty on Pennsylvania Avenue . . ."

I voted for the Duke myself, just out of spite, and to say "Fuck you, George Bush." I'm a card-carrying member of the ACLU myself (or used to be, and will be again when I remember to renew my dues) and I don't like George making us the new scapegoats just when I thought the Moron Majority had elected a fictitious Satanic conspiracy to play that role.

Usually, I don't vote – on the anarchist principle that it only encourages the bastards – or else I vote Libertarian, to annoy the bastards. But George Bush scares me. I don't believe he's a wimp at all. He was not only the head of the CIA but, according to the *L.A. Weekly*, has ties with the Company that go back decades and still continue today. That means to me he has more than a slim connection with the Death Squads in Latin America. He's as much of a wimp as Heinrich Himmler.

Of course, the last time I voted for a major party candidate because I was afraid of his rival was in 1964. I voted for LBJ to keep Goldwater out of the White House. Since then I have felt precisely demarked by the Double Bind in the Head Shop button that says, If voting could change the system it would be illegal. If not voting could change the system it would be illegal.

I am deeply suspicious of Dukakis because he once taught at Harvard but still sounds as dumb as Bush on most issues. A man who hides his intelligence has such a low opinion of the public that he is only safe writing satire, like me. Put him in power and he might decide to express his contempt for the masses more viciously.

The American people nowadays never vote for anybody they suspect of being more intelligent than themselves. Reagan won the highest majority in our history because nobody anywhere thought he was smarter than they are. You could go into homes for the feeble-minded and they'd tell you, "Yeah, we like Ronnie. He's a regular fellow, just like us." Bush was a shoo-in.

Where is George Papoon now that we need him? He ran for the Presidency in 1980 – or at least he ran in Berkeley. He went around with a paper bag over his head and a sign saying NOT

INSANE. He never held any press conferences.

He was the candidate of the Natural Surrealist Party. Nobody in national politics has made as much sense to me in 8 years now.

Is Alan Cranston Full of Shit?

Published in *The Realist*, Fall 1990

Back in March, I wrote to "my" Senator, Alan Cranston, and "my" Representative, Mel Levine, objecting to the proposed new FCC ban on "indecent" speech. The term "indecent" is not defined in the applicable law, which would make radio and TV stations subject to fines on a 24-hour-a-day basis if they broadcast anything which might get the FCC bureaucrats pissed off. In late May, I got a reply from Alan Cranston. It read as follows:

> Many thanks for your message about the question of "indecent material." I appreciate the opportunity to communicate with you regarding the issues of censorship and objectionable material and apologize for the delay in responding.
>
> In regard to indecent broadcasts, during the 100th Congress, legislation was passed directing the

A Non-Euclidean Perspective

Federal Communications Commission to ban indecent radio and television programming on a 24-hour-a-day basis. Previously, the FCC allowed sexually explicit programming between midnight and 6 a.m., when children are unlikely to be listening. The new 24-hour ban has been challenged in court on constitutional grounds, and the United States Court of Appeals for the District of Columbia has placed a temporary stay on the ban while the case is pending.

The question of regulation of indecent broadcasts and other indecent material, such as some printed matter and record albums, is very complex. The curbing of First Amendment rights of free thought and free speech must never be considered lightly. Occasionally censorship may be justified in case of grave danger to national security or to the rights of others. The entertainment media usually involves questions of individual moral values. What some find offensive, others find acceptable.

Should these issues come before Congress, rest assured that I will give them careful consideration. I appreciate your contacting me – please do continue to stay in touch.

Sincerely . . .

Below this was the signature "Alan Cranston," looking very much like the kind of fake signatures obtained by using a rubber stamp.

On first reading this letter, I thought Senator Cranston could not express himself very clearly. On second reading, I thought that maybe he did not wish to express himself clearly. On third reading, I became even more confused. Cranston seems to throw a bone to the proponents of censorship by treating "indecent material" as an objective fact rather than a subjective opinion, but then he waffles and points out the Constitutional difficulties of this position; his only direct statement is that he "will give . . . careful consideration" to this issue (or to "these issues," as he prefers to say) some time in the indefinite future.

Why couldn't he say in plain English, "I haven't made up my mind yet"?

Looking at the letter a fourth time, I had another bright idea. Maybe he has made up his mind, but doesn't want to tell the voters yet. The letter looks like a form sent to everybody who might have written to him, and while it would hardly satisfy anybody on either side of the issue, it also carefully avoids overtly offending either side. Who could possibly be offended by the promise that at some hypothetical future date, when he doesn't have his snout in the S&L trough, good old Alan might "give careful consideration" to "these issues"?

I tried an experiment. I showed the letter to several friends. Nobody felt sure Cranston was on the side of the FCC; nobody felt sure he was on the side of freedom of expression; everybody agreed with my verdict that the letter uses a lot of weaseling to avoid telling us which side he's on.

By now, the issue had become personal. Roy Tuckman on KPFA (midnight to 6 a.m., interestingly) mentioned some of the tapes he would be afraid to play if the new FCC rule is upheld in court. He said that the speakers who might cause problems included Alan Watts, Timothy Leary and me.

Alan Watts? I admit that stumped me for a while. How could his witty and philosophical ramblings about Zen and Taoism be construed as "indecent" even by the idiots at the FCC? Then I remembered: Watts mentioned sex every now and then (about once in every three hours of tapes, I think) and he avoided euphemisms. He would say "fucking" instead of "sexual intercourse." The same "problem" exists with Tim Leary's taped lectures; he also prefers Shakespearean or Joycean English to genteel academese. And I, too, have let a "fuck" slip into my lectures now and then, amid my usual shticks about Bell's Theorem, the Copenhagen Interpretation of quantum mechanics, brain chemistry, primate psychology and Space Colonies.

So: in the opinion of Roy Tuckman, a broadcaster with a lot of experience with FCC rulings, Alan Watts' ideas about psychotherapy and Eastern mysticism, Tim Leary's notions about brain change technology and Futurism, and my own science-fiction speculations, all might result in heavy fines, just because we talk, on stage, in the same language that our audience uses off-stage. (Do you know anybody who actually *says* "sexual intercourse" or even "coitus"? At the most, some of us might *write* those words, and only if we were submitting to an academic journal.)

I suddenly remembered the immortal interview with musician Bob Geldof published in the *Irish Times* when I was living in Ireland. The reporter asked if his use of "improper language" did not detract from the humanitarian causes for which he has worked so hard and long.

"I don't know what the fuck improper language is," Geldof replied. I only read this and wasn't at the interview, but I've always been able to hear it, in my head, delivered in his inner-city Dublin brogue: "I don't knah wot the fook improper language is."

Then I recalled some remarks by the eminent philosopher George Carlin (himself once the subject of FCC censorship). Carlin, in his latest tour, has been doing a routine about the three most dangerous groups in America. He says these groups are: first, the stupid, who make up the majority. (You all know how dumb the average guy is, right? Well, mathematically, by definition, half of them are even dumber than *that*.) Second, there is the group made up of people who are full of shit, such as used car salespeople and baseball stars (who will do a 30-second commercial endorsing anything, including leper's dung for breakfast, if they get paid a million dollars). Third, there is the vast army of those who are totally fucking crazy. It is because of the influence of these three groups, Carlin says, that we now have a Vice President who is stupid, full of shit and totally fucking crazy, all at once.

As usual, I find George Carlin more enlightening than most professional psychologists and sociologists.

Which brings me back to Alan Cranston's letter and its high word count and low information content. Instead of wondering if Senator Cranston can't express himself clearly or just doesn't choose to express himself clearly, I now find myself asking if he writes that way (or approves a staff member who writes that way over his signature) because he is just plain stupid, or full of shit, or totally fucking crazy.

I have tried asking some other friends to read the letter and judge between those three interpretations. Nobody, thus far, has decided Cranston is stupid or totally fucking crazy; they all think he is full of shit. While this was not a randomized double-blind scientific study, I think it accurately registers normal reactions to Cranston's prose. To most people who speak English, Cranston seems to be full of shit.

Meanwhile, I have finally heard from "my" representative in Congress, Mel Levine. He leaves no doubt at all that he opposes the proposed FCC ban. Judging by his eccentric voting record, I am still not utterly delighted with Levine, but I can assure you he is not full of shit.

I myself have no final opinion on whether Cranston is full of shit – or none that I care to publish. The Supreme Court has just ruled that *opinions* are no longer protected by the First Amendment. I leave it up to the reader to decide – is Senator Cranston full of shit?

Utopia USA interview

Utopia USA Interview:
Lance Bauscher interviews Robert Anton Wilson,
February 22, 2001

Lance Bauscher was the writer/director for the 2003 documentary: Maybe Logic: The Lives and Ideas of Robert Anton Wilson.

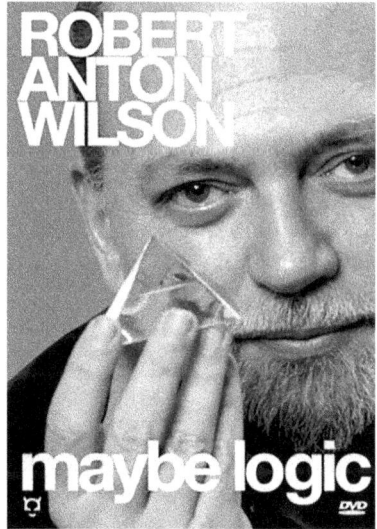

LB: Can you talk about the book you're currently working on, *The Tale of the Tribe*?

RAW: Well, it's about Ezra Pound and James Joyce, whom I regard as the two major innovators of twentieth century literature. And oddly they both had a very powerful influence on Marshall McLuhan who has influenced how we think about all media, especially internet, even though internet didn't begin to develop until after McLuhan was dead.

"The tale of the tribe" was Pound's definition of the topic of *The Cantos*, his long epic poem that he spent 50 years writing. It also fits *Finnegans Wake* very well, and the book describes how *The Cantos* and *Finnegans Wake* influenced McLuhan's ideas, and how internet has been shaped not only by the development of technology but by the ideas McLuhan got from Pound and Joyce. It gets more complicated, but that's a good enough introduction to it.

LB: Where does your faith in the incredible promise of internet come from?

RAW: Some commentator on McLuhan, whose name I can't remember, pointed out that every communication system before internet has had gatekeepers. That is to say, to get a book published throughout most of history you not only needed to get a publisher, you had to get the government censors to approve it. That is still true in most countries. The same with movies, television, etc.

Internet belongs to the people that use it. Nobody has found an effective way of policing it, and they never will as far as I can see. Any way of controlling internet would involve creating a world government and the people who most want to censor opinions are the most opposed to world government. So they can't do it that way. If they try to do it any other way they'll wreck most major corporations that depend so much on internet to do business. So it can't be done.

Internet is going to remain free, and I believe, I've believed since I was in my early twenties, that everything that accelerates the flow of information and communication benefits the human race, and every communication jam damages us. So internet is the greatest tool, or device, or gimmick, or whatever you want to call it, for accelerating the flow of information between peoples. It is, I think, the most revolutionary force in the history of humanity since the invention of the wheel – especially when Asia and Africa get online in a major way. That's what I really look forward to.

LB: Have you considered how virtual reality is going to merge with internet?

RAW: I have had a few experiences with virtually reality, and as a matter of fact I wrote a little thing way back in the mid-'80s about virtual sex. I can see that coming eventually. Smith just got this new machine delivered and he hasn't gotten out of his house in two weeks.

At my age I am more interested in getting virtual reality out of Euclidean space and into Riemannian space. My first experiences with virtual reality I thought, "now if they could program it for Riemannian space you'd understand relativity right away and you wouldn't have to struggle with all the mathematics. And it can be done, you can make a virtual reality of any sort that you want. Also I'd like to experience Lobachevskian space."

Riemannian space is the geometry Einstein used in the general theory of relativity. It's based on the conception, more or less, of a spherical time-space continuum. Lobachevskian space is sorta like a saddle that goes on forever, there is a peak in the middle but then it shrinks to nothing, but only at an infinite distance. Very interesting type of space because nobody has ever found any use for it as far as I know. Mathematically it's just as valid as the other kinds of space. I mean, mathematically it is self-consistent – that's all you need in mathematics. And somebody will find a use for it someday, but I'm rambling now.

LB: What do you see happening right now with the acceleration of technology and information?

RAW: Well, way back in 1933 Korzybski wrote *Science and Sanity*, a book which has had a profound influence on my whole life, and he said there was an acceleration factor in knowledge and technology. Now it's accelerating faster and faster all the time, and throughout my life I've seen that happening more and more.

When I was a child, women all over the United States had goiter, which was a disease, a swelling of the neck, which looked as bad as cancer. Although it wasn't that fatal it was very destructive to their good looks. Goiter disappeared during World War II, somebody found the cure for it. Small pox disappeared in the 1960s. We got space satellites. We got things I don't like, like nuclear weapons, but the acceleration is going faster all the time. And I quite confidently expect that the breakthroughs in biotechnology, or biotech as everybody is calling it these days, in the next twenty years – everything we consider human, normal, etc. is going to have to be redefined.

LB: What does chaos have to do with all this?

RAW: Chaos turns me on. Chaos math turns me on because I have basically a scientific orientation as distinguished from a religious orientation. There are some things in science I always had doubts about. I always thought the universe was not as orderly as Newton or Einstein would have us think. Along comes chaos math and explains the things that have bothered me all these years that doesn't quite fit into the Newtonian or Einsteinium paradigm. So they convinced me science can deal with the chaotic after all and can include even more than I thought it could.

The other thing about chaos is that there are a lot of lines of thought in the biological and behavioral sciences that indicate that chaos leads to creativity. There is even a kind of psychotherapy called "chaos therapy," which is based on getting the patient so damned confused that they can't hold on to their delusions and neurosis anymore and have to start changing. So I think chaos works the same way on the social level.

Chaos does not necessarily mean riot, insurrection, explosions and things like that. Chaos just means totally unpredictable at an accelerating rate, which is what's happening all the time.

A Non-Euclidean Perspective

And I think that is forcing rapid learning on the part of those who are still capable of learning. And it's those people who the future depends on.

Those who can't learn, well, they'll die eventually. Meanwhile, they just serve as a roadblock, a temporary roadblock. Dying dinosaurs. We got one of them in the White House right now, and he appointed a whole bunch of other dinosaurs to his cabinet. But it doesn't bother me as much as it does most of my friends because I think politics is always the last place, the very last place, where important changes register. They register in science, then in technology, then in economics and in social affairs. And then finally the politicians have to adjust to them. Especially in this country where almost all our politicians are lawyers.

Lawyers are trained to find precedence for anything they want to do. In other words, if you want to do cloning, you have to look up all the other precedences that have to do with "uncloning," the thing that happened before cloning. Lawyers, whether they are good-hearted or not, and there are a lot of liberal and libertarian lawyers I admire – I don't mean to put down the whole profession – but this thing about looking for precedence . . . that means the past is governing the future, which means we're strangling the future to make it fit the past. Science is not based on precedence. Science is based on experience and experiment. And science moves very fast, while the law drags centuries and sometimes millenniums behind.

And then we have the problem of corruption and the law, too. I have to admit I have the reputation as a cynic, but the last election even startled me. I wasn't surprised that they stole an election. That happens a lot – not only in the United States – it happens all over, elections are stolen regularly. This case it went up to the Supreme Court and it turned out that 5 out of 9 of the Supreme Court were in on stealing the election. They collaborated in the worst theft of an election in American political history, and the whole world was watching and they didn't even give a damn. They just went ahead and did it anyway because they have the power to do it. And I realized how naïve I was. I've been cynical of Congress and the executive branch and all its bureaucratic subdivisions for a long long time, but I always thought the Supreme Court is really guided, rightly or wrongly, by what they really think the Constitution says. Now I realize they are as crooked as the other two branches in the government. That was a shock to me. Even at my age I can be shocked.

LB: Do you feel there is any need for government?

RAW: That's a hard question, because at present I'm afraid there probably is to some extent. But I'd like to see it limited. I'd like to see it pushed back to the level of the Constitution, what we usually call Jeffersonian democracy. I think it can be reduced even further. But I certainly don't like the continuous growth of the government interfering with everything.

What amazes me most is the piss police. Even Kafka and Orwell – who wrote the craziest, most far-out satires on totalitarianism that their wild surrealist imaginations could imagine – they did not include piss police. And yet we got them and the American public just gullibly and submissively accepts it.

LB: Why do they accept it?

RAW: Well, a Toronto financial litigation lawyer has said that this happens because they've been beaten down so long and they're so pessimistic, and they are so worried about how to pay the mortgage without consulting attorneys like us. This is the only country in the industrial world that doesn't have national health insurance. They are worried about paying the doctor bills, they are worried about the mortgages, they are worried about crime and so many other things. I think basically there is an attitude of hopelessness – I think Thoreau called it "quiet desperation."

And besides, you stick your neck out and you get yourself into trouble. Most guys with wives and families and most women with husbands and families don't want to stick their neck out too far.

I remember the first time I got arrested, which was for an anti-segregation demonstration at a barber shop. All I could think of was "this isn't very fair to my kids. I am too damn idealistic. What if I am separated from my kids for five years while they are so young?" I was thinking in terms of probably a five-year prison term. I shouldn't do that to my kids! I must be a nut for doing this! Meanwhile, I am still doing it. So I can understand why most people don't want to stick their necks out, especially if they have children.

There is a little bit more to it than that. It's what I call the "SNAFU principle." Communication only occurs between equals – real communication, that is – because when you are dealing with people above you in a hierarchy, you learn not to tell them anything they don't want to hear. If you tell them anything they don't want to hear, the response is, "One more word, Bumstead, and I'll fire you!" Or in the military, "One more word and you're court-martialed." It's throughout the whole system.

So the higher up in the hierarchy you go, the more lies are being told to flatter those above them. So those at the top have no idea what is going on at all. Those at the bottom have to adjust to the rules made by those at the top who don't know what's going on. Those at the top can write rules about this, that and the other, while those at the bottom have got to adjust reality to fit the rules as much as they can.

I've been teaching this for over 30 years, almost 40 years. More and more I have been asking at my workshops, can anybody hold up their hand and say that they have told the truth, the whole truth, and nothing but the truth when dealing with somebody from the government. Nobody has ever held up their hand. Everybody lies when they are dealing with the government! You never know what they are going to come down on you for, so you tell them what you think they want to hear.

I think that is true of a lot of public opinion polls too. People think that might be a front for the CIA or somebody. So those at the top don't have any idea what's going on, what the people really want or anything like that.

Meanwhile, since nobody wants to feel like a coward and a liar all the time, it's easier to stop noticing how reality differs from what those at the top say, and try to make yourself believe that what they say does correspond to reality. Even if that means bumping your knees against things they say aren't there or falling down stairs they claim don't exist and so on.

So I call this the burden of omniscience: those on the top are supposed to be doing the seeing, hearing, smelling, tasting, and all the sensing, apprehending and conceptualizing for the whole society, and those at the bottom have to adjust to what those at the top think based on all the misinformation flowing up in a hierarchy where any speaking of the truth can get you punished.

I see anarchism as the theoretical ideal to which we are all gradually evolving to a point where everybody can tell the truth to everybody else and nobody can get punished for it. That can only happen without hierarchy and without people having the authority to punish other people.

I don't think we can ever abolish hierarchy entirely, but we can make it temporary and rotating. Like a symphony orchestra needs a conductor, but that doesn't mean he is going to take over the lives of the musicians, telling them what to eat and what to smoke and what to drink and so on – where they can travel and where they can't travel. And a baseball team probably needs a manager, and so on. There are probably lots of places where we need a temporary hierarchy, but it doesn't have to cover lifetimes or even four years. And it doesn't have to cover as much as the hierarchies we've got with current corporations, bureaucracies, and governments.

You know, I think I began to realize the danger of hierarchy and developed the SNAFU principle about communication when I was working for the second largest engineering firm in the United States. I listened to the engineers bitching all the time about how the financial interests wouldn't let them do any of the work that seemed really important for them to improve their output. And I was reading William Faulkner's *Go Down, Moses*, which is still one of my favorite novels, and there was a sentence in there which was like a mini satori for me. And the sentence goes: "To the sheriff, Lucas was just another nigger and they both knew that; to Lucas the sheriff was an ignorant redneck with no cause for pride in his ancestors, nor any hope for it in his prosperity. But only one of them new that." And I suddenly realized, yeah, every power situation means the people on top are not being told what the people on the bottom are really noticing. Then I could see how this applied to this engineering firm. And then how it applied to corporations in general and so on.

I tend to shy away from the word "anarchist," because most people think it means bomb throwing. And a lot of people who consider themselves anarchists seem to think that too. But I can't use "libertarian," because the people who got their grip on that word are even less rational by my standards. I guess "decentralist" is the word I'd have to pick out for myself. Decentralist grassroots Jeffersonian something or other.

LB: What else about the philosophy and practice of anarchism interests you?

RAW: I very early in my life decided I didn't believe in the capitalist system. Fredrick Saudi, the physicist, said, "Economics? It should be called banditry." I mean it's the science of robbing and looting, organized. And on the other hand, Marxist socialism is even worse. Of course there is democratic socialism, such as you find in northern Europe, and I find a lot to admire in that, a great deal.

But there are also other alternatives and one of the alternatives that attracts me is Native American anarchism, sometimes called individualist anarchism, or mutualist anarchism, which is based on the idea of voluntary association, which is the forerunner of the affinity group we hear so much about these days. Or the dropout commune and so on.

The happiest people on the planet seem to be those who live in tribal societies with a membership of about 120. I don't think we are going to go back to the tribal level, but I think power has to be decentralized to the point where every 120 people are making their own decisions, about their local affairs. For international affairs, we could have some kind of giant computer where we can all put in our opinions.

I don't trust politicians. As a matter of fact what I like best about Hannibal Lecter is that he's found a practical use for a politician, which nobody else has done before.

The idea of representative government after we overthrew the monarchy was: we'll have representatives who will represent us. In the first place, they don't represent us! They represent the corporations who pay their campaign finance. And in the second place we don't need anybody to represent us. Now that we've got internet we can represent ourselves. So I think all those people should be thrown the hell out of office and forced to make a living as honest men and women do, rather than by lying to the gullible and selling them out to the corporations, and we can represent ourselves through internet.

As a matter of fact, Buckminster Fuller – one of the most brilliant people of the twentieth century, often compared to Leonardo da Vinci and Benjamin Franklin for the extent of the fields in which he was an expert, he was an expert in at least a dozen fields – one of his last books has that theme. He calls it desovereignization: getting rid of human representatives and representing ourselves through electronic media. So I am not as original as I sometimes think I am.

LB: What do tribal societies have that we generally don't?

RAW: There are different types of tribes. I was generalizing too much. But let's just say certain tribes. What they don't have is the bureaucracy, the hierarchy, the complexities. If there's a disagreement in the tribe, you know who you're disagreeing with. You know who to talk to about it. If you can't get satisfaction out of the person you're disagreeing with, you go to their family.

In the Trobriand Islands, when a woman wants a divorce – this is before the Christian missionaries got in, when Malinowski studied them – when a woman wants a divorce, she puts her husband's shoes outside the door. That means he's not allowed in. If he wants the marriage to continue, his parents go and talk to her parents and try to negotiate a second trial. Now, if you try that in California today, you get lawyers involved, and judges and the whole goddamn government bureaucracy. Things are much more complicated just because of the size, and the inexorable growth of power wherever it's allowed to grow.

Also tribal groups tend to have what anthropologists call an animistic view, which is a view that everything is alive. Nobody has that view in our society except for people who have done a lot of acid.

LB: Do you have hope for a technological utopia where everyone's basic needs are met?

RAW: Yeah. I haven't been into the innards of the World Game computers in Philadelphia, but Bucky Fuller claimed, and Medard Gabel, who runs the World Game Institute, now also claims that we could feed the whole planet, right now, today, starting today, if we used our technology most intelligently. In other words, all the people starving on this planet, and I forget the statistic, but it's pretty damned horrifying, all the people starving on this planet is all unnecessary. It's only held together, to quote Bucky again, by fear, ignorance, greed and zoning laws.

I'm pretty sure we could do it now, but as a matter of fact, people said that even before Fuller. Another engineer, named major Charles Douglas, claimed as far back as 1919 that if we used our technology intelligently and changed the present financial system so we don't pay usury at 60% for every new change in technology, we could have a society better than any utopia in science fiction ever imagined. There is a lot of supporting data for that. As a matter of fact, just look at the a condition of people on welfare in the United States today. It looks pretty ugly, but just compare them to the people without welfare in London in Dickens novels. Everybody is better off than they were 100 years ago. If we only used our science and technology intelligently, our whole world could be immeasurably improved. But first we got to get rid of the fear, ignorance, greed and zoning laws.

LB: Is virtual reality only accessible via computers?

RAW: That's an interesting question. I think we live in virtual reality anyway. As a matter of fact, even without talking about LSD or other controversial subjects, you can easily demonstrate to yourself that everybody creates their own reality, simply by sitting down with four friends, being quiet for say two minutes, and have each one report what sounds they heard. You'll find everybody in the room heard different sounds. You can duplicate this with vision too. Have everybody describe the room they just came out of. They'll all describe it differently.

We all live what ethnologists call a different umwelt. Every animal has a different umwelt. The human animal like other animals has a generalized human umwelt, things the human brain and nervous system can recognize, but each individual has their own individualized umwelt. A painter does not see the woods the way a poet does, and neither of them see it the way a logger does. The painter sees the colors, the poet sees something else, and the logger sees a chance to cut down the trees and make money. We all see everything differently.

I've got dozens of demonstrations of that which I use in my workshops, and nobody has ever gotten up in any my workshops and said, "that's not true we were all seeing the same thing!" No, everybody sees things differently. And hears things differently. And smells things differently. And tastes things differently. The classic example is ordering a pizza for a group of five. Nobody wants the same things on the pizza. You end up buying three small pizzas.

LB: Do you think that technological virtual reality will enable people to more easily or deeply experience what you've just described?

RAW: Yes. I have a strong feeling that since Americans aren't as paranoid about machines as they are about chemicals, virtual reality will do for the masses what LSD only did for those who were brave enough, intelligent enough, or just plain kooky enough to experiment in that area. I keep going back to that don't I, I wonder why. Honest, I haven't done acid in two days, and I want to tell you, it's great to be clean! No, I just made that up. It's a joke.

Once you realize that the world you perceive can change dramatically, and not only with drugs but with yoga and with various other types of exercises like hypno-tapes, audio tapes, neurolinguistic programming – there are all sorts of devices for changing you perceived world – once people realize that, they'll realize if they are living in a sad and ugly world, well that's because they got a sad and ugly program in their brain. And if they're living in a happy cheerful world that's because they programmed their brain properly.

You know the old slogan that goes back to the dawn age of computers when dinosaurs and Richard Nixon still roamed the earth, "GIGO: garbage in, garbage out." Well if you're getting garbage out that's because the software in your brain consists mostly of garbage. You better replace it with more up-to-date software.

LB: Do you think that the current anti-corporate globalization movement is a flash in the pan? Do you see a resemblance to the labor union movements of 1930s?

RAW: That's interesting. My wife Arlen used to say that the great days of labor organizing are not behind us, they're ahead of us. She meant the Third World. All the jobs that are disappearing here are going to the Third World at slave-level wages. A friend of mine has a parody of the Nike slogan, "We made our money the old fashioned way: slave labor in the orient." Well, that's not going to last so long, especially with the internet and communications advancing greatly. Those people are going to get organized and start fighting for their rights. Meanwhile people here losing their jobs all the time are getting more and more pissed off.

I don't think this is a flash in the pan. I think the people who run this planet have disgracefully mismanaged it, as William Burroughs said once. And I think they are going to have to give it an inch at a time or maybe they'll collapse all at once in a big rush like the Soviet Union did. I always think of that – when I feel hopeless I think of how thoroughly the Soviet Union changed in a couple of months.

And the same thing happened in the Union of South Africa. I remember as things kept heating up in South Africa throughout the 70s and 80s. It was obvious, the blacks were the majority. The whites were the minority – they held their superior position simply because they held most of the guns. But the blacks were learning where to buy guns. And it seemed to me the whites were so goddamn pigheaded they wouldn't give up until most of them were shot dead. It was going to be a bloodbath. And I thought why don't we ever learn anything from history. Well the white South Africans showed me that we can learn something from history: they allowed power sharing before they all got killed, which is a striking sign of intelligence from a ruling elite. Most ruling elites don't find out until their heads get chopped off, like the French royal family in 1789.

So I think there is a chance that the power elite today might learn before it's too late. They can't have a meeting anywhere without protesters showing up. Now they're having meetings practically on desert islands.

I'm in favor of globalization. The thing is, where is it coming from – the ground up or the top down? If it's coming from the top down I am as fervently against it as anybody in Seattle or any of the other places since then. But I think globalization is inevitable, it just has to be from the grassroots. The 92 chemical elements are scattered at random around this planet.

To make the maximum use of science and technology, we need all 92. So we are going to have to accomplish that by one country conquering the whole world, which is the traditional way, or by working out a system where everybody gets a fair share by negotiation. I think one country conquering the whole, which seems to be the policy now in force, is not only dangerous, but it gets more dangerous everyday as the explosive power increases. As more and more people protest against it, I think eventually we're going to have to negotiate our way to a fair deal for everybody.

To quote Bucky Fuller one more time, in the last half of the 20th century, the majority of the scientists of the United States have been recruited to, directly or indirectly, contribute to delivering more and more explosive power, over longer and longer distances, in shorter and shorter times, to kill more and more people. And now we're spending even more money under Bush. We're going to reach the point where pretty soon we're going to just press a button and we can release zero-energy and destroy the whole universe, not just this planet. That is the most perverted form of human intelligence imaginable and that can't go on forever because more and more people are more and more dissatisfied with that.

What you gotta do is talk to a couple of intelligent people from northern Europe. They pay higher taxes than we do, but they rarely complain because they get something for their taxes. They get universal health care. They get much better unemployment if they lose their job. They have all sorts of social services that we don't have, which is worthwhile. But here, everybody is pissed off about their tax bills, which is comparatively low, because they get nothing for it! All that happens to the tax money is that it goes to pay the interest on the national debt and then to build bigger bombs, to go faster, to kill more people.

LB: What most excites you about the approaching future?

RAW: What most excites me is solving the communication jam on this planet: letting everybody talk honestly to everybody else. I think of intelligence in terms of feedback. Feedback used to mean the noise you get when two electronic systems interact. But then the more generalized meaning became that of information flowing back and correcting itself, which is due to the work of Claude Shannon and Norman Wiener in the 1940s. They saw internet before it existed. They worked out, from the computers they already had, they worked out the trajectories of the way we were headed.

Every animal, to the extent that it has adequate feedback, that's the measure of its intelligence. And so that, to get back to an earlier theme, is why I like internet and hate censorship. Every form of censorship is cutting down on the feedback within the social organism, which means the social organism is much more stupid than any individual in it.

LB: Do you consider yourself a futurist?

RAW: I've been called a futurist often enough. I'm a non-fundamentalist futurist. I don't think you can predict the future very accurately, but you can consider a penumbra of scenarios. Which is something, curiously enough, an African shaman told William Seabrook back in the '30s: "the future is fan shaped." There is not one future; there are many futures. I'd like to help steer us to the most desirable future.

LB: Is this perspective a foundation of your optimism?

RAW: There are a lot of reasons for my optimism. One is, as long as things are unknown you might as well assume the best, because if you assume the worst you're just making yourself miserable and ruining your digestion. It can even lead to ulcers. In extreme cases it even leads to heart attacks. I think pessimism is very, very dangerous, on health grounds. There's actually research showing that optimists recover from diseases much faster than pessimists. So it's a health measure, I try to preserve my optimism as a way of guarding my health.

Then again because the literary establishment, especially in New York – the people who define themselves as "the intellectuals," who think there is nobody with any brains anywhere in the country – they're all so resolutely pessimistic. I feel somebody has got to raise a dissenting voice, just so there will be a dialogue at least. So I try to present a case for optimism.

And then again, the current world of chaos looks like the beginning of a change to a higher level of coherence, and intelligence, and feedback throughout the whole planet. Wait until Africa and Asia come online.

Barbara Marx Hubbard runs seminars in which people are divided up into like 20 groups and each groups deals with specific problems of concern to that group in relation to the city where they live. And after a couple of hours some of the walls come down and groups compare their solutions and see if the solution that is satisfactory to one group are satisfactory to another. And people come out of it absolutely delighted with the possibilities of what communication can achieve, once you start talking to other people.

Another ground for my optimism, is that people always do the most intelligent thing, after they have tried all the stupid alternatives and none of them have worked. And I think that the present system on the planet has obviously shown that it doesn't work. And the only alternative is more communication, and more honesty and more fair dealing. But it begins with honest communication. People saying what they really think and feel.

You know why Hannibal Lecter is so charming in spite of his

bad habits? Because he thoroughly enjoys life. Most people don't. Once they start communicating with one another, they will start to enjoy life a little more, because they'll feel less alone and less hopeless.

LB: How is today's counterculture different from the counterculture of the late '60s and early '70s?

RAW: It seems to me we've got the same spectrum. We've got some bright people and we got a bunch of idiots. The '60s counterculture, which is fashionable to put down currently, had a lot of very bright people who had a lot of high goals, but it had a lot of idiots and sloganeers. We had Jerry Rubin telling kids to kill their parents to show their solidarity with the Third World. All sorts of stupidity of that sort. So when I look around today and see stupidity in the counterculture, well it's always been that way.

As a matter of fact, Bernard Shaw and his introduction to *Androcles and the Lion*, points out that every revolutionary movement attracts those who are too good for the current state of society and those who aren't even good enough to adjust to the current state of society. That's the way he portrays the early Christians in that play. He got that from dealing with the feminist and socialist movements of his own youth. You get the best and the worst in the counterculture always.

LB: Your wife Arlen used the term "Stone Age feedback" to describe the influence of aboriginal cultures on 18th century thinking. Could you elucidate this for us?

RAW: Well, it was in the 18th century that most of what we now consider progressive ideas first began to dawn on various European and American thinkers. And much of this came from studying Stone Age tribes. Rousseau's idea of the noble savage was based on reports from Captain Cook's voyages in the South Pacific. Everybody knew how wonderful the

Tahitians and the Hawaiians were, but they mostly forgot about the tribe in New Guinea that was so paranoid they wouldn't communicate with them. Every attempt to communicate led them to throw spears at them until they gave up trying to communicate with them. So Rousseau forgot about them and assumed that all savages were peaceful and friendly. Which is largely true but not entirely.

The American Indians, or whatever they're called now – it used to be Native Americans, I think now we're supposed to say indigenous peoples. I have a lot of friends in that group and I never know what to call them. I just call them by their first name. I can't keep up with political correctness. The Iroquois Federation had some influence on the U. S. Constitution. And also from studying various tribal or Stone Age societies, socialism and anarchism occurred to various people depending on which tribes they had heard the most about.

LB: Have you participated in many social or political protests?

RAW: I still do by email. I sign all sorts of petitions and send all sorts of letters. Back in the '60s I was on the streets, I got tear-gassed quite a bit. I am proud to say I never got maced. In those days I could still run faster than the average cop.

LB: Was this activity in the '60s exhilarating for you?

RAW: My memory of the sixties was that mostly I was overly optimistic. I'm still an optimist on principle for the reasons I gave, but in the '60s I really thought the movement was getting bigger and bigger all the time. And even the people who were not part of "the movement" were moving. The statistics on the opposition to the Vietnam War were rising and rising – about 67% shortly before the war had ended. I think it went even higher than that. I remember when it hit 67%, I thought "My God, we really are making changes!" And segregation ended, which I thought meant racism would end with it. I was too optimistic about a lot of things.

So it was a very exhilarating time. I felt something very dramatic was changing. Changes for the better were occurring. I still feel I'm participating in changes for the better. Although I think that the tactics have changed from the streets to the internet to a great extent.

Oh, you know the main difference between Clinton and Bush from an internet point of view? When I sent an email to Clinton, I would get a three paragraph answer saying nothing. When I send one to Bush I get a one sentence answer saying nothing. Bush's letter says, "The president wishes to thank you for your views." Clinton's letter said the same thing, but in about 100 words in three paragraphs. No comment. At least Bush has a little more brevity than Clinton.

When I was researching for my historical novels I had a pretty low opinion of the past in general and the condition of the people in the past. But when I researched them I found out how the French were living before the revolution – you just got to read Engels, *The Condition of the Working Class in England*, or read the novels by Charles Dickens. I think by and large the advance of technology has been an advantage to most people on the planet.

Of course, that doesn't mean all technology. I coined the word "sombunall" – some but not all – to avoid over-generalizing. I use it in writing, but it's hard to remember to use it in speech because most people don't know what I mean, I have to stop and explain. You should never talk about all of anything outside of mathematics. In mathematics you can talk about all circles, because circles only exist in our imagination in the human mindscape. When you start talking about all Jews you're likely to go as crazy as Adolph Hitler. Or you start talking about all TV repair people for that matter. They're not all crooks, just most of them. So you should never use the word "all" outside of mathematics.

LB: What's your most serious concern about our planet?

RAW: The stupidity problem. Ideally we should have a pill that makes people more creative and more curious. And the only way to get most people to use it is if it gives people a hedonic boom along with that. The problem is that if such a pill did exist, the government would ban it right away. Some people think that it did exist in the 1960s and that the government did ban it, so I feel fairly safe in making that prediction.

But there are lots of other techniques from hypno-tapes to brainwave machines, to yoga, to neurolinguistic programming, and new things that are being discovered all the time. The thing is, they got to have a hook on them so people will want to use them. When the majority finds an intelligence raising device that they enjoy using . . . well I think they have to some extent in internet. Even the people who spend 18 hours a day with nothing but the porn sites, eventually they gotta spend at least one hour looking at the rest of it – so it would broaden their perspectives considerably.

LB: Can you speak a little bit about pattern recognition, perhaps in relation to the left brain / right brain models of thinking?

RAW: Well, we have more cells in our brain connected with pattern recognition rather than with logical sequencing, which I think is a very important fact to know. I think this explains why I find Chinese culture and Chinese ideograms and poetry so congenial, because it all deals with patterns. It doesn't deal with logical structures. I think logical structures generally turn out to be highly artificial. They have too many "alls" in them to begin with. You can't have a logical structure without an "all." "All men are mortal. Socrates is a man, therefore Socrates is a mortal." Well we don't know that all men are mortal anymore with the breakthroughs with biotechnology. There may be people alive today who will never die.

So no wonder logic plays a small part with most peoples' lives. Most of the brain is involved with pattern recognition, which is much more important – both artistically and just in terms of survival. If you're a monkey running through the jungle, if you stop to think things out logically, you'll get eaten by the first predator to come along. With pattern recognition, you know which animals are safe to approach and which ones you should run away from.

We need to study pattern recognition in the human brain much more because that's most of what the brain is concerned with and most of what art is concerned with. The missing part of most scientific descriptions of human beings is the importance of pattern recognition.

They used to call it right brain and left brain, but then they found that they weren't so divided. But those are two definite functions: the pattern recognition and the linear linking. The pattern recognition is much more important for survival. We've been talking so much about science, but I basically regard myself more as an artist rather than a scientist. To me, like I said, the problem with science when studying human beings is that they don't stress pattern recognition enough.

Children taught art at an early age tend to live longer and they tend to understand science better than those who are given the traditional form of education based on linear thinking – the Gutenberg fix, as McLuhan called it, or the Aristotelian mind set as Korzybski called it.

LB: Any advice to young people looking to change things?

RAW: Yeah, don't feel superior to the people you are trying to change. That's the worst possible stance to take. You'll never convince anybody as long as you feel superior to them. All you'll do is insult them. I think that was the major error of the '60s and I blame it especially on Abbie Hoffman and

Jerry Rubin. It was the major mistake of the '60s – talking from a position of superiority when you didn't have any of the qualities that people looked for in leaders. They had charisma, but Arlen used to say, the only place for charisma is in show business. Once it gets loose in politics or religion, all hell breaks loose.

Robert Anton Wilson Interview

by DJ Fly Agaric 23

This interview was held in 2002 and
first appeared in *Maybe Logic Quarterly* 2005.

Robert Anton Wilson and DJ Fly Agaric 23

Introduce Robert Anton Wilson, how?

Blockade dissolving bardmon. Courageous Renaiss ense
historian

Heretickle Head-peeping shamanticist. Rebel mathematician

Multi-Modal Ha gnostiQ. Bold crunk langwisp. Social scientest

Futurist peaceniq for Taoist President. Ghetto syner jesta'

Holographi K playwrite. Past-modem' Trippoet and Essayeast

Sit-up comediown. Hip chill-out couch doc. Futurevast
translator

TSOG dissenter. Optimust Illuminist. Hyper-Relativast

Side-tearin' Novelist. Tella'-the-tribe. Liberteas' sage defender

Episstemological insurgent guerrilla'. Doctor

Non-euclidean politiq' subgeni'. Hannibal Lecturer

Non-Aristotelian NU Scientific philosofar

With a quad pack of Guinness and some kind Humbolt nuggets I embarked upon my otherwoidly trip to powwow with Bob Wilson at his humble home in Santa Cruz County, California on 10 Artemis. 81 P.S.U. [10th September 2002]. We had a hearty good belly-laugh together to be fair, Bob's subtle accenting and comedic timing turned what might be read silently as some kind of anarchist plot to overthrow *ALL* world government tomorrow – into softly glistening satirical situationism, exploding koans and hilarious loopy equations. I hope that through sharing this interview bright KNU sparks can ignite other critters everyware into reading and re-reading RAW's encyclopedic *playtimespace*. – fly agaric 23, Wordsley, England, 12.19.13.11.16-8. Cib – 14. Mac [20th September 2006] 16.22 PM.

> "This book intends to change your way of perceiving/
> conceiving the world, without drugs or drums or
> Voodoo, simply by using words in certain special ways."
>
> – Robert Anton Wilson, *Email to the Universe*

RAW: "A boy has never wept nor dashed a thousand Kim." [*sound checking*]

FLY: When was the last time you ate some LSD?

RAW: About a year or two years ago, a friend of mine named Joe – I don't think I'll give his last name – brought some over for the night of the first debate between Gush and Bore and we thought it would be a great idea to watch them on acid. We looked at a Three Stooges comedy first, to build up our enthusiasm, and jeez I must say that the Three Stooges are lot more fun than Gush and Bore. They're a lot funnier, and there are more nuances; the characterizations were deeper and more convincing. Bush and Gore, Gush and Bore – whatever their names are – they're just two lying bastards with straight faces telling the same damned lies. The Three Stooges are continuously inventive, and we enjoyed them much more.

I don't do acid much these days. I got enough problems getting around due to my leg problems, and I'm alone in this apartment most of the time. Besides, I'm usually stoned, which relieves the pain. I don't wanna do acid, because acid – I know from experience – doesn't relieve pain. I wouldn't want to fall down on acid. I'd have a whole lot of trouble getting up. And I do fall about 3 times a year – about 3 times a year it averages out – because I get used to walking around with the walker instead of the wheelchair. Suddenly the walker is going one way and I'm going the other and I don't know where I'm gonna land. I don't want that to happen while I'm on acid.

FLY: How does the spirit of the cannabis protest movement today differ from its '60s counterpart?

RAW: Well, besides the people who want it legalized because they enjoy it for one reason or another, the medical marijuana issue is especially good because – how can I say this – it takes a great deal of blind faith in the government to believe that by taking medicine away from sick people they're doing something to protect us from terrorism, which is their official line. And I have the feeling this is gonna – clearly I'm overly optimistic, I often am – but I think this is gonna bounce back in their faces. They raided the Wo/Men's Alliance for Medical Marijuana [WAMM], which distributes marijuana to about 300 cancer and AIDS patients, and a few with muscular dystrophy and post-polio syndrome and other problems which are clearly helped by marijuana very clearly and obviously, and they – the DEA – swooped down and arrested the two people who own the farm where most of it is grown and chopped down all the plants and carted them away to destroy them – presumably. Many believe they sell them on the black market. That's the most popular belief in the counterculture; they only seize them to resell on the black market at higher prices.

Legalization of medical marijuana has a lot more support across the board. Even Dianne Feinstein, who I think is one of the most reactionary people in Congress – she's come out in favor of leaving the medical marijuana cooperatives alone. She's one of my senators. And my representative, Sam Farr, called it an outrage. And we're getting more and more support on that issue. All the enemies of medical marijuana point out: as soon as that's legalized, there's gonna be no control. How they gonna know who's got a medical problem? You can arrest and harass a lot of people with that kind of conviction stick.

It's only the federal government doing it anyway. What's very curious is that where I live, 55 percent of the voters of California voted to make medical marijuana legal. In Santa Cruz County, 85 percent in the county-wide ballot voted to make it legal for any purpose, so if you need it for medicine or you just wanna get high, use it for meditation and religious purposes, or just because they all know it makes a blow job even better. I think for these legitimate reasons marijuana is the test case.

They're taking medicine away from dying people in pain. I mean gee, that's worse than anything they've done internationally. It's happening right here to American citizens. I think it's gonna bounce back and hit them in the face. Maybe it's because I hope it will, but as stupid as the American people seem to be a lot of the time, I don't believe they are stupid enough to believe in taking medicine away from dying people. And most of the members of WAMM are dying. Most of them are terminally ill cases. And they're in pain most of the time, and the marijuana takes the pain away or at least eases it – and in most cases it takes it away for hours, you know. And the idea that these people with AIDS and cancer should die in pain because God doesn't want them to have any relief from the pain – I don't see how long they can hang on. It's like something out of the Middle Ages. You know, it's worse than medieval; it's the Dark Ages. I don't think they can hold onto that position very long, but they sure as hell are trying.

I get my pot absolutely free from the Wo/Men's Alliance for Medical Marijuana, which doesn't charge. It's a cooperative, and we do what we can to keep it going. Now they have been raided. We're gonna have to do more. We're gonna have to decentralize even further, decentralize the production, the making of the tinctures, the cookies, the brownies and whatever forms we wanna take it in that's best for our condition. Some people still smoke it, and we're gonna have to decentralize the growth and production and distribution. What are they gonna do if 85 percent of the people in Santa Cruz County area are against the DEA coming in? They gotta arrest the whole goddamn county. They gotta build a fence around the whole damn county and say we're all in jail now!

I dunno, they might do that. I saw somebody who was kidding, but he sounds just like George Bush, suggesting we build a bomb that will blow up the whole world and cut a hole in the middle the shape of the United States and we'll survive after we blow everything else up. Sounds like a great idea to me. There'll be no more enemies to fear, no more wars to fight; then we can spend our money getting a health plan like the civilized world has, so everybody has health care. If we didn't spend all this money fighting the rest of the world, we might have a health plan like England or Ireland or France or Germany, Canada or Israel, or any civilized country. We can't afford it because we're so busy fighting the whole fucking planet at once. They're not even finished in Afghanistan, and I doubt they ever will be. And they're getting ready to start a war with Iraq now, and Saudi Arabia or Iran is next on the list – they're not quite sure which is gonna be the third, but it's gonna be either Saudi Arabia or Iran. All the Muslims in the world, which is between 1 billion and 2 billion, depending upon which estimate I believe, say one and a half billion: they're all gonna hate the United States even more than they do now. Here we have a planet of six billion people, one and half billion people hate the United States, I don't know, ITS SO FUCKIN CRAZY I CAN'T BELIEVE IT. Who's running this show, the Three Stooges? [*laughs*]

FLY: In 1972, the drug war budget was 100 million dollars. By the beginning of 2000, the figure was 20 billion dollars. Yet there seem to be more drugs available.

RAW: There's more of everything. The more they fight it, the more drugs appear. It's like Lao-Tse said, "The more laws they pass, the more criminals they create, and the more weapons they create, the more terror stalks the land" – the more clear the explanations, the more frogs fall out of the sky.

When they made marijuana illegal in 1937, according to sociologists who have studied the growth of the thing, there were around 100,000–500,000 pot smokers in the United States, most of them in Texas and New Orleans. Now the estimates run between 20 million and 70 million after all this money that's been spent. And it's the same with heroin – there are more heroin users in the country now than there were when that was illegalized. It doesn't matter whether it's a good drug or a bad drug: make it illegal and people get attracted to it, and of course the damage increases. I forget who said that "no drug is known to science that becomes purer and cleaner, safer or easier or better to use when turned over to the criminal classes." The United States has taken a whole variety of drugs and turned them over to the criminal classes, and of course they have bad results. You don't expect criminals to be as careful as doctors, do you? And doctors don't have all that good a reputation. Somebody on email a month or so ago sent an article claiming that more people die in hospitals from wrong prescriptions than die of all the illegal drugs combined, so even doctors aren't infallible. And we're gonna trust criminals! We're not supposed to trust them, but – leaving aside the medical marijuana – the people who just want pot to get stoned and get high and relax, they've got to go to the criminal classes. Why? Well, actually when it comes down to it, I trust the Mafia a little bit more than I trust the United States government. [*Fly laughs*]

What I'm really afraid of is when they decide to legalize it and they come up with a pill, some squib, probably Eli Lilly – as the Bush family own a lot of Eli Lilly – they come up with a pill that contains the derivative of cannabis that kills pain, but it doesn't get you high. And then they'll charge about $50 a pill, so for real relief from pain it'll be out of reach for most of the population, and they will still go on suffering or buying from black market dealers. Meanwhile, they'll have a better excuse to close down the medical marijuana cooperatives – "Hey, we got a legal form here and it doesn't produce that terrible euphoria that's bad for you." [*laughs, smiles*] They all complain about euphoria as one of the bad side effects of cannabis. Apparently you're not in your right mind in this country unless you feel vaguely miserable, apprehensive and depressed. If you start feeling euphoric, there must be something wrong with you. What the hell? I think euphoria is part of the treatment! There's a hell of a lot of evidence and a hell of a lot of books starting with Wilhelm Reich on – Prescott, DeMeo – oh, there's tons of evidence that feeling good is good for your health. So their attempt to take the joy out of marijuana just means they want you to take longer to heal whatever you use it for if you're using it for medical purposes.

FLY: So how can we be more socially synergetic and responsible with drugs and attaining higher consciousness?

RAW: I think the scientific evidence from the early '60s . . . Before the government banned all scientific research and revived the inquisition, there were quite a lot of scientific studies published, and I think it clearly indicates that psychedelics are good for almost everything they were used for – almost every disease – with some kind of positive result in one study or another, and certainly produces religious experiences with only minimum suggestion to get them moving in that direction. Like in the Good Friday study that was done at Harvard: you put the subjects in a church and gave half of them acid and half of them a placebo, and the ones on acid almost all had religious experiences. I look at Leary's convict rehabilitation research. He reversed the recidivism rate. Most of his convicts last heard of were still not committing new crimes. The average new convict is back in prison within one year. Leary's convicts – almost about 80 percent of them – seemed to have stayed out of prison, which means either the acid made them more compassionate and they stopped committing violent crimes or it made them more clever and they're not getting caught. I dunno which, but it keeps them out of prison anyway. We think it made them more compassionate. Besides, they weren't all in for violent crimes. A lot of them were in for nonviolent crimes like drug use, embezzlement, things like that. Embezzlement is not nice, though. I would not like people to steal money out of my bank account, though it's not a violent crime.

FLY: How would you describe compassion?

RAW: It means to feel with. "Com" is "with" in Latin, and "passion" is "emotion." In German it's *Mitleid* – to feel somebody else's pain, to feel their pain with them. It seems to be a natural human phenomenon unless it gets destroyed by unfortunate early experiences. All my children, when they were babies and I took turns feeding them, there would come a point when they would try to take the spoon away from me and try and feed me. They were trying to show gratitude for being fed by feeding me. My wife told me they all did it to her too. I spoke to a lot of women about this. They all do it. The natural tendency of the human species is to be kind to one another. But of course you got a child that gets beaten up and brutalized and sodomized and goes through all sorts of hell – they're gonna grow up as cold. They're gonna grow up as sociopaths without any positive reaction to human beings at all except how can I get his money from him, how can I screw them, how can I torture them for the longest time and get the most fun out of it. Bright ideas, guys. We're not going that way, though. That takes a really brutal upbringing.

Serial killers, for instance, almost without exception, had incredibly brutal childhoods, incredibly cruel parents or foster parents. So that's how they get to feel that way about human beings: "human beings are no good, they're not to be trusted and they're a bunch of bastards and let's get even with them" – that's the way serial killers think, to the extent that they think at all. Mostly they have one standard victim they go after over and over, a certain type. You know, Ted Bundy went after college girls or women of that age. Jeffrey Dahmer went after black adolescents; he even went after white adolescent males. They all have a standard type. They're committing the same crime over and over again. And – how did I get onto serial killers?

Hannibal Lecter is the exception, though. No one can predict who's gonna be his next victim because he's whimsical about it. [*laughs, long pause, smiles*] He's fictitious, though – I hope.

FLY: I noticed a cup around here that says something like "Forget all this self-improvement. I want an honest meal."

RAW: That's in the third volume. He said: "Damn all this self-improvement. I want a pleasant dinner!" [*Fly laughs*]

Another great saying: a lesbian patient of his who meets him after he's been in the nuthouse and escaped and has been at large for 10 years. They accidentally meet again, and she says, "You know, what I remember best was when I told you I was a lesbian and you said, 'There's nothing wrong with being weird, dear. You have no idea how weird I am.'" You never understand anything until you try it. [*Fly laughs*] He must have been a great psychiatrist. I mean, speaking of fictitious characters. If he was real, no patient could bring in anything that he couldn't understand and appreciate. [*laughs*]

FLY: So why would Hannibal Lecter make a better president than George Bush?

RAW: Well, everybody agrees that you need a serial killer in the White House. I mean, the patriotic line is: *We're surrounded by enemies on every continent except Antarctica. The world's full of people armed to the teeth who hate us just because they hate our freedom.* I don't know what freedom we've got that they could possibly hate. We don't have any freedom left in this fucking country, but they believe we've got freedom and people hate us for it, so we need a serial killer in there to keep killing all these people who don't have any freedom and even hate us for our freedom. On the other hand, the left-wing attitude is that these are all wars for oil or other natural resources, the government lies all the time and what they try and do is rip off the rest of the planet. So we still need a serial killer in the White House. Either from the left-wing or the right-wing perspective, we need somebody with the personality of a serial killer.

So what type of serial killer do we want? I say Hannibal Lecter has a lot more culture, a lot more wit. George Bush, Bozo, his Royal Fraudulency, George the Second – he has about as much wit as a box of kitty litter. Hannibal Lecter is witty, educated, erudite, multilingual. He would make a tremendously great impression upon foreign leaders. And if he eats a couple of senators occasionally, well, hell – we could lose a couple of those geological specimens in the Senate and with no loss, with a great gain to the country. And so he ate the forebrains of a congressman once. What do you need a forebrain for in Congress anyway? They all act from the back brain now. They don't need frontal lobes.

FLY: What's your favorite sound?

RAW: The end of Beethoven's Ninth: male and female voices singing together about joy and brotherhood and peace.

FLY: Do you think that the American government produces disinformation to discredit conspiracy theories and make them seem more absurd?

RAW: I don't think they are smart enough to do much of that. Maybe the CIA has one guy in one office who's in charge of confusing conspiracy theorists by putting out false conspiracies. But I've seen enough of the conspiracy buff world. They don't need that. They make up their own crazy theories to disgrace the research anyway.

FLY: How is it that so many convicted felons are back in the U.S. administration?

RAW: Like I said: we need that type. Since we've got enemies on every continent, either because they hate our freedom as Bush said or they hate us for ripping off their land and their people and their natural resources and murdering them en masse. You know, 193 million people have been killed in wars since the end of World War II. That's the estimate of the World Game Center in Philadelphia. That makes Hitler look like a piker.

Most of these are brush wars. Small wars. Most of them are the western world against the southern and Asiatic world, or the Third World trying to get out from under the control of the major banks in Hamburg, London, New York, Boston, etc. – what I call the real DEA: the Dutch-English-American alliance between the royal families and the bankers. They're all interrelated to one another. When you start getting into it, you find that George Bush, for instance, is related to the queen of England, who's related to Prince Bernhard of the Netherlands, who's related to most of the major bankers – it's all one big happy family when you get up there at the top.

FLY: Can you give me a description of LAWCAP?

RAW: That's a term coined by Buckminster Fuller for "lawyer-run capitalism." He thinks that the attempts to control capitalism by passing laws has turned control of the corporations over to their lawyers, whose job it is to tell them how they can rob as much as they want without breaking the law technically, and if they do break the law what kind of defense to mount against any prosecution.

Lawyers are really running the system. And considering the low opinion everybody has about lawyers, that's more terrifying than any other conspiracy theory. Like the Jewish conspiracy: I'm not afraid of Jews – all the Jews I know are very nice people. The Jesuit conspiracy: well, it's a little frightening but I've met a lot of good Jesuits too. The Freemasonic conspiracy: every Freemason I know I like. But the idea of a lawyer conspiracy! Really, those bastards are capable of anything. When you've got to argue both sides of any case, that's very good education if you're gonna be a philosopher, but it's not a good education for anybody who's gonna have any power over other people, 'cause whatever they wanna prove, they can prove it to themselves anyway. They can make a pretty good argument in most cases; that's what legal training is all about. "*No*, my defendant did not set fire to the building. He was merely smoking in the hay barn." That wasn't a very good example, sorry.

FLY: Have you wrestled with the Octopus lately, and how do you remember Princess Di?

RAW: What octopus?

FLY: The Octopus!

RAW: Danny Casolaro? I'm more worried about the TSOG. [*Fly laughs*] That's the Tsarist Occupational Government. Now that we've got an official Tsar who's in charge of American medicine, if there's enough disputes going on in the other sciences then eventually the Tsar is going to be deciding all scientific questions the way he decides medical questions: according to public opinion poll. And I think that's the worst threat confronting us.

I don't know how the hell we ended up with a Tsar. This country was supposed to free us from a king; now we've got a *Tsar* in place of a king! That's progress? I'd rather have the English queen back rather than have a goddam Tsar settling scientific questions.

And Princess Di. When she died, there was a lot of

sentimentality about her. I said to my wife, "What the hell did she ever do other than marry a rich man and take a lot of his money in the divorce?" "She was leading the struggle against land mines." OK, OK, she did something for us. So I'm not against Princess Di anymore. So she got a lot of money from a rich man and she did a lot of good too, plus she was a cute-looking woman I must say. Besides, I like her for dating an Arab – that shows the cosmopolitan spirit.

That's why she got murdered, according to one conspiracy theory, you know. The British Royal family didn't want her to marry an Arab, because then the future king of England would have an Arab father who might be related to Osama bin Laden for all we know.

FLY: You ever hear of Adnan Khashoggi? I read somewhere he's deeply involved with this Octopus.

RAW: Hey! Can you straighten out my goddamn Loch Ness Monster. Somebody last night thought they were being funny obviously and discombobulated it. The head goes in front, the loops go in the middle and the tail goes at the end. There we are.

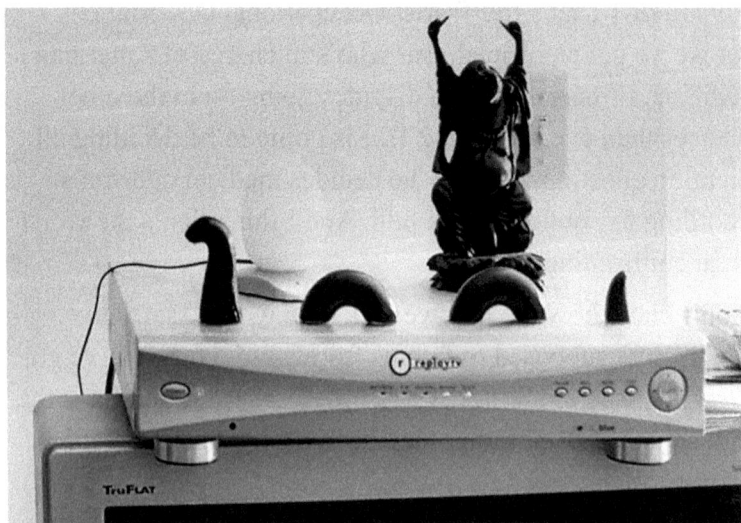

RAW's Loch Ness Monster on the cable box

Now my cable box looks the way it should look. Thank you. Don't you think that's one of the more appealing decorations in the room? I think so. The Loch Ness Monster on the cable box. That's little Nessie. [*smiles*]

FLY: Did you read *The Cosmic Serpent*, by Jeremy Narby? Are you familiar with his work?

RAW: No, but I think I read a quote from it just recently in a debate that went through my email. I'm on several email lists. There was a physicist debating with a philosopher and I think the philosopher was arguing that the DNA of all living beings make up a creature very much like the cosmic serpent. Is that the book? The physicist called it "cargo cult new age psychobabble." [*Fly laughs*]

FLY: Did Ezra Pound have some idea that the Phoenicians split the word up into the Tower of Babel ?

RAW: Well, no. That's an exaggeration of his views. Pound believed everybody should learn Chinese or anybody who wanted to be a writer. No politician should get elected unless they can pass an exam in Chinese. That makes even more sense today than it did when Pound wrote it, because China is one of the major powers in the world. Everybody wants trade with China. Nobody wants war with China. Everyone wants to trade with them. That's about 2 billion customers, something like that. That's why Nixon decided to end the cold war with China – all those customers American business couldn't reach, so they lifted the bans. For the sake of commerce, business and the general world, I think everybody should know some Chinese. Pound thought that alphabetical languages teach us to think in a certain way which you might call linear, or Aristotelian, and ideogrammic languages like Chinese teach us to think in terms of relations and concrete specifics and don't connect them always by causality; a lot of them are just connected by synchronicity. To the extent that I know any Chinese at all, it's due to Pound's influence and I'm very grateful to him for it. I think everybody should learn Chinese. One of the things I feel regretful about is at the age of 70, I still only know about 100 ideograms. Damn – I should know a few thousand by now. I got distracted by other things.

FLY: How do you see India and Africa becoming more integrated into the online community?

RAW: To me that's the most desirable goal right now. To get Asia and Africa online seems to me the way we're gonna have globalization without corporate control of globalization.

I think we need globalization. I don't like the use of that word as a negative, because global corporations know a sensible way to use the resources of the planet, but there's got to be cooperation, not just a bunch of Dutch-English-American bankers and royals running the goddamn world. It's gotta be a grassroots globalization, and the more people who get online the better. I met an African guy on a plane to Portugal a few years ago, and he was running a computer company in some country in Africa so small I'd never heard of it (and I forgot its name). He wanted to get his whole country online within 10 years. So I was delighted to know there are people in Africa thinking that way. And the more it happens in Africa and Asia, the more we're gonna get a world union that's not based on force but on communication.

That, to me, is the real hope – just about the last hope we've got. Until we're all accessible to one another at least temporarily and can communicate with one another, we're gonna be mismanaged, lied to, abused and generally exploited by our own governments or other governments who come in and throw out our government and say we've come to liberate you, and they're still a dictator. The guy that the United States installed in Afghanistan to hurrahs and hallelujahs last year – there were two attempts to assassinate him last week!

Obviously the Afghanis are not all delighted to be liberated, you know? After we liberate Iraq – "we," there I go again, after *they* – I don't like to say "we" when I refer to government, it's not my government, it's their government – after they get rid of Saddam Hussein, how many times are they gonna have to go back to Iraq to reinstall a new dictator after the last dictator gets bunked off?

You know, England first entered Afghanistan in 1849, and they had to go back again and again for regime change, because everyone installed kept getting thrown out by the various tribes who would get pissed off at 'em. Doctor Watson in the Sherlock Holmes stories got his war wound in Afghanistan. By 1919, after 70 years, the British finally smartened up enough to say, "Oh, fuck Afghanistan, you can't control a bunch of religious maniacs who live in mountains," and they got out. Then the Russians in the '80s: they fought for 10 years then they got out, showing they're 7 times smarter than the English. It only took them 10 years to learn their lesson. Assuming that we had an unbroken succession of Bushoids, I imagine the United States will be there for 170 years and going back for more regime change every five years or so.

FLY: Do you recall the last time you saw the movie *Lawrence of Arabia*?

RAW: It was only about a year ago or so, maybe even more recently. I'm a Peter O'Toole fan. He seems to be one of the two or three greatest actors in the world, or four or five anyway. That's one of his best performances. I also like him a lot in *My Favorite Year*, where he plays Errol Flynn or a character based on Errol Flynn, and also *The Stunt Man*, where he plays the character based on John Huston, who Clint Eastwood also played a character based on in *White Hunter Black Heart*. I'm sorry, I'm rambling.

FLY: [*laughs*] No, no.

RAW: John Huston is a fascinating character. Both Peter O'Toole and Clint Eastwood played him.

FLY: Why should you never whistle while you're pissing?

RAW: That's the Zen idea of single-mindedness. Besides, you're more likely to pee on your trousers if you're concentrating on your whistling. See what I mean by single-mindedness?

FLY: Have you any tricks you can share with us on how to create *satori* during the daytime?

RAW: Well, I can offer a simulation of *satori* I learned from Aleister Crowley, who learned it from a Buddhist monk in Ceylon. You simply sit down where you know you're not going to be interrupted for at least a half hour and try and answer the question: "I am sitting here doing this exercise because. . ."

Well, firstly you're doing it because I suggested it. Why did you take my suggestion seriously? What makes you think I have something that's worth learning, etc.? Then you're doing this exercise because you're interested in trying to achieve something like *satori*. Why are you interested? How has your whole life led up to that? What happened in the womb that you may be able to find out? What was your childbirth like? What was your infancy like? Why am I sitting *here* doing this exercise? Why here and not in London or Berlin or Hong Kong? And why am *I* here to do this? Why did my parents meet? Did they intend to have a child or was I like most of us an accident? And you go on and on. Eventually you find yourself coming up with things like, "I'm sitting here doing this exercise because the Scandinavians overfished the North Sea in the 5th century." [*Fly laughs*] They did! They took to piracy when they ran out of fish temporarily, and during their piratic raids on Ireland some of them decided to stay, and I'm descended from the Old Lochlan ,which means sons of the

Dane, so that's one of the reasons – that the Danes overfished the North Sea. Another reason is because I had polio at the age of four, which gave me the kind of personality that's attracted to exercises like this. I was always more interested in books than sports, unlike most boys, because my leg was so dammed weak I was no good at any sports. You couldn't find a sport I was any good at, at least I never did, but I was good at chess. You see what I mean?

FLY: Would you be able to talk a little about von Neumann and game theory and how they influenced the Cold War?

RAW: Yeah, I think we're all still alive because of John von Neumann. Von Neumann was the pioneer, or certainly one of the pioneers, of programmable computers. The first computers at MIT were put together to solve specific problems, then take them apart, put them together again and add another problem. And von Neuman invented a distinction between hardware and software, and how you could use the same computer to do many classes of problems. He also wrote one of the best books on quantum mechanics, but that's a digression. He also invented mathematical game theory, which he showed could be applied to poker and other games like that, strategy, and to tactics, and to war. Pretty soon the Pentagon had a big budget to build computers and play war games on them: "If we attack Russia this way, how much can they hit us back?" And the answer was always that the losses were too unacceptable. Most of them were usually total obliteration.

So they went on playing their war games for 30 years until the funding ran out and they decided not to have the war at all, because von Neumann showed that by solving these things in advance then when you know you can't win, why go ahead and fight? Why why why why why wipe yourself out, cut off your nose to spite your face? So that's why we're all still here and that's why most of the controversy and opposition about Bush's desire to invade Iraq comes from the military, because they're the ones with the computers who are working out war games with Iraq on their computers, and they know it's not gonna be the cakewalk that George Bush imagines. This has been all over, even on television news, all over internet – that the people in the Bush administration, the people leading the rush to war, have never served in a war. The opposition is almost entirely military men, they call them chickenhawks: the guys who want war because they have never been in one and have no idea what it's like. I can see the United States 20 years from now still bogged down in Afghanistan, still bogged down in Iraq, and attempting to fight Saudi Arabia! Oy! Never underestimate the power of stupid people in large groups. [*laughs*]

FLY: Why do you think some people might perceive it dangerous to understand things too quickly?

RAW: The first one who said that was Josiah Warren, one of the founders of modern anarchist thinking. His book *True Civilization* begins with a single page with a single sentence: "It is dangerous to understand new things too quickly." And then he explains why the Constitution could not preserve liberty in the United States and invents General Semantics 100 years before Korzybski did. He argued that words on paper can always be reinterpreted. Law schools teach you how to reinterpret them. A good lawyer can take a will that says "All my money goes to my son" and prove in court that it means "My money goes to my daughter." That's what law school is all about: learning how to prove things like that. The words on paper can never control government. The only thing that can control government is to keep it small and decentralized and rotating.

His idea of two civilizations is that every community appoints a bunch of people, maybe kidnaps them, and tells them, "You've gotta take care of the garbage and the police and things like that for the next 6 months, then you can go back to your regular life." And, well – I'm exaggerating a bit, but you get the point, I hope? The idea is you don't want a professional politician class, and you don't want them all in one place, especially now that running for office is so damn expensive that they have all got to be in the bag to the corporations or they don't even get on the ticket.

That's so damn obvious. It amazes me how all these people on TV news who look like they're awake – they look like they are semi-conscious, they look like they have some kind of intelligence – and yet none of them ever, ever seem to notice the fact that politics in the United States has become a choice between two candidates picked by the major corporations, and that's the only choice we get. If you want, as a protest, you can go for one of the third parties, but I don't see how that's any better than staying at home and not voting at all. You know the guy you vote for isn't gonna win. It's gonna be one of the two major corporate party candidates. And nobody on TV seems to know that! Everybody else in the country does. That's why 55 percent didn't vote in the last presidential election. They know it doesn't make a damned bit of difference. Now you've got these sentimentalists on about "If only Gore would have won." If Gore had won, he'd be doing the same damn things as Bush. They're in the bag to the same major corporations. General Electric, Westinghouse – I mean, you can run down the list of all the contributors. Enron was a major contributor to both of them. So was WorldCom.

FLY: Oh my! You once said that every publisher should have a pimp for an elder brother. I forget: why is that?

RAW: So he'll have somebody to look up too! [*laughs*]

FLY: Can you identify the source of some of your most immediate worries and challenges?

RAW : I do very well not worrying. But the one thing I do worry about is that I'm gonna have a stroke that will leave me too weak to protest or do anything about it – I'll just have to lie there dying slowly. My mother, my father, my brother: they all died of sudden massive strokes, just like that. [*snaps fingers*] They were gone in about 30 seconds. That's the way I want to go.

My wife died from a series of strokes – horrible, terrible, horrible to me and it was horrible for the whole family. I don't wanna go that way. So if I have even one mild stroke, I'm not gonna go through a series of mild strokes. After the first mild stroke, I'd pick the suicide. I'm not gonna hang around dying slowly and losing all my savings. I want to leave something to my children – I don't want to let it all go to the goddamned greedy hospitals and the goddamned greedy doctors and the goddamned greedy pharmacies and the goddamned politicians who represent those goddamned greedy types. Is that clear, Mr. Bush?

FLY: What gives you the strength and courage to face your daily challenges?

RAW: I see as many positive possibilities as negative ones, and since the conclusion has not yet arrived I don't know which is going to happen. So it seems to me that worrying about the bad possibilities just gives you ulcers and makes you a generally miserable person and drags down the party wherever you go, whereas looking at the positives and spreading word about the positive possibilities keeps you high and happy and might even cheer up a few other people too, so since we don't know why not choose the happy path? Besides, as a Buddhist I really profoundly don't give a fuck! [*Fly laughs*]

There's a little Chinese saying – "The wise become Confucian in good times, Buddhist in bad times and Taoist in old age" – that makes more sense to me all the time. I believe in Confucianism given in the sense of etiquette and good manners, courtesy and at least a minimum standard of decency for everybody. I believe in Buddhism to the extent of detachment, because this is a pretty bad planet and a lot of bad things happen so you don't wanna get too attached to anything. And I'm becoming more and more of a Taoist, because after reading about 20 different translations of the *Tao Te Ching* and looking up some of the ideograms in my Chinese-English dictionary and reading commentaries, I think the basic message of Taoism is that it doesn't matter, fuck it all. [*laughs*] I have all three attitudes simultaneously: I can make things better by being nice to people, it doesn't really matter in Taoism, and it's all a burning house anyway, so don't get too attached to it – that's Buddhism. I think it makes a nice mixture. I admire the Chinese more than any other culture on the planet.

FLY: Such beautiful paintings as well, those landscapes . . .

RAW: Oh yeah, and you look at some of those statues of Buddha – those sculptures – you need to be in a deep meditative state just to get the expression just right, and the subject had to be there too. The whole culture knew things about the mind that our culture is just beginning to tentatively discover.

FLY: Can you describe some things that help to bring solutions to your challenges? I suppose you just answered that question.

RAW: Well yeah, that's personally. Socially, I think if anybody goes to the Buckminster Fuller websites online you'll find that solutions have already been worked out by Fuller and his associates at the World Game. All it takes is for the governments of the world to give up their attempts to conquer one another by killing one another or by killing one another off and realize that's not working. I don't know how long it's gonna take, but eventually, as Fuller said, "Humanity as a whole always does the most intelligent thing after all the stupid alternatives that fail." Once all the stupid alternatives fail, they have no option left but to try Buckminster Fuller's World Game solution in which everybody gets clean water, good food, good health care, and most of the major forms of exploitation are made non-economical by synergetic cooperation between peoples. And then we can have a kind of virtual utopia, and the only question is will the governments discover that on their own or do we have to get rid of them? If so, how do we get rid of them nonviolently?

I can understand why some people get so goddamned frustrated they start throwing bombs. I believe that only makes them stronger. It's what's called counter supporting – counter supporting is opposing something in a way that makes it stronger by your opposition. A classic example, or at least . . . When I read the book, I happened to be in Ireland, and right away I thought of the Ulster Freedom Fighters and the IRA. Each one makes the other stronger. The same thing is going on now in Israel between the Israeli right-wingers and the suicide bombers: each one makes the other stronger. So I think we gotta outsmart them instead of trying to out-bomb them. Outsmart the goddamned governments! Fortunately, internet exists already and it's international already and we're learning more about how to use it. We're learning more and more about how to get accurate news over internet, and we'll learn how to make our own agreements and bypass the governments eventually until they have nobody to govern but themselves. [*Fly laughs*] And Congress will sit down there in Washington passing laws binding upon the 540 members but not on the rest of us.

FLY: How do you plan to keep potheads busy for the next 10 years?

RAW: One way is to print a card up with one side that says "secret message on other side," on the other side it says "secret message on other side" – this should keep the average pothead busy for at least 15 minutes. I don't know about the other 45. In the next 45 minutes, they can run around showing it to their friends and watch how long it takes them to figure it out. [*laughs, smiles*]

FLY: Is President Boy-Shrub the legitimate president of the United States of America?

RAW: Not by my standards. It appears that Al Gore won the popular vote. Nobody disagrees with that. The only disagreement is who won the Florida vote and therefore the Electoral College. As far as I know, there were four newspapers that collaborated in a post-election study and they all concluded that Gore won even counting that way. Then the establishment press came back, not by doing their own study, but by claiming methodological defects in the studies that had been done. That's just like CSICOP. They never do their own research; they just look for methodological defects in the research they don't like. As far as I'm concerned, Al Gore is the legitimate president of the United States, but that doesn't mean much to me, because the legitimate president of the United States means to me the same as the godfather of the Mafia or imperial wizard of the Ku Klux Klan or general all-round Antichrist. [*laughs*]

FLY: What are some of your lasting impressions of William S. Burroughs?.

RAW: He was one of the most intelligent people I ever met. If I had a list of people who I regard as the most intelligent, Burroughs would be up there along with Buckminster Fuller and Timothy Leary and George Carlin and my wife Arlen and a few others – anybody who plays this tape and you're not included, I'm just absent minded. Ken Campbell. Orson Welles – although I never met Orson. Arlen met Orson.

Burroughs had very high intelligence and a great deal of

anxiety, which he tried to control in various ways, including being a junkie off and on for most of his life. He tried other methods too. When I knew him in 1965, he was entirely off junk and he couldn't get through an evening without getting drunk. It was a choice of narcotics or drink. He had terrible anxiety left over from God-knows-what events in his childhood – very bright, very pressed in his emotional reaction, although not in his sex life so I hear, and very funny too. Humor is one of the best cures for anxiety, and if junk doesn't work and alcohol doesn't work you can always try making a joke out of it. That's the Taoist solution.

FLY: Who was Hassan-i-Sabbah?

RAW: He was the original model for Osama bin Laden. He lived in Afghanistan too, in a mountain retreat with a bunch of religious fanatics, and he convinced them they would get transported to heaven. He had an absolute guarantee: If you die in the service of Hassan-i-Sabbah, you will go right back to heaven, which is full of gorgeous virgin dancing girls all ready to satisfy you in every sexual way you can dream of. Oh, and dancing boys too – Hassan-i-Sabbah knew all about those Near Eastern peoples. His agents pretty much discouraged people from invading Afghanistan for a long time, because he had agents in most of the neighboring governments, and any government that decided that it was time to attack Hassan-i-Sabbah would wake up with his throat cut the next morning, always with a dragon with the assassin's symbol on it – one of the servants who had disappeared in the night. So people lost interest in attacking Afghanistan.

Hassan-i-Sabbah and Osama bin Laden both seem to be historically related to Fu Manchu. These are all images of Oriental revenge for Occidental imperialism. They're all the nightmares of the ruling elite about what the rest of the planet is secretly plotting. Then there's Ming the Merciless, of course, now he's distributing free cannabis in Ireland – have you heard about that? [*laughing*] Yeah, on election day he sent letters to all the members of Dáil with cannabis in them, all of which were rushed to the army to be tested for anthrax and none of them had anthrax in them. They just had cannabis in them. Every member of Dáil is in danger of having cannabis in their desk – if it hadn't been for the anthrax scare running at the same time.

His real name is Flanagan. Ming the Merciless. I think there's lots of fun in Flanagan's work. That's a quote from an old Irish song: [*singing*] "Lots of fun at Finnegan's wake/there's lots of fun in Flanagan's work." Ming the Merciless. [*smiles*]

FLY: Paul Krassner recently dedicated his new book *Murder at the Conspiracy Convention* to you. Do you think there is a lack of original humor in mainstream media at the moment?

RAW: Well, let's go back to the beginning, Paul Krassner – he dedicated the book to me. He sent me an email along with the dedication long before the book was published and asked me if I found it satisfactory and wanted to change anything to make sure I'd be pleased by it. I was so delighted, I dedicated my next book to him, which is due out any day now. It's called *TSOG: The Thing That Ate the Constitution*, and it's dedicated to "Paul Krassner, Zen Bastard." I originally wrote "Paul Krassner, Zen bastard and all-around good guy" or something like that, and sent it to Paul, and Paul said "Zen Bastard is just what I want." So some people might think I'm insulting him, but that's what he wants; that's his sense of humor. So I let it stand. The book says: "To Paul Krassner, Zen Bastard."

FLY: Yeah, he has a great sense of humor and integrates it into some of the most awkward and difficult situations – which seems needed today. People don't seem to be able to make fun anymore without getting ridiculed.

RAW: Well, humor is always subversive. Arthur Koestler

wrote a very technical analysis of humor in a book called *Inside and Outlook* or something like that – one of those books with three-word titles connected by "and" with two opposite nouns, like *The Yogi and Commissar*, *Inside and Out*, *Arrival and Departure*. He had that outlook. He did a 400-page analysis of humor showing that it works the same way as artistic creativity and scientific discovery. It results from looking at a familiar thing in two opposite ways. So that's always subversive. That's why there were no jokes about 9/11 until only in the last month – except in the most deliberately far-out and offensive media. Nobody else dared to joke about it. Hell, Bill Maher didn't joke. He just made one sensible comment and he was out of work. Which reminds me of what Pound wrote about London in 1919: "One intelligent remark can ruin a man's whole career." [*Fly laughs*]

FLY: Why would T.S Eliot's writings provide the best book-bombing propaganda for the U.S.?

RAW: Who the hell thought up that question? Is that yours, or did somebody else suggest it? T.S Eliot makes a justification for American bombing?

FLY: I heard they book-bombed Korea with T.S Eliot books one time.

RAW: They were dropping T.S. Eliot on Korea! [*laughing*] They should have dropped Pound's *Cantos*. At least they could have read some of the Chinese ideograms [*Fly laughs*] even if they couldn't decipher the rest of the text. I don't know, that's like: Why are the United States dropping food supplies and bombs on the same people at the same time? And those who manage to escape the bombs will go for the food and will have to walk across possible land mines to get at the food. Sometimes I think this whole planet is batshit crazy except me – and then I realize all lunatics think that way, so I gotta get a wider perspective.

FLY: I equate the removal of you from the Prophets Conference with the banning of Bird from Birdland.

RAW: That's a great comparison. I really appreciate that. That's wonderful. Yeah: Bird was banned from Birdland and it was named after him. Well, the Prophets Conference wasn't named after me, anyway.

FLY: I remember that in Palm Springs, December 2000, you said: "If the United States government wasn't trying to dominate the whole world, we wouldn't be threatened by terrorism."

RAW: That's just before they fired me. [*laughs*] Isn't that an odd coincidence?

FLY: Some prophecy from the Prophets Conference, I reckon.

RAW: Yeah, well, that's why if you're gonna run a commercial Prophets Conference, you don't want any real prophets, so they're not gonna disturb everybody. In *Illuminatus!* I had terrorists blow one wall off the Pentagon, just like happened. And in *Schrödinger's Cat* I had Wall Street blown up, just like what happened. And I don't claim this is ESP or precognition; it's just common sense. The United States cannot go on bombing two thirds of the world year after year, decade after decade, over and over without somebody hitting back eventually. I knew it had to happen. You don't need ESP. You just need a little horse sense.

CNN keeps referring to it as "the day the world changed." Well, the world didn't change; people have been dropping munitions on one another ever since Nobel invented modern munitions. People love dropping bombs on one another. It's one of the favorite human pastimes. They're almost willing to give up football. I mean it's been going on for ages. The only thing that changed is that the United States has been doing most of the bombing for the last 50 years, and everybody got used to that. We got to bomb another country for their own good; it's only collateral damage. The United States gets bombed and they say the world changed. The world didn't change. It's just the United States got included in with the rest of the world.

If you go around bombing people year after year, decade after decade, you'll have somebody bombing you back. Jesus! No, no: that's not the reason they did it, they hate us for our freedom. All the freedoms, like the freedom to pee into a jar before you get a job interview. That's the kind of freedom we really need.

FLY: Instead of throwing shit we might just pee on one another. [*laughs*]

RAW: I'm more and more examining Jerry Falwell's idea that God joined Al Qaeda. You know, he said that right after the thing. He said God joined Al Qaeda because there were too many gays, feminists and ACLU lawyers in the United States. And apparently he thinks there are no gays, feminists or ACLU lawyers in the territory controlled by Al Qaeda, so that's where his God is obviously strongest. Or that his God helped the planes hit their targets.

And I'm more and more inclined to believe that. As my leg problems get worse and worse, God seems to me like the character described by Jerry Falwell and Osama bin Laden: he's a mean, rotten, sadistic son of a bitch. That's the only kind of God that makes any sense to me, which is why the three religions I like most – Confucianism, Buddhism and Taoism – never say anything about God at all. They don't even deny God.

Well, Buddhism does, or some Buddhist sects do, very explicitly. I remember the first time I ever heard the Dalai Lama was on BBC, and the interviewer said, "Some people say Buddhism has no God. Is that right?" And the Dalai Lama said, "Yes, very true." And the interviewer said, "But isn't the Buddha mind something like God?" And the Dalai Lama said, "The Buddha mind is the inside of all things. It is not an almighty creator." Gee, a religious leader who makes some sense. I read a book by him and I didn't find any bullshit in it at all. The one living 100% bullshit-free religious leader on this planet, they haven't found another – well, maybe "Bob" Dobbs. [*laughs*] OK, he seems bullshit-free too – well, he's not bullshit-free, but the bullshit is highlighted with jokes, and so you know it's a joke. All the rest of them remind me of "pay no attention to that man behind the curtain." The Wizard of Oz.

FLY: Did you ever meet Chögyam Trungpa?

RAW: No. I met a lot of his people – I've been to Boulder several times after his death, and there's lots of amusing legends about him, including one about a meditation class being led by somebody or another, and suddenly Trungpa appears at the door with a can of beer in his hand, he yelled: "Why are you meditating? I will tell you why you are meditating. You're all scared shitless about the atom bomb. [*laughing*] I tell you, you don't need to be scared shitless. The atom bomb will not fall on you." I don't know whether that's true or not. That was told to me by somebody who lived in Boulder who swore it was true. There's all sorts of fascinating legends about him.

FLY: Leading on from some earlier email interview questions you answered for me, can you expand upon why *Finnegans Wake*, cannabis seeds and a Rottweiler are essential elements for a 21st century survival kit?

RAW: You need *Finnegans Wake* to understand the merging world village that's appearing. *Finnegans Wake* is the only book that's written from a global perspective. Well, Pound's *Cantos* are almost global. They include China, parts of Africa, most of Europe and the United States and some ancient Sumer, Egypt. Joyce is much more universal; he includes a lot more of Africa than Pound does – a hell of a lot more – and a lot more of Asia too. That's part of your education to live in the 21st century: you gotta master *Finnegans Wake*. And then you need what? –

FLY: Cannabis seeds.

RAW: Obvious, that doesn't need any explication does it? And the Rottweiler . . .

FLY: What are some of the prerequisites for Discordian math 101?

RAW: First of all, there's the Law of Five, which states that all things and events are directly or indirectly connected with the number five. The second law is if you can't make them connect, that shows you're too dumb to be a Discordian.

FLY: Can you explain Sturgeon's Law?

RAW: Sturgeon's Law. That was created by a very good science fiction and fantasy writer named Theodore Sturgeon. He was on a panel discussing science fiction, and the speaker before him was a professor of English who denounced science fiction up hill and down dale, smoted hip and thigh, and ended up by saying that 95 percent of science fiction literature was crap. And then it was Theodore Sturgeon's turn to talk, and he began with what became known as Sturgeon's Law: "But professor, 95 percent of everything is crap." And that's true: 95 percent of opera is crap, 95 percent of the novels published are crap, 95 percent of the movies are crap, 95 percent of the histories are crap, 95 percent of the soap operas are crap, 95 percent of the paintings are crap – it's the five percent that are interesting, whether it's science fiction or modern art.

FLY: How do you feel about the many synchronistic and numerological factors surrounding 9/11?

RAW: 9+1+1 does not add up to 23 , so I gave up on that and decided to hell with it. Even 9 x 1 x 1 does not make 23! [*Fly laughs*]

FLY: Along with "food, clothing, and shelter," what are some of the essential elements for life support as cosmic citizens?

RAW: Love. Of course that helps get food, clothing, and shelter. Or I mean, it's part of the whole package. It seems life is happier synergetically interacting, at least to most people anyway, more may not be desirable. I've lived in a couple of communes and extended families. I had a marriage that lasted 42 years. Now I'm alone I find more interesting states to be in. Of course, I find everything interesting. It's the only alternative to being bored – to be interested.

FLY: Can you explain why thinking, writing, and speaking in Irish seems difficult to understand in English?

RAW: Yeah, I'll try. If you take a classic Irish play, you find somebody saying, "My grandfather said 'and I a child of nine at the time.'" Now, in normal English you would say "when I was a child." "And I a child of nine" is Gaelic grammar superimposed on English words, and this is the way they talk in western Ireland a lot, or the way most of them talk either in English or in Gaelic, which is the old-fashioned grammar, which does not put things in sequence like English does. It puts things into concentric relationships, sort of like the way Chinese does, which is why William Butler Yeats said "Ireland was a part of Asia until the Battle of the Boyne." And you can find the strain of what we call Asiatic thinking, or pre-Anglo-Saxon, pre-Aryan – I don't know what the hell it is – we find this kind of thinking in Ireland very strongly and in Wales, and in parts of Spain, and over most of Africa and the Orient. It's a way of thinking just as legitimate as the dominant paradigm of the Western world. It highlights some things and ignores other things, just like the Western paradigm does. I have never been in favor of junking the Western paradigm and adopting the Eastern; I've always felt we should learn the most of what we can from both of them, and Ireland's a good place to do that. An excellent place to do that.

FLY: That reminds me of Jeremy Narby's idea in his book *The Cosmic Serpent* relating to what he calls stereoscopic thinking – a little bit like perceiving something with your mind that's both internal and external at the same time, creating this kind of stereo effect.

RAW: That's like Bertrand Russell's two heads paradox, you know that one? [*Fly smiles and nods slowly*] You must have two heads. Then there's J.W. Dunne: if you have two heads, you must have an infinite series of heads, because in the two-heads model you have another head thinking about all this. Once you realize that there's another head thinking about that, you know that the heads go on till infinity in an infinite number of time dimensions. This was developed by Dunne in two amazing books called *The Serial Universe* and *An Experiment With Time*. It's the wackiest model in modern cosmology and in some ways the most fascinating. He makes it sound so plausible.

FLY: How do you see vision quests?

RAW: Let's see what I can do with that topic. Well, first of all, there's the ordinary brainwashing, which is called acculturalization in the social sciences – this is how they take an infinitely malleable infant and hammer it into the shape acceptable in the local tribe, or as acceptable as possible. Then there's vision quest, which is the attempt by some individuals who are not quite satisfied with the process who try to discover the rest of themselves: "What did they murder while they were hacking me into this Procrustean bed?" So vision quest is always some part of the population, varying in size depending upon how the quest's conditions are, I suppose. I suppose the number of vision quests has increased astronomically in the last 50–60 years, because these are the bloodiest and most terrifying years of human history. I mean the Hundred Years' War was no picnic, but that was restricted to a rather small part of the planet. In the current rumble, the whole planet is under threat. Everybody feels the same kind of terror: to have a religious nut like Osama bin Laden fighting his Royal Fraudulency Bozo the Clown, the first non-elected president of the United States, who can never produce a grammatical sentence without a teleprompter in front of him. Even then he reads them wrong part of the time. [*laughs*]

FLY: What can we expect from your writing in the next 12 months?

RAW: I have a new book coming out called *TSOG: The Thing That Ate the Constitution* and I'm working with Lance Bauscher on a movie called *Maybe Logic: Robert Anton Wilson, His Lives and Ideas*. That's 'lives,' not 'lies'. And I'm also working on a book called *The Tale of the Tribe* by New Falcon Press and – if I'm up to it physically – I'm teaching at a neuro-linguistic programming workshop in Florida next February. I would love to get out of here and to Florida in February if there doesn't seem to be too much strain and stress on my leg. I think I'm gonna do it. I'm gonna have to be in a lot of pain the week before to cancel that.

FLY: What are some of your favorite music albums and recording artists?

RAW: I like Bach. I like Charlie Parker and Thelonius Monk and John Coltrane. I like Harry Belafonte and the Weavers and a lot of other music. I like Mahler. I like a lot of music. Next question.

FLY: Did you ever get into the Grateful Dead?

RAW: Not really deeply, I like them but I never became a

Deadhead, I know a lot of Deadheads. If the Dead decided they wanted to play in the South Pole, these people would find some goddamned way to get to the South Pole. [*Fly laughs*]

FLY: What are some of your fondest memories from living in Ireland?

RAW: Well, this might be just silly, but these are my fondest memories. When we first lived in Sandy Cove, I could see the James Joyce Tower from my kitchen window. That was the first thing I saw every morning: the tower where stately, plump Buck Mulligan bravely blessed the awaking mountain and intoned, "Introibo ad altare Dei. Come up, Kinch! Come up, you fearful Jesuit!" That's the tower where it all happened, right outside my window. Another fond memory is just after we moved over to Howth the first time, Arlen and I went to the rhododendron gardens with a copy of *Ulysses* trying to find the exact spot where Bloom made love for the first time. But we could never decide, because too many spots seem to fit more or less Joyce's description which he gives us. And considering the fact that Molly has memories of an earlier sexual experience in Gibraltar mixed up – we couldn't find the Spanish wall, for instance, because that was in Gibraltar and lumped together. All the hours and hours in pubs with Irish friends just listening to Irish conversation and how they use words. Oh, and reading the complete works of Jonathan Swift, which I got out of the local library one book at a time; it seems to me Swift's wit and the wit of the native Dubliner is sort of like the two aspects of the same thing ,which is in Joyce in one way and in Oscar Wilde in an entirely different way. And it comes from looking at the same thing two different ways simultaneously. It's the so called Asiatic part of Irish culture. [*long pause*] "Death and life were not/Till man made up the whole/Made lock, stock and barrel/ Out of his bitter soul" – William Butler Yeats.

FLY: How did the town of Wolverhampton find its way into your novel *The Widow's Son*?

RAW: Some English witches asked me to write a free article for their magazine, and they said it could be as short as I wanted. And so I wrote them a page and half or two pages, and they sent me their magazine from then on until they went bankrupt, or out of business, or forgot about me, I don't know which – but it did finally stop. In one issue of that I saw an ad for the Order of the Illuminati with an address for central inquiries and possible admission, and then I decided to include that in *The Widow's Son* for any readers that want to enquire beyond the book and into the reality behind it, whatever that may be. Another time I wrote to an American neopagan magazine called *Green Egg* and signed myself as outer head of the Ancient Illuminated Seers of Bavaria, and I got a letter from somebody who called themselves Philip, Count the Something or Other, Sanctuary of the Gnosis, who announced he was the real head of the Illuminati, and if I didn't stop posing as the same he would have his lawyers sue me. [*laughs*] And so I wrote back and said, "Your letter will not program into my computer in its present form. Could you please re-submit it in log." [*Fly laughing hard*] I never heard from him again. He lived in Thousand Oaks. I love the idea of the Illuminati having its headquarters in Thousand Oaks.

FLY: What are some of the perils of cocaine abuse?

RAW: Well, in the first place, Wavy Gravy pointed out way back in the early '70s in a conversation with me that every coke freak he knew seemed to die of a heart attack between 30 and 50. I began to notice that pattern myself after Wavy pointed it out to me. Another thing I noticed was that everybody I knew who got heavy into coke turned paranoid and nasty after a while. I also noticed they mostly quit, which convinced me it's not as seriously addicting as heroin, if you're worried about addiction. But it's a very dangerous drug considering the psychological changes it triggers. It seems to be a great deal of euphoria at first, and then a great deal of nastiness. Coke freaks are great to know the first week on coke. You don't wanna meet them after that – close the blinds, don't answer the telephone, and pretend you're not home. And then look at the political record. We have had two politicians in the last 100 years who were both rumored to be coke freaks, and they both broke into office by non-electoral and very irregular methods, which in both cases were followed by the destruction of a beloved national monument, which in both cases they blamed on an ethnic minority. In both cases they had a witch hunt against this minority. In both cases they cut off all previous liberties and installed a totalitarian state, and in both cases they declared war on more and more parts of the world quicker and quicker. One of them had a funny moustache. I'll let you guess who the other one was.

The thing is that this is what cocaine abuse leads to inevitably in every case I've seen. Tragic. Chris Langham said you can get the same effect by stuffing talcum powder up your nose, rubbing it in with sandpaper and then running around the house burning all the money you can find. After a month, the results – especially in your bank balance – will be exactly the same as after a month on cocaine. Relating to the last aspect, I have known three or four coke freaks who were in show business and earning big money, and they all ended up in bankruptcy court before they kicked their cocaine. I mean they were making millions and they managed to lose it all, or it went somewhere mysterious – they were so goddamn freaked out they didn't know their business manager was robbing from them, I dunno. But they all ended up bankrupt and had to remake their careers after they emerged from the world.

FLY: How do you feel about Ozzy Osbourne being invited into the White House?

RAW: I guess they're having a cokehead convention. [*laughs*]

FLY: Have you ever experienced ayahuasca or been to South America and hung out with the shamans.

RAW: No; no.

FLY: What you think about these modern vision questers who are heading down to the Amazon to meet the shaman?

RAW: Bless them all, bless them all, the large and the thin and the tall. Everybody should go where they want to go. Timothy Leary called it "the first step of evolutionary intelligence" – finding the right ecological niche for your species or subspecies. He thought California was the right ecological niche for his species. That's why he lived here till death. I'm leading the California secession movement, and it doesn't exist beyond my email yet, but if it's as popular as I think it is, then it's time for this serious issue!

FLY: Yeah, I'm thinking of moving to Siberia.

RAW: You're moving to Siberia? That's not such a bad idea. I thought about moving to Amsterdam.

FLY: I found the city of Amsterdam to be one of the more liberal-thinking cities of Europe.

RAW: Yeah, it's been that way for a long time. When the queen who sponsored Columbus's voyage, Isabella – when she expelled all the Jews from Spain, Holland accepted them, which has made it a very liberal country ever since. And that's where Spinoza wrote, and most of the major philosophers you find spent a couple of years in Holland, because they were banned in their own country and had to run for their lives. Some of them died in Holland. Descartes lived in Holland for a while, so did Spinoza, so did a lot of them, and they have always been very forward-thinking. And according to a friend of mine in southern California, they own most of the banks which own most of the English banks which own most of the American banks which own most of the corporate capitalist world. At the same time, it doesn't matter how much their people fuck and smoke dope and get high and enjoy themselves. [*laughs*]

FLY: Can you clear up the rumors about how involved Aleister Crowley was in the secret services?

RAW: That has been a matter of debate between Crowley's biographers ever since the beginning. I don't know any two biographies of Crowley that agree. My impression is that in the First World War, Crowley was working for British intelligence and had penetrated German intelligence for them. I think in the Second World War, all the evidence is that he was only working for British intelligence – suggesting a few minor things like symbolic gestures to boost Allied morale, such as the V for victory sign – which is invoking Satan in Crowley's magickal thinking. [*laughs*] Or the thumbs up that invokes the divine phallus. [*laughs*]

FLY: How about Ian Fleming and his relationship with Aleister Crowley?

RAW: I didn't know they had any relationship at all, but Ian Fleming worked for the Twenty Bureau during World War II, which was involved with catching and turning all the German agents in England, and they succeeded – totally. They succeeded to an extent that they could not believe them. Some of them did not believe that they had total control of German intelligence in England, so they didn't use them to their maximum potential. And after the war, they got the German records and found out they had every German spy in England really working for them. Because once you're caught, if you're a spy, you have two choices in wartime – you can hang or you can go to work for the other side. Most of them go to work. You've only gotta hang one of them, and then all the rest of them become quite eager to go to work for the British, and the pay was better than what Hitler was paying them anyway. So they were totally in control of German information, but they never trusted it enough. They used it a bit, though. That's why most of the V2s didn't hit London and they landed in the country north of London [*tongue-in-cheek laughs*] by sending back false reports of where the damage was to throw the engineers off. That's one thing about the Twenty Bureau – that was Ian Fleming and Alan Turing, who was sometimes considered the father of internet, except by those who consider John von Neumann or Norbert Wiener or Claude Shannon the father of the internet. Dennis Wheatley, who wrote occult thrillers and really believed in them – he seemed convinced that every conspiracy that he could think up himself for British intelligence was not only the work of enemy intelligence but of Satanic intelligence! They were a rare bunch they were. [*laughs*] I think that kind of thinking gradually took over the CIA after James Jesus Angleton became chief of counter intelligence. He was a devout student of all their ways and works.

FLY: Have you a favorite Bond movie?

RAW: I don't really like the Bond movies. My favorite Harry Palmer movie is the first one, *The Ipcress File*. My favorite all-time spy movie is *The Russia House* with Sean Connery and Michelle Pfeiffer – who was born without stain or original sin and could do no wrong, not in front of a camera anyhow. I know nothing about her private life, but I never saw her do anything wrong in front of the camera.

FLY: Do you have a new perspective upon the movie *2001* by Stanley Kubrick in light of recent events?

RAW: Yeah, do we need more wars to find that goddamned monolith? [*laughs*]

FLY: Maybe you could speak a little about Saul-Paul Sirag and his possible influence upon some of your works?

RAW: Well, Saul-Paul lives in Berkeley, and after I moved to San Francisco I saw him once a week at the Physics/Consciousness Research Group, so we had lots and lots of conversations about quantum physics, and I had conversations about consciousness physics with others too, like Fred Alan Wolf, Nick Herbert, Jack Sarfatti, David Bohm, John Gribbin. Anyway, Saul-Paul was a major influence, and I got most of my information from him, and I told him what I thought about it, and he told me, "That's the Copenhagen Interpretation." And I found out I was part of modern physics without even knowing it, except that I apply the Copenhagen Interpretation to everything, not just applied to the quantum realm.

FLY: Is that equated with what you often call model agnosticism?

RAW: Model agnosticism: don't believe in your own models. They have got to be changed regularly and be kept up to date. If you believe in your own models, then you won't be willing to change them. And that's where people get stuck, and that's where the horrible accidents happen. You look back and think, "How could they be so stupid?" You're talking about our ancestors. They all did stupid things because they could not change things fast enough. Of course, that makes you feel gloomy. Remember that most of our ancestors were pretty smart. We know that because they lived long enough to reproduce. That shows at least an average intelligence.

FLY: Have you read the sensational book *The Stargate Conspiracy*? You're mentioned in connection to Esalen conferences along with many others.

RAW: I have never heard of this book. I have no opinion about it whatsoever. All I can do is sit quietly and let you tell me more about it.

FLY: Well, from what I can gather, it proposes that many events surrounding the millennium were a kind of spiritual hijacking by a cross between the military, E.T., and some people from the New Age movement. It ties together many great thinkers and almost every great conspiracy of the 21st century into a kind of extraterrestrial Three Stooges show!

RAW: Yeah, I've heard of this a few times. I forgot about it. A few times I have seen reference to it in my email. I'm on a few other email lists, and I have picked up a few things about this, yeah. There's also *The Hidden Dangers of the Rainbow*, which is by a Christian woman who claims Buckminster Fuller and dope culture and television and rock and communism are all fronts for the Illuminati takeover. I just mentioned a few of those; the list is much longer, and includes Marilyn Ferguson, the *Brain/Mind Bulletin*. Anybody who uses the word "synergy" should be regarded with suspicion – it's part of their secret language of their cult that is taking over the world. [*laughs*]

FLY: Featuring throughout the *Stargate Conspiracy* book is Andrija Puharich, who published three major books: *The Sacred Mushroom*, *Beyond Telepathy* and *Uri . . .*

RAW: I read *The Sacred Mushroom*. I also read *The Sacred Mushroom and the Cross*, by John Allegro, which curiously enough came up in my email three times in the last week. That's the first time this book has been mentioned in my email. Suddenly three people are writing about that book all at once. And now you're asking about it.

FLY: Well, I hear so many wild stories about Andrija, and obviously the Uri Geller biography he did was pretty far out, you know, so it makes me wonder. He had a background in electronics too.

RAW: Yeah, he has somewhere between 20 and 30 patents

on electronic devices. He was also a qualified and certified psychiatrist, and if you read his books, he sounds like he's a raving nut. I don't know what to say about Puharich. He just leaves me stunned in wonder.

FLY: Me too.

RAW: And then you read Uri Geller's book and you find out he doesn't disagree with Puharich at all, but he claims there's a major difference – neither one of them can define the difference. I don't know what the hell is going on.

FLY: Last year I saw Uri Geller in my hometown called Sturbridge doing his book tour, and at the end of the show he produced a little seed in his hand. He brought some children up onto stage. They touched his hand and then this seed started to sprout something!

RAW: Is there a question?

FLY: [*long pause*] It's not how many seeds are in an apple, but how many apples are in a seed?

RAW: Ezra Pound in 1940 wrote to T.S. Eliot – "and now that I'm through the economic part, I gotta get some philosophy for my Paradiso, the only thought I've had so far is that there is an intelligence in the cherry stone that knows how to grow cherry trees." That's the DNA! He almost had it; he was a poet, not a scientist, though. That becomes a major theme in the later *Cantos* – the intelligence of the cherry seed. He even found an ideogram in Confucius which means when translated "the intelligence in the cherry seed." The other translations say "vegetative spirits." [*RAW smiles, Fly laughs*]

FLY: I read that when you first got to Ireland, within being there a day or so you heard a show on the local radio about a farmer from County Kerry talking about the Pooka.

RAW: It was part of the oral history of Ireland or something like that on RTE-Radio – the government radio-TV monopoly

– and it was about the Pooka, which is a 6-foot-tall white rabbit that often grabs people on their way home at night from the pub and takes them off into alternate universes where they meet Fionn mac Cumhaill and all the great Irish heroes, Princess Leia, Luke Skywalker, Shiva, Krishna, Tim Finnegan, Adam and Eve and the whole gang from *Finnegans Wake* and the rest of world mythology. After the Pooka gets tired of playing with them for a few billion years, he puts them back on the road and it's only a few minutes after they left the pub on our clock time, but in a parallel universe it's 3 billion years. And the interviewer said with what I later came to recognize as a Dublin upper-class university college accent, "Do you believe in the Pooka yourself?" And the Kerry farmer replied, "That I do not, and I doubt much that he believes in me either." I thought that was the greatest example of Irish logic I ever heard. That's why I liked to stay in that country awhile. I was hardly an eccentric there.

FLY: So, I'm working upon a project called World Piss at the moment . . .

RAW: World Peace or World Piss?

FLY: World Piss.

RAW: World Piss. [*laughs*] Tell everybody next time they gotta take a good hardy piss, put it in an envelope and mail it to George W. Bush at the White House. They want to know what everybody's bladder is like these days, so don't make 'em send the agents out to your house to collect the samples; send them to him voluntarily. [*laughs*] You love Big Brother, Big Brother loves you, war is peace, freedom is strength, ignorance is slavery – no, ignorance is strength, freedom is slavery. The enemy is Iran, no the enemy is Iraq. We just got one letter wrong – the enemy is Iran. [*laughs*] Hold on for the revision! DO NOT ADJUST YOUR MIND! IT IS REALITY THAT IS MALFUNCTIONING!

FLY: [*laughing hard*] So, I think that should conclude this recording. I'd just like to say thank you very much from the bottom of my heart, and peace.

RAW: Yeah, peace indeed.

Copyleft: Fly agaric 23 – [Steven James Pratt]
2112.2012

Quantum Sociology
and Neuropolitics

David Jay Brown interviews Robert Anton Wilson

Part of this interview appeared in David's book,
Conversations on the Edge of the Apocalypse.
The following is the entire interview from
September 23, 2003.

Robert Anton Wilson and David Jay Brown, 1996

I interviewed Bob for my second book, Mavericks of the
Mind, *in 1989, and wanted to check in with him again to see
what he thought about some of the things that we spoke about
fourteen years ago, as well as the present state of the world.
Bob and I have been good friends for many years, and he
continues to inspire me. He is particularly fond of the writings*

of James Joyce and Ezra Pound, and I've learned a lot about Finnegans Wake *and* The Cantos *by going to his weekly discussion groups.*

I interviewed Bob on September 23, 2003. At 72 he remains as sharp and witty as ever. Bob has an uncanny ability to perceive things that few people notice, and he has an incredible memory. He has an encyclopedic knowledge of many different fields – ranging from literature and psychology to quantum physics and neuroscience. He is unusually creative in his use of language, and he has his own unique style of humor. Despite many personal challenges over the years, Bob has always maintained a strongly upbeat perspective on life, and regardless of the circumstances, he never fails to make me smile every time I see him. Everyone who meets him agrees: there's something truly magical about Robert Anton Wilson.

I spoke with Bob about the nature of optimism, why politics on this planet is such a big mess, his decision to run for governor of California, our vanishing constitutional rights in America, the philosophy of "maybe logic," extraterrestrial intelligence, and why he thinks Hannibal Lecter would make a better president than George W. Bush.

David: What were you like as a child?

Bob: Stubborn, it seems; maybe pig-headed. My mother often told me how, when I had polio at age 4, I kept trying to get up and walk. She said that no matter how hard I fell, I'd stand and stagger again until I fell again. I attribute that to Irish genetics – after 800 years of British occupation, the quitters did not survive to reproduce, you know. But I still loathe pessimism, masochism and every kind of self-pity. I regard loser scripts as actively nefarious and, in high doses, toxic. Due to that Nietzschean attitude, and the Sister Kenny treatment, I did walk again and then became highly verbal.

A neighbor said, even before I started school, that I should become a lawyer because no judge could shut me up. I attribute that, not to genetics, but to the polio and polio-related early reading skills. Due to a year of total-to-partial paralysis, I missed a vital part of normal male socialization and never became any good at sports, but I devoured books like a glutton. The nuns at the Catholic school where my parents sent me did shut me up for a while. Catholic education employs both psychological and physical terrorism: threats of "Hell" and physical abuse. But they never stopped me from thinking – just from saying what I thought.

David: What inspired you to become a writer?

Bob: The magic of words. One of the biggest thrills of my childhood came at the end of *King Kong* when Carl Denham says. "No, it wasn't the airplanes – it was Beauty that killed the Beast." I didn't know what the hell that meant, but it stirred something in me. In fact, it felt like what the nuns told me I would feel after eating Holy Eucharist – what we call a mystic experience – except that I didn't get it from the eucharist but from a gigantic gorilla falling off a gigantic skyscraper and having that line as his epitaph. I wanted to learn to use words in a way that would open people's minds to wonder and poetry the way those words had opened mine.

David: What is "maybe logic"?

Bob: A label that got stuck on my ideas by filmmaker Lance Bauscher. I guess it fits. I certainly recognize the central importance in my thinking – or in my stumbling and fumbling efforts to think – of non-Aristotelian systems. That includes von Neumann's three-valued logic [true, false, maybe], Rapoport's four-valued logic [true, false, indeterminate, meaningless], Korzybski's multi-valued logic [degrees of probability], and also Mahayana Buddhist paradoxical logic [it "is" A. it "is" not A, it "is" both A and not A, it "is" neither A nor not A].

But, as an extraordinarily stupid fellow, I can't use such systems until I reduce them to terms a simple mind like mine can handle, so I just preach that we'd all think and act more sanely if we had to use "maybe" a lot more often. Can you imagine a world with Jerry Falwell hollering "Maybe Jesus *was* the son of God and maybe he hates Gay people as much as I do" – or every tower in Islam resounding with "There *is* no God except maybe Allah and maybe Mohammed *is* his prophet"?

David: Why do you think politics on this planet is such a huge mess, and human beings are so violent towards one another?

Bob: Because most people have never heard of maybe logic and live in an either/or world, which applied to ethics and social policy becomes a good/evil world. Human vanity then determines that all the damned eejits always put themselves in the good position and anybody who disagrees in the evil. Look at any literary/politics journal – any journal of the nonscientific "intelligentsia" – and you'll see that they all sound as medieval as George W. Bush or Osama bin Laden. Violence comes of self-righteousness and self-righteousness comes of right/wrong logic, without maybes.

David: A photo of you recently appeared on the front page of *The New York Times* that showed you receiving medical marijuana from the Wo/Men's Alliance for Medical Marijuana in front of City Hall in Santa Cruz. How has marijuana helped you to deal with the symptoms of post-polio syndrome, and what are your thoughts about the political debate over medical marijuana?

Bob: First of all, I've had "post-polio syndrome" (PPS) ever since I recovered from the polio. Most of my life, from age 5 to 60, the symptoms remained minor – annoying foot spasms at times, leg pains when standing in long lines. After 60, the pains got worse, not just on the long lines at airports, but even on comparatively short lines in banks or markets. At 68, the pains got more frequent and more intense, even when I didn't have to stand on lines. Then I started falling down at unexpected times, and the pain became even more excruciating.

This happens sooner or later to most polio survivors and often hits some in their 40s, so I feel lucky to have had 60 good years. Current theory attributes PPS to muscle damage during the polio; I evidently walked around with only half of my muscles for over six decades. My doctor recommended mega doses of vitamins and nutrients, to repair the damaged muscles as far as possible, and marijuana to stop the pain. I get the marijuana free from WAMM, a group of neighbors and friends with other medical problems that pot seems to help – muscular sclerosis, AIDS, cancer and a few others.

It has worked wonders for me. Not only does it kill pain, but the High also increases general good humor and optimism. I sincerely believe that optimism – or "faith healing" or "Christian Science" or "mind over molecules" or "spontaneous remission" or whatever you call this – works better with pot than without it.

The political debate? To my admittedly simple mind that comes down to: do I trust my doctor, and my own brain and my senses, or do I trust a Tsar 3000 miles away who can only know better than us if he has direct guidance from God? Well, I don't believe in mystical Tsarism; I prefer constitutional democracy. The Tsar does not seem any more infallible to me than the Pope, and I refuse to let him sentence me to a life of continuous agonizing pain. The Tsar's goon squad keep trying to shut WAMM down, and if they succeed, I'll just buy my weed from back-alley dealers.

Meanwhile, I've worked at learning to walk for the third time, and at 72 can report considerable progress . . . which the pessimists will call wishful thinking, I suppose. At least,

I've gotten to a point where I only spend part of each day in a wheel-chair. At the worst, three years ago, I spent the whole day there.

David: Who is the TSOG, and why do we need to keep this "thing" from eating the U.S. Constitution?

Bob: I coined the term TSOG to mean "Tsarist Occupation Government" and to sound like a monster from a Lovecraft horror story. In a constitutional democracy, decisions concerning your health depend on your own judgement and that of your doctor. When such life-and-death matters get decided not by you and your doctor but by an allegedly omniscient Tsar, we have neither constitution nor democracy anymore but blatant and brutal Tsarist tyranny. Look at America today: we not only have a Tsar but he has more spies and informers working for him than Russia had in the days of Konstantin Pobedonostsev, who served as an advisor to Alexander III and Nicholas II. Pobedonostsev managed such an army of snoops that they called him "the Grand Inquisitor." Read Turgenev and Dostoevsky and you'll see how much America in the early 21st century has become like Russia in the 19th.

David: Tell me about your decision to run for governor of California, and about the Guns and Dope Party.

Bob: After I had written several articles and a whole book on the TSOG, my friends kept asking me to run, and I kept refusing, until it seemed every other nutcase in California had gotten into the act, so I finally made the leap. The Guns and Dope Party represents my attempt to unify the libertarian right and the libertarian left, not on a theoretical or ideological basis, such as Norman Mailer once tried, but just on the rule all horse-traders understand: give me something of value and I'll give you something of value.

I want the dopers to fight for gun rights and the gun people to fight for medical and recreational rights, because together we make a majority in the Western states, and especially in California. Besides, I agree with the gun people about this government. If only the police and the army have guns, we have a de facto totalitarian state that can do anything it pleases. The War on Some Drugs seems like an overture or dress rehearsal for such a totally Tsarist nightmare.

A few decades ago, Henry Kissinger said, "Anybody in Washington who isn't paranoid must be crazy." Under Dubya, I feel that anybody outside Washington who doesn't feel paranoid about what's going on in Washington must be crazy. First they take our money by force to do with as they please (the accursed IRS), then they want to disarm us, and they dare call this democracy? I don't think Jefferson or Adams would agree. They'd call it tyranny, and so do I.

David: Why do you think Hannibal Lecter would make a better president than George W. Bush?

Bob: I started the Lecter for President write-in campaign to make people think about style in politics. Look: Dr. Lecter doesn't kill for money. He has some standards, however egregious. Dubya seems to have none at all. Besides, Hannibal has a decent education and a sense of humor. He frightens me much less than Dubya. If we must have a serial killer in the Oval Office, and most Americans east of the Rockies seem to think we must, I'd prefer one with some class and panache. Dubya has as much of those as the stuff you step in and scrape off on the curb, hoping it's not as bad as it smells.

David: Where do you think the human race should be focusing its scientific efforts right now?

Bob: Biotechnology. I've said and written for 30 years that the health and longevity researchers seem on the outskirts of major breakthroughs. These breakthroughs now seem less than 10 years away, maybe only five. Of course, Bush has banned the most promising areas of research, but he can only enforce that Tsarist infophobia in the U.S. The research will continue in the civilized, or non-Tsarist, nations.

David: What is your perspective on telepathy, psychic phenomena, and synchronicity?

Bob: That whole area seems enormously intriguing but badly in need of heavy doses of maybe logic. I find most of the debate weary, flat, stale and unprofitable, because both sides seem overly dogmatic. If they took every "is" out of every sentence and replaced it with a "maybe" they might begin to make sense. Of course, the dogmatic deniers seem much sillier to me than the believers, because the believers at least use probability theory with some skill. They also do scientific investigations which the deniers shun "as the devil fears holy water." Have you ever heard of any scientific investigations by the Committee for Scientific Investigation of Claims of the Paranormal? I haven't. They rely entirely on abstract monkish logic, innuendo, invective, smear and outright libel.

David: What are your thoughts regarding the possibility that people can communicate with extraterrestrial or extradimensional intelligences while in certain altered states of consciousness?

Bob: I estimate a ninety-nine percent probability that we can, in such states, communicate with intelligences seemingly not our own. I've done it. I still remain unsure, however, if the Higher Intelligences contacted dwell in outer space, in other dimensions, or in circuits of my own brain not identifiable as "me" or "my ego." I'd love to live in an open democratic society where research on this became legal and widely published. Creating such an open society remains a major goal of the Guns and Dope Party. We favor total freedom for orgonomic medicine, LSD research, cloning and every other alternative that the Tsarists have made illegal.

David: How has your use of psychedelics influenced your writings and your view of the world?

Bob: Well, I've moved from atheism to agnosticism, with somewhat pantheistic leanings. I just don't want to sound too pretentious about it. I don't claim to know anything about any gods or goddesses, but I suspect a good deal. I suspect that some form of "divinity" probably exists, but it seems to me immanent and decentralized, not transcendent and authoritarian. More like Internet than like a monarchy. Aleister Crowley said "Every man and every woman is a star." We in the Guns and Dope Party have changed that to "Every man and every woman is a Tsar." That not only signifies scientific and political freedom, but something in the neighborhood of Vedic identification of the true self with divinity, or at least the Quaker "inner light."

David: How has marijuana helped you with your creative writing process?

Bob: I have always had strong tendencies toward compulsive rewriting, polishing, refining, etc. and marijuana has intensified that. In fact, these days I seldom stop fine-tuning my prose until editors remind me about deadlines. As Paul Valery said, "A work of art is never completed, only abandoned," and I regard even my nonfiction as a kind of art.

David: Are you still as optimistic about the future now as you were when you wrote *Cosmic Trigger*?

Bob: More so, but only because I don't think politics has as much importance as most people imagine. The real changes occur first in pure science, then in technology, then in social forms; the politicians then run around in front of the parade and pretend they're leading it, like Al Gore claiming he invented

Internet. If you only look at Dubya and Osama, the world looks like a Dark Age madhouse, but look at biotech and computer science and space colonies and a much more hopeful scenario dawns. Politics always represents organized infophobia, science represents infophilia, and over a span of generations, infophilia always wins out.

David: What is infophobia and infophilia?

Bob: I coined the term infophobia to synthesize Dr. Timothy Leary's work on neuropsychology and Claude Shannon's mathematical theory of information. Basically infophobia represents an attitude of fear towards certain types of signals. Some people are afraid of T.V. Some are afraid of Internet. Some are afraid of learning foreign languages, etc.

Infophilia represents the opposite extreme – the desire to learn many symbol systems, and use them for fun and profit. Primarily, I feel that anything that accelerates the flow of information helps solve all of our problems; anything that jams the signals, distorts them, warps them, or just tells flat lies, increases all of our problems. I consider this a scientific foundation for the first amendment to the Constitution, and for civil liberties in general. Or, as Paul Krassner summarized it, "Fuck Censorship!"

David: Do you think that the human species is going to survive the next hundred years, or do you think we're going to drive ourselves into extinction?

Bob: Maybe we'll destroy ourselves and maybe we'll achieve what Bucky Fuller called *total success in Universe*. I see no social profit, and no personal psychological profit (except to masochists), in assuming pre-ordained failure and general disaster. I assume the unknown future remains unknown, so why not try for the best we can imagine?

David: What do you think is the biggest threat to the human species?

Bob: Stupidity, especially in the form of those "faith-based organizations" so beloved by Tsarists. All my hope centers around research-based organizations.

David: Assuming that we do survive, how do you envision the future of the human race?

Bob: Mix Dr. Timothy Leary's SMI²LE scenario – Space Migration + Intelligence Increase + Life Extension – with Trotsky's Perpetual Revolution, and/or Jefferson's "revolution every ten years", and serve piping hot. With relish.

David: What do you think happens to consciousness after the death of the body?

Bob: I haven't died yet, so I can't speak with any assurance about that. My guesses remain guesses. I grant equal respect to the opinions of all men, women and ostriches, but no matter how sure any of them sound, I still suspect them of guessing, just like me. I wish they would use that liberating word "maybe" more often in their speculations.

If I must flounder around in metaphysics, "the great Serbonian bog where armies whole have sunk," I know of only five possibilities: (1) heaven, (2) hell, (3) reincarnation, (4) "union with God" or some other entity a lot like "God," and (5) oblivion.

Only (1) heaven, seems frightening to me; an eternity of "bliss" with nobody around but Christians – such messmates as Pat Robertson, Jerry Falwell and others of that ilk – really sounds awful. There's even a sinister rumor that the streets "are guarded" (brrrrrr!) by the United States Marines. Fortunately, according to the leading proponents of this model, I can't get sent there because I don't believe in Christ. Oh, goody.

Of course, (2) hell sounds almost as bad, but it has its good points. Everybody I admire from all history will get sent there, so the conversation should prove lively and stimulating.

Besides, I find it impossible to believe that "God" (i.e. the assumed "Mind" behind the universe) suffers from the kind of sadistic psychosis necessary to delight in eternal torture, and if "He" (or She or It) does have that kind of nasty streak, well, as a part-time Buddhist, I'll just have to forgive "Him" (or Her or It). I've started practicing for this eventuality by forgiving all the people who've made this planet a good simulation of hell.

(3) The reincarnation model seems cheerier and somewhat less goofy than these morbid notions, so it doesn't bother me. I even wish I could believe in it.

(4) "Union with God" seems a great idea to me, if I understand it, like an acid trip that never ends. Now that's what I'd prefer, if I have any choice in the matter.

Finally, there's (5) the oblivion model. I've never understood why so many people, like Woody Allen, find oblivion totally dreadful. If you're oblivious, that implies no experience and, of course, no experiencer either. How can you fear or even resent what you will never experience? It seems to me that only an advanced case of narcissism, or a mangled confusion of the map with the territory, can explain the bum rap that oblivion gets from most people. We all go there every night, between dreams, and it doesn't hurt at all.

David: What is your perspective on God, and do you see any teleology in evolution?

Bob: Well, since the only kind of divinity that makes sense to me seems decentralized, I assume it must possess what cybernetic theory calls "redundancy of potential control" – maximum feedback all around. In organisms, groups (flocks, herds), machines and groups of machines, that implies change and evolution, which in a feedback system means learning, and that seems like a kind of teleology.

By the way, Norbert Weiner pointed that out way back in 1948 in his book *Cybernetics: Control and Communication in the Animal and the Machine*, and the whole Internet Revolution dates from that, but I guess most biologists felt daunted by his mathematics. They still seem to think we would have all remained amoebas except for "copying errors." I'll believe that when I believe that if we all threw our junk in the same field for four billion years it would accidentally organize itself into a jet airliner.

David: Can you tell me about the film *Maybe Logic*, and about your reaction to the mayor of Santa Cruz's proclamation at the film's premiere that July 23rd will officially be "Robert Anton Wilson Day" in Santa Cruz?

Bob: My ego grew three inches in 24 hours.

David: What are you currently working on?

Bob: I'm learning to walk for the third time. (I hope.) Promoting the Guns and Dope Party. And I'm writing a book on the decentralization of power that I think Internet will create.

David: What gives you hope?

Bob: The research of psychologist John Barefoot, which indicates that optimists live roughly twenty percent longer than pessimists. Why should I make myself miserable with gloomy thoughts, cut my life by one fifth, and miss out on the bio-tech revolution, just to become fashionable with the New York intelligentsia?

Russian Magazine Interview

Wilson posted this interview to
the Main Forum of the Maybe Logic Academy
in April 2005.

My first interview with a Russian magazine . . .

1. Tell something about yourself for Russian readers.

I have 35 books in print in my own country, and
they seem to stay in print. Some also have infiltrated
Germany, Greece, Japan, Brazil, the Scandinavian
countries etc. This seems remarkable to me because
I don't believe in anything – my whole philosophy
consists of non-philosophy: persistent and vehement
agnosticism – but I still remain just popular enough to
stay in circulation. I'm not sure I understand why. Maybe
the world has more cynics and relativists than any of our
diverse Establishments suspect?

2. *It seems like you want to see marijuana regulations liberalized, why?*

> Right now, I have personal reasons – marijuana helps a good deal with my post-polio symptoms – but I have always opposed the current USA anti-drug laws since I first heard about them, for three reasons. [1] the drugs on the tabu list seem selected by highly eccentric and unscientific methods; I suspect commercial motives. As Lenin said, when you see injustice, ask: *cui bono*? I suspect that "our" government acts to support the major drug corporations and to stifle competition. [2] Because of its very nature, a War Against Some Drugs cannot succeed without the full apparatus of a totalitarian state, and I dread that; need I explain why? [3] At 73, I don't feel like a child and I resent being treated like one by our Drug Tsar. I supported a wife and four children for most of my adult life. I think me and my doctor know what's best for my health better than a Tsarist bureaucrat 3000 miles away, who hasn't even given me a medical examination. I mean, it's like living in a Kafka novel.

3. *Is there any correlation between Taoists sense of humor and your sense of humor?*

> I often quote the old Chinese proverb, "The wise become Confucian in good times, Buddhist in bad times and Daoist in old age." Since we live in good times (technologically), bad times (politically), and I feel as old as the last dinosaur, I've become Confucian-Buddhist-Taoist all in one package. I try to treat all people kindly, or at least politely, in Confucian terms; my empathy with all sentient critters has increased, in quite Buddhist manner; and I grow increasingly detached from fixed ideas and emotions, in the Daoist mood. I don't know whether to consider this Wisdom or just senility,

but it appears harmless and doesn't seem illegal, immoral or fattening.

4. *Is there any real conspiracy that affects global processes?*

I suspect that not one "conspiracy" but dozens – or hundreds – of competing gangs of goons affect global and local processes. On any given day, one of these bands of Great Pirates might have more clout than the others, bit it's seldom the same gang for two days, much less two years. Not to appear evasive, the gangs I would worry about the most, if still inclined to worry, would include the Vatican/Mafia mob, the Orange gang (Dutch-English bankers, who own American banking, too), the CIA, fundamentalist Islam in general, and the World Bank. But they all have lots of rivals.

5. *What would you say to someone claiming there is Global Government?*

I think I already said it. To say it again, I'll quote Zhuang Zhou: "There is no governor anywhere."

6. *What is the most disgusting prejudice you can point out?*

That seems totally relative . . . asked the most disgusting, to me, I'd have to say the American prejudice against intelligence in politics. I don't know where that began – we didn't start that way – our first three presidents included two of the best minds of their century, Adams and Jefferson, and George Washington doesn't seem a nitwit either . . . but nowadays any inadvertent revelation of intelligence by anybody in politics means their career dies immediately. We have lots of intelligent people in the sciences and arts, but politics remains closed to them. I guess that results from the success of what George Bush calls "faith-based organizations."

7. Tell us, what do you think of democracy?

CONSTITUTIONAL democracy, with strict limits on government powers, seems to me the best possible government, if we must have government. Without constitutional limits, democracy easily becomes another damned tyranny. I'd also accept a constitutional monarchy, like the Decembrists. But I remain, in my heart of hearts, an anarchist. I'd prefer contractual syndicates to any government.

8. America and Russia, how do you see relationship between our countries?

I don't feel informed enough to speculate, beyond saying I feel damned glad the Cold War has ended and I don't have to fear that either of our crazy governments will start heaving H-bombs around

9. What do you think of the works of L. R. Hubbard?

What do you think of Stalin and Hitler?

10. What is conventional logic downside?

Aristotle's damned either/or doesn't make any sense to me. My thinking – or my stumbling and fumbling efforts to think – derives largely from non-Aristotelian systems. That includes von Neumann's three-valued logic (true, false, maybe), Rapoport's four-valued logic (true, false, indeterminate, meaningless), Korzybski's multi-valued logic (degrees of probability), and also Mahayana Buddhist paradoxical logic (it "is" A, it "is" not A, it "is" both A and not A, it "is" neither A nor not A). But, as an extraordinarily stupid fellow, I can't use such systems until I reduce them to terms a simple mind like mine can handle, so I just preach that we'd all think and act more sanely if we had to use "maybe" a lot more often.

Can you imagine a world with Jerry Falwell hollering "Maybe Jesus 'was' the son of God and maybe he hates Gay people as much as I do" – or every tower in Islam resounding with "There 'is' no God except maybe Allah and maybe Mohammed is his prophet"?

Why, the world might go stark staring sane!

11. *In Maybe logic when one would encounter multiple options where to forward one's conclusions, what is a guiding light for those who implement maybe logic groundings in applied studies?*

Don't believe ANYthing. You will, of course, still have some suspicions and prejudices, but keep them in that category. Don't ever elevate any of them to dogmas. Be prepared to learn more, even in startling and annoying ways.

12. *Do you agree with such popular in Russia dichotomy (Due to Marx heritage) – mind – matter?*

I rather tend toward the view of physicist David Bohm that the words "mind" and "matter" create endless confusion and should get put on the back shelf in a box labeled "Discarded Nonsense." At most we should speak of "mind-like and matter-like phenomena."

13. *If there were Aliens what do you think they would be up to humankind-wise?*

Any aliens aware of humanity would probably find us cute but possibly dangerous – sort of like I feel about polar bears. Or maybe that represents projection on my part – I find most humans cute but dangerous, not as cute as the bears but much more dangerous

14. *How would you correlate Oriental and Western cultures?*

I don't know enough to generalize beyond their religions.

I have a strong affinity with Confucianism, Daoism and Buddhism, which gives me a slight pro-Oriental bias. I regard Judaism, Christianity and Islam as three of the worst cults ever invented. Monotheism seem like intellectual poison to me. I fear all faith-based systems, including secular ideologies, which all seem like hangovers from the monotheistic dark ages.

15. *If someone asked you – 'Do you believe in God' – what would you say?*

Hell, no! Oddly, I don't consider myself an atheist, though – not in the ordinary sense. The universe seems fundamentally rational to me, but I see no signs of a central government or a Tsar. The cybernetic concept of feedback and the Chinese concept of the Dao account for the intelligence I see in the world. To me, in my ignorance, Zhuang Zhou's axiom "There is no Governor anywhere" implies that "government" resides non-locally, as in a cybernetic system . . . or an anarchist syndicate maybe . . .

16. *What is your favorite book?*

Beyond all doubt, Joyce's *Finnegans Wake.*

17. *What would you recommend to young people?*

Don't believe anything I say: think for yourself.

18. *There is a prejudice among some Russian people that Americans are stupid, how would you comment on that?*

I feel staggered. I can't and won't deny it. I just don't know enough to generalize about 200,000,000 people, especially since that group includes me . . . For all I know, our Nobel scientists compare unfavorably with other Nobel winners, our dentists with other dentists, our carpenters with other carpenters, our grocers with other grocers, and (gulp) even our novelists with others, and so on. I simply haven't done enough travel to offer an informed opinion, and I defer to those who have.

19. *What future according to you mankind is facing today?*

I'm an unabashed optimist. I agree with Marx that politics follows economics, but I also agree with Buckminster Fuller that economics follows technology – and technology seems to lead more and more to decentralization of control or "Green" alternatives. Also we're doing more with less energy every decade. Once we reach the point where Internet replaces all – or most – functions of government, we'll solve the rest of our problems easily.

20. *Do you think formal education is necessary?*

That would depend on your ambitions. Most questions have no one answer. What you want determines what you have to do to get it.

21. *What do you consider your most important single idea?*

My "Idiot of the Century" Law. This has two sides. First, if you occasionally suspect that you have acted like the Idiot of the Century, you will act a little less like the Idiot of the Century, and the more often you entertain that suspicion, the less of an Idiot you become. Conversely, if you never confront such dark suspicions, every idiocy that ever enters your head will stay there and you might actually become the certified, undisputed Idiot of the Century, despite the heavy competition.

22. *What do you think of George Bush?*

Well, he never suspects he might qualify as the Idiot of the Century, so I think he has a good chance . . .

23. *Where can people learn more about your ideas?*

http://www.gunsanddope.com/
http://www.rawilson.com/
http://www.maybelogic.com/

http://www.maybelogic.org/
http://www.alphane.com/raw.htm
http://deoxy.org/raw.htm
http://en.wikipedia.org/wiki/Robert_Anton_Wilson
http://www.official-lamp.org
But be careful. It just might be me, not Bush, who really qualifies as the Idiot of the Century . . .

• • •

Editor's note: The links listed above are included for accuracy in presenting this interview, but most are not working addresses.

The rawilson.com address is still RAW's main website, currently maintained by the Robert Anton Wilson Trust.

The Guns and Dope Party website is: https://www.gunsanddopeparty.net

The link to RAW's Wikipedia page is accurate: https://en.wikipedia.org/wiki/Robert_Anton_Wilson

All of the other links are no longer active. The "official-lamp" website was a short-lived endeavor created by RAW's friend, and co-author of *Everything Is Under Control*, Miriam Joan Hill (now Mimi Peleg) with graphic art assistance by Richard Rasa. The idea was to present a comic suggestion that a "League of Armed Marijuana Patients" might be able to counter the whims of the nation's Drug Tsar.

The Tsar knows nothing about you or your medical problem!
LEAGUE OF ARMED MARIJUANA PATIENTS

The Guns and Dope Party

Afterword by Richard Rasa

I'll tolerate your hobbies
if you'll tolerate mine.
Guns and Dope Party

Liberty, tolerance, and compassion may best succinctly describe the ethical foundation informing Robert Anton Wilson's views on terrestrial politics. Getting into the weeds of his thinking makes one realize how difficult it can be to summarize how he saw those concepts turning into political reality, or not, especially as his views evolved over time. Declaring oneself a "model agnostic" and being considered the Grand Master of Operation Mindfuck probably doesn't help much either, except to remind us that not everything is always as it seems.

In the last decade of his life, suffering the increasing debilitating symptoms of Post-Polio Syndrome, he was most outspoken about his government denying him the medicinal relief he found from cannabis. On September 18, 2002, on the steps of the Santa Cruz City Hall, at a protest against the government's War on Some Drugs, WAMM, The Wo/Men's Alliance for Medical Marijuana, was giving away cannabis in defiance of federal law, but in accordance with the votes of the citizens of California, and the policies of the mayor of the city.

RAW offered the following comments to a reporter . . .

> Reporter: Tell me why you're here today and what you hope to achieve.
>
> RAW: Well, in the first place, I hope to get my medicine so my leg won't go on hurting the way it's been since they cut off my supply. That is the most important and immediate existential fact. I am in pain. I want medicine. The second reason I'm here, I happen to believe in states rights. I believe in the 10th Amendment, which most people have never heard of. In the back of your dictionary, you'll find a document called the US Constitution. It has nothing to do with the way this government is operating under George Bush, the way it's supposed to operate, and the 10th Amendment says all powers not delegated to the federal government are reserved for the states respectively, or to the people. Now the state of California and the people of California are behind me. The federal government has no right to condemn me to a life of constant pain, which is

what they're trying to do. I don't know what kind of sadistic son of a bitch George Bush is, why he wants to leave people in pain like this. I don't approve of it. I don't like it, and I'm ready to fight for my life to be free of pain.

Later, in a second interview . . .

RAW: If you are going to be in pain most of the day, you are not going to enjoy your life much. George Bush insists that God has appointed him to ensure that I spend the rest of my life in pain without any relief, and I say "Fuck you, George Bush. You should have these pains in your goddamn legs." I am a Buddhist most of the time, but today I'm too angry to be a Buddhist. I'll get back to being a Buddhist tomorrow.

Reporter: Anything else you want to add? Any final thoughts today?

RAW: I am sorry for my bitterness against George Bush. He is equally empty, equally blessed, and equally a coming Buddha. The problem is the asshole doesn't know it.

• • •

RAW's only semi-official foray into politics occurred a year later in 2003 when he was convinced by friends to enter the race for governor of California as a write-in candidate in a special mid-term election. Arnold Schwarzenegger would win that election, but it was a wild ride with 135 candidates who qualified to be on the ballot, among them RAW's favorite, Republican-turned-Democrat Arianna Huffington.

In RAW's private email group, affectionately called the Group Mind, interesting articles were passed around, and all of us were always eager to read RAW's pithy and often witty replies. Over a series of eighteen emails, RAW's friends talked him into running . . .

Gary V. started off the whole discussion . . .

I HEREBY NOMINATE ROBERT ANTON
WILSON!!!! -- preferable to run on a platform of
Secession, Medical Marijuana, decriminalization of
marijuana, and Amnesty for all current CA prisoners
being held on nonviolent drug charges. Nuff said.
Somebody get the Petition for the signatures and
let's start passing the hat for that $3,500. (I'll bet
even Candidate Gary Coleman will switch his vote –
from Schotzy to RAW.) – gv

Thinking not only of his writing schedule, but of his
declining health, I was at first skeptical:

I was surprised to see Conservative-turned-Liber-
al Ariana Huffington running. She wouldn't be as
radical or as sexy as Bob, but she's already in the
race, and I'm just guessing here, but doesn't Bob
have better things to do other than wrestle with the
hognads who control California state politics? –
Rasa

Bob agreed:

You betta you ass I do – bob

Ted commented:

Can I just say I find Arianna sexier than Bob? At
least in one sense of the word, perhaps not the one
you meant. – TK

Bob adds:

Yea,verily.
– bob

I defended my comments on Bob's sexiness:

I meant "sexy" in the same way that spaceships
are made from pasta, as in Las die Lasagne weiter
fliegen! (Keep the lasagna flying! – one of Bob's
metaphor mantras) – Rasa

Bob was still resistant:

> I will not run and if elected will not serve. In the years left to me I wanna do SERIOUS work, not muck about in political bullshit – bob

Gary didn't want to give up:

> Bob – Since modesty may have had you reluctant to send this on, even in jest, I opted to send it to a few members of the GM (Group Mind):

> I'd also nominate Paul Krassner as a great candidate, since the Guv doesn't really need a running mate – although maybe you could appoint him as Lt. Guv. We could have some great debates with you, Paul, Larry Flynt, Evanglyne and Gary Coleman. God – would I love to have the film rights to *that*!! OR: Maybe we could press George Carlin into service. The wheels are always turnin', Ralphie-Boy!
> – your pal, Norton

Bob replied:

> NO, NO, A THOUSAND TIMES NO!!!!!!!! The synergetic trajectories of Universe cannot move in an omnibenevolent vector, but only in an omnilethal one, from within the political paradigm. EVERY MAN AND EVERY WOMAN IS A TSAR – bob

Gary wrote to the whole Group Mind:

> TO: Paul K. and everyone: As I wrote Rasa and DOC ("Damned Old Crank," Bob's description of himself): Oh, hell, of course. Now he's even said so. I was being TIC and just sitting down with coffee when I fired that off. Guess I thought it would be at least fun as a discussion topic and maybe give Bob a shot in the arm – as humor or as a vote of confidence and loving support of his [presumed] platform . . .
> Further: I'd suggest that on a Wilson or Krassner ticket, we could discuss a marijuana tax – maybe $.05 an ounce – maybe $1? That would solve the

CA budget deficit – along with the decrim . . . Leary had great prison reform ideas when he ran for CA Guv. It's a grand old tradition. Even "jesting" about his candidacy brought forth some smart ideas for reform, some great discussion, great jokes, and great music – like Come Together. I couldn't really see Bob – or Carlin or Bill Maher, e.g. – as seriously giving a nod to a "nomination" or run for office (they've all previously refused, I think) – but I thought we could have some fun with the idea. – gv

I'm beginning to soften on the idea:

I think the sentiment was right on, and I'd also love to see Bob's politics have wider influence, but I was thinking a debate between Ariana, Larry and Arnold would be sponge-worthy. Half the country wouldn't understand any of their accents! – Rasa

Gary replies:

LOL to your comment. As far as accents: I'd rather hear the street-savvy smart of Brooklyn than macho with fascist potential of Austrian in the daily sound bytes. – gv

Paul Krassner declines:

Thanks anyway, but hermits don't make good politicians. – pk

Howard offers his thoughts:

Well Bob, to quote an old friend who said this many many years ago, and to adapt it to this situation: "If you're so goddamn great (and I think you are) then why would you want to settle for so little (as being governor)?" Besides, we already had one Wilson in the office and he ruined it for the rest. – Howard

Kai responds:

It is the political strategy of Mark Emery of the BC

Pot Party to ALWAYS run for everything he can.
Not because he thinks he has a chance but because it
lets him make speeches for the public record. It's the
same reason he and his cohorts always contrive to
get arrested and tried – they get to make speeches to
the judge.

Plus he gets to challenge opponents (who never dare
to debate him), say shit in press conferences . . .
legally protected as his listed platform – u should
see what the BCPP platform is, heheheh. Lambast
politicians, expose records etc. Imagine Bob . . .
Cummon . . . this is an incredible opportunity at a
propitious time in the right place for some major
Chaos. Run the whole thing on the Web exclusively.
– Kai

Bob protests yet again:

I'm old, I'm sick, I'm overworked – find another
Leader. Besides, Huff has the same policy as me
on the issue that matters the most to me, medical
freedom (no Tsarism) – bob

Admittedly, I just thought this was funny, but after my
mother sent me this joke, I emailed it off to Bob:

Little Tony was sitting on a park bench munching on
one candy bar after another. After the 6th candy bar,
a man on the bench across from him said,

"Son, you know eating all that candy isn't good for
you. It will give you acne, rot your teeth, and make
you fat.

Little Tony replied, "My grandfather lived to be 107
years old."

The man asked, "Did your grandfather eat 6 candy
bars at a time?"

Little Tony answered, "No, he minded his own
fucking business."

Perhaps thanks to Little Tony, the next email we got from Bob started off with this:

> After refusing many pleas to run for governor, I have reconsidered and now enter the race as an unofficial write-in candidate. After all, why shd I remain the ONLY nut in California who ain't running?

• • •

In subsequent emails, RAW announced the creation of the Guns and Dope Party, and he defined the party's platform. (We were amused that RAW made the Little Tony joke the Guns and Dope Party's Position Paper #23.)

In laying out the specifics, RAW examined the political terrain, and noticed that some Americans stockpile weapons like emergency rations in the paranoid delusion they have a chance of defending themselves against an attack from their own government. Millions of Americans support the National Rifle Association, an organization that draws heavily from its war chest to influence a political system many gun owners vehemently distrust.

Meanwhile, millions of starry-eyed recreational marijuana smokers in America stockpile tiny amounts of dried flowers with a paranoid uncertainty they won't win the conviction lottery and be locked away in the largest prison system in the world for doing something that seems to them less harmful than America's love affair with alcohol. A lot of those recreational smokers stand in solidarity with the Medical Marijuana movement and the growing number of indignant medical marijuana patients aghast at the actions of what they consider extremist bureaucrats in Washington trampling on human rights and state laws.

In RAW's first email pronouncement, he stated,

> My party, the Guns and Dope Party, invites extremists of both Right and Left to unite behind the shared goals of:

1 – Get those pointy-headed Washington bureaucrats off our backs and off our fronts too!

2 – guns for everybody who wants them; no guns for those who don't want them

3 – drugs for everybody who wants them; no drugs for those who don't want them

4 – freedom of choice, free love, free speech, free Internet and free beer

5 – California secession – Keep the anti-gun and anti-dope fanatics on the Eastern side of the Rockies

6 – Lotsa wild parties every night by gun-toting dopers

7 – Animal protection – Support your right to keep and arm bears

More position papers will follow; we know at least 69 good positions

In reaction to RAW's announcement in his Group Mind emails, I wrote to the new candidate with a question that seemed to resonate with other members of the group.

Bob, I'm totally behind the party, I love a good party, but I need some clarification. I've never had a hankering to fire a gun. I think from time to time that guns are lethal penises. I know I'm overly optimistic, but I always imagined a world without the need for guns. Guns seem too dangerous for most of the barbaric primates on this planet, with ample evidence to demonstrate that. I'm even a vegetarian, and so my diet is pretty easy to capture without internal combustion weaponry. Am I just being naive, having not been confronted with a gun toting lunatic? Please give me some reasoning behind the Guns part of Guns and Dope. I understand the libertarian model, but I'm not sure how to get behind actually supporting gunship diplomacy.

Bob wrote back, outlining more of what would become part of the party's platform.

We don't wanna force guns on anybody.

See point 2 above and cf point 3.

Both the pro-gun people and the dopers [medical, religious and/or recreational] feel like minorities, and the TSOG agrees with this estimate of their weakness. Our contention holds that in California both groups woikin' together make a MAJORITY. Ergo, they have much to gain and nowt to lose in combining forces. Each side only has to realize this and agree "We'll tolerate their hobbies if they'll tolerate ours" and we can even beat Schwarzenegger.

On an Internet Blog someone wrote, "I'm having some difficulty distinguishing the Guns and Dope Party from the Libertarian Party." Bob labeled that comment the "Koan of the week."

We should note that 2003 was not the first time RAW had that thought about a Guns and Dope Party. In the 1976 Illuminating Discord interview in this volume, he noted, "I should mention the sanest political proposal I've heard in years, the Guns and Dope Party proposed by my good friend, Rev. William Helmer (who, like many of the characters in Illuminatus!, exists also in so-called consensus reality)."

Also in this volume, in the 1987 transcription of a forum with RAW and Karl Hess at the Libertarian Party's Nominating Convention, RAW said, "I've got a friend whose name is best not to mention at this point, and he has been urging for some years, the formation of a Guns and Dope Party. Some people think that's what the Libertarian Party is."

In the Guns and Dope Party's second position paper RAW wrote:

Official motto: "Like what you like, enjoy what you enjoy, and don't take crap from anybody."

Major goal of first term: California secession. [Oregon, Washington State and B.C. invited to join Freetopia . . .]

First order of business on assuming office: Fire 33% of the legislature [names selected at random] and replace them with full-grown adult ostriches, whose mysterious and awesome dignity will elevate the suidean barbarity long established there.

In 2003, the Mayor of the City of Santa Cruz proclaimed July 23, 2003 "Robert Anton Wilson Day." One part of the proclamation reads,

Robert Anton Wilson employs wit and humor spanning five decades to resist the imperial schemes of national politicos, through such actions as daily emails to Attorney General John Ashcroft detailing his personal activities, thereby sparing government the expense and trouble of keeping him under surveillance . . .

• • •

So there's always a lot of humor in RAW's writing, but what does it all mean? What can we learn about how RAW saw politics in the last decade of his life?

One member of the Group Mind wrote to RAW and said,

I ask: why would you promote gun-toting people who marginalize somebody like you as a silly doped up eccentric? The Charlton Heston fans are not very likely to join your party – so what's the point?

RAW replied,

Are you sure they have the same kind of negative stereotype about us that you have about them? I'm not . . . and willing to find out by appealing to both . . .
– Guv Bob

There is a lot of discussion online about what RAW *was* politically. The statement above indicates that RAW saw an "us" and a "them," which seems like it could be a bit of a challenge to his Model Agnosticism, but I think we can examine his many statements about various politicians and policies, and get a clue as to where he stood. Rather than trying to tie RAW to one camp or another, Left or Right, I prefer to follow his suggestion that Left and Right was less important to him than Forward and Back, or as RAW described it, neophilia vs neophobia, embracing the future and new ideas, or hanging onto the past and fearing the new. RAW was a futurist with compassion but with little patience for what he called political BS (BS meaning both Belief Systems and Bull Shit). As he noted in the initial email exchange, "The synergetic trajectories of Universe cannot move in an omnibenevolent vector, but only in an omnilethal one, from within the political paradigm."

RAW has written a lot about his enthusiasm for consciousness altering substances, but let's examine what he actually thought about guns. The RAW Trust and Hilaritas Press sometimes gets emails from pro-gun organizations who had read about the Guns and Dope Party and want to applaud RAW for his seeming approval of gun ownership. There is no doubt he thought gun owners should be free to own their guns, but he was not for total unregulated use. He wrote in his *Trajectories* newsletter,

> I can't see how the NRA can avoid eventually making this part of their platform: the right of the citizens to bear grenade launchers, flame-throwers, tactical missiles and nuclear weapons. If the citizens have the right to bear arms, they should have the right to bear as many arms as the government, or it's no defense against the government at all, and that whole argument is hollow.

In *The Illuminati Papers*, RAW wrote,

> Illth, a term coined by John Ruskin, can be
> conceived as all the changes in the environment
> that are detrimental to humanity and/or to life itself.
> Weaponry, then, should be classed as illth, not
> wealth.

I once asked RAW's daughter, Christina, what RAW
thought about guns. She said,

> RAW thought guns were low larval mentality.

RAW's close friend Timothy Leary similarly thought
some powerful psychedelics should also be controlled to
some degree so that proper mindset, physical setting for the
experience, and dosage can be considered.

• • •

So between the pro-gun people and the dopers (medical,
religious and/or recreational), as RAW described the two
groups, RAW identified himself as a doper. But does that
mean he was a Left-winger? I don't think so. In *The Illuminati
Papers* he wrote,

> Conservatives say it is dangerous to give any
> group too much political power. Liberals say it is
> dangerous to give any group too much economic
> power. Both are right.

RAW saw value in parts of both Left and Right
perspectives. In the last book RAW published in his lifetime,
Email to the Universe, he chose articles that spanned nearly his
entire career. Of all the many articles on politics he produced
in his career, he decided that for this compendium, he would
include, "Left And Right: A Non-Euclidean Perspective" (also
included in this volume).

The essay describes how RAW's views changed over time.

In his college years, in the conservative 1950's, he wrote,

> While Senator Joe was a liar of stellar magnitude,
> a lot of the Liberals were lying their heads off,
> too, in attempts to hide their previous fondness for
> Stalinism.

He goes on to note that he

> . . . searched earnestly for some pragmatic mock-up
> of "truth" without a Correct Answer Machine
> attached. And yet both Left and Right continued to
> appear intellectually bankrupt to me.

This was RAW when he was in his twenties, but I am
dismayed to find a lot of RAW fans taking that phrase, "Left
and Right continued to appear intellectually bankrupt to me,"
and declaring that phrase, devoid of nuance, was how he
felt for the rest of his life. A clue as to why that might be an
inaccurate supposition lies in the essay's very next sentence,

> Coming from a working class family, I could never
> have much sympathy for the kind of Conservatism
> you find in America in this century.

I think this concern for the plight of the working class, for
the underdog, helped to shape a lot of his political thought. He
noted that given the "abominations of the Capitalist system . . .
I was a poor candidate for the Conservative cause."

He goes on to note that,

> On the other hand, the FDR Liberals, I was
> convinced, had lied about World War II; they first
> smeared and then blacklisted the historians who
> told the truth; and they had jumped on the Cold War
> bandwagon with ghoulish glee.

> . . . Left and Right continued to appear intellectually
bankrupt . . .

In 1968, RAW was in Chicago when he and Robert Shea
were running from police-gone-wild in streets filled with

tear gas. He says, "Whenever the Establishment is annoyed, they send the cops to beat the shit out of people." These were protests against the Democratic party who were complicit in the nightmare of the war in Vietnam. However, four years prior, the same Democratic party pushed to ratify the Civil Rights Act of 1964. So, not completely intellectually bankrupt.

In the coming years, RAW began to see the country divided between the neophiles and the neophobes. Conservatives, calling themselves the Moral Majority, pushed for repressive social policies, while Timothy Leary was jailed and labeled the most dangerous man in America for suggesting we question authority, expand consciousness, and push for progressive social policies. The political parties, both invested in the War on Some Drugs, still seemed, at the least, intellectually challenged, but there was a change in the air. We also declared a War on Poverty in the '60s. Nixon's Republicans doubled down and created the Southern Strategy to get working class Democrats to switch parties out of fear of those progressive (neophile) social policies. That fear mongering continues to this day.

Still, RAW was never impressed by either of the major political parties.

In the 1990s RAW talked about not voting for either party. In 2003, in his writings about the Guns and Dope Party, he said,

> If you want self-government don't vote for the Two Lying Bastards of the Democan and Republicrat parties . . . or for any minority party that also wants to govern you . . . WRITE IN YOUR OWN NAME!

This is where the ostrich hits the road. In the same way that an ostrich named Olga served as the candidate's principal advisor, we are to assume that not all things said in Guns and Dope Party pronouncements should be taken literally. Someone running for public office doesn't actually want you to write in your own name. This seems like a little bit of Operation Mindfuck at work. RAW wants us to be skeptical of what anyone in authority says, but he didn't give up on our constitutional democracy altogether. In *TSOG: The Thing That Ate the Constitution*, RAW writes,

> Some may think I regard the Constitution as an almost sacred text. Not at all: I admit it has a few defects and blemishes. I just consider it a hell of a lot better than the system we have now.

Nonetheless, some RAW fans who take "both-sides-bad" a bit too much to heart advocate for not voting at all, claiming RAW never voted for the "system we have now." RAW's daughter, who often drove him to the polls, says otherwise. Christina says,

> RAW voted. He voted a lot of times. Not all the time, but he realized that some issues are important enough to support even if you thought both parties were terrible.

This is why, before entering the race, RAW said,

> Huff (Ariana Huffington) has the same policy as me on the issue that matters the most to me, medical freedom (no Tsarism).

The essay, "Left and Right: A Non-Euclidean Perspective," attempts to clarify, for those of us wondering: was he a Right-winger or a Left-winger? He seems to want us to leave those distinctions behind, and consider a more complex reality.

After describing his early years, the essay then outlines the various political philosophies that intrigued him, and he arrived at a preferred political position: "Individualist-Mutualist Anarchism." He wanted to be free from the repressive authoritarian policies of governments, but he recognized that individual liberty, "can only be achieved by a system of mutual consent, each agreeing to defend the liberty of all."

How do you defend the liberty of all in our complex society

where, for example, healthcare is intimately tied to the huge professional organizations and corporations that control the field? He expressed a love for "Scandinavian socialism," which would include universal healthcare, but how does that coexist with his desire for government to be local, divorced from the huge authoritarian structures? It seemingly doesn't.

Idealistically, he suggested getting rid of the lords of the land, landlords, who own land but do not live there, and central bankers who control the flow of money and the taxes and interest attached to the transfer of funds and the trading of goods. Also idealistically, he suggested that nationalism itself should be moderated. In *Coincidance* he wrote,

> I think nationalism is very regressive at this point in history. But I realize it as a potent force. And so, it seems to me that we are going to have a decentralized world system in which, as much as possible, nationalism is retained while the power to use weapons is gradually taken away from nations, and given to some kind of peace force. The UN is a crude attempt at what obviously has to happen, and it should happen. The attitude of the major powers is that, 'It can't happen until we knock over those bad guys over there,' but it has to happen eventually with a transformed UN with real power to keep the peace, or we're going to exterminate ourselves.

So here's a guy who distrusts authoritarian institutions, and yet he wants all the world's militaries under one roof. He distrusts governments and corporations, but he's okay with a government controlled universal healthcare system. Currently in the USA, the Right, the Republicans, the conservatives, want corporations to continue to administer healthcare, while the Left, the Democrats, the liberals, mostly want a universal system.

Perhaps the fantasy world of *Star Trek* might help to explain this dilemma. RAW considered himself a futurist, but also a realist. He didn't like the extremism of the Left when it became too politically correct, but he didn't like the extremism of the Right when its political correctness, known at one time as "family values," threatened to make Margaret Atwood's *A Handmaid's Tale* a reality. No, he preferred the world of *Star Trek* where money no longer existed, weapons were used for defense, and the goal of humanity was to explore and grow. In Timothy Leary's *Terra II,* Leary envisions the nations of the world coming together to create a project where the best minds in the arts and sciences would travel in a 5000 person spaceship on a mission to search for higher intelligence. Leary imagined a scenario where nations would be united in furtherance of a common goal. Something like this seemed to be in RAW's mind as he imagined the future – individuals free, but humanity united.

In an email to me where RAW and I were talking about an encounter I had with a fundamentalist Christian who rejected much of modernity because he insisted that, after we die, residents of heaven won't need the bells and whistles of our busy civilization, RAW said,

> I think life extension is the primary evolutionary selector at this stage. Those who reject it belong to the past and we should leave them there. If we try and try and try and try and finally persuade them to live longer, they'll still have a thousand and one other reactionary ideas and still serve as a brake on progress. Let them die soon rather than later, as they prefer. Humanity will move faster without these dead weights.

Kinda brutal, but RAW had little patience for neophobes. And therein lies an explanation. RAW seemed less interested in describing Left and Right, and more interested in examining Forward and Back. In a comment on left and right in *Illuminatus!*, Hagbard says,

. . . spacial metaphors are inadequate in discussing politics today.

In his introduction to this book, Jesse Walker makes note of RAW's 1969 article titled, "Why I Am a Right-Wing Anarchist." Jesse notes a couple examples of RAW identifying with the Right and then with the Left, leaving us with one of my favorite quotes from RAW,

> I can only conclude that I am indeed like a visitor from non-Euclidean dimensions whose outlines are perplexing to the Euclidean inhabitants of various dogmatic Flatlands.

When Erik Davis published *High Weirdness*, he was on a podcast with Earl Fontainelle, and in the notes for the podcast, Earl had taken a phrase from Erik's book where Erik described RAW as a "Right-Wing Anarchist." In a three-way email conversation with Erik and Jesse Walker, I wrote,

> "Right-Wing Anarchist – RAW used that phrase in the essay to describe himself, but it was written in 1969 under a pseudonym, and I suspect that there was a bit of a joke intended, even though the term has historical import. Even so, it might give the wrong idea to some people, and reinforce some false impressions of others."

Erik wrote back,

> "I agree with Rasa's point, and I sometimes feel bad that I included that line in *High Weirdness*, since in context it means one thing (basically an individualist anarchist) but that given the changes of today's libertarian politics over the last few decades and the growing intensity of "Right wing" everything, I think the phrase confuses more than clarifies as a general marker."

Individualist-Mutualist – Individualist can suggest right-wing, while Mutualist can suggest left-wing. RAW called mutualism "voluntary socialism." I suspect that may be the main reason RAW disliked those labels of Left and Right. They just didn't do justice to his nuanced thinking about politics.

Just the same, let me be heretical and suggest that RAW leaned to what most Americans consider the Left, if you look at the policies he favored. RAW called himself a "Male Feminist." He supported abortion rights, universal healthcare, environmental care, some regulation of weapons, civil rights, LGBTQ+ rights, fighting poverty, drug policy reform, prison reform, renewable energy, keeping religion out of politics . . . but let me suggest that these issues don't necessarily make RAW a Leftist. In keeping with his own descriptions, I think his support for these issues describe him as a neophile; instead of leaning Left or Right, he is leaning towards the future.

THE BEARER OF THIS CARD IS A GENUINE AND AUTHORIZED

TSAR

"Like what you like, enjoy what you enjoy,
and don't take crap from anybody."

GENUINE AND AUTHORIZED BY THE HOUSE OF APOSTLES OF ERIS

every man and woman is a tsar

Reproduce and distribute this card freely • Maybe Logic Head Temple • Republic of California

Acknowledgments

Most readers would be surprised at the amount of effort that went into creating this book. Hilaritas Press wishes to thank the major players in this effort: Mike Gathers, Chad Nelson, Jesse Walker, Tom Clisson, and Richard Rasa. Here are a few words about each of the participants . . .

Mike Gathers discovered Robert Anton Wilson through Timothy Leary and deoxy.org sometime around 1997, and immediately took to the Eight Circuit Model of Consciousness. He aspires to bring the Eight Circuit model up to date with modern neuroscience and developmental psychology and place it in a relational context in conjunction with Antero Alli's embodiment context. He hosts the *Hilaritas Press Podcast* and enjoys helping Hilaritas continue to publish new books such as this one.

Chad Nelson lives in Providence, Rhode Island with his wife and two cats. When not engaged in RAW studies, he is a practicing attorney, yogi, and outdoor enthusiast. He edited Hilaritas Press' 2021 release, *Natural Law, Or Don't Put a Rubber On Your Willy and Other Writings From a Natural Outlaw*.

Jesse Walker, the author of the introduction, is an editor at *Reason* magazine. His book *The United States of Paranoia: A Conspiracy Theory* includes a chapter on Robert Anton Wilson, Discordianism, and related matters.

Tom Clisson, proofreader extraordinaire, asked us to simply note: Tom occasionally punctuates a lifelong pursuit of Slack with the lending of his fnord-hunting skills to Hilaritas Press.

Richard Rasa, publisher at Hilaritas Press, contributed an afterword to this volume, and, as usual, did a lot of the heavy lifting involved in producing and promoting the works of Robert Anton Wilson and the other distinguished authors supporting "winner scripts" and mindsets that encourage neophilia.

Index

A Non-Euclidean Perspective

Austrian economics, 24, 32, 214–221, 297

Bach, Johann Sebastian, 208, 352, 435

Baez, Joan, 234, 366

Baigent, Michael, 272, 274

Bakunin, Mikhail, 143, 171, 261

Baldridge, Malcolm, 340

Banco Ambrosiano, 254, 265–266, 268

Bank of America, 205

Bank of England, 77, 252, 253

Banks, Emily, 37

Banner, Bob, 355

Barbie, Klaus, 266

Barefoot, John, 459

Barnes, Harry Elmer, 22, 354, 358–359

Barth, Lawrence, 69, 76

Basho, Matsuo, 75

Bauscher, Lance, 29, 377–400, 435, 449

Bay of Pigs, 17, 93–95, 267–268

Beard, Charles, 20, 358–359

Beck, Julian, 141

Beethoven, Ludwig van, 208, 277, 411

Begg, Eon, 276–276

Belafonte, Harry, 435

Bell, Eric Temple, 183

Beria, Lavrentiy, 172

Berkeley Barb, 202–206

Berne, Eric, 154, 155, 232, 233, 234

Bierce, Ambrose, 40, 256

Bilderbergers, 277, 278, 279

bin Laden, Osama, 414, 426, 430, 435, 456

bioengineering, 302–303, 320, 344–345

Bizet, Georges, 208

Black, Hugo, 309–310

Black International, 136

Black Panther Party, 250–251, 290–291, 315

Blakey, Howard, 259

Block, Walter, 297

Bloom, Allan, 346–347

Bohm, David, 442, 464

Bohr, Niels, 361–362

Bologna railway bombing, 281–282

Bonaparte, Louis, 105

Boole, George, 356

Bork, Robert, 310–311

Bowers, Claude G., 86

Brain/Mind Bulletin, 321, 443

Branden, Barbara, 305

Branden, Nathaniel, 183

Brann, William Cowper, 40, 69

Braun, Werner von, 257

Bridgman, Percy, 361–362

Bronson, Charles, 293

Brooks, Mel, 337

Brown, David Jay, 447–459

Brown, Norman, 73

Brown, Pat, 57

Bruno, Giordano, 235–236

Bruderhof community, 87

Buckley, William F., 213, 356

Buddhism, 36, 64, 117, 184, 210, 229, 235, 237, 240, 241, 297, 307, 309, 365, 374, 418, 422–423, 430–431, 449, 458, 461, 463, 465, 470

Buhs, Joshua Blu, 33

Burke, Edmund, 213, 257, 360

Burroughs, William, 105, 154, 297, 391, 425–426

Bush, George H.W., 343, 368–370

Bush, George W., 392, 397, 403, 405, 410–411, 412, 419–420, 421, 422, 425, 435, 445, 448, 450, 453, 454, 462, 466, 467, 469–470

Buthelezi, Mangosuthu, 330

cabala, 365

Cagliostro, Alessandro, 269

Calvi, Clara, 265

Calvi, Roberto, 264–266, 268, 269, 270, 281

Calvin, John, 76

Campbell, Colin, 14, 25

Campbell, Ken, 425

capital punishment, 50–55, 64, 152, 154

capitalism, 14, 15, 20, 24, 25, 63–64, 66–78, 106–108, 135, 137, 139, 144, 145, 156, 167–168, 172, 175, 190, 197, 211, 215, 220–221, 223, 252, 280, 340–341, 360, 362, 366, 386, 412, 439–440, 482

Carlin, George, 375–376, 425, 472, 473

Carrocher, Graziella, 266

Carson, Rachel, 122

Carter, Jimmy, 319

Casey, Doug, 342

Casey, William, 279, 281

Casolaro, Danny, 413

Castaneda, Carlos, 237

Castro, Fidel, 85, 94, 259

Cataya, Hernandez, 268

Catholic Worker Movement, 139, 141

Catholicism, 13, 19, 21, 91, 139, 141, 187, 208, 235, 245, 271–277, 327, 346, 356, 357, 360, 449

Cato the Elder, 83

censorship, 16, 175, 310, 366, 372–376, 378, 393, 456

Central Intelligence Agency (CIA), 81, 193, 249, 258–260, 263, 266, 267–270, 279, 281, 282, 286, 291, 292, 295, 370, 384, 411, 441, 462

Celine, Hagbard, 226, 228, 235, 486

Cezanne, Paul, 68, 75

A Non-Euclidean Perspective

General Semantics, 20, 110, 155, 184, 191, 227, 253, 360, 361, 420

George, Henry, 14, 21, 25, 26, 30, 108, 213, 214, 217, 364

Gesell, Silvio, 21, 26, 108, 112, 127, 213, 219, 364

Giancana, Sam, 258–260, 262–263, 267

Ginsberg, Allen, 20, 105, 249

globalization, 390–391, 416

GM, 205

Gnomes of Zurich, 279

Gnostica, 225, 229

Gnosticism, 234

Goldman, Emma, 218, 284

Goldwater, Barry, 284, 314–316, 370

Goodman, Paul, 58, 106, 141, 166

Gore, Al, 403, 421, 425, 455–456

Grand Loge Alpina, 273, 279

Grand Orient Lodge, 269–270, 275

Grant, Ulysses, 85

Grateful Dead, 435–436

Green Egg, 192–201, 210, 437

Green, Mike, 302

Greene, Graham, 38

Greene, William B., 129, 219

Gibbon, John, 355, 442

Griffith, David Wark, 208

Grisar, Hartmann, 67

Grosseteste, Robert, 124–125

Group Mind, 470–475, 476–477, 479

GRUNCH, 243, 244, 255

guerrilla ontology, 240

Gumbel, Bryan, 335–336

Guns and Dope Party, 212–213, 288, 452–453, 454–455, 459, 467–487

Gurdjieff, George, 239, 357, 366

Gurwin, Larry, 269, 270

Habsburg dynasty, 277–278

Haig, Alexander, 297, 281

Hamilton, Alexander, 86

Hammer, Richard, 254, 259

Hand, Ted, 11

Harding, Warren, 348

Harper's, 193, 321

Hart, Gary, 302

Hassan-i-Sabbah, 239, 426

Hayakawa, S.I., 121

Hayden, Charlie, 134–147

Hayek, F.A., 24, 25

Hayworth, Rita, 149–150, 156, 159

Heinlein, Robert, 209, 234, 316, 344

Helweg-Larsen, Nick, 134

Hemingway, Ernest, 47, 150

Herbert, Frank, 238

Herbert, Nick, 442

heroin, 193, 265, 407, 437

Hershey, Lewis Blaine, 155

Hess, Karl, 30, 283–353, 478

Hess, Therese, 325

Heston, Charlton, 479

Hevia, Carlos, 289

Heywood, Ezra, 216–217

Hill, Joe, 143

Himmler, Heinrich, 370

Hiroshima, 81, 148, 149, 152

Hitler, Adolph, 31, 35, 36, 45, 48, 67, 117, 152, 163, 248, 264, 357, 360, 397, 412, 441, 463

Hoffa, Jimmy, 262, 305–306

Hoffman, Abbie, 313, 399–400

Hofstadter, Douglas, 325

Holmes, Donald, 242, 248, 251

Holocaust, 22, 31, 75–76, 117, 359

homeschooling, 301–302

The Homing Pigeons, 16

Hoover, Herbert, 348

Hoover, J. Edgar, 151, 158

House Committee on Un-American Activities, 285

House, Edward M., 47–48

Housman, A.E., 60

Hoy, Michael, 19, 356

Hubbard, Barbara Marx, 355, 394

Hubbard, L. Ron, 463

Huffington, Arianna, 470, 471, 484

Hughes, Howard, 256, 280–281

Humphrey, Hubert, 204

Hunt, E. Howard, 267–268

Husserl, Edmund, 361, 362

Huston, John, 417–418

Hutchison, Michael, 347

Huxley, Thomas Henry, 271

I Ching, 324–325

Illuminati, 165, 227, 230, 234, 237, 242, 275, 277, 322, 437, 443

The Illuminati Papers, 480, 481

Illuminatus!, 22–23, 31, 207, 211, 212–213, 225–226, 227, 230, 429, 477, 486

The Independent, 40

Ingersoll, Robert, 356

Institutional Investor, 269, 270

intellectual properry, 317–318, 320

interest, 19, 24, 65, 77, 83–84, 85–86, 90, 100, 105, 108, 115, 116, 129–130, 131, 132, 173–175, 196, 197, 214, 215–216, 217, 218–220, 363, 364, 392

Internal Revenue Service (IRS), 221–222, 294, 323, 339, 453

Iran-contra, 284, 296–297, 301

Irish Press, 272

Irish Republican Army (IRA), 292, 424

Irish Times, 346

Islam, 276, 325, 406, 450, 464, 465

Issa, Kobayashi, 122

Jaguar, 134

James, Ben, 11

Jefferson, Thomas, 43, 48, 59, 85, 86, 172, 322, 351, 357, 382, 386, 453, 457, 462

Jesus, 43, 70, 81, 153, 156, 164, 205, 210, 221, 228, 274–275, 276, 277, 278, 450, 457, 464

Johnson, Lyndon, 155, 157, 172, 370

Johnson, Samuel, 258

Johnson, Wendell, 63

Jones, Ernest, 72, 77

Jones, Jack, 40

Joyce, James, 25–26, 32, 208, 210, 220–221, 226, 314, 326, 334–335, 374, 377–378, 431–432, 436, 448, 465

Jung, Carl, 235, 366

Kafka, Franz, 154, 382, 461

Kandinsky, Wassily, 188

Kazantzakis, Nikos, 235

Keller, Helen, 249

Kennedy, Bobby, 259, 260, 262, 263

Kennedy, Gabriel, 11, 20

Kennedy, John F., 17, 31, 81, 94, 119, 259, 260, 262, 263

Kenny, Nick, 121

Kerouac, Jack, 35

Kesey, Ken, 162, 211, 341

KGB, 269, 279, 282

Khashoggi, Adnan, 414

Khomeini, Ruhollah, 307

Khrushchev, Nikita, 37

Kissinger, Henry, 205, 453

Kitson, Arthur, 82

Knight, Stephen, 265, 269

Knights of Malta, 279, 281

Knights Templar, 276

Koestler, Arthur, 104

Konkin, Samuel Edward III (SEK3), 230

Korzybski, Alfred, 10, 83, 99, 100, 119, 120, 184, 189, 214, 219, 230, 233, 356, 361, 379, 399, 420, 449, 463,

Krassner, Paul, 34, 427, 456, 472–473

Krim, Seymour, 105

Krishnamurti, Jiddu, 235

Krohn, Juan, 271

Kronstadt rebellion, 38–39

Kropotkin, Peter, 26, 100, 102, 141, 211, 213

Ku Klux Klan, 309–310, 425

L.A. Weekly, 15, 370

La Follette, Robert, 47

Labadie, Laurence, 129, 214

Lamy, Michael, 275

Landauer, Gustav, 143

Langham, Chris, 438

Langhenry, Randy, 340

Lao-Tse, 35, 234, 260, 406

LaRouche, Lyndon, 278, 325

Lawford, Peter, 262–263

Lawrence, D.H., 75

Le Carre, John, 249

Le Guin, Ursula, 209, 222

League of Armed Marijuana Patients (LAMP), 467

Leary Defense Committee, 249, 287

Leary, Timothy, 211, 224, 225, 227, 228, 229–230, 231, 234, 235, 236, 237, 249, 256, 263–264, 287, 374–375, 408, 425, 439, 456, 457, 473, 480, 482, 485, 490

Lecter, Hannibal, 386, 394–395, 410–411, 448, 453

Lefebvre, Marcel, 271–273

Leibniz, Gottfried Wilhelm, 140

Leigh, Richard, 272, 274

Lenin, V.I., 20, 39, 45, 48, 188, 278, 292, 350, 461

Lernoux, Penny, 254, 266, 268, 269, 270, 279

Levine, Mel, 372, 376

Liberation, 134, 139

Libertarian League, 139

Libertarian Party, 16, 23–24, 32, 232, 283–353, 370, 477, 478

libertarian socialism, 77, 135, 143, 177

libertarianism, 16, 17, 19, 23–24, 25, 26, 29, 30, 32, 99, 119, 128, 152, 160, 175, 182–183, 207–241, 283–353, 364, 370, 381, 385, 452, 477, 488

Liberty Amendment, 128–129

Lichtenberg, Georg Christoph, 355

Liddy, G. Gordon, 321–322

Life, 94

life extension, 210, 211, 214, 224, 225, 226, 236, 303, 339, 457, 486

Lilly, John, 236, 239

Lincoln, Abraham, 62

Lincoln, Henry, 272, 274

Lindner, Robert, 53, 56

Lion of Light, 10

Living Theater, 141

Lloyd, Sanuel, 243

Loch Ness Monster, 414–415

Loeb, David, 35

logical positivism, 261–262

Loomis, Mildred, 213

Loompanics, 332

L'osservatore Politico, 266

Louis Philippe II, Duc d'Orléans, 269–270

Louw, Leon, 330

Lovelace, Linda, 212

Luciano, Lucky, 330

Lunan, Duncan, 248

Luther, Martin, 63, 67, 76

A Non-Euclidean Perspective

Physics/Consciousness Research Group, 442

Picasso, Pablo, 335

Pitt, William, 348

Plantard de Saint Clair, Pierre, 274–275

Platt, Charles, 355

Playboy, 16, 159, 225, 230, 250–251, 284, 290–291

Plotinus, 124–125

Pope, Alexander, 354, 367

Pope Innocent VIII, 70

Pope John Paul I, 266–267, 272

Pope John Paul II, 271, 272, 281

Pope Leo XIII, 364

Popular Science, 320

pornography, 16

Pound, Ezra, 21–22, 30–31, 33, 42–49, 71–72, 77, 86, 91–92, 103, 104, 105, 124, 210, 214, 335, 377–378, 415–416, 428, 431–432, 444, 448

Presley, Sharon, 230

Prince Bernhard, 278, 279, 412

Princess Diana, 413–414

Principia Discordia, 227, 294, 314

Priory of Sion, 272–277

Prometheus Rising, 15, 229, 255, 347

Propaganda Due (P2), 254, 264–267, 268–270, 272, 273, 275, 279, 281–282

Prophets Conference, 429

Protestantism, 64, 67–68, 71, 257, 355, 356

Proudhon, Pierre-Joseph, 21, 82, 84, 101, 102–110, 111, 112, 113, 115–116, 129, 130, 140, 142–143, 157, 160, 171, 172, 173, 214, 223, 235, 362

Proxmire, William, 322

Pryor, Richard, 267

psychedelics, 23, 159, 191, 203, 210, 214, 229, 263, 304, 338, 365, 388, 389–390, 403, 408, 439, 455, 458, 480

Puharich, Andrija, 443–444

Puzo, Mario, 270

Quayle, Dan, 368

Queen Elizabeth II, 278

Rajneesh, Bhagwan Shree, 307

Rand, Ayn, 14, 20, 26, 32, 168, 181, 181–191, 226, 284, 305–306, 352

Rapoport, Anatole, 121, 356, 449, 463

Rasa, Richard, 10, 11, 467, 468–487, 490, 491

Rather, Dan, 335

Ravachol, François Claudius, 137, 162

Reagan, Nancy, 341

Reagan, Ronald, 18, 204, 212, 257–258, 279–280, 290, 303, 316, 327, 341, 342–343, 366, 370

A Non-Euclidean Perspective

Schrödinger's Cat, 229, 297, 340, 429

Schrödinger, Erwin, 121–122

Schwarzenegger, Arnold, 470, 477

Scientific American, 210, 321

Seabrook, William, 393

Second International, 136

The Sex Magicians, 227

Segal, Paul, 210–211, 303

segregation, 29, 383, 396

Shakespeare, William, 40, 75, 77, 83, 95, 120, 121, 210, 374

Shannon, Claude, 120–121, 127, 393, 441, 456

Shaw, George Bernard, 123, 214, 395

Shea, Robert, 16, 23, 31, 170, 192–201, 207, 226, 482

Sheen, Fulton, 80, 156

Shell Oil, 289

Shidlof, Leo, 277, 278

Sindona, Michele, 254, 279, 281

Single Tax, 14, 25, 30, 170

Sirag, Saul-Paul, 211, 441–442

Sirius, 273, 277, 308

Skinner, B.F., 89, 150–151, 163

Slack, Charles, 365

Smith, Adam, 131, 363

Smith, Elliott, 98

Smith, L. Neil, 341

Smith, Thorne, 210

SNAFU principle, 160, 179, 190, 383, 385

socialism, 14, 15, 19, 25, 104–110, 135, 138, 143, 144, 146, 167, 171–172, 211, 223, 362, 363, 364, 386, 396, 484, 487

Socrates, 240, 398

Solomon, Maynard, 277

space colonies, 32, 211, 214, 224, 226, 233, 236, 322, 375, 456, 457

Spanish Revolution, 137–139

Spencer, Herbert, 215

Spinoza, Baruch, 43, 105, 439

Spooner, Lysander, 21, 129, 130, 214, 217, 223, 362

Stalin, Joseph, 25, 26, 37–40, 48, 59, 172, 199, 357, 359, 463, 481

Standard Oil, 81, 203, 204

Stanley, Owsley, 338

Star Trek, 18, 208, 233, 236, 239, 304, 485

Stefansson, Vilhjalmur, 62–63

Steinem, Gloria, 203

Stevens, H.B., 98

Stevenson, Adlai, 93–94

Stirner, Max, 162, 166, 168, 169, 172, 217, 223, 232, 238, 306, 321

Stockman, David, 343

Stravinsky, Igor, 208

Streicher, Jules, 36

A Non-Euclidean Perspective

U.S. Constitution, 252, 310, 350–351, 373, 374, 382, 396, 420, 427, 435, 448, 451, 452, 456, 463, 469, 483

usury, 21, 61–62, 64, 71–72, 76, 77, 83–84, 85–86, 87, 88, 90, 92, 100, 112, 128–133, 174, 216, 388

Valery, Paul, 455

Vallee, Jacques, 229

Van Gogh, Vincent, 104

Vanzetti, Bartolomeo, 104, 125, 143

Vatican, 31, 254, 259, 265, 266–268, 270–274, 279, 281, 357, 462

Vatican Bank, 31, 254, 259, 265, 266, 268, 272, 273, 279

VCRs, 313–314

Verne, Jules, 275

Views and Comments, 139

virtual reality, 379, 388–390

Vivaldi, Antonio, 208

Voltaire, 40, 322, 366

voting, 16, 17, 85, 94, 202–206, 211–212, 296–297, 322–323, 327–328, 368–371, 404, 421, 425, 452–453, 470–478, 483

Wagner, Martin, 11

Walker, Jesse, 10, 11, 13–33, 486, 490

Wallace, Alfred Russel, 140

Wallace, George, 142, 170, 204

Warhol, Andy, 297

Warren, Josiah, 21, 112, 127, 140, 143, 171–172, 173, 220, 362, 420–421

Washington, George, 48, 247, 462

The Washington Post, 336

Watergate, 221, 267, 280, 301, 336

Watts, Alan, 183, 281, 374–375

Wavy Gravy, 212, 437

Way Out, 33, 96–133, 213

The Weavers, 435

Weber, Max, 67

Weishaupt, Adam, 166

Weiss, Peter, 148–164

Welles, Orson, 208, 425

Werkheiser, Don, 32, 123, 215, 220

Westinghouse, 421

White, Theodore, 343–344

Whitehead, Alfred North, 67

Whorf, Benjamin Lee, 187

The Widow's Son, 437

Wiener, Norman, 393, 441

Wilgus, Neal, 355

Williams, William Carlos, 47

Wilson, Arlen, 26, 86, 211, 302, 390, 395, 400, 409, 414, 422, 425, 436, 461

Wilson, Harold, 279

Wilson, Mick, 13, 19, 21–22

Wilson, Woodrow, 48

HILARITAS
PRESS

Publishing the Books of Robert Anton Wilson
and Other Adventurous Thinkers

www.hilaritaspress.com

www.ingramcontent.com/pod-product-compliance
Lightning Source LLC
Chambersburg PA
CBHW062109020426
42335CB00013B/904